London

5th Edition

Michael Jackson, Leonie Glass and Fiona Duncan

Prentice Hall Travel

New York • London • Toronto • Sydney • Tokyo • Singapore

THE AMERICAN EXPRESS ® TRAVEL GUIDES

Published in the United States by
Prentice Hall General Reference
A division of Simon & Schuster, Inc.
15 Columbus Circle
New York, NY 10023

PRENTICE HALL and colophon are
registered trademarks of
Simon & Schuster, Inc.

First published 1983 in the United
Kingdom by Mitchell Beazley
International Ltd, Michelin House
81 Fulham Road, London SW3 6RB as
*The American Express Pocket Guide
to London,* reprinted 1985. Second
edition 1986. Third edition 1989.
Fourth edition 1991. This edition,
revised, updated and expanded,
published 1993.

Edited, designed and produced by
Castle House Press, Llantrisant
Mid Glamorgan CF7 8EU, Wales

Library of Congress Catalog Card
Number 92-082889
ISBN 0-671-84750-3

The editors thank Neil Hanson of
Lovell Johns, Sharon Charity, David
Haslam, Sally Darlington, Melanie
Gould, Anna Holmes and Andrea
Thomas for their assistance during the
preparation of this edition.

FOR THE SERIES:
Series Editor:
  David Townsend Jones
Map Editor: David Haslam
Indexer: Hilary Bird
Gazetteer: Anne Evans
Cover design: Roger Walton Studio

FOR THIS EDITION:
Edited on desktop by:
  David Townsend Jones
Art editor: Eileen Townsend Jones
Illustrators: Jeremy Ford (David
  Lewis Artists), Illustra Design Ltd.,
  Rodney Paull, Karen Cochrane,
  David Baird, Sylvia Hughes-Williams
Cover photo: Aberham/Britstock IFA

FOR MITCHELL BEAZLEY:
Art Director: Tim Foster
Managing Editor: Alison Starling
Production: Matthew Batchelor

PRODUCTION CREDITS:
Maps by Lovell Johns, Oxford,
  England
London Underground map
  © London Regional Transport
Typeset in Garamond and
  News Gothic
Desktop layout in Ventura
  Publisher
Linotronic output by
  Tradespools Limited, Frome,
  England

Contents

Culture, history and background

Basic information

Planning

London's districts

Walkers' London

Sights and places of interest

Where to stay

Eating and drinking

Nightlife and entertainment

Shopping

Recreation

Excursions

279: Bath. **284:** Brighton. **287:** Cambridge. **291:** Canterbury.
294: Oxford. **298:** Stratford-upon-Avon. **301:** Windsor and Eton.

Maps

London Underground

How to use this book

Few guidelines are needed to understand how this book works:

- For the general organization of the book, see CONTENTS on the pages preceding this one.
- Wherever appropriate, chapters and sections are arranged alphabetically, with headings appearing in **CAPITALS.**
- Often these headings are followed by location and practical information printed in *italics.*
- As you turn the pages, you will find subject headers, similar to those used in telephone directories, printed in CAPITALS in the top corner of each page.
- If you still cannot find what you need, check in the comprehensive and exhaustively cross-referenced INDEX at the back of the book.
- Following the index, a LIST OF STREET NAMES provides map references for all roads and streets mentioned in the book that are located within the areas covered by the main city maps.

CROSS-REFERENCES
These are printed in SMALL CAPITALS, referring you to other sections or alphabetical entries in the book. Care has been taken to ensure that such cross-references are self-explanatory. Often, page references are also given, although their excessive use would be intrusive and ugly.

FLOORS
We use the European convention in this book: "ground floor" means the floor at ground level (called by Americans the "first floor").

KEY TO SYMBOLS

☎	Telephone	▭	Secure garage
Fx	Facsimile (fax)	⌂	Quiet hotel
★	Recommended sight	⬍	Elevator
☆	Worth a detour	♿	Facilities for disabled people
i	Tourist information	▢	TV in each room
⇐	Parking	▱	Telephone in each room
🏛	Building of architectural interest	🐕	Dogs not allowed
		≋	Swimming pool
▣	Free entrance	☘	Garden
▩	Entrance fee payable	⊰	Good view
✗	Photography forbidden	♆	Gym/fitness facilities
↗	Guided tour	⅄	Bar
▣	Cafeteria	▭	Mini-bar
✳	Special interest for children	⟁	Sauna
❧	Hotel	⚇	Conference facilities
▪	Simple hotel	≡	Restaurant
⬜	Luxury hotel	●	Simple restaurant
♣	Good value (in its class)	⌂	Luxury restaurant
▢	Cheap	⌂	A la carte available
▢	Inexpensive	▰	Set (fixed-price) menu available
▣	Moderately priced		
▤	Expensive	➤	Good wines
▥	Very expensive	⊖	Open-air dining
AE	American Express	○	Disco dancing
⊡	Diners Club	♪	Nightclub
◉	MasterCard/Access	♫	Live music
VISA	Visa/Barclaycard	❦	Dancing

HOTEL AND RESTAURANT PRICE CATEGORIES

These are denoted by the symbols ▢ (cheap), ▢ (inexpensive), ▣ (moderately priced), ▤ (expensive) and ▥ (very expensive). They correspond approximately to the following actual local prices, which give a guideline **at the time of printing**. Naturally, prices tend to rise, but, with a few exceptions, hotels and restaurants will remain in the same price category.

Price categories		Corresponding to approximate prices	
		for **hotels**	for **restaurants**
		double room with	*meal for one with*
		bath + breakfast; singles	*service, VAT and*
		are slightly cheaper	*house wine*
▥	very expensive	over £170	over £45
▤	expensive	£130-170	£30-45
▣	moderately priced	£100-130	£20-30
▢	inexpensive	£70-100	£15-20
▢	cheap	under £70	under £15

About the authors

Michael Jackson, writer and presenter of the television series *The Beer Hunter* (commissioned for Britain's Channel 4 and seen on Discovery Channel in the US), wrote the original *American Express Pocket Guide to London,* which won the 1983 London Tourist Board Guide Book of the Year award. His other books include *The Pocket Beer Book, Michael Jackson's Pocket Cocktail and Bar Book* and *The World Guide to Beer* (all three published under different titles in the US).

Joint authors of *3-D London* (with Caroline Sharpe), *3-D Manhattan* and *3-D Amsterdam,* **Leonie Glass** and **Fiona Duncan** have collaborated on revisions of this guide in its earlier format since the second edition. The third edition won the London Tourist Board's Best General London Guide Book of the Decade award in 1990. In this new, redesigned edition they have refocused and greatly expanded the scope of the guide.

John Roberts contributed SIGHTS AND PLACES OF INTEREST to the first and second editions. Other contributors to this edition were **Catherine Palmer** (BASIC INFORMATION, RECREATION and CALENDAR OF EVENTS) and **Jonah Jones** (who reshaped LONDON'S ARCHITECTURE).

A message from the series editor

In designing *American Express London* we aimed to make this brand-new edition simple and instinctive to use, like all its sister volumes in our new, larger paperback format.

The hallmarks of the relaunched series are clear, classic typography, confidence in fine travel writing for its own sake, and faith in our readers' innate intelligence to find their way around the books without heavy-handed signposting by editors.

Readers with anything less than 20:20 vision will doubtless also enjoy the larger, clearer type, and can now dispense with the mythical magnifying glasses we never issued free with the old pocket guide series.

Months of concentrated work by the updating authors and our editors have been dedicated to ensuring that this edition is as accurate and up to date as possible as it goes to press. But time and change are forever the enemies, and in between editions we very much appreciate it when you, our readers, keep us informed of changes that you discover.

As ever, I am indebted to all the many readers who wrote during the preparation of this edition. Please remember that your feedback is extremely important to our efforts to tailor the series to the very distinctive tastes and requirements of our sophisticated international readership.

Send your comments to me at Mitchell Beazley International Ltd, Michelin House, 81 Fulham Road, London SW3 6RB; or, in the US, c/o American Express Travel Guides, Prentice Hall Travel, 15 Columbus Circle, New York, NY 10023.

David Townsend Jones

London

London: a city for explorers

To see the pageantry of London, or the architecture, to visit the theater or the places of government and jurisdiction, is to be immersed for a moment in a city that was capital of half the world, and enjoyed that position rather more recently than Athens, Rome or Constantinople. Nor has London yet cast aside the robes of her eminence. She may be wrinkled in some places, face-lifted in others, and over-painted here and there, but she has retained dignity in her middle age.

The attitude of Londoners to their own city can puzzle the newcomer. There is a defiant defensiveness in the proclamation, "I love New York"; Londoners are cooler and seem more detached, but are inclined nevertheless to be deeply and irremovably in love with their city. They will rightly evince anger at the handiwork perpetrated by planners and developers in the postwar period, but the irony is that such licensed vandalism prospered so long without restraint simply because the profusion of fine and historic architecture seemed inexhaustible.

To the newcomer, London is an overwhelming jumble of antiquity, a labyrinthine junk store with "finds" hidden all over the place, often apparently unnoticed and gathering dust. Sometimes it seems that every house was the birthplace of someone famous, or the scene of an invention, each corner the site of an important speech, a battle or an especially vile crime, each name one that has passed into the language.

The irrepressible curiosities of London manifest themselves from Greenwich in the east to Richmond in the west, two of the most interesting and pleasant little towns in England. Both maintain their identities while remaining parts of London, although they stand about 20 miles apart (London is at some points 35 miles from end to end), and each can be reached by pleasure boat from the heart of the capital.

TWO CITIES

London grew from the river; the Thames was its first thoroughfare, its lifeline and its means of social irrigation. Because the first route to London was up the river, successive waves of immigrants, Italians, Jews, Huguenots and many others settled in what became known as the "East End," a series of waterside, working-class communities which has nurtured its own culture, patois and social mores. They settled in the east because, being foreigners, they had been barred in times past from entering the city. Yet there were older immigrants in London from the beginning; Romans founded the settlement nearly 2,000 years ago, and many a Cockney today has a discernibly Roman nose.

This is how the city was born. Yet when Londoners talk about "the City," they mean specifically and exclusively that part that was originally walled and still vestigially is, and which covers no more than one square mile, located between Tower Bridge and Blackfriars Bridge.

The City is the financial district, the "Wall Street" of Britain. The Lord Mayor of London represents only this square mile, and its streets are patrolled by the separate City Police. The City does not include the famous shopping streets, or theaterland, and does not care. It is an entity within itself, parochial yet worldly, with its own rituals and customs, and its preoccupation with bulls and bears and commodity prices.

London is governed not from the City but from the town halls of its more than 30 boroughs. Britain is governed not from the City but from Westminster, a mile upriver. Westminster, once a small city too but now spread far from the river, today takes in Covent Garden, Soho, theaterland and the main shopping streets of central London. Yet, because of its geographical relationship with the original walled city, we call today's center the "West End."

While the City remained fiercely independent and introspective, Westminster was the royal seat, and London has good reason to be grateful. The royal residences of Westminster (St James's, Buckingham Palace and Clarence House) are joined to those of Kensington (Kensington Palace) by a long swathe of royal parks. Through St James's Park, Green Park, Hyde Park and Kensington Gardens, you can walk miles across the great metropolis amid the greenery. With Holland Park, Regent's Park, and the Georgian and Victorian squares of Bloomsbury, Chelsea and Kensington, London has a remarkably green inner city.

A CITY OF VILLAGES

Born from two separate cities on the river, modern London is, not surprisingly, a complex patchwork of villages. To anyone from outside, Chelsea is probably the most familiar district name in the capital. It is also a neighborhood that perfectly demonstrates London's enigmatic charm, contriving simultaneously to be grand and yet to be a pristine, dollhouse village. At one moment, it spreads itself elegantly on the riverside; in another it hugs itself in narrow streets, cozy as a cat. It has been smart, then bohemian, and is now both, and yet richer than ever. It has the most discreet streets in London, yet its main thoroughfare, King's Road, if no longer quite as outré as in the 1960s, remains bereft of caution. It is always unmistakably Chelsea, yet, like London itself, it has many moods.

The changes of mood can be sudden. South Kensington has some of the wealthiest streets in Britain, North Kensington some of the poorest. Yet deprivation has not bred dullness, nor isolation. Take Brixton, south of the river. Less than a ghetto, despite occasional tensions, it has a delightful market, for jellied eels, an old cockney delicacy, as well as yams and breadfruit.

The river may no longer influence population trends. Indeed, with the decline of river transport and the flood of Victorian road-building along its banks, it became woefully neglected. (There are, however, signs of improvement, with developments such as Chelsea Harbour and Docklands beginning to utilize its great potential.) The underground railway lines had more influence on where people settled. Parts of South London became places of cheap housing when they were ignored by the underground systems; but when the new Victoria line went south in 1969, these neighborhoods suddenly became attractive to a new generation of young, professional people who no longer wished to live out in the suburbs. The contemporary equivalent was the 1980s boom in London's

Docklands. The same "gentrification" has taken place in several districts that were built for the artisan; the social classes are as identifiable in London as they are anywhere else in Britain, but nowhere else do they quite so readily live together.

Strangers get lost in London. So do Londoners, unless they are cab drivers. It is a city in which to lose oneself, an engrossing experience. People who are afraid of getting lost, who believe that every city should be built as a piece, at a single stroke, to a well-ordered plan, should not come. London was not built for efficiency. It is a city for explorers.

London, that great sea, whose ebb and flow
At once is deaf and loud, and on the shore
Vomits its wrecks, and still howls on for more
(Shelley, *Letter to Maria Gisborne,* 1819)

Culture, history and background

Landmarks in London's history

AD43: The invading Romans under Claudius defeated the Celtic tribes of Southeast Britain and bridged the Thames close to the site of the later London Bridge. By **AD60**, London was a thriving port and settlement at the center of the Roman road network. **AD60**: A revolt by Iceni tribe from East Anglia, under Queen Boadicea, culminated in the destruction of London.

200: England's capital, and a prosperous city of traders, London was fortified by the Romans. Walls ran from the modern sites of the Tower to Aldgate, along London Wall to the Barbican and down to the river at Blackfriars. **200-400**: The Romans used Germanic mercenaries to help defend this outpost of their weakening empire. **410**: The Romans withdrew, and London reverted to a farming town under the Angle and Saxon warrior kings.

700-820: England gradually reunited under the kings of Wessex, from Winchester. London was an important provincial market town. Christianity was slowly reintroduced, stimulating learning.

836: London was sacked by the Vikings. For almost two centuries it was a borderland pawn in their struggle with the western Saxon kingdoms. **1014**: London was taken by storm for the last time; Olaf, an Anglo-Saxon, tied his boats to London Bridge and sailed downstream to destroy it. (Hence the song *London Bridge is Falling Down*.)

1052: Disgusted by London's switching of support to his enemies, King Edward the Confessor started to build a new abbey and palace named Westminster on the Isle of Thorney. The tension between the City and the Crown was born.

1066: The Norman invasion. William did not attack the well-fortified London, but forced it into submission by destroying the surrounding farmlands. **1066-1100**: London accepted and thrived under the civilized Norman rule. William I built the Tower of London.

1140-90: As the king and powerful barons feuded, undermining political stability, London exacted a price for its support. It won the power to raise taxes and elect its own governors. The powerful guilds, confederations of merchants, controlled trade. **1215**: London accepted the Charter of Incorporation from King John, confirming the authority of the Lord Mayor, who was elected annually by 24 aldermen. Displeased by heavy taxes, London supported the barons in drafting Magna Carta. **1217**: The first stone bridge over the Thames, London Bridge, was built. **1263**: Trade guilds took control from the aldermen during the turbulent period of baronial wars, reinstituting Government by citizens' assembly (an Anglo-Saxon idea).

1269: Henry II began the construction of the new Westminster Abbey after a boundary dispute with the City. **1280**: Old St Paul's Cathedral was completed, half as tall again as the current St Paul's. The precincts housed a sports arena, markets and a brewery. Inside the city, 126 parish churches plus monasteries displaced the population.

1326: The new urban pressures of the city erupted in riots against the king. Foreigners and Jews were attacked. **1338**: Edward III made Westminster the regular meeting place of Parliament. Previously it had met only irregularly. **1348**: The Black Death: half the city's 60,000 population died.

1381: The Peasants' Revolt. Seeking an end to feudalism, a working-class "army," led by Wat Tyler from Kent, took over London for two days. Tyler was killed by the mayor. **1399**: London supported Parliament in forcing the deposition of the absolutist and heavily-taxing Richard II.

1411: Work began on the Guildhall, the city's "royal palace." Professional soldiers and tradesmen formed a new wealthy class threatening the old feudal aristocracy.

1461: London's support was essential to Edward IV, victor of the Wars of the Roses, in the struggle to restore stability to the country and its trade. The king knighted many London citizens in return for their support.

1500-1600: London's population exploded from 50,000 to 200,000 during the economic boom born of the relatively stable Tudor period. New slum areas arose outside London, all of them ungoverned suburbs, including the red-light district of Southwark.

1533: Henry VIII's Reformation. The new gentry class snapped up land vacated by the dissolution of the monasteries. Henry founded downriver naval bases. **1553-58**: Queen Mary reinstated Catholicism. Citizens were martyred at Smithfield. London subsequently supported the parsimonious Protestant Elizabeth I for 45 years.

1600-70: The new gentry, now an aristocracy, began to develop their new land, moving westward, building on the edge of the countryside in Piccadilly and Leicester Square. **1603-42**: Puritanism flourished in the city as a reaction against the autocratic Stuart kings, James I and Charles I. **1642-49**: London financed Parliament in the Civil War. London and Westminster were both embraced by new fortifications, and the citizens manned the defenses. In **1649**, London was the setting for Charles I's execution. **1649-60**: The Commonwealth republic. London traders gradually reacted against the religious radicals' egalitarianism, and supported the restoration of Charles II in **1660**.

1665-66: The Great Plague. In this last and worst outbreak, at least 100,000 died in just over a year. **1666**: The Great Fire. Medieval London was destroyed after a fire that started in a baker's shop in Pudding Lane. **1666-1700**: Reconstruction with stone buildings and wider streets. Wren's visionary plan of a grid of streets with piazzas infringed too many property rights; private ownership was the true interest that shaped the new landscape. Instead Wren built 51 churches, culminating in St Paul's.

By **1700**, the 300,000 population was widely dispersed after the fire.

1700-50: Both the new urban poor and the fashionable elite pushed up the population to 675,000 by **1750**. The villages of Knightsbridge and Marylebone were incorporated, and St James's and Mayfair were developed. To the E and S were slums, where gin consumption averaged two pints per person per week and only one child in four lived beyond the age of five.

1774: The City, still self-governing, elected the radical John Wilkes as Mayor after he was expelled from Parliament three times. It still distrusted the cultured West End and the almost omnipotent Parliament. **1780**: The Gordon Riots. Anarchy in London lasted for a week, but still there was no police force with day-to-day authority. **1780-1820**: The middle and upper classes moved ever more to the suburbs in the W, as slums and urban pressures increased. No comprehensive system of local government had yet emerged. **1829**: The Metropolitan Police or "Peelers," the first police force, was founded. In **1835** the City founded its own force. **1820-38**: The Prince Regent, later George IV, and architect Nash developed Regent's Park and Regent St., Buckingham Palace and The Mall.

1835: Britain was given local councils, but London was exempted from this and continued to be "governed" by more than 150 parishes, encompassing 300 administrative bodies. Slum clearance was still partially executed by the Commissioner for Woods and Forests. **1839**: The new Palace of Westminster, the present one, was started after the old one was burned down. **1844**: The controlling monopoly in the printing of money was granted to the Bank of England. **1832-66**: Cholera killed thousands: various Public Health Acts had no effect on London, until the Metropolitan Board of Works was founded in 1855. Destitution was worsened by the clearance of land for railways.

1851: The Great Exhibition in the Crystal Palace in Hyde Park celebrated British supremacy in trade, science and industry. It was consolidated by Prince Albert's development of the museums and learned institutions of South Kensington. **1863**: Railways became available to the working class for the first time. The first underground line was opened. Increased mobility and belated public health and education measures improved Londoners' quality of life.

1889: The London County Council was formed, giving London comprehensive local government for the first time.

1897: Queen Victoria's Diamond Jubilee. London was described as the "centre of an empire on which the sun never sets."

1900-05: The opening of four new electric underground lines began a rapid expansion of the city into sprawling suburbs. **1914-18**: Women took over many public services in London during World War I, and the suffragettes won the vote in **1918**. **1920-30**: The "Homes for Heroes" program was part of the growth of vast new estates, which quadrupled the size of London. **1940**: The Blitz. London was bombed, mainly in the City and East End; St Paul's stood alone amid the rubble.

1945-55: Private and local government redevelopment of the city resulted in its fast modernization. **1951**: The Festival of Britain, one of the first world fairs. **1955-65**: Boom years for property developers, who erected prestigious skyscrapers, while London County Council concentrated on housing in the suburbs. The population of Central London stood at its lowest for centuries. **1956**: The Clean Air Act created smokeless zones and marked the end of central London as an industrial area.

1960-70: "Swinging London." An economic boom, immigration and changing values and wealth patterns made London more cosmopolitan. In 1965, the Greater London Council succeeded the LCC.

1970-80: Local government gained strength throughout the Greater London area. **1986**: The Labour GLC was abolished by the Conservative government. The London Stock Exchange was reformed — the "Big Bang." **1987**: Margaret Thatcher's Conservative government was re-elected for a third term of office. The first black MPs were elected. **1989**: First televising of the House of Commons.

1992: Britain joined the European Single Market. Deep recession signaled the end of the booming **1980s** and the start of a more sober decade. New building slowed; house prices tumbled. Conservative Party won fourth successive General Election.

Who's who

A list of the famous whose names are linked with London would be endless. The following personal selection pays particular attention to those mentioned in this book.

Adam, Robert (1728-92)
The great Scottish Neo-Classical architect and designer brought new refinement to the town and country houses of London.

Albert, Prince (1819-61)
Queen Victoria's consort endeared himself to Londoners, despite his German origin. He left his stamp on the capital in the massive KENSINGTON museum and learned society complex.

Bacon, Sir Francis (1561-1626)
The great philosopher and statesman of the Elizabethan and Jacobean period was a member of GRAY'S INN.

Boadicea (died AD61)
Now considered a national heroine, the warlike queen led her Iceni tribe against the Romans, razing London to the ground before her defeat. Her statue graces Westminster Bridge.

Browning, Robert (1812-89)
Apart from 15 years spent in Italy with his wife Elizabeth Barrett of Wimpole St. fame, the Victorian poet spent most of his life in London, largely by the REGENT'S CANAL at Little Venice.

Carlyle, Thomas (1795-1881)
Author of *The French Revolution* and in many ways the essential Victorian intellectual, Carlyle lived for 47 years in CHELSEA in preference to his native Scotland. CARLYLE'S HOUSE is as he left it.

Charles I (1600-49)
The most ambitious of Britain's royal patrons ended his reign on the scaffold after defeat in the Civil War with Parliament. He was led to his execution from his own BANQUETING HOUSE.

Charles II (1630-85)
Perhaps the most flamboyant of kings, Charles II enjoys enduring fame thanks to his indiscreet relationships with the likes of Nell Gwynne. More significantly, he was a great patron of the London theater, developed the royal parks and presided over the rebuilding of the CITY.

Chaucer, Geoffrey (c.1340-1400)
The greatest of the medieval English poets was for many years a senior customs official of the port of London. The pilgrims of *The Canterbury Tales* set off from a Southwark inn.

Churchill, Sir Winston (1874-1965)
The steadfastness of the wartime national leader helped Londoners endure the horrors of the German bombing of their city — the Blitz. This he successfully organized from his secret Cabinet War Rooms bunker in WHITEHALL.

Constable, John (1776-1837)
The great painter of the English countryside lived for many years in HAMPSTEAD. Several of his finest works, on view at the VICTORIA & ALBERT

MUSEUM, show views of the Heath. He is buried in Hampstead parish churchyard.

Coram, Thomas *(c.1668-1751)*
This bluff sea captain became one of the 18thC's leading philanthropists in his retirement, setting up the Foundling Hospital. The CORAM FOUNDATION displays works by the artists whom Coram enlisted into his fund-raising efforts.

Cubitt, Thomas *(1788-1855)*
To this energetic man can be credited some of the finest housing in London. Establishing the first modern building firm and inventing the concept of "speculative builder," he constructed much of BLOOMSBURY and BELGRAVIA.

Dickens, Charles *(1812-70)*
In novels such as *Oliver Twist* and *The Old Curiosity Shop,* Dickens drew attention to the appalling social deprivations of Victorian London.

Edward the Confessor *(c.1002-66)*
This pious king began the Normanization of England that culminated in the Conquest. He also reinforced the importance of London by establishing his palace at WESTMINSTER.

Flamsteed, John *(1646-1719)*
The first Astronomer Royal, working largely at the Royal Observatory at GREENWICH, recorded no fewer than 3,000 stars.

Garrick, David *(1717-79)*
The English stage's greatest actor/manager, Garrick established the naturalistic style that modern acting takes for granted. Most of his performances were in COVENT GARDEN.

Gibbons, Grinling *(1648-1721)*
Wren's master-carver decorated many of the great architect's outstanding buildings with incomparably naturalistic flowers, leaves, fruits, musical instruments — all sculpted in wood or stone with Baroque exuberance. The greatest profusion is to be seen at ST PAUL'S CATHEDRAL or HAMPTON COURT.

Gibbs, James *(1682-1754)*
Continuing where Wren had left off, this Scottish architect introduced some of the more theatrical elements of the Italian Baroque to London church building. Excellent examples can be seen at ST MARY-LE-STRAND and ST MARTIN-IN-THE-FIELDS.

Gresham, Sir Thomas *(1519-79)*
Founder of the Royal Exchange in the CITY, Gresham was one of the great merchants and financiers of the Elizabethan age, when London began to establish its dominance in international commerce.

Henry VIII *(1491-1547)*
The heavy hand of this powerful monarch was repeatedly felt in London — not least in the dissolution of the monasteries. Among more positive achievements, he moved the chief royal palace to WHITEHALL (giving Westminster to Parliament) and built up ST JAMES'S PALACE and HAMPTON COURT.

Hogarth, William *(1697-1764)*
With the sharpest of all eyes for any kind of social foible or moral

weakness, Hogarth in his paintings and engravings has given us an unforgettable picture of the seamier sides of life in 18thC London. HOGARTH'S HOUSE at CHISWICK is now a museum.

Johnson, Dr. Samuel *(1709-84)*
The giant of 18thC letters patronized the pubs of FLEET STREET, the coffeehouses of COVENT GARDEN and wrote his famous dictionary at DR. JOHNSON'S HOUSE nearby.

Jones, Inigo *(1573-1652)*
With this architect, the ideas of the Italian Renaissance came to England with extraordinary sureness and originality. Examples of his bold vision can be seen in the Queen's House at GREENWICH, the BANQUETING HOUSE and COVENT GARDEN.

Keats, John *(1795-1821)*
The perfect romantic poet, and a consumptive to boot, wrote much of his best work at HAMPSTEAD (see KEATS' HOUSE).

Marx, Karl *(1818-83)*
Writing in German in the BRITISH MUSEUM, the political economist whose theories split the world down the middle lived for most of his life as an exile in SOHO and North London. People still flock to his grave in the Cemetery at HIGHGATE.

Nash, John *(1752-1835)*
MARBLE ARCH, REGENT'S PARK and Carlton House Terrace in THE MALL are the visible legacies of this Regency architect. Just as significant is the fine town planning scheme of which Regent St. forms the main axis.

Pepys, Samuel *(1633-1703)*
Recording the Great Plague and Fire of London, Pepys' diary is an outstanding social document, presenting an irresistible account of daily life in the 17thC city.

Prince Regent *(1762-1830)*
In many ways a ludicrous figure, the Regent (later George IV) led the nation in fashion and sport, and backed the ambitious town-planning schemes of John Nash.

Rogers, Richard *(born 1933)*
Innovative contemporary architect who, having won acclaim for his Pompidou Center in Paris, was commissioned to build the controversial Lloyd's Building in the CITY. His recent work includes the restoration and conversion of Billingsgate Market.

Shakespeare, William *(1564-1616)*
The London stage saw the first productions of almost all the bard's plays — usually in the theaters of SOUTHWARK, where he worked, although sometimes in the halls of the INNS OF COURT.

Sloane, Sir Hans *(1660-1753)*
The BRITISH MUSEUM, NATURAL HISTORY MUSEUM and MUSEUM OF MANKIND all ultimately owe their existence to this successful physician's vast collections, bequeathed to the nation.

Tyler, Wat *(died 1381)*
After his capture of the TOWER OF LONDON, the leader of the great Peasant's Revolt of 1381 was killed by the Lord Mayor of London while attempting to parley with Richard II at Smithfield.

Wellington, Duke of *(1769-1852)*
The leading British general of the Napoleonic Wars, Wellington ultimately defeated Napoleon at the Battle of Waterloo. He went on to become an authoritarian prime minister, during which time he lived at APSLEY HOUSE, now the Wellington Museum.

Whittington, Dick *(1358-1423)*
A rich merchant and the greatest medieval Lord Mayor of London, Whittington has passed into legend. In the quintessential rags-to-riches story, he paused in flight from the City on Highgate Hill (accompanied by his famous cat), when the bells of ST MARY-LE-BOW called him back to greatness.

William the Conqueror *(c.1027-87)*
Having defeated the English and declared himself their first Norman king, William consolidated by building the massive TOWER OF LONDON.

Wolsey, Cardinal *(c.1473-1530)*
Promoted by Henry VIII but falling from grace when he failed to secure the king's divorce, this powerful churchman's palaces at WHITEHALL and HAMPTON COURT were confiscated and became the favorite royal residences.

Wren, Sir Christopher *(1632-1723)*
The dazzling career of the greatest British architect includes a staggering number of major buildings, most of them in London — a feat made possible by the ravages of the Great Fire of 1666. Numerous city churches, ST PAUL'S CATHEDRAL, major parts of HAMPTON COURT and ST JAMES'S PALACE testify to his genius.

London's architecture

London was not the vision of an emperor or king. Surprised visitors, knowing by repute its showcase architectural masterpieces, find not a city of grand avenues and broad boulevards but a family of villages, offering delightfully distracting details more often than panoramic views. A uniquely pervasive grandeur derives from this blending of a rich heritage of fine buildings into the everyday life, past and present, of a bustling city.

A CHRONOLOGY OF ENGLISH ARCHITECTURAL STYLES

London has been settled continuously since Roman times. For the Romans, Londinium was a fording place and the strategic nodal point of the radiating road system that enabled effective government. London therefore reflects throughout the ages a microcosm of the succession of architectural styles that have adorned Britain since Norman times, for the Roman settlement has been overlaid by the concentration of subsequent building in the city.

Styles merge, of course, and nowhere is the tension between Classical and Gothic more in evidence than in the mass of building that took place with the advent and extension of Empire.

Norman (1066-1200)   Sturdy buildings based on mass and volume. Round, massive piers, round arches (often with "dog-tooth" or chevron ornament), plain barrel vaulting. Secular building mostly consists of square towers and keeps.

Gothic (1180-1540)   Lighter, more dynamic structures. Flying buttresses, crockets (carved ornaments in the form of a curled leaf), pointed arches and windows, spires. Galleries and arcades replace internal walls. Main periods are **Early English** (1180-1260), marked by simplicity and airiness; **Decorated** (1250-1370), using more extensive surface decoration and window tracery, with the advent of stained glass; and **Perpendicular** (1300-1540), with long slender columns stressing vertical line, elaborate fan-vaulting and paneled windows.

Tudor (1540-1603)   Influence of Italian Renaissance in decoration, especially plasterwork and carved gables. Extensive use of red brick, often on geometrical **E** and **H** plans. Flat, pointed arches; large mullioned windows with leaded glass in lozenge pattern.

Jacobean (1603-25)   Greater extravagance in wood and plaster decoration; paneled interiors of dark oak. Wider use of Italian motifs, more for their manner than their meaning, in both building and furniture.

Classical (1615-66)   Inigo Jones introduces more austere Palladian style from Northern Italy. After Great Fire of 1666, Christopher Wren and Hawksmoor return to Classical simplicity and develop it toward a dignified, sophisticated Baroque.

English Baroque (1690-1720)   Fluidity and elaboration of Continental Baroque tempered by English moderation. Classical pediments over niches, wall embrasures, doors, windows and facades, with accent on symmetry. Heroic monuments, e.g., to Nelson in St Paul's.

Georgian (1720-1820)   Italianate buildings, columns and porticoes, often quite plain, combined with the new art of landscape gardening. Classical elements persist, based on Greek orders of Doric, Ionic and Corinthian, but on a more domestic scale in London squares.

Regency (1780-1820)   Development of Georgian style with delicate interior ornament and often panels of stucco relief, light-hearted and owing much to Rococo shells, trees and flowers.

Victorian (1830-1900)   Extravagantly treated Neo-Gothic themes, with heavily ornamented facades to public buildings, contrasting with structures in iron and glass in industrial sites and rail terminals, along with a rash of streetscapes.

Edwardian (1905-1920)   Direct simplicity in domestic buildings; honest use of brick, stone and wood. Rather plainer than Victorian, but in its soundness reflecting the stability and wealth of Empire at its height before the Great War. Elements of **Art Nouveau** introduced from the Glasgow and Viennese schools.

Modernist (1930 to present)   Influence of Bauhaus, based on rationalism and function. Reduction of ornament; airy interiors with glass facades and often on green sites. Conversely, brutalism in concrete, with accent on basic sculptural form, often at expense of human considerations. Imaginative use of new materials, aluminum, stainless steel and plastics.

Post-Modernist (1970 to present)   Eclectic and hi-tech, with Neoclassical elements. Much use of reflecting-glass facades, with emphasis sometimes on engineering features. Uninhibited use of color and materials: highly pictorial. In corporate projects, the building is the message — a sort of three-dimensional logo.

LONDON

Especially near the Barbican, London is still blessed with the stones and mortar of its Roman founders in the remnants of the 2ndC city wall. Defense was still the vital consideration when the Norman conquest of 1066 was followed by the construction in 1078 of the huge, square White Tower (in the Tower of London), which today provides one of Europe's finest surviving examples of a Norman keep.

Westminster Abbey, begun in 1245, is London's finest remaining medieval building, the abbey's E arm epitomizing the elegant Early English style, with the later nave built in the Perpendicular style. Timber roofing, one of the glories

The White Tower

of the English Gothic, survives in the hammer-beam roof of Westminster Hall (see the drawing on page 191), in the Great Hall of Hampton Court (1536), and also in St James's Palace, a superb red-brick example of the ornate Tudor adaptations of Gothic.

Inigo Jones, born in 1573 in Smithfield, brought the vigor and sophistication of Italian Renaissance styles to London, most notably the elegant symmetry of Andrea Palladio. Jones' particular contribution to the building of London was the development of Covent Garden, especially the Piazza (1631-39), and the first two Palladian buildings in London, the Banqueting House in Whitehall, based on a double cube, dating from 1619-22 and illustrated on page 100, and the delightful Queen's House in Greenwich.

The west end of **St Paul's Cathedral**

Sir Christopher Wren (1632-1723), an Oxford-educated scientist, and later Surveyor of the King's Works, was entrusted with the rebuilding of the City after the Great Fire. On the churches of the City he designed towers and steeples to lead the eye to the dome of St Paul's Cathedral. In his buildings, Wren used elements of the Classical Renaissance style, but was obliged to adapt its geometrical grandeur and piazzas to the framework of the medieval city's alleys and courtyards.

Wren's secular buildings include the Royal Naval Hospital, Greenwich (1696-1702), and the Royal Hospital, Chelsea (1681-91). His assistant **Nicholas Hawksmoor** designed several churches that are increasingly appreciated; a fine example is St Mary Woolnoth (1716-24). Wren also influenced **Sir James Gibbs**, a leader of the English Baroque, and the combination of styles is exemplified by St Martin-in-the-Fields (1722-26).

> *Si monumentum requiris, circumspice.*
> If you seek a monument, look around you.
> (Sir Christopher Wren's epitaph in St Paul's Cathedral)

In the Georgian period, fashion swung away from Baroque back to the rules and conventions of Classical architecture, a move typified by Palladian Chiswick House (1725-29), illustrated on page 111, which also has a garden landscaped by **William Kent**. The same notions of refine-

Nash's west wing of **Buckingham Palace** can only be seen from the palace garden.

ment and good taste were evident in the Georgian terraces built at this time. The dominant designer was **Robert Adam** (1728-92), one of a family of influential architects, whose terraced town houses were unified by an elegant facade.

In the later part of the Georgian period, the Regency architect **John Nash** (1752-1835) used these themes to give a sense of shape and elegance to the heart of modern London. Seen from Piccadilly Circus, the bold, sweeping curve of Regent St. echoes Nash's plan for a triumphal "Royal Mile" from the Prince Regent's residence at Carlton House to Regent's Park. At either end of this mile are two pristine examples of Nash's work: Carlton House Terrace (1827-32) and Park Crescent (1812-22). His original design for Buckingham Palace was partly concealed by later additions, and the surviving w wing, overlooking the palace garden, remains hidden from outside view. Nash's elegant terraces and crescents were mirrored in the development of Belgravia and Chelsea, largely by **Thomas Cubitt**, in the 1820s and 1830s.

The sterner values of the Victorian period were reflected in church-like buildings such as the Houses of Parliament (1840-50, **Sir Charles Barry**

St Pancras Station as it appeared in 1926.

and **Augustus Pugin**), pictured on page 189. This Gothic Revival architecture had moments of fantasy, as the spires and complex details of St Pancras Station (1868-74, **Sir Gilbert Scott**; illustrated on the preceding page) happily demonstrate.

The railway era also brought some breathtaking examples of civil engineering, and the interior of Paddington Station (1850-4,

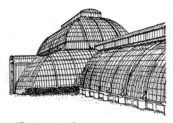

The Kew Gardens conservatorium

Isambard Kingdom Brunel) remains a good memorial to the best of these. Similarly inspired use of cast iron and sheet glass is seen in the magnificent conservatorium at Kew Gardens (1844-48, **Decimus Burton** and **Richard Turner**).

The 20thC has produced some of London's least attractive architecture, although the passing of time is leading to a greater appreciation of surviving industrial buildings from the 1910s to the 1930s such as the Art Nouveau-influenced Michelin building (1910) on the Fulham Rd.

The Hoover factory

(pictured on page 83), the Art Deco Hoover factory (1932, **Wallis, Gilbert & Partners**) on Western Ave., and the now sadly abandoned Battersea Power Station (1932-4, **Giles Gilbert Scott**). Bauhaus refugees founded the design group **Tecton**, which designed Highgate's Highpoint Flats (1936), described by Le Corbusier as "a vertical garden city."

Notable postwar buildings, all of which have provoked controversy, are Oxford Street's dominant Centrepoint (1965, **Richard Seifert**), which became a symbol of profligate speculation, the National Theatre (1967-77, **Denys Lasdun**), in the cold, horizontal style of the South Bank complex (illustrated on page 250), and the vast glass and tubular steel Lloyd's Building (1986, **Richard Rogers**).

Most recently attention has focused on the Broadgate complex of shops and offices in the City, on the 800-foot tower at Canary Wharf, Docklands (**Cesar Pelli**), and on the Sainsbury Wing at the National Gallery, designed by American husband and wife team **Robert Venturi** and **Denise Scott-Brown**, of which the interior, at least, has been greeted by universal acclaim.

Although the Prince of Wales' outspoken criticism of modern architecture in the capital has infuriated contemporary architects, it has succeeded in focusing attention on the subject, and has helped to accelerate the trend away from the brutalism of the 1960s and 1970s. Curves have replaced hard lines, steel, glass and brick have replaced concrete, and architects are employing Classical motifs — pediments, porticoes, columns, moldings — within the context of modern architecture. Plans are afoot to rectify some of the worst mistakes, such as the dismal walkways of the South Bank complex and the barren wastes of Paternoster Square.

In the end, London's sheer scale and history easily absorb these occasional slights to her essential spirit, and the eye is forever entertained by the variety of styles, from **Robert Smirke's** British Museum to **J.F. Bentley's** neo-Byzantine Westminster Cathedral, from Alexandra Palace (from which BBC Television broadcast in its early days) to **Robert Adam's** Kenwood House.

The Lloyd's Building

You look out from the 'City of the Dead' [Highgate Cemetery] on the top of Highgate Hill at an enormous London spread out before you. It is a *living* city. You can see Canary Wharf, the Tower of London, the Natwest Tower, St Paul's, St Pancras Station, Big Ben and the Telecom Tower; between them are a dozen tower blocks and a hundred church spires and towers by Wren, Hawksmoor, Gibbs, Smirke, Nash, Wyatt, Barry, Pugin, Scott, Street, Butterfield and Waterhouse; and all around are hundreds of thousands of slate roofs, each protecting a private world, but together giving London life, and creating one of the world's great cities.
(Richard Trench, *London — Architecture, History, Art,* publ. George Philip, 1991)

London and literature

The resonances of a city through its life are caught and retained in its literature. Few pavements echo these sounds as pervasively as those of London. The streets are dotted with blue plaques to mark the birthplaces, homes and workplaces of writers, and the British Museum is heavy with the manuscripts of classics.

> London is enchanting. I step out upon a tawny
> coloured magic carpet . . . it takes up the private life
> and carries it on, without any effort . . . .
> (Virginia Woolf in her diary, 1926)

From London, English literature began its journey; from the Tabard Inn in Southwark, whence **Geoffrey Chaucer** (1340-1400), a court official and customs officer in London, dispatched his garrulous pilgrims with their *Canterbury Tales*. In so doing, he created a specifically English literature, graphically realistic and vernacular. The Tabard became the Talbot Inn, a survivor until the 1870s; Talbot Yard is still there, with six centuries of exits and entrances to remember. It is easy to perceive Chaucer's London in his descriptions of the walled city of Troy in *Troilus and Criseyde* — there is something familiar about a city surrounded by countryside but bursting inside with wonders such as those detailed in the contemporary but anonymous *Piers Plowman*.

A tradition was established. Even for the great Renaissance writers, steeped in Classical learning, London, noisy, fast and aggressive, dictated its own style of drama. **William Shakespeare** (1564-1616) worked in the circular galleried theaters of Southwark, thought too rowdy for the City proper, where art was brought for almost the first time to the working class, the "groundlings" who stood in the "pit" (see SHAKESPEARE GLOBE MUSEUM). He would also perform for more exclusive audiences — both *Twelfth Night* and *A Midsummer Night's Dream* may first have been performed privately in the Inns of Court.

The plays of his contemporary **Ben Jonson** give perhaps the best idea of London, where the cunning and clever prosper, especially *The Alchemist, Bartholomew Fair* and *Every Good Man in his Humour,* which includes a scene in Paul's Walk, the central aisle of St Paul's. Jonson and others would often retire to The Mermaid Tavern, which stood where Bread St. meets Cheapside, but they sometimes wound up in Southwark's prisons, The Clink and Marshalsea, for writing plays that displeased the Crown. Others met a worse fate: much of **Sir Walter Raleigh's** finest writing was done during his 13 years in the Tower before his execution in 1618, and in 1593 **Christopher Marlowe** was stabbed to death in a tavern in Deptford.

John Donne (1573-1631), whose early lyrics have such sense of place, is claimed by some to symbolize London's temporary "decline" into intellectualism by turning to religious poetry. In 1621 he became Dean of St Paul's. Admittedly, London only housed and did not inspire **John Milton** and the great metaphysical poets. Yet from the ashes of the medieval city (burned down in 1666) and Puritanism rose arguably the greatest works about London, certainly two of the best diaries ever written, both social history and literature: those of **Samuel Pepys** and **John Evelyn**.

> The stones of St Paul's flew like grenades, and the lead
> melted down the streets in a stream. The very pavements
> glowed with fiery redness, and neither horse nor man
> was able to tread on them.

Evelyn's physical description is outstanding, but in both diaries everyday life is also vividly pictured; Pepys' account is so honest that he wrote in a secret shorthand, not deciphered until 1820.

With the 18thC post-fire development of the West End came a new Augustan "Age of Reason," when London, a new Rome or Athens, inspired learned, urbane works. But its vigorous, down-to-earth character shone through. Satire became the new mode: irreverent modern classics about people, not gods, such as *The Dunciad* by **Alexander Pope** (1688-1744), often to be found at CHISWICK HOUSE with his patron Lord Burlington; or *London* by **Dr Samuel Johnson** (1709-84), an archetypal English blend of common sense and Classicism (see JOHNSON'S HOUSE).

> Sir, the noblest prospect that a Scotchman ever sees,
> is the high road that leads him to London.
> (Dr. Samuel Johnson)

Cliques need meeting places, and the most famous surviving one is the Cheshire Cheese on Fleet St.; Russell St., Covent Garden, housed the most renowned coffeehouses. But the age of reason was not all it thought itself. In 1679 **John Dryden** was beaten up outside the Lamb and Flag pub in Rose St., WC2 (since nicknamed "The Bucket of Blood"), having offended the Earl of Rochester, a fellow writer, in a satire.

At Jonathan Swift's suggestion, **John Gay** wrote *The Beggar's Opera* in 1728 as a "Newgate pastoral," depicting with a new moral stringency the slums of Covent Garden and the notorious Newgate prison. **Henry Fielding**, a pioneer of the new novel form with *Tom Jones,* was an innovative magistrate in Bow Street, trying to protect the same slum dwellers. Even writing had its seamy side — buried under the Barbican is the site of Grub Street, still the imagined habitat of ill-paid hack writers.

Although **William Wordsworth** was moved to write "Earth has not anything to show more fair" (*On Westminster Bridge,* 1802), and **John Keats** (1795-1821) found peace enough in Hampstead to write *Ode to a Nightingale* (see KEATS' HOUSE), it was urban squalor that moved **Charles Dickens** (1812-70), the most obsessive writer about London. Like that of his own Sam Weller, Dickens' "knowledge of London was extensive and peculiar." In his novels London is most often a brooding, malevolent presence, too powerful for the people in it, a city of slum tenements, an evil ruling class, prisons and "London particulars" or "pea-soupers," poisonous mixes of fog and smog.

> London. Michaelmas Term lately over, and the Lord Chancellor
> sitting in Lincoln's Inn Hall. Implacable November weather . . . .
> Fog everywhere. Fog up the river, where it flows among
> green aits [river islets] and meadows; fog down the river,
> where it rolls defiled among the tiers of shipping, and the
> waterside pollutions of a great (and dirty) city.
> (Charles Dickens, *Bleak House*, 1853)

To balance this, there is the comedy and vitality of his unforgettable Cockneys, such as Sam Weller, Mr Micawber and Bill Sykes, with their own unique language. Yet underneath speaks the morally appalled social reformer. The references are endless (see DICKENS' HOUSE), but some idea of his feelings can be gained from his treatment of the Thames, along which Abel Magwitch tries in vain to escape in *Great Expectations* and which is so often the recipient of corpses — as in the superb opening scene of *Our Mutual Friend*.

By the interwar years, things had changed. **Virginia Woolf** (1882-1941) wrote: "I ask nothing better than that all the reviewers . . . should call me a highbrow. If they like to add Bloomsbury, WC1, that is the correct postal address." In Bloomsbury's leafy Georgian squares, where dark brick houses surround pleasant gardens, **D.H. Lawrence**, **W.B. Yeats**, **T.S. Eliot** and **E.M. Forster** found a calming peace, which is still there and pervades the modernist literature they helped to forge in the area.

More recently, aspects of London have been memorably portrayed in two novels by **Paul Theroux**, *The Family Arsenal* and *The London Embassy;* in **Peter Ackroyd's** chilling *Hawksmoor;* in *London Fields* by **Martin Amis**; and in *Mother London,* **Michael Moorcock's** fantastical portrayal of London from the Blitz to the present day.

Suggestions for further reading

The Architecture of London by Edward Jones and Christopher Woodward
Betjeman's London by John Betjeman
The Blue Plaque Guide to London (Journeyman Press)
London: A Literary Companion by Peter Vansittart
London (Architecture, History, Art) by Richard Trench
London (The City and Westminster) by Nikolaus Pevsner
London (excluding the City and Westminster) by Nikolaus Pevsner
London Encyclopaedia, ed. Ben Weinreb and Christopher Hibbert
London's Riverside (1975) by Susanne Ebel and Doreen Impey
Louise Nicholson's Definitive Guide to London by Louise Nicholson
The Time Out Guide to London
3-D London by Fiona Duncan, Leonie Glass and Caroline Sharpe
The Tower of London by A.L. Rowse
A Walk Around London's Parks (1983) by Hunter Davies

Royal London

Like the pussycat in the nursery rhyme, people go "up to London to look at the Queen." For the visitor from other parts of the realm, the rituals, pageantry, and palaces of royal London are the tangible demonstration not only of a heritage but also of stability. The monarchy has survived not because the kingdom is quiescent but because the Crown itself is a stabilizing influence. It has had its low points, of course: it was replaced by the Commonwealth from 1649 to 1660; and more recently the abdication of Edward VIII in 1936, before his coronation, provoked something of a crisis of confidence in the institution. But today, despite further tremors caused by the revelations, true or otherwise, about the less-than-perfect lives of the younger Royals, most Britons regard the monarchy as the keystone of the State.

The kingdom is not, of course, England, otherwise the Queen's husband and her son and heir would not be Duke of Edinburgh and Prince of Wales. The Queen is also head of state of many countries in the Commonwealth. But arguably the most important job of the monarchy is to represent the family of nations that together, and by consent, compose the United Kingdom. Because they have smaller populations, Scotland and Wales are numerically less represented in Parliament than England, but they are equal in the sight of the Crown. In countries of less age, national unity can be an objective in itself. But Britain, being neither young nor one nation, needs some means to articulate its wholeness.

At the time of the Prince of Wales' wedding in 1981, *The Times* conceded that the Queen has "almost no executive function to perform," but concluded that she has "a 'presence' in the highest reaches of the political process." Before a general election can take place the Queen must dissolve Parliament. After the contest, she appoints as Prime Minister the leader of the victorious party and invites him or her to form a government. The monarchy, *The Times* pointed out, "is not yet constitutionally allowed to slip back into a world of sumptuous ceremonial."

WHERE TO SEE THE ROYAL FAMILY

The daily Court Circular, which gives details of all the Royal Family's public engagements, is printed in *The Times, Daily Telegraph* and the *Independent*. Apart from this, the Queen presides at certain annual events, often accompanied by other members of her family.

The State Opening of Parliament, at the beginning of each new session of Parliament, usually late October, is the most apparently political of the Queen's regular duties, in that she announces in her speech a program of proposed legislation. In fact, the measures outlined are put forward not at the discretion of the Queen but on behalf of her government.

Remembrance Sunday, on the Sunday nearest November 11, sees the Queen placing wreaths on the Cenotaph in Whitehall to commemorate the dead of the two World Wars.

Trooping the Colour takes place on a Saturday in mid-June to honor the Queen's official birthday. Each year a different Guards regiment presents itself for inspection; the "colour" is its regimental flag. The Queen rides in a landau to Horse Guards Parade, off Whitehall, receives the salute amid marching bands, and often makes an appearance on the balcony of Buckingham Palace on her return.

ROYAL RESIDENCES

BUCKINGHAM PALACE did not become the principal royal residence until the time of Queen Victoria (1836-1902), although it had been used by monarchs since George III bought it in 1762. However, the palace is in every sense the center, home and headquarters of the British monarchy.

Before Victoria, **ST JAMES'S PALACE**, built for Henry VIII (1509-47), was the sovereign's official residence. Its status is still honored in the accreditation of foreign diplomats to "the Court of St James," and it is the headquarters of the Gentlemen at Arms, who form a personal bodyguard for the Queen, and the home of the Yeomen of the Guard. These, rather than the Tower Yeomen, are the true "Beefeaters," a word probably derived from "buffetier," meaning an attendant at royal buffets. St James's Palace also includes **Clarence House**, home of Queen Elizabeth the Queen Mother, one of the most dearly loved members of the Royal Family in recent decades.

KENSINGTON PALACE was acquired as a home by William III, who wanted a place in the country around London. It was the home of the sovereign from 1689 to 1760, and is now the London home of the Prince and Princess of Wales, and the home also of Princess Margaret, the Queen's sister, and of other royals. **Windsor Castle** (SEE EXCURSIONS) is still used extensively by the Royal Family. Originally the home of Edward the Confessor (1042-66), it is a country home much closer to London than **Balmoral** in Scotland, or **Sandringham** in Norfolk.

There will soon be five kings left — the Kings of England,
Diamonds, Hearts, Spades and Clubs.
(King Farouk of Egypt, 1951)

Portrayed *left to right* are a **Life Guard** (scarlet tunic, white helmet plumes), a member of the **Blues and Royals** (blue tunic, red helmet plumes), and a **Grenadier Guard** (white plume on the left side of the bearskin cap).

Basic information

Before you go

DOCUMENTS REQUIRED

A valid national **passport** is often all that is needed to visit Britain, since citizens of the US, Commonwealth and most European and South American countries do not need visas.

Vaccination certificates are not required, but you should check if one is needed on re-entry into your own country.

Only your full valid national **driver's license** is required to drive personal or rented cars. If you are bringing your own car make sure it is properly insured, and bring the **vehicle registration certificate** (logbook) and an **insurance certificate** or **international green card**. A **national identity sticker** is also required.

TRAVEL AND MEDICAL INSURANCE

Be sure to take out an insurance policy covering loss of deposits paid to airlines, hotels, tour operators, etc., and emergency costs such as special tickets home and extra nights in a hotel.

Visitors from countries with no reciprocal health agreement are not covered for any medical help other than accidents or emergencies, and even then will be expected to pay if they have to stay the night in hospital. They should be properly insured. No charge is made for visitors from countries with a reciprocal arrangement, such as EC member countries.

The **IAMAT** (International Association for Medical Assistance to Travelers) is a nonprofit organization that has a directory of English-speaking doctors who will call, for a fixed fee. There are member hospitals and clinics throughout the world, including several clinics in London. Membership is free, and other benefits include information on health risks overseas. For further information write to **IAMAT** headquarters in the US or in Europe *(417 Center St., Lewiston, NY 14092, USA, or 57 Voirets, 1212 Grand-Lancy, Genève, Switzerland).*

MONEY

There is no exchange control in Britain, so you can carry any amount of any currency through customs in or out of the country. The unit of currency is the **pound sterling** (£), divided into 100 **pence** (p). There are coins for 1p, 2p, 5p, 10p, 20p, 50p and £1, and notes for £5, £10, £20 and £50.

Travelers checks issued by American Express, Thomas Cook, Barclays and Citibank are widely recognized; make sure you read the instructions included with your checks. **It is important to note separately the serial numbers of each check and the telephone number to call in case of loss.** Specialist travelers check companies such as American Express provide extensive local refund facilities.

Major international **credit and charge cards**, such as American Express, MasterCard (linked in Britain with the Access Card), Visa (linked with Barclaycard) and Diners Club are widely accepted for most goods and services.

American Express also has a **MoneyGram**® money transfer service that makes it possible to wire money worldwide in just minutes, from any American Express Travel Service Office. This service is available to all customers and is not limited to American Express Card members. Payment can be made in cash, or with an American Express Card with a Centurion Credit Line, an American Express Optima (SM) Card, Visa or MasterCard. For the location nearest you ☎1-800-543-4080 (in the US and Canada).

CUSTOMS

If you are visiting the United Kingdom for less than six months, you are entitled to bring in, free of duty and tax, all personal effects that you intend to take with you when you leave, except tobacco goods, alcoholic drinks and perfume. Ensure you carry dated receipts for valuable items, such as cameras and watches, or you may be charged duty.

Since January 1993, the limits for goods bought duty-free and tax-paid within the EC have been virtually abolished. The much higher thresholds, above which you must be able to prove that the goods are for your own personal use, have been set at 800 cigarettes, 400 cigarillos, 200 cigars, 10 liters of liquor or strong liquor, 90 liters of wine (no more than 60 sparkling), 20 liters of fortified wines and 110 liters of beer.

Other allowances

For goods bought anywhere outside the EC, or duty- and tax-free within the EC, including purchases from a UK duty-free shop, the limits remain as follows: 200 cigarettes *or* 100 cigarillos *or* 50 cigars *or* 250g tobacco; 1 liter liquor or strong liquor (more than 22-percent alcohol by volume) *or* 2 liters of alcoholic drink (less than 22-percent alcohol), fortified wine or sparkling wine *plus* 2 liters of still table wine; 50g/60cc/2fl.oz perfume and 250cc/9fl.oz toilet water; and other goods to the value of £32.

Restrictions and recommendations

- Travelers under 17 are not entitled to the allowances on tobacco goods and alcoholic drinks.
- Prohibited and restricted goods include narcotics, weapons, obscene publications and videos, as well as animals and birds.
- If you have anything in excess of the duty-free allowances, pass through the channel with red "Goods to declare" notices; otherwise pass through the green "Nothing to declare" channel.
- For exemption from Value Added Tax (VAT) on goods bought in Britain for export, see page 255.

GETTING THERE

London's **Heathrow Airport**, w of the capital, is one of the busiest in the world, and there are regular flights from most countries on a wide range of international airlines. **Gatwick**, to the s, the city's second international airport, is also heavily used. To the NE, London's third and most modern airport, **Stansted**, is becoming increasingly popular as US and European airlines take up spare capacity there, while **Luton** airport, N of London, is mainly a major air charter destination.

All four are within an hour of the city center, and **London City Airport**, which connects with many European cities from Docklands, is highly convenient for the business traveler. See FROM THE AIRPORT TO THE CITY, opposite.

Air fares vary enormously, so consult your travel agent.

Only Cunard now operates frequent **transatlantic sailings**, but it is possible to sail to English ports (usually Liverpool or Southampton) on other less regular routes. An efficient network of short-distance passenger, car and train **ferries** links Britain with France, Belgium, the Netherlands, West Germany, Ireland and Scandinavia. The main ferry ports are Dover, Folkestone, Harwich, Felixstowe, Portsmouth, Plymouth, Holyhead and Fishguard, but there are a good many others. Road or rail connections to and from ferry ports, and the length, time and availability of ferry sailings, are all important factors in choosing your route: again, consult your travel agent.

The projected completion date for the **Channel Tunnel**, linking Dover and Calais, is winter 1993. The British Rail passenger terminal, due to open in 1994, will be located at Waterloo.

CLIMATE

English weather is rarely given to extremes, but it is unpredictable and can change character several times a day. Indeed, it is a constant and characteristic topic of British conversation. Average daytime temperatures range from 6°C (43°F) in winter (December to February) to 26°C (79°F) in summer (June to August), only occasionally going below 0°C (32°F) or above 30°C (86°F). Annual rainfall is 24 inches (60cm), most of it in winter but likely at any time. There are, of course, considerable regional variations.

CLOTHES

In summertime light clothes are adequate, but remember to include some protection against showers, and a sweater or jacket for cool evenings. During the rest of the year, bring warm clothes and hope you won't need them all, although in winter overcoats, gloves etc. will usually be necessary. Be sure to be equipped with comfortable, water-resistant footwear: London is a great city for walking, and you don't want to be defeated by damp conditions underfoot.

London has given the world some bizarre fashions and is consequently relaxed about dress. But restraint is expected in some institutional buildings, the older hotels and restaurants, casinos and some clubs. If you are attending any formal or notably grand occasion, full evening dress, which the British refer to simply as "black tie," may be expected; check first.

GENERAL DELIVERY (POSTE RESTANTE)

General delivery mail can be addressed to any post office. (See POST OFFICES on page 46 for the two main locations.)

Getting around

FROM THE AIRPORT TO THE CITY

Heathrow is the w terminus of the underground's Piccadilly Line; trains link the airport within about 40 minutes with all parts of the city between 5am (6.45am on Sunday) and 11pm.

The M4 motorway is the other main link, the trip to the center taking 30 minutes to one hour depending upon traffic. London Transport operates a 24-hour bus service (including the Airbus service) to points in Central London, various coach companies run services to Victoria Coach Station, and some airlines run buses to meet arriving flights and connect with their various passenger terminals in Central London. A more expensive alternative is to take a taxi, always readily available at the airport, but make sure you take a black metered cab and not one of the "pirate" operators, who may overcharge.

Gatwick, in the s, is farther out of the city. The easiest way into London is to take the Gatwick Express, the fast, comfortable British Rail service from the airport station. This reaches Victoria Station in London in 30 minutes, and all parts of the city can easily be reached from there. The airport is next to the M23 motorway, an hour or more from Central London, and there are bus services around the clock. Because of the distance from London, a cab is not a realistic proposition for most travelers, and could be expensive; ask first how much the fare will be.

Stansted, NE of London, is linked by rail to Liverpool Street Station, 40 minutes away, and by road via the M11 motorway, within an hour or so of Central London. **Luton**, N of the capital, is near the M1 motorway, with fast bus and excellent rail links to London. From the inner-city **London City Airport**, take the Courtesy Shuttle, which connects with the RiverBus service and the Docklands Light Railway (only 8 minutes to the City).

ARRIVING BY OTHER MEANS

By rail: London's several major stations encircle the center (this is clearly shown on the ORIENTATION MAP on pages 60-61), and all have underground interchanges, taxi stands and bus stops. (See RAILWAY SERVICES on page 41.)

By road: The roads into London plow through the sprawling suburbs, after which signposting for "West End" indicates the center. Try to avoid driving anywhere in the rush hours (8-9.30am and 5-7pm). The biggest bus terminus in London is at Victoria, and most cross-country coaches arrive there.

PUBLIC TRANSPORT

London Regional Transport's network of buses and underground trains (often referred to as "tube trains" or simply "the tube") is extensive and efficient. But as in all great cities, try to avoid traveling in the rush hour.

Free bus and tube maps and details of services are available at the Travel Information Centres located at the following tube stations: **Heathrow Central**, **Euston**, **King's Cross**, **Piccadilly Circus**, **Oxford Circus** and **Victoria**. There is also a 24-hour telephone information service (☎ *(071) 222-1234):* you may have to wait a while for an answer as the calls are stacked and dealt with in rotation.

The London Transport system is divided into six fare zones. Zone 1 covers the Circle Line of the underground and a small area beyond, and incorporates most of the places you are likely to visit. A small flat-fare is payable for every zone you enter. Children under 16 pay a reduced fare, and those under 5 travel free. Children aged 14-15 must have a Child Rate Photocard; proof of date of birth is needed to obtain this.

If you are feeling intrepid and intend to use the public transport system, it is worthwhile buying a special ticket. The most convenient is a Travelcard, which gives unlimited travel on the bus and underground (and on British Rail's Network South East trains and the Docklands Light Railway) within the zones selected on purchase and is valid for one day or seven days. A passport-sized photograph is needed for a seven-day Travelcard. Travelcard Seasons are available for longer periods.

One-day Bus Passes, valid only on the buses for selected zones, can be bought in advance. The date of travel is scratched off on the first journey of the day on which you decide to use it. For seven-day Bus Passes, a passport-sized photograph is needed.

All special-rate tickets are available from underground stations, London Tourist Board Centres and many newsagents. Bus Passes can also be bought from the larger bus stations. The Visitor Travel Card, on sale only at travel agents outside London both in the UK and abroad, allows unlimited travel on buses and underground for three-, four- or seven-day periods.

The alternative to these special tickets is to buy individual single or return (one-way or round-trip) tickets at the beginning of each journey. For public transport, remember to stand in line in the queue.

The underground

The underground (see map at back of book) is the easiest and fastest way to get around the city, if not the most pleasant or interesting. The stations (which are gradually being modernized) are easily recognized by the London Transport symbol, a red horizontal line through a red circle. On maps, each line always has its own color (the Circle Line is yellow, the Central Line red, etc.), so it is easy to plan your journey, noting where you have to change lines.

The fare depends on how many zones you enter. Buy your ticket before boarding, either from a ticket office or a machine in the station, where the fares will be on display. Show your ticket to a collector or, if it is a yellow one, put it in the automatic entry gate and walk through, picking it up as you go — you will need to present it at the end of your journey. Follow the signs to the platform for the line and direction you want. Check with the indicators above the platform and on the front of the train that it is going to your station; some trains do not go to the end of the line, and some lines divide into two or more branches.

Trains stop at every station, with only a few exceptions on weekends. The first tube trains run at about 5am, and they begin to close down after 11.30pm, when you might have trouble with connections. Smoking is forbidden throughout the underground system.

Docklands

The **Docklands Light Railway** *(information ☎ (071) 538-0311, operates Mon-Fri only)* links the City with the rapidly developing Docklands area.

Buses

London's red buses are usually slower than the tube, but can be cheaper and are more interesting, offering a good view from the upper deck. Do use them and don't be discouraged by the complex network of routes: people waiting in the line will usually help you, and the conductor will answer your questions and tell you if necessary when you have reached your destination.

Each bus runs along part or all of a numbered route — find out which route you want from the map at the bus stop, and look at the indicator on the front of the bus to check that it is going far enough along the route for you. There are two types of bus stop: a normal stop, with the red LT symbol on a white background, where all buses stop; and a request stop, with a white LT symbol on a red sign bearing the word "Request," where the bus will stop only if you raise your hand or, if you are on the bus and want to get off, ring the bell.

On some buses the conductor will come around and collect your fare or check your Travelcard or Bus Pass during the journey, but on others you will have to pay as you enter. Smoking is allowed only upstairs on double-decker buses. The buses run between about 5am and 11.30pm, although there are a few night buses on special routes, running once an hour or so.

In Central London, small "midi" buses have been introduced on selected routes, specially designed to give speedier rides to people traveling just a few stops. Green Line Coaches run from Central London into the country outside London Transport's area. They stop only rarely in London, and are more expensive than red buses. Ask at a Travel Information Centre for details of routes.

Taxis

London's distinctive black taxis (other colors are now being introduced on the modern metrocabs) are driven by some of the best drivers in the world, who have to pass an examination to prove their detailed knowledge of the city before they get a license. They can be hailed as they cruise the streets (a cab that is free illuminates its yellow light), and you will also find them on stands at stations and outside hotels and large shops, etc.

Once they have stopped for you, taxis are obliged to take you anywhere you want to go within 6 miles of the pick-up point, provided it is within the metropolitan area. The fare, always shown on the meter, consists of a basic rental charge and subsequent additions according to the length of your journey; there are additional charges for extra passengers, night or weekend journeys, and for baggage. In all cases, notices are displayed inside the taxi with details of all charges. Give the driver a 10-15 percent tip.

Private taxis (usually sedans and known as "minicabs") cannot be hailed but must be ordered by phone. You will find the numbers by some public telephones and in the *Yellow Pages* directory under "Taxis and Private Hire Vehicles." It is best, however, to stick to the black taxis if possible; the strict regulations governing fares for black taxis do not apply to minicabs, so if you have to use a minicab try to fix the fare with the driver at the start of the journey to avoid problems when you reach your destination.

GETTING AROUND BY CAR

Driving in London is not as aggressive as in most large cities, but the difficulty for foreign visitors is that everyone appears to be on the wrong side of the road, and that the city has a totally unplanned road system with an abundance of one-way routes. If you can face all of that, make sure that you are carrying your license, that your tires have at least 1.6mm of tread, and that all your lights are working. There are strong penalties for driving under the influence of alcohol.

You must drive on the left and you must pass only on the right. The speed limit in London and all built-up areas (i.e., streets with lampposts) is 30mph (48kph) unless otherwise indicated. Standard international road signs are generally used. Pedestrian crossings are marked by black and white zones across the road and are sometimes controlled by traffic lights. In either case, pedestrians have the right of way and traffic must stop to let them cross, unless there is a green traffic light showing, in which case drivers have priority. Observe lane division rules: slower traffic keeps to the inside (left) and faster traffic passes on the outside, and be sure to get into the correct lane coming up to an intersection, as different lanes may be controlled by different traffic signals. Horns must not be used from 11.30pm-7am except in emergencies, and the wearing of seat belts in both front seats is compulsory, as is the wearing of rear seat belts if the car is fitted with them.

Parking is extremely difficult on streets in Central London, and is usually possible only at meters for a maximum of 2 hours. Two yellow lines or, more rarely, a red line by the roadside means no parking at all; one yellow line means no parking during the work day (8am-6.30pm, Monday to Saturday). Always look for an explanatory sign in the restricted zones: one will give details of the maximum stay allowed, or indicate that the space is for residents only. Parking is always prohibited near pedestrian crossings and intersections.

If you violate parking regulations, you may be fined (but not on the spot). Or you may have your car immobilized by a wheel clamp; instruction on how to get it released will be displayed on the windshield, but you will have to pay a fine, on the spot, and wait until it is unlocked.

Sometimes the police may tow away your car: go to the nearest police station to ask if this has been the case.

Off the streets, there are various parking lots and garages, often indicated by a blue sign with a large **P**. Charges for these should be set out clearly somewhere near the entrance.

If you belong to an FIA- or AIT-affiliated automobile club, you are entitled to free roadside assistance from the **Royal Automobile Club** *(for breakdowns ☎freephone 0800-828282; for information ☎(081) 686-2314).* Britain's other major automobile club, the **Automobile Association** *(for breakdowns ☎freephone 0800-887766; for information ☎(0345) 5006000)* assists only affiliated members of the AIT.

RENTING A CAR

It is probably not worthwhile if you do not intend to go outside London. You must be over 21 and hold a full valid national license. Opt for either a daily rate plus a mileage charge, or a weekly rate with unlimited mileage, often more economical. Insurance is usually included, but check first. You may need a cash deposit larger than your likely eventual overall charge: the difference will be refunded when you return the car. Using a charge or credit card overcomes this problem.

Car rental can be arranged through travel agents or at desks in airports, major stations and large hotels. Or make a telephone reservation through one of the major companies, such as **Avis** *(☎(081) 848-8733)*, **Europcar** *(☎(081) 950-5050)* or **Hertz** *(☎(081) 679-1799)*. All these companies can arrange for cars to be waiting if you arrive by air or train.

GETTING AROUND ON FOOT

It is in the back streets of a city that an area's individual character is formed. A gentle stroll in the narrow streets of such areas as Covent Garden, Soho or the City may be rewarded by unusual surprises in the form of specialist shops and some beautiful buildings. For a really energetic walk, however, a wander in some of London's larger parks can be challenging.

Although many Londoners ignore them, it is best to cross the street using zebra crossings, where pedestrians have priority, or underpasses.

Some outer areas are unsafe for pedestrians after nightfall: if outside the city center after dark, stick to the main streets.

RAILWAY SERVICES

British Rail offers a fast InterCity service between major towns throughout the UK, as well as Motorail and sleeper trains over longer distances. First-class and, on some routes, Pullman tickets are available. Reduced-rate tickets are available for off-peak day or weekend trips, and the BritRail Pass, on sale only outside the UK through travel agents, offers unlimited travel on the whole network for periods of four days up to one month.

British Rail Travel Centres (visitors only)
4-12 Regent St., SW1 *(map 9 G10)*
407 Oxford St., W1 *(map 8 F8)*

Major British Rail stations in London

- **South and Southeast England, East Anglia (information ☎(071) 928-5100)**
  Charing Cross, Strand, WC2 *(map 9 G11)*
  Waterloo, Waterloo Rd., SE1 *(map 10 H13)*
  Victoria, Buckingham Palace Rd., SW1 *(map 16 J9)*
  Liverpool Street, Liverpool St., EC3 *(map 12 E16)*
- **Southwest and West England, South Wales (information ☎(071) 262-6767)**
  Paddington, Praed St., W2 *(map 6 F5)*
- **Midlands, Northwest England, North Wales, West Scotland (information ☎(071) 387-7070)**
  Euston, Euston Rd., NW1 *(map 3 C10)*
  St Pancras, Euston Rd., NW1 *(map 3 C11)*
- **East and Northeast England, East Scotland (information ☎(071) 278-2477)**
  King's Cross, Euston Rd., NW1 *(map 3 B11)*

DOMESTIC AIRLINES

The principal airline operating from London to other major cities is British Airways. Others include Air UK, British Midland Airways and Dan-Air. Unless you wish to go to one of the country's extremities, such as Aberdeen in Scotland, it is often easier to go by car or train and arrive directly in the city center. London City Airport, situated in Docklands, catering mainly to businessmen, serves only European destinations, including Paris, Amsterdam, Zurich, Stockholm and Brussels *(for information ☎ (071) 474-5555)*.

FERRY SERVICES

Apart from the pleasure cruises on the Thames, the only ferry service is the frequent RiverBus, which runs between Chelsea Harbour and Greenwich with stops at Cadogan Pier, Charing Cross, South Bank, Swan Lane for the City (weekdays only), London Bridge and Docklands. The service does not operate during weekends October to March. *(For RiverBus information ☎ (071) 987-0311.)*

River cruises start from Westminster or Charing Cross pier for trips to Greenwich or the Thames Barrier. From October to Easter, trips start from Greenwich only. *(For Riverboat Information Service ☎ (071) 730-4812.)*

On-the-spot information

PUBLIC HOLIDAYS

New Year's Day, January 1; **Good Friday**; **Easter Monday**; **May Day** (first Monday in May); **Spring Bank Holiday** (last Monday in May); **August Bank Holiday** (last Monday in August); **Christmas Day**, December 25; **Boxing Day**, December 26. Most places are closed.

TIME ZONES

London time is Greenwich Mean Time (GMT) in winter and changes to European Summer Time (EST), one hour ahead of GMT, from the end of March to late October. In winter this puts it 5 hours ahead of Eastern Standard Time and 6-8 hours ahead of other US time zones; in summer, add another hour's time difference.

BANKS AND CURRENCY EXCHANGE

All banks are open Monday to Friday 9.30am-3.30pm. On Saturday a handful of Central London branches are open, such as **Barclays** *(208 Kensington High St., W8, map 13I2, open 9.30am-noon)*. Money can also be exchanged outside these hours at foreign exchanges, found as small separate shops and in hotels, railway stations, travel agencies and airports, but their exchange rates are poorer and they charge service fees.

Along with banks, **American Express** and **Thomas Cook** offices give the best rates of exchange for their respective travelers checks. For your nearest American Express office ☎(071) 930-4411 (Travel Services); for Thomas Cook ☎(071) 408-4286. It is also possible to withdraw cash with a Visa or similar credit card from the many 24-hour cashpoint machines, situated just outside or in the foyers of many major banks.

Travelers checks are widely accepted in hotels and large stores, but not so much in smaller shops and restaurants; the exchange rate is roughly the same as for cash. Most widely accepted in lieu of cash is, of course, an internationally recognized charge or credit card.

SHOPPING HOURS

Most shops are open Monday to Saturday 9am-6pm. Many large city-center shops and supermarkets stay open late on Wednesday or Thursday, and some on other weekdays as well (see SHOPPING). Many shops, such as grocers and newsagents (newsdealers), a few stores and supermarkets open on Sunday. In the weeks before Christmas, many larger stores may be open on Sunday.

Outside the city center, shops may close at lunchtime, usually 1-2pm, on Saturday afternoons, and for one afternoon during the week.

RUSH HOURS

During the working week (Monday to Friday), the rush hours are approximately 8-9.30am and 5-7pm. Unlike some cities, London does not become totally choked, but traffic congestion is worsening. If your last visit to London was, say, five years ago, allow more time now than you did then for getting around at peak times.

POST AND TELEPHONE SERVICES

Post offices are usually open Monday to Friday 9am-5.30pm, Saturday 9am-12.30pm. A notable exception is the post office in William IV St., off Trafalgar Sq. *(map 9 G11),* open Monday to Thursday, Saturday 8am-8pm, Friday 8.30am-8pm.

Stamps are available at post offices, some shops and, occasionally, from machines. There are two classes of inland mail, but the second class is sometimes a lot slower and more unreliable. You will also have to specify which rate you want for international mail, as it will not automatically go air mail. When sending a parcel out of the country you will have to fill in a customs form declaring the contents. Besides the boxes in post offices, mail can be posted in the red boxes placed at regular intervals on main streets. There are various special services available, such as express or recorded or guaranteed delivery.

Public telephones are found in booths on main streets and in post offices, hotels, pubs, stations, etc. If you need a number either inside or outside London, dial **192** or **142** and Directory Inquiries will supply it. There is always an area code, which may have up to six numbers. It is not necessary for local calls but must be used when telephoning from outside the area.

There are two area codes for London, one **(071)** for inner London, and the other **(081)** for outer London. If you are dialing within one area you do not need to use the code, but dialing from one area to another requires the relevant code.

Most international calls can be dialed direct (IDD) from public telephones. If in difficulty call **155** for the International Operator or **153** for International Directory Inquiries.

Some public telephones take coins; others take phonecards, which can be bought from post offices and shops displaying the phonecard sign. Follow the instructions displayed by the telephone; you will be refunded any unused coins. The ringing tone is a repeated double trill, and an intermittent shrill tone means that the line is busy.

See also TELEPHONE SERVICES, page 47.

FAXES
If you are staying in a hotel, the hotel's fax facilities will be at your disposal (fax numbers are given in this guide where appropriate). Alternatively, major post offices, such as those at 181 High Holborn, WC1 (☎ *(071) 239-5896* ℻ *(071) 242-4893, map 4 E12)* and 110 Victoria St., SW1 (☎ *(071) 834-0509* ℻ *(071) 834-0293, map 17I10)* will send and receive faxes on your behalf. For a small charge, they will deliver incoming faxes to your door.

The *Yellow Pages* telephone directory lists other addresses under "Facsimile Bureaux."

PUBLIC LAVATORIES (REST ROOMS)
With some exceptions, the public lavatories found in main streets (often in French-style, automated "superloos"), parks and tube stations can often be dirty and vandalized. Well-maintained lavatories that can be used by anybody will be found in all larger public buildings, such as museums and art galleries, large department stores and railway stations. It is not acceptable to use the lavatories in hotels, restaurants and pubs if you are not a customer. Public lavatories are usually free of charge, but you may need a small coin to get in or to use a proper washroom.

ELECTRIC CURRENT

The electric current is 240V AC, and plugs have three square pins and take 3-, 5- or 13-amp fuses. Foreign visitors will need adaptors for their own appliances: buy them before departure.

CUSTOMS AND ETIQUETTE

The English are a tolerant people and London is a cosmopolitan city, so foreign visitors are unlikely to offend by tripping up on some part of etiquette. An important custom is "queuing" — the British line up for everything, and you must wait your turn.

The British tend to hide behind their newspapers on public transport rather than indulge in the art of conversation. However, one topic that readily concerns them all is the weather, and this is a standard and acceptable topic with which to initiate a conversation.

TIPPING

Tipping is customary in a few cases. A tip of 10-15 percent is usual in hotels and restaurants, unless a service charge is already incorporated into the bill. Taxi drivers also expect about 10-15 percent of the fare. You need only give small tips to porters, hairdressers, rest room attendants and doormen.

DISABLED VISITORS

Ensure you are well briefed before you set out. A useful publication is *Access in London,* published by Nicholson and readily available from bookstores such as W.H. Smith, and there is an Information Department run by **The Royal Association for Disability and Rehabilitation (RADAR)** *(write to 25 Mortimer St., London W1N 8AB ☎(071) 637-5400, map 8E9).* The **London Tourist Board** also produces a number of helpful information sheets for disabled people *(☎(071) 730-3488).*

Can-be-Done Ltd *(write to 7-11 Kensington High St., London W8 5NP ☎ (081) 907-2400, map 13I3)* arranges tours around London and England for disabled and able-bodied visitors. Guided tours around London in an adapted minibus are run by **William Forrester** *(☎(0483) 575401).*

LOCAL AND FOREIGN PUBLICATIONS

The weekly entertainments magazines, such as *Time Out, City Limits* and *What's On & Where to Go,* are the most comprehensive guides to events and entertainments of all sorts. London's daily evening newspaper, the *Evening Standard,* also features a wide range of entertainments. Programs of special events (free concerts, ceremonies, etc.) are usually available from Tourist Information Centres and are listed in *The Times.* National newspapers do not necessarily cover local London events.

Foreign newspapers are widely available from newsagents, the *International Herald Tribune* and many others on the day of publication, and most of the others a day or two later.

Useful addresses

TOURIST INFORMATION/TICKETS/ HOTEL RESERVATIONS

- **London Tourist Board and Convention Bureau information centers:**
  Harrods (basement), Knightsbridge, SW1, map **15**I6
  Heathrow Central Underground Station, Heathrow Airport, map **19**D2
  Liverpool St. Underground Station, map **12**E16
  Selfridges (basement), Oxford St., W1, map **8**F8
  Victoria Station Forecourt, SW1, map **16**J9
  West Gate, Tower of London, EC3 (summer only), map **12**G17
- **LTB Tourist Information** ☎(071) 730-3488
- **Telephone hotel reservation service:** Call in advance of your arrival ☎(071) 824-8844. A small reservation charge will be made.
- **Written inquiries and hotel reservation service** (write 6 weeks in advance):
  Accommodation Services, London Tourist Board, 26 Grosvenor Gdns., SW1W 0DU, map **16**I8
  On-the-spot hotel reservations can be made at LTB centers at Victoria Station, Heathrow and Selfridges.
- **British Travel Centre** 12 Regent St., W1, map **9**G10
- **American Express Travel Service** 6 Haymarket, London SW1 ☎(071) 930-4411, map **9**G10; a valuable source of information for any traveler in need of help, advice or emergency services
- **City of London Information Centre** St Paul's Churchyard, EC4 ☎(071) 260-1456, map **11**F14
- **London Transport Information Centre** 55 Broadway, SW1; 24-hour telephone service ☎(071) 222-1234, map **17**I10
- **Travel Information Centres at the following stations:**
  Euston, Heathrow Central, King's Cross, Oxford Circus, Piccadilly Circus, Victoria.
- **British Tourist Authority** and **English Tourist Board** Thames Tower, Black's Rd., W6 ☎(071 846-9000
- **Kidsline** ☎(071) 222-8070
- **Visitorcall** ☎(0839) 123456; operated by the London Tourist Board, it delivers recorded messages on specific subjects, such as "What's on," places to visit, entertainment and accommodation. Calls are charged at a higher rate than normal local calls.

POST OFFICES

Poste restante (general delivery) mail can be addressed to any post office in London.

The two main post offices are **Trafalgar Square post office** (24 William IV St., WC2N 4DL ☎ (071) 930-9580, map**9** G11) and **City post office** (King Edward Building, King Edward St., EC1A 1AA, map**11** E14 ☎ (071) 239-5047 for general inquiries).

TELEPHONE SERVICES
Dial the following numbers for the services indicated:
Operator 100
Directory inquiries 142/192
International operator 155
Time 123 (from London numbers only)
Telemessages and International Telegrams 190
Weather forecast, Greater London (0898) 500-401, **national** (0898) 500-400

EMBASSIES AND CONSULATES
Australia   Australia House, Strand, WC2 ☎(071) 379-4334, map **10**F12
Canada   1 Grosvenor St., W1 ☎(071) 629-9492, map **8**G8
Ireland   17 Grosvenor Pl., SW1 ☎(071) 235-2171, map **16**I8,
Japan   101-104 Piccadilly, W1 ☎(071) 465-6500, map **8**G8
New Zealand   80 Haymarket, SW1 ☎(071) 930-8422, map **9**G10
USA   24 Grosvenor Sq., W1 ☎(071) 499-9000, map **8**G8

SIGHTSEEING TOURS
London Transport *(☎(071) 222-1234):* London sightseeing tour in open-top double-decker bus departs every half-hour 10am-4pm from Victoria St., Baker St., Marble Arch, Trafalgar Sq.; commentary in eight languages.
Cityrama *(☎(071) 720-6663)* also departs every half-hour from several points; 8-language commentary.
Harrods *(☎(071) 581-3603),* very luxurious; commentary in eight languages.
Frames Rickards *(☎(071) 837-3111)* and **Evan Evans** *(☎(071) 930-2377)* all offer various sightseeing tours by coach.
    All the above tours can be reserved through the **London Tourist Board Centres** at Victoria, Harrods or Selfridges.

PRIVATE GUIDED TOURS
If you would like to go sightseeing in the company of a qualified Blue Badge Guide (many of them driver-guides), you should contact **Tour Guides Ltd** *(☎(071) 839-2498),* **Take a Guide** *(☎(081) 960-0459)* or **British Tours** *(☎(071) 629-5267).*
    For a list of operators offering walking tours, see WALKS IN LONDON.

MAJOR PLACES OF WORSHIP
Church of England churches cover the whole city, and Roman Catholic, Baptist and Methodist churches also abound.
American Church in London (Interdenominational)   79 Tottenham Court Rd., W1 ☎(071) 580-2791, map **3**E10
Central Synagogue (Orthodox)   36 Hallam St., W1 ☎(071) 580-1355, map **8**E9
London Central Mosque   146 Park Rd., NW8 ☎(071) 724-3363, map **1**C6

Emergency information

EMERGENCY SERVICES (FROM ANY TELEPHONE)
For **Police**, **Ambulance** or **Fire** ☎999 or 112. No coins are needed. The operator will ask which service you require.

HOSPITALS WITH CASUALTY (EMERGENCY) DEPARTMENTS
Charing Cross Hospital   Fulham Palace Rd., W6 ☎(081) 846-1010, off map **13**K1
St Mary's Hospital   Praed St., W2 ☎(071) 725-6666, map **6**F5
St Thomas's Hospital   Lambeth Palace Rd., SE1 ☎(071) 928-9292, map **18**I12
St Bartholomew's (Barts)   West Smithfield, EC1 ☎(071) 601-8888, map **11**E14
Westminster   Adults: Horseferry Rd., SW1 ☎(081) 746-8080, map **17**J11); children: Udall St., SW1 ☎(081) 746-8080, map **17**J10

OTHER EMERGENCIES
If your complaint does not warrant an ambulance or hospitalization you will have to ring up a doctor or dentist. Consult the *Yellow Pages* of the telephone directory under "Doctors (Medical Practitioners)" and "Dental Surgeons."

LATE-OPENING CHEMISTS/PHARMACIES
Every pharmacy has the late-opening roster for its immediate area displayed in its window. For even later requirements, go to the following:
Bliss   50 Willesden Lane, NW6 ☎(071) 624-8000 and 5 Marble Arch, W1 ☎(071) 723-6116, map **7**F7, both open daily 9am-midnight

HELP LINES
Capital Help Line   ☎(071) 388-7575. Referral service.
Release   ☎(071) 603-8654. Drug problems, legal and practical.
The Samaritans   46 Marshall St., W1 ☎(071) 734-2800 (24-hour). Map **8**F9. Personal callers 9am-9pm. Talk out problems.

AUTOMOBILE ACCIDENTS
- Do not admit liability or incriminate yourself.
- Ask any witnesses to stay and give a statement.
- Contact the police.
- Exchange names, addresses, car details and insurance companies' names and addresses with other driver(s).
- Give a statement to the police. Insurance companies will accept the police report as authoritative.

CAR BREAKDOWNS
Call one of the following from the nearest telephone:
- The nearest garage/breakdown service.
- The police, who will put you in touch with the above.
- The number you have been given if you rented the car.

LOST PASSPORT
Contact the police immediately, and your consulate (see page 47) for emergency travel documents.

LOST TRAVELERS CHECKS
Notify the local police at once, then follow the instructions provided with your travelers checks, or contact the issuing company's nearest office. Contact your consulate or **American Express** *((071) 930-4411)* if you are stranded with no money.

LOST PROPERTY
Report your loss to the police immediately (many insurance companies will not recognize claims without a police report). There are some special lost-property offices:
British Rail   At main stations (see RAILWAY SERVICES, page 42)
Heathrow Airport Lost Property Office   ☎(081) 745-7727
London Transport   200 Baker St., NW1 ☎(071) 486-2496 (recorded message), map **1D7**
Taxi Lost Property Office   15 Penton St., NW1 ☎(071) 833-0996, map **4B13**

CONVERSION FORMULAE

To convert	Multiply by
Inches to Centimeters	2.540
Centimeters to Inches	0.39370
Feet to Meters	0.3048
Meters to feet	3.2808
Yards to Meters	0.9144
Meters to Yards	1.09361
Miles to Kilometers	1.60934
Kilometers to Miles	0.621371
Sq Meters to Sq Feet	10.7638
Sq Feet to Sq Meters	0.092903
Sq Yards to Sq Meters	0.83612
Sq Meters to Sq Yards	1.19599
Sq Miles to Sq Kilometers	2.5899
Sq Kilometers to Sq Miles	0.386103
Acres to Hectares	0.40468
Hectares to Acres	2.47105
Gallons to Liters	4.545
Liters to Gallons	0.22
Ounces to Grams	28.3495
Grams to Ounces	0.03528
Pounds to Grams	453.592
Grams to Pounds	0.00220
Pounds to Kilograms	0.4536
Kilograms to Pounds	2.2046
Tons (UK) to Kilograms	1016.05
Kilograms to Tons (UK)	0.0009842
Tons (US) to Kilograms	746.483
Kilograms to Tons (US)	0.0013396

Quick conversions

Kilometers to Miles	Divide by 8, multiply by 5
Miles to Kilometers	Divide by 5, multiply by 8
1 meter =	Approximately 3 feet 3 inches
2 centimeters =	Approximately 1 inch
1 pound (weight) =	475 grams (nearly $\frac{1}{2}$ kilogram)
Celsius to Fahrenheit	Divide by 5, multiply by 9, add 32
Fahrenheit to Celsius	Subtract 32, divide by 9, multiply by 5

Planning your visit

When to go

Unlike the folks of some cities, Londoners do not all choose to take their vacations at the same time, so the capital never "closes down." It does, on the other hand, become very crowded at the height of summer. Consider sidestepping this stampede: the British climate may be unpredictable, but it is rarely extreme, and London, being in one of the mildest parts of the country, can be very pleasant in the spring and fall. Moreover, a whole series of outdoor sporting (and social) events takes place from March onward (see CALENDAR OF EVENTS, below).

Outdoor institutions, such as the open-air theater in REGENT'S PARK, begin to brave the elements in May, and in the same month Glyndebourne's opera season starts. The crowded months are July and August, but theater-lovers will want to avoid the summer in favor of fall and winter, which are often better times for new shows and certainly for hotel accommodation.

Even in winter, London remains alive with activity, and several of the main exhibitions take place at this time of year. One famous winter institution that London cast aside many years ago is the pea-soup fog, vanquished by clean-air legislation, and little else remains to stop Londoners going about their daily rounds.

Calendar of events

For exact dates of events, telephone the **London Tourist Board and Convention Bureau** (☎ *(071) 730-3488)* or the **City of London Information Office** (☎ *(071) 260-1456)*. See also SPORTS AND ACTIVITIES on pages 271-4 and PUBLIC HOLIDAYS on page 42.

JANUARY
1st week: **January sales**. Most shops offer good reductions; the most voracious shoppers camp out overnight so as to get in first. Many sales now start in late December.
  International Boat Show, Earls Court, SW5. Leisure boats.
  Last Sunday, 11am: **Charles I Commemoration**, Whitehall, SW1. On the anniversary of his execution, the unofficial King's Army parades from St James's Palace to the Banqueting House.

January/February: **Chinese New Year**, Chinatown, around Gerrard St., W1. Dragons, lanterns, flags, torches and the Lion Dance.

January/March: **Rugby Union Internationals**, Twickenham. On two Saturday afternoons England play.

FEBRUARY

First Sunday, 4pm: **Annual Clowns Service**, Holy Trinity Church, Beechwood Rd., Dalston, E8. The Clowns International Club attends its church in full costume to honor founder Joseph Grimaldi. All welcome to free **clown show** afterwards.

Shrove Tuesday, noon: **Pancake races**, Covent Garden, followed by a **band performance**; also in Carnaby St.

MARCH

March 1: **St David's Day**, Windsor Castle. A member of the Royal Family usually presents the Welsh Guards with the principality's national emblem, a leek.

Ideal Home Exhibition, Olympia, W14. A huge exhibition of everything, but everything, found in and around the home.

Camden Jazz Festival always attracts big jazz names.

2nd Tuesday, noon: **Bridewell Service**, St Bride's, Fleet St., EC4. The Lord Mayor and Sheriffs attend this thanksgiving service for the Bridewell children's home, now moved out of London.

3rd or 4th Thursday: **Oranges and Lemons Service**, St Clement Danes, Strand, WC2. As a reminder of the nursery rhyme, children are presented with the fruits during a service. The church bells ring out the rhyme daily at 9am, noon, 3pm, 6pm.

March/April: **Head of the River Race**, Mortlake to Putney. Racing between teams from all over Europe.

March/April: **Boat Race**, Putney to Mortlake. Oxford and Cambridge University eights battle upstream with awesome power.

APRIL

Maundy Thursday (Thursday before Easter): **Maundy Money**. At a different church every year, not necessarily in London, the Queen presents specially minted coins to the elderly and to groups of children.

Good Friday: **Butterworth Charity**, St Bartholomew the Great, Smithfield, EC1. After 11am service, hot cross buns and coins are laid out on tombstones for local children.

Easter Sunday: **Easter Parade**, Battersea Park. Climax of the day-long fair is the huge colorful parade at 3pm. Also **fairs** on Hampstead Heath and Blackheath, which is scene of a **kite festival** as well. **Tower Church Parade**, Tower of London, EC3. After 11am service, Yeoman Warders have official inspection.

Easter Monday: **Procession and Easter carols**, Westminster Abbey, SW1. **London Marathon**, from Greenwich Park to Westminster Bridge. 30,000 competitors, from very fast to very mad.

Harness Horse Parade, Regents Park, NW1. A morning parade of heavy working horses in superb, gleaming brass harnesses and plumes.

2nd Wednesday after Easter: **Spital Sermon**, St Lawrence Jewry, EC2. A service attended by all the City's pomp, Lord Mayor included, in full regalia.

April 21: **Queen's Birthday**. 21-gun salutes in Hyde Park and on Tower Hill at noon. Troops in parade dress.

April/May: **FA Cup Final**, Wembley Stadium. Showpiece soccer match.

Rugby League Cup Final, Wembley Stadium. Showpiece rugby league match.

MAY

2nd Sunday: **May Fayre and Puppet Festival**, Covent Garden. Procession at 10am, service at St Paul's at 11.30am, then Punch and Judy shows until 6pm at the site where Pepys watched England's first show in 1662.

Ascension Day: **Beating the Bounds**. The boundary stones of parishes were traditionally "whacked" with a stick in defiance. Today it happens around the Tower, and All-Hallows-by-the-Tower, EC3, one of the marks of which is in mid-river but is whacked notwithstanding.

Glyndebourne Opera Season, Sussex. Exclusive performances in a country house, with champagne picnics during intervals. To August.

Royal Windsor Horse Show, held at Home Park, Windsor Castle.

Chelsea Flower Show, Royal Hospital, Chelsea, SW3. A massive and superb 4-day horticultural display.

May 29 or soon after: **Founder's (Oak Apple) Day**, Royal Hospital, Chelsea, SW3. The Chelsea Pensioners' annual parade.

Late May: **Samuel Pepys Memorial Service**, St Olave, EC3. Lord Mayor and Co., 17thC band, all flock to Pepys' own church.

May/June: **Summer Exhibition**, Royal Academy, Piccadilly, W1. An extensive potpourri of much that is happening in British art. To August/September.

Private Fire Brigades' Competition, Guildhall Yard, EC4. They spray targets with hoses. Again in September.

JUNE

Beating Retreat, Household Division, Horse Guards Parade, SW1. Military massed bands and marching.

1st Wednesday: **The Derby**, Epsom Downs. This great horse race is on common land, and so is attended by fairs, Gypsies, and huge crowds.

Beating Retreat, Scottish Division, Horse Guards Parade, SW1. Military massed bands and marching, by a different regiment each year.

Test match, Lords, NW8. Five-day international cricket match.

2nd week: **Stella Artois Tennis Championships**, Queen's Club, Baron's Court, W14. A warm-up for Wimbledon.

June 11 or nearest Saturday: **Trooping the Colour**, Horse Guards Parade, SW1. The Queen leaves from Buckingham Palace in procession to receive the Colour from her Foot Guards amid full pageantry.

Biggin Hill International Air Fair, Kent. International flying displays.

3rd week: **Royal Ascot**. The Berkshire racecourse sees some fine racing; but the event is more important for royalty on parade and "society" out to impress each other and have fun.

Monday during Ascot week: **Garter Ceremony**, St George's Chapel, Windsor Castle. The 24 members of The Very Noble Order of the Garter attend a service, invest new members, and pay homage to the Queen.

June 22 or near: **Election of the Sheriffs of the City of London**, Guildhall, EC2. Full pageantry and procession.

Last Sunday: **Kite festival** at Blackheath.

June/July: **Wimbledon Tennis Championships**. The world's top players.

Outdoor concerts, in all major parks, Kenwood Lakeside, Marble Hill Park and Crystal Palace Bowl. Until September. Military bands perform in royal parks.

JULY

1st week: **Henley Royal Regatta**, Henley, Oxfordshire. Another sporting event (rowing) that is also part of the "season."

City of London Festival, at various venues throughout the City.

Hampton Court Palace International Flower Show. A widely acclaimed 5-day international show.

Royal Tournament, Earls Court, SW5. All the Armed Forces join in displays of gymnastics, motor-cycling and military skills. On the Sunday before it begins, they all parade along a chosen route, sometimes in and sometimes outside London.

Promenade Concerts, Royal Albert Hall, SW7. Until September. See CLASSICAL MUSIC on page 248.

3rd week: **Swan Upping**, the Thames, from Temple Stairs to Henley. The Dyers' Company and Vintners' Company, which share ownership of all swans with the Queen, take six boats upriver counting and marking the birds.

2nd Wednesday: **Vintners Roadsweeping**. Wine porters sweep the road in front of a procession, from Vintners' Hall, Upper Thames St. to St James's Garlickhythe, EC4, at 11.58am, marking the inauguration of their new Master.

Doggett's Coat and Badge Race. A race for single sculls rowing from London Bridge to Chelsea against the tide, founded in 1714.

AUGUST

American Bowl, Wembley Arena. Exhibition American football game between two top NFL teams.

London Riding Horse Parade, Rotten Row, Hyde Park. Moss Bros cup goes to best turned-out horse and rider.

Bank Holiday Weekend (last in August): **Horse Show**, Clapham Common. **Bank Holiday Fair**, Hampstead Heath. A traditional fairground. The **Notting Hill Carnival**, Ladbroke Grove, W11. West Indian street carnival.

August/September: **Test match**, Kennington Oval, SE11. Five-day international cricket.

SEPTEMBER

First Saturday: **The Great River Race** from Richmond (9.30am) to Greenwich (approximately 1pm) between traditional craft, ranging from Hawaiian canoes to Viking longboats.

2nd weekend: **Farnborough Air Show**, Hampshire.

Last Night of the Proms, Royal Albert Hall, SW7. See page 248.

Chelsea Antiques Fair, Chelsea Old Town Hall, King's Rd., SW3.

3rd Sunday: **Horsemen's Sunday**, St John's, Hyde Park. Gathering of horses for a service.

September 21: **Christ's Hospital Boys March**. After a service at St Sepulchre-without-Newgate, Holborn Viaduct, EC1, pupils and band of this ancient school march to Mansion House in 16thC "bluecoats."

Private Fire Brigades' Competition, EC4. See MAY.

September 28: **Admission of Sheriffs**. See JUNE. In another ceremony, they are admitted to the Guildhall.

September 29: **Election of the Lord Mayor**, Guildhall, EC2. Beforehand, the whole corporation processes between Guildhall and St Lawrence Jewry.

OCTOBER

October 1 or 1st Monday: **Judges Service**, Westminster Abbey, SW1. At the start of the legal year, the judiciary processes from Westminster Abbey to breakfast in the Palace of Westminster, and then parades in the afternoon at the Royal Courts of Justice in the Strand, WC2.

1st Sunday, 3pm: **Pearly Harvest Festival**, St Martin-in-the-Fields, WC2. The brightly caparisoned Pearly Kings and Queens, Cockney folk leaders, in full uniform.

Punch and Judy Festival, The Piazza, Covent Garden. Several Punch and Judy shows to watch 10.30am-5.30pm.

Horse of the Year Show, Wembley Arena. Show jumping, featuring top international competitors.

Sunday in early October: **Harvest of the Sea Thanksgiving**, St Mary-at-Hill, EC3, 11am. Billingsgate dealers fill the church with fish, and the City attends in state.

Late October: **Quit Rents Ceremony**, Royal Courts of Justice, WC2. An official receives token rents on behalf of the Queen; ceremony includes splitting sticks and counting horseshoes.

October 21, or nearest Sunday: **Trafalgar Day**. National Service for Seafarers at St Paul's Cathedral, attended by Admiralty top brass; and a naval ceremony in Trafalgar Sq., WC2.

National Brass Band Championships, Royal Albert Hall, SW7. A type of music at which the British excel.

October/November: **State Opening of Parliament**. The processional route is Buckingham Palace, The Mall, Horse Guards Parade, Palace of Westminster. The entire Royal Family attends; full regalia, ancient gilded coaches.

NOVEMBER

1st Sunday: **London to Brighton Veteran Car Run**, beginning at

Hyde Park Corner, SW1. An early start (8am) for the aged cars.

November 5: **Guy Fawkes Night**. To celebrate the 1605 Gunpowder Plot to blow up Parliament, fireworks and bonfires all over town, with effigies of the conspiracy's leader burned on top.

Sunday nearest November 11: **Remembrance Sunday**. The Queen and State attend an 11am ceremony at the Cenotaph, Whitehall, SW1. The previous evening there is a moving **Festival of Remembrance** at the Royal Albert Hall, SW7.

Friday nearest November 12: **Admission of Lord Mayor Elect**, Guildhall, EC2. The outgoing mayor hands over the insignia.

Saturday nearest November 12: **Lord Mayor's Show**, Guildhall to Law Courts, Strand, WC2. The state coaches follow the many colorful floats in this huge carnival.

London Film Festival, National Film Theatre, South Bank. To December.

Late November: **Switching on of Christmas lights** in Regent St. and Oxford St. Until January 6.

DECEMBER
Royal Smithfield Show, Earls Court, SW5. Agricultural show.

Norwegian Christmas Tree, Trafalgar Sq. Carol-singing on most evenings beneath the tree.

Mid-December: **International Showjumping Championships**, Olympia.

December 31: **Watch Night**, St Paul's Cathedral. Scots gather on steps for Hogmanay. Trafalgar Sq. is the other traditional spot for high-spirited revelers, and Parliament Sq. for watching Big Ben strike at midnight.

WEEKLY EVENTS
Monday: Bric-a-brac and antiques at **Covent Garden** market.

Wednesday and Saturday: **Camden Passage** antique market. Late-night shopping in **Knightsbridge** (see SHOPPING, page 259). Some theater matinees.

Thursday: Late-night shopping in **Oxford St.** and **Regent St.** Some theater matinees.

Friday: **Bermondsey** (New Caledonian) antique market (see SHOPPING, page 266).

Saturday: **Portobello Rd.** antique market and **Covent Garden** crafts market (see SHOPPING, page 265). Theater matinees. Evening open-air concerts during June and July at **Kenwood House**, Hampstead Heath.

Sunday: **Petticoat Lane**, **Camden Lock** markets (see SHOPPING, page 266).

DAILY EVENTS
11am (10am Sunday): **Changing the Guard**, Horse Guards Parade.

11.30am (only alternate days in winter, and canceled if weather is bad): **Changing the Guard**, Buckingham Palace.

9.50pm: **Ceremony of the Keys**, Tower of London. Ceremonial changing of guards. Write to Resident Governor for free ticket.

Organizing your time: 5 days in London

No two visitors to this diverse city will have exactly the same idea of how best to spend their time. The following itinerary can only be selective, but it aims to reflect the many faces of London, and to make a varied program for a first visit.

DAY ONE
- Morning: To familiarize yourself with the city center's layout, and to see some of the most famous sights, at least from the outside, take a sightseeing bus tour (see USEFUL ADDRESSES, page 47). This will take in TRAFALGAR SQUARE, the Houses of Parliament (see WESTMINSTER, PALACE OF), WESTMINSTER ABBEY and BUCKINGHAM PALACE.
- Afternoon: Explore the NATIONAL GALLERY, one of the world's greatest repositories of Western art, now further enhanced by its superb Sainsbury Wing. Then, to contrast the sublime with the frivolous, take a short stroll along the STRAND for tea in COVENT GARDEN.

DAY TWO
- Morning: WALK 2 (see page 91) picks up where you left off the day before, taking you from Covent Garden into the entirely different academic and elegant atmosphere of BLOOMSBURY, and passing the BRITISH MUSEUM, the highlights at least of which should not be missed. If lunch looms, you could retrace your steps, or curtail your walk in bookish Museum St. at the MUSEUM STREET CAFÉ (see RESTAURANTS;

reserve ahead). Afterwards, a visit to the delightfully idiosyncratic former home of SIR JOHN SOANE in nearby Lincoln's Inn Fields is highly recommended.

- **Afternoon:** After the stuffiness of Bloomsbury, green open spaces beckon. Head for ST JAMES'S PARK, the most artfully pretty of all London's parks, for a gentle stroll around the lake, and for the lovely view from the bridge. Perhaps wander past ST JAMES'S PALACE into Green Park and treat yourself to tea at the RITZ (see HOTELS — but be sure to reserve ahead) or at Fortnum's (see CAFÉS AND TEAROOMS).

DAY THREE

- **Morning:** The day for a trip on the river. Take a cruise from Westminster or Charing Cross Pier (see FERRY SERVICES, page 42) to GREENWICH, with its peerless Neoclassical buildings and the magnificent tea clipper *Cutty Sark* moored alongside Greenwich Pier.
- **Afternoon:** After lunch in Greenwich, cross underneath the Thames by the little-known pedestrian tunnel, which connects Greenwich Pier with the Isle of Dogs. Here you can pick up the amusing Docklands Light Railway *(check that it is operating that day* ☎ *(071) 538-0311)* for a trip through that modern mayhem, DOCKLANDS. You might stop at Canary Wharf, with its soaring tower, for a cup of tea, or a trip to the top for an unrivaled view over and beyond Greater London. But if time is short, carry straight on to Tower Gateway Station, and make your way to the TOWER OF LONDON to find the Beefeaters, the Bloody Tower, the ravens and the Crown Jewels.

DAY FOUR

- **Morning:** Begin the day not in the West End, but in one of the ancient villages that have amalgamated to make London so diverse and characterful. Take the underground to Sloane Sq., and then a No. 11 or No. 22 bus along the King's Rd. as far as Oakley St., and alight here to explore the delights of CHELSEA. CARLYLE'S HOUSE, Chelsea Physic Garden, and Wren's ROYAL HOSPITAL, home of the Chelsea Pensioners, are all worth visiting; choose which according to time and inclination.
- **Afternoon:** From Sloane Sq., head for classy Knightsbridge and the wonders of Harrods' food halls (see SHOPPING, page 262), thence to South Kensington with its plethora of great museums. Some will be drawn to the SCIENCE MUSEUM, others to the NATURAL HISTORY MUSEUM, but no one can fail to find satisfaction among the treasures of the VICTORIA AND ALBERT MUSEUM.

DAY FIVE

- **Morning:** A day of grandeur and ceremony to end your visit. Watch the Changing the Guard at BUCKINGHAM PALACE in the morning (see CALENDAR OF EVENTS, page 56), not omitting to visit the Royal Mews with its beautiful state coaches (if it is open).
- **Afternoon:** Head for the CITY, exploring as much or little of it as you feel like, but keeping a visit to Wren's masterpiece, ST PAUL'S CATHEDRAL, for a climactic end to your trip. As a footnote, attend the Ceremony of the Keys (see CALENDAR OF EVENTS, page 56) at the Tower of London, which begins at 9.50pm (arrive by 9.30pm).

London's districts

An overview

This introduction to the chapter is intended to be read in conjunction with the ORIENTATION MAP, overleaf. You can look up the entries for districts printed in BOLD CAPITALS, later on in this chapter.

The main **airport**, Heathrow, is on the western side of the city, and the longer **rail** and **road** routes run into the west and north. Those compass points have a powerful influence on activity in London. The greatest number of **hotels** is found in the west, in suburbs such as CHISWICK, inner districts such as KENSINGTON, CHELSEA and Victoria, or in the West End, the area that most Londoners regard as the center by virtue of its **shops**, **restaurants** and **theaters**.

Farther east, the CITY, although it is jeweled with historical sights, is seen by the Londoner as being primarily a **business district** that empties in the evenings and on weekends. In much the way that the City is a buffer to the east, so is the river to the south. The implantation of the Barbican Centre in the City and the South Bank Arts Centre across the river were both conscious attempts to extend the geographical spread of **nocturnal life**. Beyond these outriders, however, Central London fades in the City and only half-heartedly crosses the Thames. **Central London** does not formally define itself, but most inhabitants would probably accept the Circle line on the tube system as a fair boundary.

Few Londoners live within that circle, however, and their **residential districts** outside it are the source of much local rivalry. Not only does the topography of fashionable northern suburbs such as HAMPSTEAD and HIGHGATE provide their inhabitants with elevated notions, but it is also true that many Londoners feign disinclination to cross the river. In the past, many "south-of-the-river" districts closer to London have had little to recommend them to visitors, but a number of excellent **restaurants** have opened in recent years in some now fashionable residential enclaves. Nevertheless there is only one recommended tourist hotel at present south of the river; and indeed there are not many to the east of Tower Bridge. So for **hotel accommodation** the visitor has generally to stick to the center, the north or the west.

POSTAL CODES AND STREET SIGNS
Each of the compass points appears in the beginning of the postal codes and is also printed on street signs. Much of the West End is W1 (West One), addresses in the City are usually EC (East Central), and so

on. Nevertheless the system is not as logical as it might be, and spoken directions will tend to be given by Londoners in terms of the area's or the district's name.

The main areas

London grew from two ancient cities on a meandering river. Villages, many of considerable historic importance, dotted the countryside around and between them. The metropolis that coalesced from these once separate entities is today the largest urban area in Europe.

It is not an easy city to grasp in the abstract. London lacks the clearly defined historic core that in Paris or Rome groups so many visitor attractions and historic highlights within a walkable radius; and where Manhattan Island gives New York a defining reference point to hold in the mind's eye, London at first sight seems to sprawl formlessly. Not only is this city very large; it is also substantially unplanned.

Naturally, many of the most important sights lie within the area generally recognized as Central London. But a great many more, from the ROYAL AIR FORCE MUSEUM in Hendon to HAMPTON COURT PALACE, or the ROYAL BOTANIC GARDENS in Kew to the WILLIAM MORRIS GALLERY in Walthamstow, lie well away from the center. So the first challenge awaiting the visitor is to form a mental map of the city and a realistic idea of its scale.

The city center is customarily divided into two areas, **THE CITY** and the **West End**. These are surrounded by **Inner London** and then the sprawling hinterland of **Outer London**.

THE CITY
This is home not only of Mammon (in the Bank of England and the financial institutions) but also of God (in ST PAUL'S CATHEDRAL and the numerous churches). The ROYAL COURTS OF JUSTICE and the OLD BAILEY are to be found in the City, and the whole square mile is guarded by the TOWER OF LONDON.

THE WEST END
Unlike the City, the West End has no precise borders, but is divided by its main thoroughfares into clearly defined neighborhoods. Simply by crossing the street it is possible to leave behind a neighborhood of one quite distinct character and enter what seems to be another world. The ORIENTATION MAP on pages 60-61 shows the area limits.

MAYFAIR is the neighborhood of exclusive hotels, expense-account restaurants, embassies, haute couture houses and casinos, and its denizens usually ride in chauffeur-driven cars. Its "village" shopping street is Bond St., with South Molton St. for the younger folks, and North and South Audley Sts. for the extra-extravagant. In hilly, elegant Brook, Mount and Curzon Sts. are smaller, old-established, conspicuously exclusive shops. The alleys of Shepherd Market offer sidewalk cafés for rest and refreshment on sunny days.

SOHO is seductive not for its sex stores, which are no more inviting nor less sleazy than those in any other city, but for its delicatessens, pâtisseries, moderately priced restaurants, and a gossipy confluence of Italian waiters, Cockney editors, lengthy lunchers and other miscreants. Its trendiness has long attracted media folk. Across Shaftesbury Ave., its cosmopolitanism hardens into Chinatown.

COVENT GARDEN has, despite the misgivings of purists, proved to be one of the most successful examples anywhere of a discarded facility (in this instance a wholesale fruit-and-vegetable market) being turned into an area for strolling, eating and shopping. The most fiercely community-conscious of all the inner city areas, it has come to stand for everything opposed to big business and development.

BLOOMSBURY has a bookish dignity that once hid all manner of intensity. It also has the BRITISH MUSEUM and the nucleus of London University, whose visitors and students find peace in its many green squares.

BELGRAVIA is the most elegant part of the West End, with its early 19thC houses; Belgrave Sq., from which it takes its name, has beautiful gardens. Even the very rich who have always lived here are feeling the pinch, and today the area is dominated by embassies. Belgravia's "neighborhood shop" is Harrods; around the corner is Knightsbridge.

ST JAMES'S is gentlemen's clubland, with Jermyn St. as its shopping thoroughfare. The name is broadly applied to the neighborhood around St James's St., and St James's Sq., on the hill running down from Piccadilly to ST JAMES'S PALACE, constituting an area that has perhaps changed less than any other over the last 50 years.

WESTMINSTER is media shorthand for Parliament, in much the way that WHITEHALL is used to denote the Civil Service and DOWNING STREET to suggest the Prime Minister. Apart from WESTMINSTER ABBEY, all the dominant buildings in this area are concerned with government. There are no shops and very few residents — just a rich seam of pomp and circumstance.

INNER LONDON

Beyond Central London, several inner districts make their own unique contributions to metropolitan life. The most obvious are the two that give their name to the Royal Borough of Kensington and Chelsea. **KENSINGTON**, with its famous museums, also extends to Notting Hill and Portobello Rd., eventually giving way to Hammersmith, which has a couple of respected theaters. **CHELSEA**, elegant and fashionable, with its clothes stores and restaurants, spills over into Fulham.

All these districts are in the W; in the N, Islington has emerged as the outstanding example of the arty rejuvenation of London's old working-class inner boroughs.

OUTER LONDON

Intellectual **HAMPSTEAD** and **HIGHGATE** in the N, maritime **GREENWICH** in the E, villagey **DULWICH** in the S, riverside **RICHMOND** in the W . . . . All are to varying degrees outer districts, although London stretches yet farther in an exhausting sprawl of mainly 1930s suburbs.

London's districts A to Z

In this edition, for the first time, we list and describe the most interesting and typical districts of London here, in their own section. These are separate from the dozens of individual sights and places of interest, which form their own chapter starting on page 96.

This allows visitors staying for longer periods, or making a return visit, to explore the city as Londoners do: wandering on foot through the districts of the living city, and visiting the major attractions of each area as a coherent group. For many, this makes a welcome alternative to a series of high-speed, unconnected expeditions to tourist highlights.

Each district entry is comprehensively cross-referenced to individual sights listed in SIGHTS AND PLACES OF INTEREST.

BATTERSEA
Map 10D4. Train to Battersea from Waterloo, or bus no. 19, 39, 45, 49.
Little remains of the old Thameside village of Battersea, part of which is now an industrial sprawl and part a gentrified residential area. Down by the river, **Battersea Park** is well laid out, with sculptures by Henry Moore and Barbara Hepworth, and is the site of the Easter Parade (see CALENDAR OF EVENTS, page 52). Overlooking the river is an attractive **Japanese Peace Pagoda** completed in 1985.

A dominant and increasingly admired landmark is Sir Giles Gilbert Scott's vast **Battersea Power Station**, brick-built in the modern, monumental style of the 1930s. Sir Nikolaus Pevsner thought it "one of the first examples in England of a frankly contemporary industrial architecture." It is currently a sad although still proud shell, its proposed conversion into a huge indoor theme park having been halted several years ago due to lack of finance.

A newer Battersea landmark is the vast marble-faced *Observer* **newspaper building**, erected on the s side of Battersea Bridge.

BELGRAVIA
Maps 15-16. Tube: Hyde Park Corner, Knightsbridge, Sloane Square, Victoria.
London's most magnificent terraces, once the town houses of dukes, make up the great squares of Belgravia, the area around Belgrave Sq. developed by Thomas Cubitt in a frenzy of activity following the establishment of nearby BUCKINGHAM PALACE as the royal residence in the 1820s.

Belgrave Square itself forms the centerpiece of the fairly regular plan, with its massive Classically decorated blocks by George Basevi and grand corner houses by other architects surrounding the private sunken gardens. **Eaton Sq.**, to the s, is a long rectangle, with the King's Rd. running through the middle of its stuccoed terraces. To the s again is **Chester Sq.**, to some eyes the most appealing of the three.

In Motcomb St., Seth-Smith's Doric-fronted pantechnicon of 1830 looks back on Wilton Crescent, built by the same architect three years earlier. For refreshment, head for **The Grenadier** (see PUBS, page 241).

BLACKHEATH

Map 20D5. Train to Blackheath from Charing Cross.

This common near the royal residences of GREENWICH and ELTHAM PALACE used to be as grim a place as its name suggests. In the 18thC it became a fashionable country address. Now the refreshingly open, high clearing is surrounded by the fine, plain and elegantly unadorned Classical houses of that period. On the SE side, a semicircular row of buildings, known as the **Paragon**, is quite stunning. Probably dating from the 1780s, it consists of a series of blocks linked by single-story colonnaded arcades.

To the NE of Blackheath is the magnificent red-brick **Charlton House** (✫ ☎ *(081) 856-3951* ▣ ✔ *open by appointment only, Mon-Sat),* the best Jacobean house in London (now a community center). Built in 1607-12, it is entirely regular, with a central arched doorway, exuberant Mannerist carvings, and flanking towers.

BLOOMSBURY

Map 3, and WALK 2 map (page 91). Tube: Euston, Russell Square, Holborn.

Bloomsbury, like so many other areas of London, is a "village" with a reputation. The Bloomsbury Group was as well known for its mores as for its writings, but its patch of London remains the literary capital, housing a host of publishing companies and centered on London University and the BRITISH MUSEUM. WALK 2 (pages 91-2) explores Bloomsbury's Georgian squares, and includes a map.

One of the most fashionable addresses in the 18thC, Bloomsbury was an inconspicuous residential area when Virginia and Leonard Woolf, Roger Fry, Lytton Strachey and Maynard Keynes made it their fortress from 1904-39. Before long, other voices were heard there: T.S. Eliot, Bertrand Russell and D.H. Lawrence were inevitably drawn to the center of the action, even if they did not agree with "The Group."

Bloomsbury Sq. is where it all began, when the Earl of Southampton built a palace there in 1660. No original building survives, although the gardens are pleasant. **Bedford Square**, to the W past ST GEORGE'S, BLOOMS-BURY, was built in 1775; it survives virtually intact as London's finest square. Its terraces of plain houses are built of dark brick with stucco pedimented centers. The lush garden is exquisite, although private.

The much larger **Russell Sq.**, at the top of Bedford Pl., with its huge plane trees, has fared less well. South of the square, the enchanting streets around Museum St. are full of secondhand bookstores. To the N, **Woburn**, **Gordon** and **Tavistock Squares** all boast good gardens and some terraces surviving from the early 19thC. A short walk to the E brings you to the **Jewish Museum** *(☎(071) 388-4525* ▣ *open Tues-Fri, Sun 10am-4pm, Oct-Mar Fri, Sun 10am-12.45pm)* and **Cartwright Gdns.**, with a fine crescent-shaped terrace. A little farther on is **Brunswick Sq.**, a major modern public housing development with brutal but interesting architecture, and the CORAM FOUNDATION.

The University has buildings throughout Bloomsbury, of which the best is the oldest, the original **University College** in Gower St. It is a splendid Classical building with dome and portico, dating from 1827-29.

The Senate House in Malet St., by contrast, is an essay in 1930s Classicism. Also within this "open campus" is the **University Church of Christ the King** in Gordon Sq., 1853 Gothic with a cathedral-like interior. Also in Gordon Sq. is the PERCIVAL DAVID FOUNDATION OF CHINESE ART.

Looming over Bloomsbury, the BRITISH TELECOM TOWER in Cleveland St. is a familiar landmark.

CHELSEA ★
Maps 14-15. Tube: South Kensington, Sloane Square.
Chelsea is London's most fashionable address. On the one hand, the pretty, well-maintained houses in its quiet streets retain the feel of an elegant backwater, almost a country village; by contrast, the **King's Road** is *outré*, noisy and Bohemian in a way nowhere else can imitate.

Only in the later 18thC did the quiet village nestling on the river's edge become a part of London. Charles II built the ROYAL HOSPITAL from 1682 as a restful place of retirement for old soldiers. The military connection remains, with two large barracks and the NATIONAL ARMY MUSEUM.

In 1673 the Society of Apothecaries established **Chelsea Physic Garden** *(Swan Walk ☎(071) 352-5646, map 15L6-7 ▨ open late Mar/early Apr to mid-Oct Wed and Sun 2-5pm, daily during Chelsea Flower Show)* to grow plants for the study of medicine. With its exotic trees and shrubs, aromatic herbs, rock garden, tranquil pond and greenhouses, it is still a delightful place in which to stroll.

Apart from the Hospital and Physic Garden, little remains of old Chelsea. The area around CHEYNE WALK includes the few old houses there are, such as **Lindsey House** of about 1674, and Cheyne Row of 1708, where CARLYLE'S HOUSE can be visited. Most of Chelsea's housing dates from the 19thC, some of it very grand (**Cadogan Sq.**), and some of it mere artisans' cottages, which are now so sought after.

In the late 1800s, Chelsea became known as an artists' colony. Pre-Raphaelites such as Rossetti, Burne-Jones and Morris lived here; Whistler settled here, called it "the wonderful village," and quarreled with Oscar Wilde, who lived in Tite St.; and Americans, such as Henry James and Jack London, were attracted to the area. Everywhere you look, blue plaques mark the former abodes of the famous.

After World War II the avant-garde again made this their home. The "angry young men" grabbed attention at the **Royal Court Theatre** in 1956 (see THEATERS, page 251), artists crowded into Finch's pub in the Fulham Rd., and, most significantly, Mary Quant began selling clothes in the King's Rd., subsequently a major center for cult fashion.

On the Chelsea/Fulham borders, off Lots Rd., the luxury development of apartments, restaurants and private marina, **Chelsea Harbour**, has sprung up. Its tall tower block can be seen from far away; the golden ball on top moves up and down to indicate the tide level.

CHISWICK
Map 19C3, and WALK 3 map (page 93). Tube: Turnham Green.
Although on the main routes out of the capital to the W, parts of the old riverside village of Chiswick survive. A still and dreamy quarter is to be

found by turning sharp left into Church St. at the monster Hogarth Roundabout where the Great West Rd. traffic is forced to pause. **St Nicholas** church has a 15thC tower, although the rest is a Victorian reconstruction; buried in the churchyard are the painters James McNeill Whistler and William Hogarth.

Back on the Great West Rd. is HOGARTH'S HOUSE, and just beyond it CHISWICK HOUSE. Chiswick can be explored as part of WALK 3 — see pages 92-95, which include a map.

THE CITY ★

Maps 11-12. Livery company halls do not have regular opening hours and will admit visitors only on open days. For information, contact i *City of London Information Centre, St Paul's Churchyard, EC4* ☎*(071) 260-1456.*

For centuries it was just what its name suggests, and although London has now vastly outgrown it, the City retains its identity, its influence, and, to a degree that invariably surprises newcomers, its unique form of self-government.

Today, "the City" is shorthand for money; this is where the great banking, insurance and commodity trading concerns are based. During the day, more than 300,000 people work here, but at night and on weekends it can be a concrete and glass desert, with a resident population of less than 5,000. As a result, it may be best to visit the City on a weekend, when it is easier to find and enjoy the hidden, almost secret places that give the area its appeal. Be warned, however, for while the streets may be free of traffic, it can be hard to find a pub or restaurant that is open. Even the famous Wren churches are often closed on Sunday — the best time to visit them is weekday lunchtimes.

The City does not easily yield up its past. First the Great Fire of 1666, then the bombs of 1940 and, most recently, the zeal of developers have swept away much that was old. In its place, there is an ostensibly haphazard collection of office buildings, for the most part demonstrating the poverty of modern architecture. As Sir Nikolaus Pevsner has pointed out, the skyline has none of the excitement of New York or Chicago, but has more in common with that of an unimportant Mid-West town. On the other hand, ST PAUL'S CATHEDRAL is too great a building to be dominated by its taller neighbors, Wren's churches too interesting not to be visited, and history proclaims itself too loudly even from the street names to be ignored. And, of course, the City does have its own unique geography, described by a uniquely English phrase — nooks and crannies.

The key to exploring the City is not to content yourself with its obvious beauties. To an astonishing extent it retains elements of its medieval character. Within the area bounded by the old walls (the gates were at Ludgate, Newgate, Aldersgate, Cripplegate, Bishopsgate and Aldgate), one can easily work out what was where. Cheapside, for example, with the surrounding Milk St., Poultry and Bread St., marks the site of the main medieval market.

The government of the City has not even changed on the surface. The Guildhall is still its parliament, and Mansion House the palace of its head, the Lord Mayor. He is selected annually by a complex system based on ancient privileges rather than mere residence. City livery companies, descended from medieval trade guilds, have an important part to play in choosing and providing the aldermen and sheriffs from whom the Lord Mayor must come. The liveries still have their own halls, their own constitutions, and their own regalia, even though they are hardly ever connected with their original trades. The City still has its own police force (look at the badges on the helmets, different from those elsewhere in London), and on royal ceremonial occasions the monarch will not enter the City unless greeted on its borders by the Lord Mayor.

The square mile is a large area to visit on foot, with its many sites of interest widely scattered. To make it more manageable, it has here been divided into four parts, each viewed separately.

The City: east

The City to the E of a line taken from London Bridge to Liverpool Street Station in the N includes many fine churches, but the predominant tone is set by the great maritime trading interests. Until the 19thC almost all the trade goods landed at London were brought ashore between London Bridge and the Tower of London.

Lloyd's (🏛 ☎ *(071) 623-7100),* the headquarters of a business largely founded on insuring ships and their cargo, is in a controversial new building in Lime St., designed by Richard Rogers and opened in 1986. Lloyd's grew, amazingly, from a coffeehouse; now its huge underwriting room, simply called "the Room," but housed in a massive glazed atrium (200 feet high), is a beehive of activity, centered around the 18thC Lutine Bell, traditionally struck once for news of disaster of a missing ship, and twice for a safe arrival. The atrium is the core of Rogers' striking glass, steel and concrete structure. From the Room on the ground floor, illuminated glass-sided escalators ascend to three galleries, the floors of the market. All the services are contained in six satellite towers, up and down which slide glass-sided observation elevators (see the illustration on page 27). There is a viewing gallery and exhibition on the role of Lloyd's past and present (🔲 ☎ *(071) 327-6210, map 12 F16, open Mon-Fri 9.30am-12.30pm, 2-4pm by appointment with 7 days' notice, written confirmation, and name list for groups of 4-30 people).*

Lloyd's Shipping Register, where the capacity and whereabouts of all the world's shipping is monitored, is in nearby Fenchurch St. In Mincing Lane is the **Commodity Exchange** of Plantation House.

In the SE corner of the City is the TOWER OF LONDON. Just to the N is **Trinity Square** with, at its E side, a well-preserved portion of Roman wall. Opposite is **Trinity House**, headquarters of the charity operating Britain's lighthouses and lifeboats.

To the W of Trinity Sq., in Byward St., is the church of **All-Hallows-by-the-Tower**; the attractive tower dates from 1658-59. The church is actually much older, dating back to the 7thC, and there is a Saxon arch at the tower base, revealed by bomb damage. Inside is a quite beautiful **font cover** of 1682 by Wren's great carver Grinling Gibbons. All Hallows also has a **Brass Rubbing Centre** (▣ *open Mon-Sat 11am-4pm, Sun 12.30am-4pm* ▣) and an **Undercroft Museum** (▩ *✗ by appointment; same opening times*), where displays include carved Saxon stonework, part of a Roman pavement, a model of Roman London, the baptism record of William Penn, and marriage lines of John Quincy Adams.

Farther W along the riverfront toward LONDON BRIDGE is the large **Customs House** of 1812-25, its Classical facade best seen from London Bridge. Opposite, up St Dunstan's Hill, is the ruined church of **St Dunstan-in-the-East**, converted into a delightful garden; Wren's extraordinary spire of 1698, supported on flying buttresses, still stands.

Back on Lower Thames St., the next building along from the Custom House is **Billingsgate Market**, a typical 19thC covered market, closed in 1982, when the fish market that existed there since medieval times moved farther E into Docklands. It has now been beautifully converted by Richard Rogers into the headquarters of an American bank. A little farther along is the church of **St Magnus Martyr**, designed by Wren in 1671-76 although altered since. The tower is massive, with a spire of 1705.

Over Lower Thames St. is Fish St. Hill and Wren's THE MONUMENT. At the top of Fish St. Hill is the major thoroughfare of Eastcheap, site of a medieval market. Some fanciful Victorian commercial buildings deserve study — **nos.33-35**, for example, all brick Gothic and gables. To the S is the splendid Wren church of **St Mary-at-Hill**, hidden in a maze of charming lanes, which forms a moving contrast to the great space and harmony of Wren's beautiful interior, built in 1670-76. The church is unusual in that it still has box pews, and is noteworthy for some wrought-iron sword-rests and a carved organ screen.

Back on Eastcheap, another Wren church will be discovered a little farther along on the left, **St Margaret Pattens**, named after a special type of shoe made here. This time the exterior, with a fine spire of 1687, has more to offer than the interior. A pretty, early 19thC shop and house (now an American bank) next to the church completes an attractive corner. To the N is the **Commodity Exchange**, with its facade in Fenchurch St., and behind the new **Clothworkers' Hall** up Mincing Lane on the left is the small 15thC tower of **All Hallows Staining**, incongruously surrounded by large buildings.

Nearby in Hart St. is **St Olave**, an attractive 15thC church (*lunchtime recitals held here Wed, Thurs 1-2pm*). Untouched by the Great Fire of London, it was damaged in the Blitz but well restored. It contains several good monuments, especially those to Sir James Deane (1608) and Peter Cappone (1582). Samuel Pepys the diarist used the church, and there is a monument to his wife (1669). Hart St. leads into Crutched Friars, which passes under Fenchurch Street Station ("crutched" means "crossed" — there was a priory here). **No. 42** is a fine early 18thC house.

North of Fenchurch St., **Leadenhall Market**, off Lime St., provides City workers with a welcome shopping area. Leadenhall St., a little farther N, contains the churches of **St Andrew Undershaft**, mostly early 16thC, and **St Katharine Cree**, a survivor from the early 17thC, but with a medieval tower.

This section of the City, straddling the course of the Roman and medieval wall along Camomile St. and Bevis Marks, contains three churches. **St Helen Bishopsgate** is an outstanding convent church dating back to the 13thC. Its many interesting features include an attractive w front topped by a little 17thC bell tower, a poor box of about 1620 in the form of a one-armed beggar, and remarkable monuments. The other churches in Bishopsgate are **St Ethelburga**, with medieval fragments and a tower of 1775, and **St Botolph-without-Bishopsgate**, a pleasant 18thC building where Keats was baptized. The **Spanish and Portuguese Synagogue** in Bevis Marks deserves a visit; it dates back to 1700-1, and contains some lavishly decorated appointments of that period.

The City: south

This is the central area between ST PAUL'S CATHEDRAL and London Bridge, s of Cheapside, Poultry and Cornhill.

The waterfront w of London Bridge, Upper Thames St., is now one of London's least attractive roads, bearing great quantities of traffic through a windy and noisy desert. The narrow alley of **Broken Wharf**, however, leads down to a good view of the river and the **Samuel Pepys pub** in an old warehouse. There is also a riverside walk to the w of this. But to the N, only the slender pinnacled tower of **St Mary Somerset** and the much-restored church of **St Nicholas Cole Abbey**, both by Wren, relieve the monotony.

Just beyond Queen St., the approach to Southwark Bridge, there are some smaller and older streets around Mansion House tube station. Wren's **St James Garlickhythe** (1676-83) in Garlick Hill (where the herb was sold) has a fine tower, looking rather like a lighthouse with a stone lantern on top; it contains some good ironwork. **Beaver Hall** in Great Trinity Lane is the center of the fur trade, the premises of which cluster in these narrow streets. Facing Upper Thames St. is the **Vintners' Hall**, one of the best of a number of livery company halls in this area. It was built in 1671, and although much restored has a fine paneled hall and a superb carved staircase. Queen St. itself contains two magnificent Georgian houses (**nos. 27** and **28**).

Between Queen St. and Cannon Street Station there is another maze of little lanes, around the church of **St Michael Paternoster Royal**, built by Wren but much restored after war damage. Some good interior fittings have survived, including a carved pulpit and reredos. Three livery companies have their halls in Dowgate Hill, just w of St Michael: the **Skinners** (with a late 18thC facade), the **Dyers**, and the **Tallow Chandlers** (the last two are Victorian).

Between Cannon Street Station and King William St. (which leads onto LONDON BRIDGE) is yet another fascinating maze of small streets, with several historic pubs and wine bars. **Laurence Pountney Hill** to the E has two of the most beautiful 18thC houses in London, dated 1703, with elaborately decorated doorways and cornices. Other attractive buildings are found around the pleasant little **churchyard** left by the vanished church of St Laurence. Next to London Bridge is the **Fishmongers' Hall** of 1831-34, the best-sited and grandest livery company hall, with an imposing Classical facade overlooking the river.

Just N of Cannon St. are **St Clement Eastcheap**, containing some superb wood carving, and the extraordinary ST MARY ABCHURCH, both by Wren. Farther N is Lombard St., an important banking street named after the Italian money-lenders who set up business here in the 14thC. It contains two fine churches: **St Mary Woolnoth** and **St Edmund the King**. The latter is again by Wren, with a harmonious exterior and well-preserved woodwork inside. St Mary Woolnoth was built by Nicholas Hawksmoor in 1716-27 and occupies its prominent corner site with a dramatic monumental facade. The interior, with massive Corinthian columns, is Baroque in character.

North of Lombard St. are several attractive lanes: St Michael's Alley, Castle Court and Ball Court. Old hostelries tucked away in this enclave include **Simpson's**, the **George and Vulture** and the **Jamaica Wine House**. There are two churches on the S side of Cornhill: **St Michael Cornhill** has a pretty churchyard, but is itself an unhappy mixture of styles by Wren and later architects; **St Peter-upon-Cornhill** by Wren is best seen from its little churchyard.

Moving w, large offices again dominate the area S of Cheapside and Poultry. The remains of the **Roman Temple of Mithras** (see the marvelous sculptures in the Museum of London, described under LONDON, MUSEUM OF) can be seen in Queen Victoria St. Nearby is the church of **St Mary Aldermary**, completed by Wren in 1692 in an extraordinary version of Gothic, with a tall tower, nave and aisles. The fan-vaulted roof uses a very free interpretation of the medieval style, with shallow domes between the fans, all richly covered with delicate tracery.

On Cheapside is the major church of ST MARY-LE-BOW, with the grandest of Wren's steeples. Where Cheapside joins Poultry is the MANSION HOUSE, the Lord Mayor's official residence, with the important ST STEPHEN WALBROOK behind.

The City: north

The northern part of the City contains a number of important institutions and a great many lesser offices. As a result, it is less an area to stroll through than other parts of the City. In the N are the spectacularly redeveloped **Liverpool Street Station**, with its Victorian hotel, and the postwar developments of **Broadgate** — where, incongruously, there is now an open-air ice rink *(open mid-Nov to Mar ☎(071) 588-6565)* — London Wall, and the BARBICAN (pictured overleaf), incorporating the ambitious and sumptuous **Barbican Centre**.

Just to the N of Liverpool Street Station and Spitalfields Market is the remarkable **Dennis Severs' House**. Mr Severs gives a 3-hour "performance" tour of his 18thC house in the evening, or you can simply wander around yourself during the day *(18 Folgate St., map 12 D17, by appt. only ☎ 247-4013 before noon Mon-Fri for details)*.

The **Barbican** (begun 1955), a housing and social development with walkways between many levels and gardens.

To the s, forming the real center of the City, are the financial and administrative institutions, the GUILDHALL, the **Bank of England**, the **Stock Exchange**, where technology has taken over from face-to-face trading and which is now closed to the public, and the **Royal Exchange** building.

In Foster Lane, N of Cheapside, is **St Vedast**, a Wren church built in 1670-97 but reconstructed after war damage. Its finest feature is the elaborate and effectively sinuous spire. To the N is **Goldsmiths' Hall**, built with a massive Classical exterior by Philip Hardwick in 1829-35. Occasional open days *(details from City Information Centre ☎ (071) 260-1456)* make it possible to see the livery company's unmatched collection of historic and modern plate, as well as the hall's palatial interior, with its tremendous dome-covered staircase of colored marble.

On nearby Gresham St. is the interesting Wren church of **St Anne and St Agnes**, built of brick in 1680 on a square with a central dome supported on columns. In Wood St., to the E, which was completely devastated during the Blitz, there is a lonely Wren tower in the Gothic style, all that remains of the Church of **St Alban**. Next to the GUILDHALL in Gresham St. is **St Lawrence Jewry**, again by Wren (1671-87).

Lothbury, next to the Bank of England, contains Wren's **St Margaret Lothbury**. Good features include the 17thC screen brought from another Wren church, with its beautiful twisted columns. Look for **no. 7 Lothbury**: Victorian architecture at its imaginative best. Lothbury leads into Throgmorton St. (the **Stock Exchange** is on the right), which then becomes Old Broad St. Here stands the tallest, perhaps most exciting and dramatic of the City's contemporary office buildings, the **National Westminster Bank tower**. Its soaring height, emphasized by vertical ribbing, balances unnervingly on a narrowed base with a clear glass facade.

The nation's controlling bank, the **Bank of England** *(Threadneedle St. ☎ (071) 601-5545, map 12 F16 ▣ open Mon-Fri 10am-5pm, Easter to late Sept Sun, bank hols 11am-5pm)* has a museum, which charts the history of the bank from its Royal Charter in 1694 to the present day. Exhibits include Roman gold bars and coins, a collection of banknotes, the re-creation of Sir John Soane's Stock Office, and an interactive video taking you live to the Dealing Desk.

In Bishopsgate is **St Botolph-without-Bishopsgate**, rebuilt in 1727-29 and with a 19thC interior. **All Hallows London Wall** (1765-67) to the W has a simple and light interior with an ornate plaster ceiling.

The City: west

Most of the western part of the modern City falls outside the old Roman walled town, including the whole section w of Ludgate Circus to the beginning of the STRAND and Smithfield Market, the capital's wholesale meat market, housed in a fine Victorian building, to the N. Of prime interest are FLEET STREET, the Inner and Middle TEMPLE extending s to the river, and ST PAUL'S CATHEDRAL.

The stretch of riverside to the s of St Paul's is disfigured by the traffic of Upper Thames St., although **St Benet's** (1677-83) remains as one of the most delightful and best preserved of Wren's churches, small and simple in the Dutch style with charming garlanded windows. Nearby in Queen Victoria St. is the 17thC COLLEGE OF ARMS. The church of **St Andrew-by-the-Wardrobe** stands on St Andrew's Hill to the w. Built by Wren in 1685-93, it is abutted by the offices of the men who maintained the state apparel.

To the s is the **Mermaid Theatre**, surrounded by the raging traffic of Puddle Dock. In Queen Victoria St. is the extraordinary **Black Friar** pub, decorated in high Arts-and-Crafts style (see PUBS, page 240). In Blackfriars Lane next to the station is the **Apothecaries' Hall**, a fine livery company building with a facade of 1684 (altered in 1779). North again is Ludgate Hill, site of the medieval "Lud Gate" until 1769-61; it offers the best view of the portico of St Paul's. **St Martin Ludgate**, a Wren church of 1677-87, has a most attractive lead-covered spire and some good carved wood-work inside. Just behind is the **Stationers' Hall**, a building of about 1667 with a stone facade of 1800.

Another of the old roads out of the City passed through Newgate, site of the notorious jail and now the OLD BAILEY. Newgate St. leads into Holborn Viaduct, built to span a little valley in 1863-69. Its heavy, ornate ironwork can be seen best from Farringdon St. The church of **St Sepulchre** on the N side of Holborn Viaduct is unusually large, with a great (although restored) 15thC tower. **St Andrew Holborn** on the s side is a Wren church with a 15thC tower restored in 1703.

To the N of Holborn Viaduct is Smithfield, long the site of the famous medieval St Bartholomew's Fair, about which Ben Jonson wrote his play in 1614, and the place where Wat Tyler and his rebel peasants confronted Richard II in 1381; Lord Mayor Walworth showed the City's customary independence by simply drawing his sword and killing Tyler. Nearby are **Smithfield Market** and ST-BARTHOLOMEW-THE-GREAT. **St Bartholomew's Hospital** opposite dates back to the Middle Ages. Its church, **St Bartholomew-the-Less**, has another 15thC tower.

To the E of St Bart's, as it is known, at the end of Little Britain, is **St Botolph Aldersgate**, rebuilt in 1788-91 and with a well-preserved interior. Behind this little church is the charming oasis of **Postman's Park**, with a heart-rending wall of plaques dedicated to late-Victorian child heroes and heroines and the various ways in which they met their sorry ends.

The **National Postal Museum** is in King Edward St. (◨ *open Mon-Fri 9.30am-4.30pm).*

COVENT GARDEN ★

Maps 9-10, and WALK 2 *map (page 91). Tube: Covent Garden.*

Until 1974, London's fresh fruit and vegetable market was Covent Garden's chief fame, and the pubs stayed open all night for the thirsty workers (and others). When the market and its heavy traffic left to go to a new building s of the river at Nine Elms, a bitter struggle for the future of Covent Garden began. Conservationists and local residents were ranked against the developers, for whom this was a prime site for office buildings (dressed up, of course, with token community schemes).

To the enormous relief of everyone but those who stood to profit, the attempt to turn the delightful and historic chaos of decaying buildings into a "planned" desert was defeated. Although over recent years new buildings have eaten away at the old, and the population of the area has fallen, the best buildings remain, and although the many youth-oriented shops and bars have brought a huge influx of mainly young visitors, the district retains an earthy feel of real old London, with some discerningly tasteful modern patronage.

Until the 16thC, Covent Garden was an enclosed kitchen garden belonging to Westminster Abbey. The land was granted to Sir John Russell, later Earl of Bedford, in 1630, and a descendant of his obtained the right to develop it under the aegis of the great Classical architect Inigo Jones in 1670. The plan was ambitious — a huge piazza on the Italian model surrounded by arcaded houses. All that survives today is the church of ST PAUL'S, COVENT GARDEN. The present **market buildings** appeared in 1828-32, with the fine iron and glass canopies added later. In its restored state, the marriage of its severe Classicism to the more ornate roof creates a stunning effect. Other later market buildings surround the piazza. The best, the **Floral Hall** (1858) is to the NE, a superb example of the iron and glass architecture that sprang up in emulation of the 1851 Crystal Palace.

The **market** itself is now given over to trendy shops and restaurants, with market stalls in the middle and in Jubilee Market to the s; it is at its liveliest at lunchtime. In among the shops is the **Cabaret Mechanical Theatre** *(33-34 The Market),* displaying contemporary automata that all move at the touch of a button. On the s side of the piazza, the old Flower Market (1897) now houses the LONDON TRANSPORT and THEATRE MUSEUMS. Leave the piazza by Russell St. to the E, lined with fashionable wine bars thick with young advertising executives and publishers, not so different from the *monde* who congregated in its famous coffeehouses in the 18thC.

Russell St. crosses Bow St., so notorious for its street crime in the 18thC that it saw the foundation of the first police force, the Bow Street Runners. Its inspiration was the novelist Henry Fielding, a magistrate at the busy courts that are still there in a newer building. To the left is the splendid facade of the Floral Hall. Next to it (and, amazingly, by the same architect, the Victorian E.M. Barry) is the **Royal Opera House** (see page 246), the third theater on the site, built 1857-58; its grand Corinthian portico has a frieze by J. Flaxman and statues from the previous building of 1809.

Fittingly for a quarter of such vitality, Covent Garden is traditionally London's theater area, and its church, ST PAUL'S, is the actors' church. (For THEATERS, see pages 249-251).

Continuing along Russell St. will take you to the other old royal theater, the **Theatre Royal, Drury Lane**, founded in 1663 by Charles II, whose Nell Gwynne was, of course, an orange-seller in Covent Garden. The present building dates from 1810-12, and is by general agreement London's most beautiful theater. Covent Garden is also bordered by two of London's main theatrical streets; to the S is the STRAND and, to the W, St Martin's Lane, where the largest theater is the imposing **London Coliseum** of 1904, now home of the English National Opera (see page 246).

A good example of an ornate late Victorian pub, complete with cut glass and mirrors, is the **Salisbury**, a little farther up on the left (see PUBS, page 241). At the top of St Martin's Lane, Garrick St. to the right includes the solemn and grimy building of the famous Garrick Club, a gentlemen's club with theatrical associations. Up tiny Rose St. on the left is the **Lamb & Flag**, the area's oldest and best pub (see page 241).

The northern continuation of St Martin's Lane is drab Monmouth St., which leads to Seven Dials, the scene of Hogarth's "Gin Lane" of drink and vice in the 18thC and the cholera outbreaks of the 19thC. The sundial monument, which was removed in 1773 to break up gatherings of criminals, has recently been replaced. A little to the NW is **St Giles-in-the-Fields**, a fine Classical church of 1731-33, with a supremely calm interior. Near Seven Dials is **Neal's Yard** and Neal Street, with craft stores, vegetarian restaurants and health-food stores. Another craft market opened in 1987 in nearby Endell St. Housed in a glass-domed building, **Endell Street Place** has craft workshops, a shop and special exhibitions.

WALK 2 (pages 91-92) explores Covent Garden and nearby BLOOMSBURY.

DOCKLANDS
Map 20C5. Tube: Tower Hill, then Docklands Light Railway.

With the demise of the British Empire, London's docks fell into decline, and by the late 1960s Docklands was derelict: an area of poverty, slums and high unemployment. In 1981 the London Docklands Development Corporation (LDDC) was formed to redevelop Wapping, the Isle of Dogs, the Royal Docks and Surrey Docks in the largest, most ambitious scheme of its kind in Europe. Office space in the City was at a premium, so Docklands attracted businesses as well as private investors, who were prepared to plunge millions of pounds into offices, houses and recreation facilities. Since then, many businesses have moved to the area, including most FLEET STREET newspapers.

But in many respects the Docklands dream has not yet been realized. Still a building site, it is criticized for being difficult to live and work in, and architecturally it is a mishmash. The slump in property prices in the late 1980s and '90s hit Docklands particularly hard, and the Canadian developers, Olympia & York, who are funding the multimillion pound Canary Wharf project, have run into financial crisis, throwing doubt on its planned next phase.

Covering a vast 450 acres, Docklands is a 21stC river city in the making.

Since it is an official enterprise zone, architectural restrictions are suspended. Hence the variety of styles in evidence, from office buildings clad in tinted glass, framed by bold primary colors, to mellow brick buildings that recall the past with Gothic windows or a hint of pediment. Within the maze of modern architecture, it is still possible to stumble across a beautiful old church, such as Hawksmoor's **St George in the East**, a pretty terrace of Georgian or Victorian houses, or a listed building, such as the ancient and allegedly haunted *pissoire* in the Royal Docks.

The conversion of old warehouses in Wapping and Limehouse have made these fashionable residential areas, with **Tobacco Dock**, a vast but soulless complex of restaurants and leisure facilities, conveniently nearby. Moored at Tobacco Quay are two impressive life-sized copies of **pirate ships** (*open Wed-Sun 11am-6pm*), containing exhibitions that disclose the gruesome truth about piracy and Robert Louis Stevenson's adventure classic, *Treasure Island.*

On the Isle of Dogs, the grand and extraordinarily ambitious **Canary Wharf** ( ), still under construction and with an unstable future at present, is intended to be the heart of Docklands. This huge 71-acre site at least has the advantage of having been designed as a whole. It is dominated by a 800-foot-high tower, the tallest building in the UK, designed by Cesar Pelli, of which Prince Charles asked, "But why does it have to be so high?" For a fairly awesome view of London and the countryside beyond in all directions, take the elevator ( ) to the top floor, though the most conspicuous landmark of all, Canary Wharf itself, is of course missing. The country's largest and best-equipped sports complex, **London Arena**, has opened nearby in Limeharbour. Opposite is the **Docklands Visitor Centre** (*(071) 512-3000*).

Farther E are the **Royal Docks**, the least developed part of Docklands, and still in a state of flux while awaiting the area's much-vaunted potential to be fulfilled. They comprise Royal Victoria Dock, Royal Albert Dock and King George Dock; although these are still mainly strange, desolate places, a number of watersports projects have started up here recently, offering rowing, canoeing, sailing, windsurfing, waterskiing and jet-biking (see page 274). Here too, **London City Airport** provides businessmen with fast access to Europe.

On the S side of the river at Surrey Docks, the Victorian warehouses of **Butler's Wharf** have been refurbished by Sir Terence Conran to provide offices, workshops, houses, shops and restaurants, and include the DESIGN MUSEUM. Farther E is the fascinating **London Glass Blowing Workshop** (*109 Rotherhithe St., SE16* *open Mon-Fri 11am-6pm*), where hand-blowing is demonstrated and a warehouse has pieces for sale. Still farther E, **Surrey Docks Farm** (*Rotherhithe St., SE16* *open Tues-Fri 10am-5pm, Sat, Sun, school hols Tues-Thurs 10am-1pm, 2-5pm*) is one of three working farms in Docklands (see LONDON FOR CHILDREN, page 270) and sells its own delicious organic produce.

The best way to see Docklands is from the **Docklands Light Railway** (*Mon-Fri 5.30am-9.30pm* *(071) 538-0311*), which was opened in September 1987. Suspended 20 feet above the ground for much of its route, it affords panoramic views of the area. The red, white and blue computer-driven trains look even more like toys than the buildings below. The railway is closed on Saturday and Sunday for further building.

The LDDC arranges guided tours by bus for groups (☎ *(071) 512-3000 ext. 3513),* and **Dockland Tours** (☎*(071) 252-0742)* offers walks, coach and minibus tours with local guides.

DULWICH
Map 20D5. Train to West Dulwich from Victoria.

The charming village of Dulwich, with wooden signposts, broad open spaces and historic buildings, is a jewel preserved in the rock face in a way that is typical of London. The presence of DULWICH COLLEGE is strong here: in **College Road** there are several 18thC houses of considerable style, nos.103-107 dating from around 1700, and nos.57 and 97, and also substantial Georgian homes. College Rd. heads s across the agreeable Dulwich Common through a toll gate.

In Lordship Lane is the **Horniman Museum** (☎ *(081) 699-2339*☒ ₲ *open Mon-Sat 10.30am-5.50pm, Sun 2-5.50pm*▣), in an Art Nouveau building of 1902. It houses a bizarre variety of objects: dolls, tribal art, even stuffed animals, and a fine collection of musical instruments. Its new *Living Waters Exhibition* explores the ecology of the underwater world and, among fascinating displays, includes a tropical rainforest, shown in cross-section, and a living coral reef.

GREENWICH ★
Map 20C5, and overleaf. Best approached by river boat (see page 42); or train to Greenwich from Charing Cross. Can also be approached by traveling through the Isle of Dogs to the Island Gardens terminus of the Docklands Light Railway, then walking through the Victorian-tiled Greenwich Footway Tunnel under the Thames.

It is no longer regarded as the center of the world, despite the continuing primacy of the Greenwich Meridian (0° longitude) and Greenwich Mean Time (GMT), and yet the sheer self-confidence of this most easterly of the Thames-side royal residences suggests otherwise. Bold and grand in every way, the metropolis' most spectacular architectural ensemble sweeps down to the riverside through fine parkland, unifying its blend of splendid buildings in an elegant Classicism.

It owes its prominence to its position as the capital port of a great seafaring nation, and its maritime character strikes the disembarking visitor in the tall form of the masts of the *Cutty Sark* (☒ ✱ *open Oct-Mar Mon-Sat 10am-4.30pm, Sun noon-4.30pm, Apr-Sept Mon-Sat 10am-5.30pm, Sun noon-5.30pm),* built in 1869, one of the greatest of the graceful tea clippers that raced to bring back tea from the Orient. Inside the hold is a display on the ship's history and a collection of old ships' figureheads. Nearby is the diminutive *Gypsy Moth IV* (☒ *open Apr-Sept Mon-Sat 10am-5.30pm, Sun noon-5.30pm),* in which Sir Francis Chichester sailed around the world in 1966.

Dominating the river is the magnificent Baroque creation of the **Royal Naval College** (▥ ★) It was begun in 1664 as a replacement for the old royal palace, was designated a royal hospital for navy seamen in 1694,

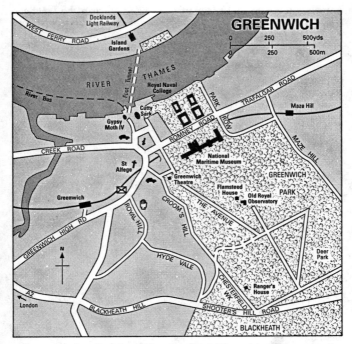

GREENWICH

and not completed until well into the 18thC. The original plans were by Wren, but other leading architects, including Vanbrugh and Hawksmoor, made substantial contributions. Of the interior, the amazing **Painted Hall** and the **chapel** can be visited (▣ *open Mon-Wed, Fri-Sun 2.30-4.45pm, closed Thurs*). Sir James Thornhill's **hall** of 1708-27 is a Baroque tour de force. The enormous painting on the ceiling represents the glory of the Protestant monarchy, the effect increased by the rich gray columns and pilasters, with illusionistic painted flutings. The **chapel** opposite is in a much lighter Neoclassical style; it was redecorated in 1779-89 after a fire.

Farther back from the river are the main buildings of the **National Maritime Museum** (▥ ★) centered on the **Queen's House** (☎ *(081) 858-4422* ▣ & ✗ *in Queen's House* ↟ *by appointment; open Apr-Sept Mon-Sat 10am-6pm, Sun noon-6pm, Oct-Mar Mon-Sat 10am-5pm, Sun 2-5pm* ▉). Henry VIII was born here, as were his two daughter queens, Mary and Elizabeth. James I gave the palace to his queen, Anne of Denmark, in 1613, and it was completely rebuilt to the designs of Inigo Jones between 1616 and 1635.

The Queen's House is a building of extreme Classical simplicity, in the Palladian style quite revolutionary in its day. Most interesting are the entrance hall, a perfect cube, and the graceful circular stairwell. To the sides are two wings added from 1807-16. In the Queen's House, the royal apartments have been carefully re-created to look as they might have done during the residence of Henrietta Maria, widow of Charles I, around 1662. The vaulted basement contains the Treasury of the National Maritime Museum and a miniature *son-et-lumière* based on an Inigo Jones court masque etched on glass screens.

The National Maritime Museum is the greatest seafaring museum in the world. Its extensive collections range from the finds of marine archeology to an entire paddle tug. The main entrance is in the East Wing, where galleries house temporary exhibitions. The West Wing is dominated by the New Neptune Hall, with its 1907 paddle tug, *Reliant*. Exciting displays here include two decorated royal riverboats, Queen Mary's shallop of 1689 and Prince Frederick's barge of 1632.

On the top floor of the West Wing, a gallery entitled *Discovery and Seapower 1450-1700* charts England's transition from economic obscurity to its position, by the end of the 17thC, as one of the great naval and commercial powers in Europe. The exhibition traces the voyages of discovery, the origins of the Royal Navy and the exploits of Elizabethan seamen such as Drake and Hawkins, and includes artifacts from the *Mary Rose*. On the ground floor of the recently refurbished South West Wing, a new gallery called *20thC Sea Power* displays all the museum's 20thC material, models of ships, paintings, uniforms, medals, sextants and charts, which had previously been in store, and highlights the national need for a merchant navy.

After the Queen's House, you pass into **Greenwich Park**, crowned with several hills and sloping down steeply toward the river. One hill is topped by a Henry Moore statue, others by the buildings of the Royal Observatory.

The **Royal Observatory** (🔊 *same hours as Maritime Museum)* was established in 1675-76, when Wren was commissioned by Charles II to build a house for the first Astronomer Royal, John Flamsteed. A well-proportioned red-brick building with a fine octagonal room on the top floor, Flamsteed House commands extensive views down over Greenwich and the river. On top of one of the towers can be seen a large red ball mechanism erected in 1833. Each day the ball falls at exactly 1pm to enable ships in the river to set their clocks accurately. At the rear of the house is a 19thC extension topped by a huge bulbous dome of 1894, which houses a 28-inch refracting telescope, one of the largest in the world. The astronomers moved to more modern equipment, first in Sussex and then in Cambridge, and Flamsteed House is now a museum, with exhibits that include clocks and telescopes used by Halley, Herschel and other royal astronomers.

Next door is the mid-18thC **Meridian Building**, where there is a display on the theme of time. This is the site of the meridian on which all the world's clock time is based through Greenwich Mean Time; visitors can have a foot in each hemisphere.

At the top end of the park is **Ranger's House** (📷 🗲 *with flash; open daily Apr-Sept 10am-1pm, 2-6pm, Oct-Mar 10am-1pm, 2-4pm),* its front fringing BLACKHEATH on Chesterfield Walk. Built of red brick, the stone center framing the main doorway dates from the early 18thC; the bow-front wings were added by the Earl of Chesterfield in about 1754. The best room, in the s wing, contains pictures of the Suffolk Collection, including several attributed to William Larkin of Jacobean aristocrats.

Chesterfield Walk leads into Croom's Hill, which proceeds back down to Greenwich town. This old road has several detached houses and terraces of the 17th-18thC along its steep slope. Near Ranger's house are **Macartney House** and the **Manor House**, both of the early 1700s. At Nos. 10-12, the **Fan Museum** (☎ ♿ ✆ *with flash* ✗ *open Tues-Sat 11am-4.30pm, Sun noon-4.30pm*) boasts over 2,000 mostly European fans and a workshop, where the craft of fan-making is demonstrated.

Greenwich has an attractive town center a little inland from the *Cutty Sark*, with wine bars and antique stores and an excellent weekend market (see SHOPPING, page 266). Its massive and monumental parish church of **St Alfege** was built in 1711-30.

Downstream is **Woolwich**, with a large naval dockyard. It is also the traditional home of the Royal Artillery. The **Royal Arsenal**, **Military Academy** and **Artillery Barracks** of the 18th-early 19thC are extraordinarily large and imposing buildings. Nearby is the **Rotunda** (☎ *open Apr-Oct Mon-Fri noon-5pm, Sat, Sun 1-5pm, Nov-Mar Mon-Fri noon-4pm, Sat, Sun 1-4pm*), a strange tent-shaped building of 1814 moved here from St James's Park in 1820, which now houses a collection of artillery pieces from the 17thC to the present day. There is an intriguing collection of relics from the Great Eastern Railway, including coaches and a locomotive at the **North Woolwich Old Station Museum** (*Pier Rd., E16* ☎ *open Mon-Wed, Sat 10am-5pm, Sun, bank hols 2-5pm);* working steam engines can be seen on the first Sunday of every month.

The river is straddled by the **Thames Barrier**, an extraordinary engineering achievement opened in 1984, which will protect London from flooding. An exhibition (☎ *open daily 10.30am-5pm)* demonstrates how it works.

HAMPSTEAD
Map 20C4. Tube: Hampstead.
Hampstead Heath's high and hilly grassland, scattered ponds and dense woodland seem much farther than just 4 miles from a great city center. Hampstead "village" itself still follows the street patterns of an earlier time: around the hills wind convoluted lanes lined with attractive 19thC and earlier houses, now favored by successful academics, artists and media folk, who give Hampstead its arty reputation.

In the 17thC, a few large out-of-town residences were established in the rural village of Hampstead; FENTON HOUSE is a notable survivor. The craze for health-giving waters in the 18thC boosted the village into a fashionable spa, which began to spread down the sides of the hill, becoming in the process a favorite haunt for artists: George Romney lived in Holly Bush Hill and John Constable at Lower Terrace, Downshire Hill and Well Walk.

The best-preserved part is to be found around the parish church of **St John** to the w of the High St. The massive cedar trees of its calm churchyard shade Constable's grave. **Church Row**, which leads down toward the modern center, has superb terraced houses of 1720, reflecting the period of expansion following the discovery of the spa. To the N of Church Row are a number of charming little streets, most notably **Holly Walk** with its early 19thC cottages.

A later fashionable period is represented to the s, with the Victorian and Edwardian mansions of Frognal and Fitzjohn's Ave. Look out for **Kate Greenaway's Cottage** in Frognal, in a fairy-tale style appropriately similar to her illustrations. Farther s toward Swiss Cottage is the fascinating **Freud Museum** *(20 Maresfield Gdns. ☎(071) 435-2002 ▨ open Wed-Sun noon-5pm, bank hol Mon 2-5pm).* Freud escaped here from Nazi Austria in 1938, with his extensive library, his furniture, rugs and collection of Greek, Roman, Egyptian and Oriental antiquities. After his death in 1939, his daughter Anna preserved the house exactly as it was in his lifetime.

The winding, hilly streets of Church Row lead to the wild, densely wooded **West Heath**. To the E, on North End Way, is **Jack Straw's Castle**, an old weatherboard inn rebuilt in the 1960s, named after the peasant leader who supposedly gathered his rebels here in 1381. Farther N on the same road is the equally famous **Bull and Bush** of the music hall song (see PUBS, page 242).

Back into the village, most shops are concentrated in Heath St. and High St. The **Flask** (see page 242) in Flask Walk is a good lunch spot, and in Well Walk, **Burgh House** *(☎(071) 431-0144 ▣ open Wed-Sun noon-5pm ▣)* mounts local exhibitions. These streets lead past attractive cottages toward **East Heath** and the strange enclave of the **Vale of Health**, a wooded valley crammed with 19thC houses. Down the Heath to the s (right) are **Downshire Hill**, with an interesting church, and **Keats Grove**, both with cottages and houses of around 1820, including KEATS' HOUSE.

The Heath itself stretches across to HIGHGATE, some parts wild and open, others enclosed and wooded. Across to the N is the **Spaniards**, an 18thC inn in Spaniards Rd. with a toll house, and the Georgian splendor of KENWOOD HOUSE, a good focus for a walk. To the s is **Parliament Hill**, festooned with kites on weekends and offering a fine view across the dense housing of Kentish Town to the City beyond.

HIGHGATE ☆
Map 20B4. Tube: Highgate, Archway.
This twin village of HAMPSTEAD, looking down on London from the N, takes its name from a tollgate that used to be near its center, and its dizzying height, which is best appreciated by approaching steep Highgate Hill or Highgate West Hill. Highgate Hill has a few fine mansions, most notably **Cromwell House**, a red-brick house in Dutch style of about 1637-40. Here also is **Whittington Stone** where, according to legend, Dick Whittington rested on his way home in c.1390, gazed down at the City and heard the bells chiming, "Turn again Whittington, thrice Mayor of London."

The High St. has good 18thC terraced houses, and South Grove on the

ractive Waterlow Park and Pond Sq. to the intersec-
and **The Grove**, with an attractive terrace built around
ommemorates Coleridge, who lived in one of the houses;
h   ue aisle of the nearby **church of St Michael**, an imposing
19th   . (1832) edifice with Highgate Cemetery (see below) behind
it. In co   plete contrast with these charms are two large and architecturally influential blocks of apartments to the N on North Hill, the
Highpoint Flats, constructed in 1936 and 1939 by the Tecton group.

Highgate Cemetery is one of the most extraordinary relics of Victorian London gone to seed, a romantic wilderness that pays tribute to
nature's power to reclaim its own. A tour of the W side (✗ *compulsory*
☎ *(081) 340-1834 for current times* ◄€) takes you to Christina Rossetti's grave, a weird Gothic Chapel and the Egyptian catacombs. The
most famous grave on the newer E side is the **grave of Karl Marx**, now
surmounted by an ugly monument erected in the 1950s. Many other
well-known people are buried here, including George Eliot.

KENSINGTON ☆
Maps 13-14. Tube: South Kensington, High St. Kensington.
Pleasant and prosperous, Kensington has a few enclaves of ostentatious wealth, but the predominant pattern is of good 19thC terraces and
villas, large late-Victorian and Edwardian apartment buildings, major
shopping streets that include the better department stores, and little
roads of classy boutiques and antique stores. Good taste abounds.

In the 17thC, two great houses emerged from the manors scattered
among the fields: HOLLAND HOUSE AND PARK, and Nottingham House, which
became KENSINGTON PALACE in 1690 when William and Mary moved there
and gave the impetus to a new crop of aristocratic houses. **Kensington
Square** was one such development, of about 1700, and a few attractive
houses are preserved, such as **no. 29**. The part just S of Kensington Palace
is a lovely enclave, **Canning Place** in particular. **Kensington Palace
Road**, running W of the palace, is known as "Millionaires' Row"; it was
begun in 1843 and consists of grand detached mansions, now largely
occupied by embassies or their staff, and is a private road.

The public road running N from **Kensington High Street**, a busy
shopping area, to Notting Hill Gate is **Kensington Church Street**, with
its many good antique stores and clothes boutiques. Along or near
Kensington High St. are LEIGHTON HOUSE, the COMMONWEALTH INSTITUTE and
Linley Sambourne House *(18 Stafford Terr., W8* ▨ *open Mar-Oct
Wed 10am-4pm, Sun 2-5pm; run by the Victorian Society, 1 Priory Gdns.,
W4* ☎ *(081) 994-1019),* where an engraving on the brass mailbox reads:
"Mr Linley Sambourne Not At Home." The home of the well-known
Punch cartoonist, great-grandfather of the Earl of Snowdon, has changed
little in three generations. Crammed with Victoriana (photographs, chim-
ing clocks, china and glass), the walls covered in William Morris wall-
paper, the windows hung with heavy Victorian drapes, it feels a long way
from the late 20thC.

The central part of Kensington, thought of as **South Kensington**
since that is the name of the tube station serving it, is dominated by a

complex of museums and colleges set up on land bought with the proceeds from the Great Exhibition held in Hyde Park in 1851. Albert, Prince Consort to Queen Victoria, sponsored the scheme, and much of the character of this monument to Victorian optimism comes from his vision. He is commemorated by the ALBERT MEMORIAL and ROYAL ALBERT HALL.

Next to the Albert Hall is the **Royal College of Art**, a supposedly "brutal" but in fact dull building of 1960-61. A little to the E of the Albert Hall is the **Royal Geographical Society**, an attractively informal house in Dutch style designed by Norman Shaw in 1874. There are statues of David Livingstone and Scott of the Antarctic, both fellows of the RGS.

To the S is Prince Consort Rd. Here, at the center of the large 20thC buildings of **Imperial College** (London University's leading science department), is the **Royal College of Music**, a red-brick pseudo-medieval building of 1883-84. Its lovely collection of musical instruments is on view (*open Wed in term-time 2-4.30pm, at other times by appointment with curator* ☎ *(071) 589-3643).* The 280-foot **Queen's Tower** is a survivor of the 1887-93 Imperial Institute buildings, but is no longer safe to climb and is now closed to the public.

South of Imperial College are the great museums that, together with the colleges, represent the fulfillment of Albert's dream: the SCIENCE MUSEUM, the NATURAL HISTORY MUSEUM, one of London's finest buildings, the Geological Museum, now known as the Earth Galleries of the Natural History Museum, and the VICTORIA & ALBERT MUSEUM.

The eastern part of Kensington is predominantly residential. Beyond the Victoria & Albert Museum is the BROMPTON ORATORY, with the shopping center of the Brompton Rd. beyond, and the incomparable **Harrods** department store. Behind the main road, attractive 19thC housing stretches up to Knightsbridge and S into Brompton.

An interesting building, well worth a detour, is **Michelin House**, an Art Nouveau gem of 1910, on Fulham Rd., containing the Conran Shop (see SHOPPING, page 264) and BIBENDUM restaurant (see RESTAURANTS). Its ceramic decorations include panels with charming scenes of early auto races.

KEW
*Map **19**D3. Tube: Kew Gardens; or train to Kew Bridge from Waterloo.*
Close to the ideal of an English country village, Kew Green is not as rustic as it first seems. It is actually flanked by 18th-19thC detached and terraced houses that lend an air of substantial prosperity, and its unusual parish church, **St Anne's**, was built under royal patronage in 1710-14 (and extended in 1770). An interesting feature is the Royal Gallery above the W door, donated by George III in 1805.

Charming and pleasant though all this is, it is only a curtain-raiser to the ROYAL BOTANIC GARDENS, more popularly known simply as Kew Gardens. The greatest scientific institution of its kind in the world, it is also a garden of matchless delight and beauty.

MARYLEBONE
Maps 7-8. Tube: Baker Street, Great Portland Street.

During the 18thC, the fashionable West End expanded N to surround the village of St Marylebone (St Mary-le-bourne, meaning St Mary-by-the-brook). The streets form a near-perfect grid, with the major ones running N-S from REGENT'S PARK toward Oxford St. It now consists largely of smart houses and apartment blocks, with some busy shopping streets. Although it has several squares and some good buildings, it is a curiously anonymous area.

The earliest square is Cavendish Sq. (1714). **St Peter's Chapel** nearby in Vere St. was designed in 1721-24 by James Gibbs, and prefigures ST MARTIN-IN-THE-FIELDS. The finest houses are **no. 20 Portman Square**, (Robert Adam, 1775-76), and **Hertford House** in Manchester Sq. (the WALLACE COLLECTION). Other famous addresses are **Harley Street**, home of top doctors and clinics, **Baker Street**, of Sherlock Holmes fame, and **Wimpole Street**, where Robert Browning wooed Elizabeth Barrett. On Marylebone Rd. are MADAME TUSSAUD'S and the PLANETARIUM.

MAYFAIR ☆
Maps 7-8. Tube: Bond Street, Green Park.

The very name is synonymous with wealth and elegance — nowhere in London will you see more Rolls Royces or more diamonds. It was not always so. The annual fair that lent its name to the area was suppressed by George III in 1800, so riotous had it become. Mayfair today is a roughly square-shaped section of the West End, bordered by the shopping streets of Oxford St., Regent St. and Piccadilly, and Park Lane, lined by large 20thC hotels and the backs of grand 19thC mansions. Inside this area are expensive shops, luxurious hotels, casinos, and homes of the rich.

The development of this area began in about 1700, and by 1800 it was largely filled with squares and terraces. **Grosvenor Square** is the largest, without its original houses and with the large United States Embassy of 1961 at its western end. Of the squares, **Hanover Square** is the oldest (about 1715); original houses survive in **St George's Street** to the s. **Berkeley Square** is best known, thanks to its mythical nightingale; it has huge plane trees (almost 200 years old) in its fine gardens and attractive 18thC houses surviving in the sw corner.

Only one really grand mansion remains among the houses: **Crewe House** in Curzon St., begun in 1730. Two churches date back to the early development of the area: **St George's, Hanover Square**, in St George's St. (1721-24; notice the grand portico and bronze hunting dogs standing guard); and **Grosvenor Chapel** in South Audley St., a more modest edifice from about 1730. The Jesuit **Church of the Immaculate Conception** (1844-49), in the same street, is worth a visit, with a high altar designed by Pugin.

The shopping streets scattered through Mayfair best preserve its reputation for high living. Around Bond St. (New and Old) are the best art and antique dealers. Savile Row has the world's finest gentleman's tailors (see SHOPPING, page 259). 19thC **Shepherd Market** is an enclave of alleyways lined with smart shops and cafés, and perhaps a few ladies of the night, plying a trade that was once well-established in this area.

RICHMOND ☆
Map 19D3. Tube: Richmond.

The Palace of Sheen, first occupied by Henry I in 1125, began an important royal connection that fostered the growth of this still beautiful Thameside town. The name came later; after a fire in 1499, Sheen was rebuilt as Richmond Palace by Henry VII, the title coming from his former title as Earl of Richmond (in Yorkshire). Henry died in the palace, as did Elizabeth I in 1603. Charles I was the last king to live there, moving his court during a 1634 plague. In due course the palace fell into decay.

Of the great Tudor palace, the most magnificent before the building of Wolsey's nearby HAMPTON COURT, very little remains. What there is can be seen on the western side of **Richmond Green**. A Tudor gatehouse marks the position, but within are private houses of later date, which, in some cases, incorporate portions of the old brickwork: the fine early 18thC pedimented facade of **Trumpeters' House** predominates. Richmond Green itself boasts exceptional 18th-19thC houses on all four sides — most notable is **Maids of Honour Row** of about 1724, built for the companions of Caroline, wife of the future George II, who then lived at Richmond Lodge in Old Deer Park in KEW to the N. **Richmond Theatre**, built in 1899 and recently lavishly restored, lies across the green to the W. Old Palace Lane leads down to the river, where the attractive ocher **Asgill House**, a mansion of the 1760s, is on the left.

Richmond's busy and crowded shopping center, with its infuriating traffic system, contains some 17thC almshouses in The Vineyard near the parish church of **St Mary Magdalene**, with its interesting 16thC tower, and, up Hill Rise, the fine Queen Anne houses of Ormond Rd. To the E, **St Matthias** by Sir George Gilbert boasts one of the finest Victorian Gothic spires in London, and by the river, the attractive Quinlan Terry development (1988) is a skillful blend of original and "new" Georgian architecture.

To the S of the noble 18thC bridge rises **Richmond Hill**, offering one of London's most remarkable views. Preserving this unspoiled vista over MARBLE HILL HOUSE and HAM HOUSE across the wooded expanse of the Thames Valley was a rare triumph of planning control. The view has been painted by several of Britain's greatest artists, such as Reynolds, Turner and Constable. Some good 18thC houses stand at the top, including **Wick House**, built for Reynolds by Sir William Chambers in 1772.

Richmond Park is the most telling reminder of Richmond's royal connection; with more than 2,000 acres first enclosed by Charles I and still a royal park, it is the most natural stretch of green land in London. Its rough heath and woodland contain a great variety of native plants (particularly in the **Isabella Plantation**), birds and animals, even protected herds of red and fallow deer. The highest points offer excellent views NE across London. The several private houses in the park include **White Lodge**, built for George II in 1727-29, now the Royal Ballet School, and **Pembroke Lodge** of about 1800.

ST JAMES'S
Map 9G10-H10. Tube: Piccadilly Circus, Green Park.

Despite being unprotected by conservationists, there are still in the world examples of that strange breed, the English gentleman. Come to St James's, and you would never know that they are rare, for this is *their* district, still existing to provide the quiet, comfortable and dignified life long enjoyed by the upper class.

Occupying the area between ST JAMES'S PARK and PICCADILLY, the land was granted to the Earl of St Albans in 1665 in recognition of his loyalty while the king was in exile. The earl at once began building, and the proximity of the palace ensured that his square and streets soon became fashionable. The centerpiece was **St James's Square**, with a large central garden. No 17thC houses survived, but there are several fine examples from the 18thC: **Lichfield House**, no. 15, and Robert Adams' **no. 20** are the best. At the center of the gardens is an equestrian statue of William III from 1807. To the N up Duke of York St. is the area's church, ST JAMES'S PICCADILLY.

20 St James's Square

To the s, running parallel to the park, is PALL MALL, a splendid road lined with gentlemen's clubs. ST JAMES'S PALACE is at the western end, with **St James's Street** stretching N to Piccadilly. Here are many more of the gentlemen's clubs built in the 19thC: **White's** for hard-drinking Conservatives; **Boodles**, a famous gambling club in the days of Beau Brummell, the Regency dandy; **Brooks'**, the Whig club founded in 1788; and the **Carlton**, the Conservatives' club. **St James's Place** leads off to the w toward Green Park, a quiet street lined with 18thC houses: at the end, magnificent SPENCER HOUSE (1756-66) overlooks the park. Opposite is an interesting office development, aggressively modern and built in 1959-60. Adjacent is the **Economist** complex, built around a central plaza just to the w of St James's St.

St James's is justly famed for its shops, with the most traditional approach to service and quality in London. Try the Victorian **Red Lion** pub in Duke of York St. (see PUBS, page 241).

SOHO ★
Map 9F10. Tube: Piccadilly Circus, Tottenham Court Road, Leicester Square.

Every city has its low-life area, of course, but in few are the red lights woven into a texture of such richness and variety as in London's Soho. These densely packed little streets in the heart of the West End, bounded by Oxford St., Regent St., Shaftesbury Ave. and Charing Cross

Rd., are famous for their nightlife, their restaurants, the best delicatessens in London, their seedy but famous pubs, and, above all, for the gloriously cosmopolitan mix of their people and trades.

A decade ago, much was heard about the decline of Soho, when its thriving sex industry threatened to engulf the area's other amenities, and even a pub where Dylan Thomas used to drink himself into oblivion became a sex cinema. The destruction has now largely been halted. Respectable businesses have returned, and fashionable restaurants and shops prosper. And Soho wouldn't be Soho without a scattering of sex parlors.

Two squares remind us of Soho's early development in the 17thC. **Golden Square** in the E was founded in 1673, and some 18thC houses survive around its undistinguished gardens with a 1720s statue of Charles II. More impressive is **Soho Square**, laid out in 1681, with the few survivals of early buildings largely disguised by later additions, but offering a pleasant garden with a 17thC statue of Charles II. On its s side, in Greek St., is Soho's finest house, **The House of St Barnabas** (*☒ open Wed 2.30-4.15pm, Thurs 11am-12.30pm*), a luxurious 1746 town house with a plain exterior but a magnificently decorated Rococo interior, with rich plasterwork on walls and ceiling. Soho's other public open space is **St Anne's churchyard**, a little park in Wardour St. overlooked by a splendid tower of 1801-3 surviving from the bombed church.

The southern part of Soho crosses Shaftesbury Ave., a busy street of many theaters, to London's **Chinatown**, centered on Gerrard St., small, authentic and packed with excellent restaurants. But Soho's heart, with marvelous French and Italian delicatessens, together with fine butchers, fish stores and wine merchants, is found farther N on **Brewer St., Old Compton St.** and **Berwick St.**; the latter is also an excellent open-air fresh food market, becoming more expensive and exotic at its continuation in Rupert St., s through Walker Court.

To the N of Old Compton St., **Dean St., Frith St.** and **Greek St.** have fine little restaurants, pubs and clubs, such as **Ronnie Scott's** for jazz (see PERFORMING ARTS, page 249). In Wardour St., the British movie industry has its center. Throughout, blue plaques mark apparently rundown buildings with famous associations: Blake was born in Marshall St., Chopin gave recitals in Meard St., and in Frith St., Marx worked, Baird first demonstrated television, and Hazlitt died . . . .

The northwestern part of Soho has less character: **Carnaby St.** was the Mecca of the Swinging Sixties, but most of its current visitors wonder why everyone else is a tourist.

WESTMINSTER
Map 17. Tube: Westminster.
Even the visitor who has never heard of Westminster can instantly appreciate the significance of this most stately of London's districts, for, like its long-time rival the CITY, it has remained almost free from residential invasion and is devoted to business, in this case government. Its activity is dominated by the mother of parliaments at the Palace of

Westminster (see WESTMINSTER, PALACE OF), attended by the officialdom of WHITEHALL. Next to the Houses of Parliament is the great church of WESTMINSTER ABBEY.

Parliament Square, an open space created at the time of the building of the Palace of Westminster, is appropriately studded with statues of great statesmen: Disraeli, Palmerston, Abraham Lincoln, Winston Churchill. Surrounding the square, apart from Westminster Abbey and the Palace of Westminster, there is the **Middlesex Guildhall** (Neo-Gothic, of 1906-13) and the **Home Office**.

In front of the abbey is the smaller church of **St Margaret**, founded as the parish church of Westminster possibly as early as the 11thC and now the parish church of the Houses of Parliament, and always a fashionable place for weddings (Pepys, John Milton and Churchill were all married here). The present building dates from the early 16thC but was restored almost out of recognition in the 18thC. Its interesting monuments include the tomb of Sir Walter Raleigh; the E window is Flemish 16thC.

To the E of Parliament Sq., just E of Birdcage Walk and ST JAMES'S PARK, is **Queen Anne's Gate**, with some of the best early 18thC houses in London, and a statue of Queen Anne dated 1708. In Victoria St., two important landmarks are WESTMINSTER CATHEDRAL and **New Scotland Yard**, the Metropolitan Police's modern headquarters. There is an attractive enclave to the S of Westminster Abbey, with Georgian houses in Cowley St. and Lord North St. The latter opens into **Smith Square**, which includes some 18thC survivors on its E side, and in the center of the square is one of the most magnificent Baroque churches in London, **St John's**, built in 1714-28. It was burned down in World War II but has been restored and often hosts concerts.

Back in Birdcage Walk lies Wellington Barracks. Here the **Guards Museum** *(open Mon-Sat 10am-3.30pm* ☎*)* traces the history of $3\frac{1}{2}$ centuries of the five Regiments of Foot Guards (Grenadier, Coldstream, Scots, Irish and Welsh); both their fighting record and their famous ceremonial role is covered.

WIMBLEDON
Map 20D4. Tube: Southfields, Wimbledon, Wimbledon Pk.
The modern tennis duels, which have made this suburb of SW London world-famous, had an earlier counterpart, on **Wimbledon Common**, a large expanse of heath once notorious for settling disputes of honor. The **All-England Tennis Courts** themselves are in Church Rd., and the two-week championships in June and July transform the area, attracting both tennis fans and those who come for the copious strawberries and cream and champagne.

Inside the splendid ivy-clad main building is a **Lawn Tennis Museum** *(* ☎ *open Tues-Sat 11am-5pm, Sun 2-5pm* 🍽 *).*

Walkers' London

Exploring on foot

Although London is vast in area, it is also a marvelous city for taking a walk. Perhaps the chief reason for this is the close proximity of its many separate and characterful neighborhoods, and a number of these — CHELSEA, HOLLAND PARK, LITTLE VENICE, GREENWICH, HAMPSTEAD, among others — make walks in themselves (see LONDON'S DISTRICTS and SIGHTS AND PLACES OF INTEREST).

In a city that reached its prime before the days of motor transport, walking is also, naturally, the most effective way to see and learn about London. For information about walks for this purpose — routes, subjects of theme walks, starting times — contact the **London Tourist Board and Convention Bureau** (☎*(071) 730-3488*). The following companies organize walking tours:

* **Original London Walks**   ☎(071) 624-3978
* **Citisights of London**   ☎(081) 806-4325
* **Historical Tours**   ☎(081) 668-4019
* **Cockney Walks**   ☎(081) 504-9159
* **Footloose in London**   ☎(071) 435-0259 (minimum number in group: 6)

The walks described in detail on the following pages have a quite different and special purpose: to give a taste of a Londoner's London — its river, parks and pubs (WALKS 3 and 4), and its cultural, especially literary, heart (WALK 2).

There is no quick way of getting to know London. But as an introduction to this historic city, or to refresh the memory after a long absence, the following stroll (WALK 1) through the City of Westminster, center of government and tradition and the cornerstone of the West End, links many of London's most famous landmarks and also serves as a convenient orientation tour.

WALK 1: INTRODUCTION TO LONDON
*Allow 2-3hrs. Tube: Westminster. Maps **8-9**.*

Begin by walking along Bridge St., past the statue of Queen Boadicea, symbol of patriotism, on to Westminster Bridge itself, from where the best view of the PALACE OF WESTMINSTER and **Big Ben** can be gained. Look also to your right along the Victoria Embankment to see the fine government buildings. Let your gaze move around in full circle to cross the river with Hungerford railway bridge; beyond it is the SOUTH BANK ARTS CENTRE and, on this side, County Hall, former headquarters of the now defunct Greater London Council. The panorama continues past the huge stone lion at the E end of Westminster Bridge to the modern St Thomas' Hospital, and crosses the river again by Lambeth Bridge.

From the foot of Big Ben, walk back around the W side of the Palace of Westminster past Westminster Hall. Then cross over the road to St Margaret's Church to arrive at WESTMINSTER ABBEY.

Continue around Parliament Sq. almost to Bridge St. again, before turning left into Parliament St., which leads to WHITEHALL. The second street on the left, past the Cenotaph, is DOWNING STREET, where the policeman at the door identifies "Number 10." Going N along Whitehall, the BANQUETING HOUSE (1622) is on the right, nearly opposite the Whitehall entrance to HORSE GUARDS PARADE. At the N of Whitehall is TRAFALGAR SQUARE, which is dominated by **Nelson's Column** and is a crowded area of constant activity.

As you cross the square toward the NATIONAL GALLERY, with its controversial new Sainsbury Wing extension, notice also James Gibbs' beautiful church of ST MARTIN-IN-THE-FIELDS (1726). St Martin's Pl., in front and to the right of the church, has the central Post Office on its right; to the N, up St Martin's Lane, is the globe-topped spire of the **London Coliseum**, home of the English National Opera (see PERFORMING ARTS, page 246). Leading around to the left, past the entrance to the NATIONAL PORTRAIT GALLERY, is Charing Cross Rd. Follow this road as far as Leicester Square tube station, then turn left along Cranbourn St. into **Leicester Sq.** itself.

The route continues along the N side of Leicester Sq. as far as the Swiss Centre, where a right turn up Wardour St. leads past Lisle St. and Gerrard St., the two main arteries of **Chinatown**, to Shaftesbury Ave., the heart of theaterland and the southern boundary of SOHO. Turn left on Shaftesbury Ave. and walk down to **Piccadilly Circus**.

Arriving at Piccadilly Circus, pause a moment to orient yourself between Shaftesbury Ave., Regent St., curving majestically to the W and N and PICCADILLY itself, leading W toward MAYFAIR, BELGRAVIA and Knightsbridge. It is the fourth major street that you must follow: go down Lower Regent St. to the S, which borders ST JAMES'S on the right, and crosses Pall Mall to the Duke of York Monument, at the top of the steps down past the elegant and imposing **Carlton House Terrace** to THE MALL.

At the foot of the steps look left toward Admiralty Arch, and Trafalgar Square beyond it. Notice also the ivy-clad wartime extension to the Admiralty, the Citadel, beyond which can be seen the expanse of Horse Guards Parade. Then walk W along The Mall, with ST JAMES'S PARK on your left, toward the gilded **Victoria Memorial** and beyond it BUCKINGHAM PALACE, passing MARLBOROUGH HOUSE, ST JAMES'S PALACE, Clarence House and LANCASTER HOUSE on the way. Walk around the S side of Buckingham Palace to Buckingham Gate and Buckingham Palace Rd., to the entrances to the **Queen's Picture Gallery** and the **Royal Mews**.

To complete the walk, either continue along Buckingham Palace Rd. to Victoria Station, or retrace your steps to follow Birdcage Walk along the s side of St James's Park in front of the recently restored Wellington Barracks. The first street on the right, **Queen Anne's Gate**, leads to St James's Park tube station. Or continue along Birdcage Walk into Great George St., which takes you to **Parliament Square** and Westminster tube station, where the walk began.

WALK 2: LONDON'S CULTURAL HEART
Allow 1-2hrs. Tube: Temple. Maps 9 & 3, and see map below.

The central areas of COVENT GARDEN and BLOOMSBURY have always been nurseries of artistic endeavor and achievement, as this walks reveals.

Begin by walking up Kingsway, which is directly opposite **Bush House**. From this appropriate symbol of British cultural prestige the BBC runs its foreign radio services. The first turning right off Kingsway is Portugal St., with **The Old Curiosity Shop** a little way up on the left. It is not certain that Dickens based his novel on this antique store, but he knew it well.

Back on the Aldwych, turn up **Drury Lane**. The **Theatre Royal**, down Russell St. to the left and on the corner of Catherine St., was founded in 1663. Also in **Russell St.** were the famous coffeehouses of the 18thC; Dr Johnson and Boswell first met in a bookstore at no. 8 in 1763. Drury Lane continues until it turns into Museum St. and pushes on into more elegant BLOOMSBURY, passing on the right in Bloomsbury Way the church of **St George**, which was used by Dickens as the setting for his Bloomsbury christening in *Sketches by Boz*.

Return to Museum St. and turn right. At the far end is the **Museum Tavern**, at different times favored by Karl Marx and Dylan Thomas. Turn

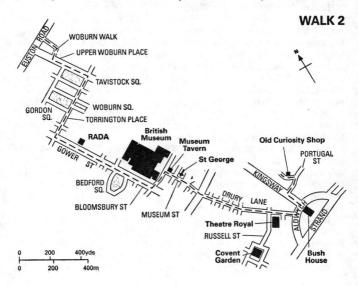

WALK 2

0 200 400yds
0 200 400m

left here, past the BRITISH MUSEUM, and then right into Bloomsbury St., passing the peaceful and unspoiled **Bedford Sq.**, the home at times of many distinguished people and therefore of a crop of blue plaques. Continue down Gower St., pausing to see the statues of tragedy and comedy outside the **Royal Academy of Dramatic Art**.

A right turn into Torrington Pl. passes Dillon's University Bookshop and Woburn Sq. on the right. Gordon Sq., on the left, was a stamping ground of the Bloomsbury Group. Torrington Pl. leads on to Tavistock Sq.; the garden in the square has as its focal point a statue of Mahatma Gandhi, and a tree planted by Pandit Nehru.

Turn left along the far side of the square to Upper Woburn Pl. On the right, a blue plaque marks the site where Dickens lived from 1851-60, now the headquarters of the British Medical Association. Farther on the right, turn into **Woburn Walk**, with its bow-front shops and brass plaque in memory of the poet W.B. Yeats, who lived here at the turn of the century.

A left turn leads back to Euston Rd., for a bus or tube.

WALK 3: A RIVERSIDE STROLL

Allow 1-4hrs, depending on route. Tube: Hammersmith (Piccadilly/District line). Map 20C4, and see map opposite.

Upstream from Central London, the Thames gradually abandons business for pleasure, and this suggested route takes you along the N bank of the Thames, past some fine Georgian houses, or along the footpath on the S bank. Much of this route is unpaved, so you will need suitable footwear. Consult PUBS for several of the pubs mentioned here.

Leave Hammersmith District/Piccadilly line tube station and head S via the underpass to Queen Caroline St., which leads you straight to the river within seven or eight minutes. On the traffic circle you will see the frontage of the Art Deco **Hammersmith Odeon**, formerly one of the largest cinemas in London and with its huge auditorium still intact, thanks to its conversion, some years ago, into a major concert venue.

In Queen Caroline St., a short detour almost immediately to your left across the main Fulham Palace Rd. will reveal a recently completed and rather remarkable 10-story building, designed by Ralph Erskine. It houses a community center, the **London Ark**. Its curved copper roof, observation dome, inclined glass curtain walls and traditional brick and timber facings, suggest a hi-tech Noah's Ark.

Make a small detour left into Crisp Rd. to visit the **Riverside Studios** arts center, where you can have a drink or snack, look around the art gallery or bookstore, or check out the schedule of performances for a later visit. As you emerge onto the river bank, **Hammersmith Bridge** is straight ahead. This stately, Victorian suspension bridge, built in 1887, is one of the most attractive on the river.

If you stay on the N bank, the walk offers historical and architectural interest. Just under the bridge are several balconied houses and boat-houses, and there are a couple of pubs next door to each other on this stretch of the river; the most interesting is the **Blue Anchor**.

As you emerge just beyond the pubs, a small area of park opens out,

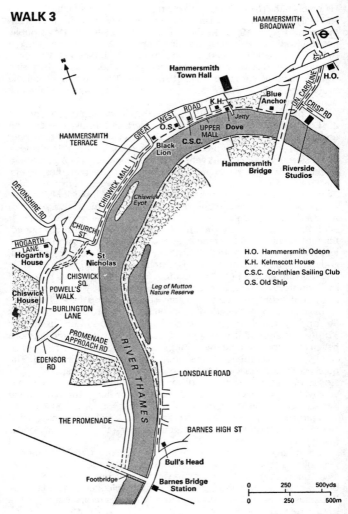

WALK 3

HAMMERSMITH BROADWAY

HAMMERSMITH Town Hall

H.O.

K.H.

Blue Anchor

CRISP RD

GREAT WEST ROAD

O.S.

Jetty

UPPER MALL

Dove

HAMMERSMITH TERRACE

Black Lion

C.S.C.

HAMMERSMITH Bridge

Riverside Studios

DEVONSHIRE RD

CHISWICK MALL

Chiswick Eyot

CHURCH ST

HOGARTH LANE

Hogarth's House

St Nicholas

CHISWICK SQ.

POWELL'S WALK

Chiswick House

BURLINGTON LANE

Leg of Mutton Nature Reserve

H.O. Hammersmith Odeon
K.H. Kelmscott House
C.S.C. Corinthian Sailing Club
O.S. Old Ship

RIVER THAMES

PROMENADE APPROACH RD

EDENSOR RD

LONSDALE ROAD

THE PROMENADE

BARNES HIGH ST

Bull's Head

Footbridge

Barnes Bridge Station

0   250   500yds
0   250   500m

with a view over to the right, across the busy Great West Rd., of the handsome rear facade of **Hammersmith Town Hall**, dating from the 1930s.

On the river, an ugly iron jetty marks the spot, indicated by a plaque, where a creek and a small natural harbor gave birth to the village of

Hammersmith. The path winds to the right, then an inlet to the left leads suddenly into a tiny Georgian street that once lay at the heart of Hammersmith, **Upper Mall**. On the left is the low-ceilinged **Dove** public house (worth arriving near opening time for a seat in the window overlooking the tidal waters), and on the right is **Kelmscott House**, once the home of William Morris. Over the coach-house door is a sign commemorating the Hammersmith socialists. The building is still the headquarters of the William Morris Society, and also witnessed the first demonstration of the electric telegraph.

The riverside pathway continues past the crow's-nest lookout post of the Corinthian Sailing Club, through a modern cloister-like construction under a block of apartments, past the balconied **Old Ship** pub, the Upper Mall Open Space and another pub called the **Black Lion**; this 400-year-old hostelry has associations with the humorist and essayist A.P. Herbert.

Leaving behind a panoramic view of the river, the path then deserts the Thames for a moment, to follow the fine Georgian **Hammersmith Terrace**. As the river comes back into view, from Chiswick Mall a view is possible, across the gardens, of a small island, **Chiswick Eyot** (pronounced "eight"). On the right is the rear of Fuller's brewery, then **St Nicholas** church, where the artists Whistler and Hogarth are buried. Enter the churchyard from the river and the tomb of Hogarth is on the left, surrounded by a railing. Walk around the church into the graveyard, and the bronze tomb of Whistler is near the ivy-covered wall.

The path leading out of the church, Powells Walk, leads to a main road, Burlington Lane. Make the detour across this busy road to CHISWICK HOUSE and its fine park only if you have the time to do the visit justice.

Back on the opposite side of the church, Church St. leads to **Chiswick Sq.**, on the left, which is said to be the setting of an episode in Thackeray's *Vanity Fair*. Around the corner is HOGARTH'S HOUSE, a now incongruous haven of tranquility amid the roaring traffic on Hogarth Lane.

Once you have reached this point, several options lie ahead. The quickest though least interesting route is to cross Burlington Lane at Hogarth Lane and head N along Devonshire Rd. After about 5 minutes you will cross Chiswick High Rd. Continue N along Turnham Green Terrace, to arrive at Turnham Green (District line) tube station.

Alternatively, you can retrace your steps back along the route toward Hammersmith Bridge, pausing for a drink along the way in one of the many pubs.

If you have the stamina to double the distance traveled, continue heading s past the cemetery, along Chiswick Walk and onto The Promenade. This leads along the river's edge for almost $\frac{3}{4}$ mile until the river can be crossed by the footbridge at Barnes Bridge. Welcoming on the far bank is Barnes Bridge railway station, from where there are trains back E toward Central London.

The final option, having crossed the bridge, is to turn N toward the celebrated riverside pub, the **Bull's Head**, which is, and always has been, a haven for jazz fans. The half-hour stroll along the southern bank, from the Bull's Head back to Hammersmith Bridge, is a surprisingly rustic one, along a tranquil, often muddy towpath.

If the southern towpath route, with its more rural perspective on the Thames, is more to your taste, cross over Hammersmith Bridge and then turn right, past the playing fields and the Leg of Mutton ponds, an old reservoir, now a nature reserve. It takes about half an hour to reach Barnes.

This stretch of the river remains the province of local strollers, courting couples and hopeful fishermen. It is also the scene, each spring, of the Oxford and Cambridge Boat Race. The 4-mile race begins at Putney, and once the competing crews have passed the top of the U-bend at Hammersmith Bridge, the long, nearly straight stretch down to Barnes usually gives the advantage to one team or the other as they strike out toward the finish around the next bend at Mortlake.

WALK 4: THE PARKS
Allow 1-3hrs. Use maps 5-9 to enjoy the parks and wander off this skeleton route. Tube: Piccadilly Circus.

A few minutes' walk from Piccadilly Circus tube station, London's royal parks begin. They spread themselves airily to KENSINGTON.

Stroll down Lower Regent St. to its end, passing the Crimean War memorial and crossing PALL MALL into **Waterloo Pl**. Descend the steps to THE MALL, with the **Institute of Contemporary Arts** on the left and the Admiralty building diagonally across the road. Cross the road, and enter ST JAMES'S PARK.

This small but pretty park is dominated by its lake, alive with waterfowl. Follow the lake to the opposite end of the park to leave by the gateway to the right, in front of BUCKINGHAM PALACE. Renegotiate The Mall to enter **Green Park**, opposite. Walk diagonally across this hilly little park, and bear left to enter the pedestrian subway passage at Hyde Park Corner.

The tunnel emerges by the triumphal **Wellington Arch**, on an island of history surrounded by a tangled urban road system. It is best to leave this island, after a look at its imposing monuments, by another subway, this one signposted for Hyde Park Corner tube station. Bypassing the station itself, emerge by HYDE PARK, backtracking to enter by the triple archway, then take one final tunnel to arrive in grassy safety. On this corner is APSLEY HOUSE.

Inside the park, the thoroughfare to the left is **Rotten Row**, for horseback riders. Straight ahead is the path leading to the **Serpentine**, the descriptively named lake popular for boating (*adequate* ≡). Follow the lake as far as the bridge carrying the main road, and cross to the other bank. A few steps beyond the bridge is the **Serpentine Gallery**, noted for exhibitions of contemporary artists. Behind it are paths to the bandstand and Round Pond, with a striking panorama to the S of the ALBERT MEMORIAL AND ROYAL ALBERT HALL.

Return to the water's edge, on the Kensington side, to see the Art Nouveau statue of Peter Pan, whose whimsy pervades the gardens. At the head of the waters is a paved garden, and beyond them the Elfin Oak, a tree-stump carved with elves. Don't leave without visiting KENSINGTON PALACE. From here, it is not far to Queensway or Kensington High St. tube stations, to the N and S respectively.

Sights classified by type

ANCIENT BUILDINGS (all 🏛)
Apsley House ☆
Banqueting House ★
Buckingham Palace ☆
Chiswick House ★
The College of Arms
Dulwich College ☆
Eltham Palace ☆
Fenton House ☆
Gray's Inn
Guildhall ☆
Ham House ☆
Hampton Court Palace
  ◁€ ★
Horse Guards Parade
Kensington Palace
Kenwood House ★
Lambeth Palace
Lancaster House
Leighton House
Lincoln's Inn ★
Mansion House
Marble Hill House
Marlborough House
Orleans House
Osterley Park ☆
Royal Academy of Arts
Royal Courts of Justice
Royal Hospital, Chelsea
  ◁€ ☆
Royal Navy College,
  Greenwich ★
St James's Palace ★
Spencer House
Staple Inn
Syon House
Temple ☆
Tower of London ★ ♣
Westminster, Palace of ★
William Morris Gallery

CHURCHES (all 🏛)
Brompton Oratory
St Bartholomew-the-Great ★

St George's, Bloomsbury
St James's, Piccadilly
St Martin-in-the-Fields
St Mary Abchurch
St Mary-le-Bow
St Mary-le-Strand ★
St Paul's, Covent Garden
St Paul's Cathedral ◁€ ★
St Stephen Walbrook ☆
Southwark Cathedral ☆
Westminster Abbey ★
Westminster Cathedral
  ◁€ ☆

GENERAL INTEREST
Barbican
British Telecom Tower
  🏛
Canary Wharf 🏛
Guinness World of
  Records ♣
Horse Guards Parade 🏛
Lloyd's Building 🏛
London Bridge
London Bridge City
London Dungeon
Old Bailey
Regent's Canal ★
Registry of Births, Deaths
  and Marriages
Rock Circus ♣
Royal Albert Hall
Royal Courts of Justice
  🏛
Royal National Theatre
  🏛
St Katharine's Dock ☆
St Pancras Station 🏛 ☆
South Bank Arts Centre
  ◁€
Speakers' Corner
Tower Bridge ♣ ◁€
Tower Hill Pageant ♣
Trocadero ♣

Sights classified by type (continued)

MONUMENTS
Albert Memorial 🏛
Charing Cross
Cleopatra's Needle
Marble Arch
The Monument 🏛 ⇐ ★
Nelson's Column

MUSEUMS AND GALLERIES
HMS Belfast ♣
Bethnal Green Museum ★ ♣
British Museum 🏛 ★
Carlyle's House
Commonwealth Institute
  🏛 ♣
The Coram Foundation ★
Courtauld Institute
  Galleries ★
Design Museum 🏛 ⇐
Dickens' House ★
Dulwich College/Picture
  Gallery 🏛 ★
Florence Nightingale
  Museum
Geffrye Museum 🏛
Hogarth's House
Imperial War Museum ★ ♣
Iveagh Bequest 🏛 ★
Dr. Johnson's House
Keats' House
London Canal Museum
London, Museum of ★ ♣
London Toy and Model
  Museum ♣
London Transport Museum
  ♣
Madame Tussaud's ★ ♣
Mankind, Museum of
Moving Image, Museum of ♣
National Army Museum ♣
National Gallery ★
National Maritime Museum,
  Greenwich 🏛 ★
National Portrait Gallery ★

Natural History Museum
  🏛 ★ ♣
Percival David Foundation of
  Chinese Art
Planetarium ♣
Public Record Office
  Museum 🏛
Royal Academy of Arts 🏛
Royal Air Force Museum,
  Hendon ♣
Science Museum ★ ♣
Shakespeare Globe Museum
Sherlock Holmes Museum
Sir John Soane's Museum ★
Tate Gallery ★
Theatre Museum
Victoria & Albert Museum
  ★ ♣
Wallace Collection ★
Wellington Museum 🏛 ★
Whitechapel Art Gallery
  🏛
William Morris Gallery

PARKS/GARDENS
Holland Park
Hyde Park ⇐
Regent's Park ⇐ ★
Richmond Park ★
Royal Botanic Gardens
  (Kew Gardens) ★ ⇐ ♣
St James's Park ⇐ ★
Zoo 🏛 ★ ♣

SQUARES AND STREETS
Cheyne Walk ★
Downing Street
Fleet Street
The Mall ⇐ ★
Pall Mall
Piccadilly
Strand
Trafalgar Square
Whitehall

Sights and places of interest

Introduction

London's major sights are every bit as enjoyable as their worldwide reputation suggests, but this is also a city of wonderful diversity, so try to take in some of the less well-known attractions too.

Many readers will share our sadness at the prolonged struggle for survival by that long-standing family favorite, THE ZOO. But they should welcome the new entries to this edition, six visitor attractions that run the gamut of London's different flavors: the GUINNESS WORLD OF RECORDS (amazing superlatives); the LONDON CANAL MUSEUM (a strange tale, indeed); the WILLIAM MORRIS GALLERY (Pre-Raphaelite delights); the SHERLOCK HOLMES MUSEUM (intrigue and detection); the TOWER HILL PAGEANT (a ride through historic tableaux); and SPENCER HOUSE (Neoclassical splendor).

We describe LONDON'S DISTRICTS in a separate chapter of their own, commencing on page 59, with the alphabetical listing, from BATTERSEA to WIMBLEDON, starting on page 64.

USEFUL TO KNOW
Opening hours are fairly regularly adhered to, and where there is a last admission before closing time, that has been given. Churches' hours vary rather more, especially in the CITY, and they are always subject to closure for services. Rules on photography vary, but often only flash is prohibited: look for the 📷 symbol.

HOW TO USE THIS CHAPTER
In the following pages, London's sights are arranged alphabetically. Look for the ★ symbol against the outstanding, not-to-be-missed sights. If you have a little more time, look for the ☆ symbol, indicating places that in our view are definitely worth a visit. Places of special interest for children (♣) and with outstanding views (◀€) are also indicated, as are buildings of architectural interest (𝔪). For a full explanation of symbols, see page 7. A classified list of headings in this chapter, sorted by type, appears on pages 98-99.

Some lesser sights do not have their own entries but are included within other entries: it is easiest to look these up in the INDEX.

Bold type is mostly employed to indicate monuments, buildings or other highlights. Places mentioned without addresses and opening times are often described more fully elsewhere: check whether they are **cross-references** to other headings, which are printed in SMALL CAPITALS.

London's sights A to Z

ALBERT MEMORIAL AND ROYAL ALBERT HALL ⅢⅢ
Kensington Gore, SW7 ☎*(071) 589-8212. Map **14**I4. Tube: Knightsbridge,*
South Kensington, Kensington High Street.
These fine examples of Victoriana are dedicated to Victoria's consort,
who encouraged the institutionalization of arts and sciences that gives
this corner of KENSINGTON its character. The **Albert Hall** was erected in
1867-71. Its bold, simple red outline is offset by a solemn ceramic
frieze showing the triumph of the arts and sciences. The huge amphitheater is used for everything from boxing to concerts, notably the
summer "Prom" season (see PERFORMING ARTS, page 248); visitors are
allowed in when the hall is not in use.

Although the ornate spire of the **Albert Memorial** across the road sits
uneasily on the huge Gothic canopy, and although the statue of Albert
himself is utterly uninspired, there are endless details to admire in the
inventive *mélange* of granite, marble, bronze and semiprecious stones,
concealed at present by scaffolding, as the memorial is in the process of
lengthy refurbishment.

APSLEY HOUSE, THE WELLINGTON MUSEUM ⅢⅢ ★
149 Piccadilly, W1 ☎*(071) 499-5676. Map **8**H8. Closed for refurbishment until*
late 1993/early 1994. Tube: Hyde Park Corner.
Once the first of a row of aristocratic houses a traveler from the W
would encounter when approaching the city, and hence known as
"No. 1, London," Apsley House still puts on a brave show, despite
being surrounded on three sides by London's busiest roads. Although
the house is currently closed to visitors while restoration work is in
progress, inside, calm pervades the majestic rooms once occupied by
the Duke of Wellington, Britain's greatest soldier.

Built by Robert Adam in 1771-78 for Baron Apsley, the brick-fronted
mansion was bought in 1807 by Lord Wellesley, Wellington's elder
brother, who sold it to the duke in 1817. Wellington transformed the
elegant house into a palace with the help of his architect Benjamin Wyatt,
who clad the exterior with Bath stone and added the large portico in 1828;
the house was clearly intended to impress at a time when the duke's
political career was at its height (he was prime minister from 1828-30).
And impress it did — during the Reform crisis of 1832, a mob stoned the
house, and iron shutters replaced the windows.

Because of the transformation, two complementary styles are to be
found in the interior. Adam's work has a delicate elegance, whereas
Wyatt's changes and additions are on a grander scale. This contrast is not
too obvious on the ground floor, where the duke's fine collection of
porcelain and dinner services are displayed in rooms that retain some air
of domesticity, but it strikes one forcibly on reaching the stairwell, where
the graceful curve of Adam's design is offset by Wyatt's heavy and ornate
banister. The stair now houses Antonio Canova's massive Neoclassical
statue of the nude *Napoleon as a Roman Emperor*.

The best example of Adam's interior work is the **Piccadilly Drawing**

Room at the top of the stairs, with its vaulted ceiling, decorated with characteristically delicate Classical moldings, and curved apsidal E end. Wyatt's work is best seen in the splendid **Waterloo Gallery**, with an elaborate ceiling in his grand "Versailles" manner. The eight large windows have shutters that slide out to reveal mirrors, turning the room into a glittering hall of light in the evenings.

The **Dining Room**, also on the first floor, was adapted by Wyatt from 1816-29 to house the fantastic table service given to Wellington to commemorate his Portuguese victories by the Prince Regent of Portugal in 1816. The complete service consisted of about 1,000 pieces, of which the most important is the centerpiece, on the large oak table.

The fine paintings at Apsley House are largely those of the first duke, with a few additions and loans. Velázquez dominates the Spanish collections with *A Spanish Gentleman* and the profoundly serene *Water Carrier of Seville* (Waterloo Gallery). Murillo and Ribera are also represented, as are many Dutch and Flemish artists: look for Jan Vermeer of Haarlem's *Landscape with Bleaching Grounds* (Yellow Drawing Room) and Elsheimer's haunting *Judith and Holofernes* (Piccadilly Drawing Room). There are many portraits of Wellington's illustrious contemporaries, including several of Napoleon and an equestrian study of the duke himself painted by Goya (Waterloo Gallery).

A new gallery in the basement is devoted to the duke himself, using prints, costumes and other memorabilia. The museum also stages public concerts and lectures, as well as two annual festivals, a Christmas festival and a Battle of Waterloo festival. The latter, held around June 15, brings history alive with costumed re-enactments of the events of 1815.

BANQUETING HOUSE ⅏ ★

Whitehall, SW1 ☎*(071) 930-4179. Map* **9H11** 📷 ✍ *with flash. Open Mon-Sat 10am-4.30pm. Closed sometimes on short notice. Tube: Westminster, Charing Cross.*

A superb Palladian building, Banqueting House was originally the focal point of the great royal palace of Whitehall. The single hall to survive a fire of 1688, it is today in a very different setting, across busy WHITEHALL from HORSE GUARDS PARADE and dominated by large government offices. Built by Inigo Jones in 1619-22, the Banqueting House has a flamboyance, but also a Classical solemnity and clarity of design, based on a double cube, that was entirely novel in its day.

On the ceiling are the giant canvases commissioned from Rubens by Charles I of the apotheosis of his predecessor and father, James I. Installed in 1635, their incredible scale and vigorous movement are entirely Baroque in feeling, contrasting strongly with Jones' Classicism. Rubens received a knighthood and a pension; Charles I, ironically, was led to his execution in 1649 from the window of this hall.

BARBICAN
☎*(071) 638-8891 (box office), (071) 638-4141 (information). Map 11E15. Tube: Barbican, Moorgate.*

The Barbican now rises as London's boldest piece of Utopian planning. It was a barren bomb site when, in 1956, it was chosen to reintroduce housing to the almost totally commercial center of the City. On a bad day, it can seem grim and forbidding, a monument to the failed dreams of modern architecture, but it does have a certain excitement, with angular towers soaring upward and walkways sweeping across, as shown in the illustration on page 72.

And sometimes the concrete comes to life: the **Barbican Centre** contains the London Symphony Orchestra's concert hall, the Royal Shakespeare Company's two theaters in the BARBICAN THEATRE (see page 250), a cinema, a gallery, conference halls, a roof garden, and cafeterias and restaurants; there are also lobby concerts and exhibitions. Opened in 1982, its complex design and sumptuous interior constitute the largest social and arts center in Europe. Here too is the superbly designed **Museum of London** (see LONDON, MUSEUM OF).

Incongruously, bastions remain of the old City wall, and the church of **St Giles Cripplegate**, whose gutted shell survived the fire-bombing. The 15thC tower is surmounted with a brick top story of 1683 and an attractive central turret and weather vane.

BATTERSEA
The main landmark of this Thameside district is Sir Giles Gilbert Scott's great **Battersea Power Station**. See LONDON'S DISTRICTS, page 64.

HMS BELFAST
Morgan's Lane, Tooley St., SE1 ☎*(071) 407-6434. Map 12G17* 🔳 ✱ *Open daily late Mar-Oct 10am-5.20pm; Nov-late Mar 10am-4pm. Tube: London Bridge.*

One of several attractions in LONDON BRIDGE CITY, this World War II warship, a Southampton-class cruiser, saw action in the Battle of North Cape in 1943, when the *Scharnhorst* was sunk, in the Normandy landings and even in the Korean War. Now she is a floating tribute to all that, and to wartime naval life in general. Conditions on board were cramped, and the visitor has to weave and duck through hatches and up ladders (very tricky with young children), but the imagination can run riot on the navigation bridge or next to the massive main guns.

There is a display on the Falklands War, including memorabilia. An audio commentary tour allows you to experience the atmosphere and sounds of active service *(for hire for a small extra charge)*.

BELGRAVIA
The area around **Belgravia Square** contains some of London's finest terraces. See LONDON'S DISTRICTS, page 64.

BETHNAL GREEN MUSEUM OF CHILDHOOD ✮
Cambridge Heath Rd., E2 ☎*(081) 980-2415. Map 20C5* 🔳 ✱ ♿ *Open Mon-Thurs, Sat 10am-5.50pm; Sun 2.30-5.50pm. Tube: Bethnal Green.*

In the heart of the authentic East End, off the usual tourist track, this museum was opened in 1872 as a branch of the VICTORIA & ALBERT MUSEUM. There are numerous old toys to study, from many periods. The **Tate Baby House** stands out, a fully furnished Georgian mansion in miniature dating from about 1760.

The galleries upstairs include wonderful collections of children's clothes, books, educational toys and furniture.

BLACKHEATH
An open area on a plateau lying SE of GREENWICH, Blackheath is surrounded by elegant 18thC houses. See LONDON'S DISTRICTS, page 65.

BLOOMSBURY
The literary heartland of London, Bloomsbury boasts the superb **Bedford Square**, one of the very few complete Georgian squares left in London. See LONDON'S DISTRICTS, page 65.

BRITISH MUSEUM 血 ★
Great Russell St., WC1 ☎(071) 636-1555. Map 9E11 ☒ K Mon-Sat 10.30am, 1.30pm, Sun 2.45pm, 3.30pm ☛ Open Mon-Sat 10am-5pm; Sun 2.30-6pm. Tube: Russell Square, Tottenham Court Road.
Despite its age and venerable traditions, the British Museum is constantly changing, for this is one of the most adventurous of the world's great museums. It was founded in 1753 around the 80,000 items collected by Sir Hans Sloane, a successful physician. Sloane's will allowed the nation to purchase his collection for £20,000, well below its value, thus beginning a sequence of generous bequests. The nucleus consisted of Sloane's broad-ranging cabinet of curiosities: zoological and mineral specimens, antiquities, manuscripts, books and drawings. Natural history was best represented, but in time the museum became oriented more toward archeology.

In 1823 George III's huge library was given to the nation by his heir and the decision was taken to build a new and grand edifice to display the nation's collected treasures. With the young Robert Smirke as architect, the intention was to create a Neoclassical structure around a quadrangle, completed by 1838, and later filled-in with the British Library's famous Reading Room (see page 106).

The move of the natural history exhibits to the NATURAL HISTORY MUSEUM in the 1880s and the ethnographic exhibits to the Museum of Mankind (see MANKIND, MUSEUM OF) in 1970 has solved much of the museum's space problem. The British Library will also be moving to a new purpose-built site during the mid- to late 1990s.

A comprehensive catalog would fill a bookcase. However, a selective visit should include the following.
Greece and Rome ★
The best place to start a visit; turn left in the entrance hall and for the moment pass through the Assyrian section. This leads to one of the best-laid-out sections, offering an excellent chronological survey and including some of the finest examples of Greek art in the world.

It starts with simple idols of the 3rd and 2nd millennia BC (**Rm. 1**) found in the Cyclades. Bronze Age Greek art (**Rm. 2**) is followed by early ceramics (**Rm. 3**) that show a developing sophistication; so too does the fine wine jar by Exekias (c.540BC), decorated with mythological scenes in black on a red-earth background. The exit is through a display of Greek vase decoration (**Rm. 4**). In **Rm. 5**, ceramics of about 500BC, now with red figures on black, demonstrate that Greek artists fully understood the forms and movements of the human body.

The next room chronologically is the **Duveen Gallery (Rm. 8)**, home of some of the finest examples of Greek art: a sizeable group of the sculptures that once adorned the Parthenon in Athens, dating from c.440BC when Pericles was beautifying Greece's greatest city. World-famous as the **Elgin Marbles (★)**, they are now the subject of controversy, with the Greek government making strenuous appeals for them to be returned to Athens. The Parthenon was ruined by an explosion in 1687; in 1803 Lord Elgin rescued the shattered fragments of the pediment sculptures, frieze and metopes and brought them to London. The **frieze**, displayed at eye level around the outside of the gallery, consists of marvelously natural figures and horses in a rhythmic procession to Mt. Olympus. The superb **pediment sculptures** recount the birth of Athena and the foundation of Athens.

Among the innumerable treasures of this collection is a **caryatid from the Erechtheum** in Athens (c.410BC) in **Rm. 9**. In **Rm. 7** are fragments of the great **Nereid Monument** (5thC BC) from a Greek colony at Lycia in Asia Minor, reconstructed into a facade. The Nereids themselves, wind spirits, are portrayed as dancing maidens with flowing garments clinging to their energetically moving bodies. In **Rm. 12** is a **frieze of the Battle of the Greeks and Amazons** from the Mausoleum of Halicarnassus, an extraordinary tomb of the late 4thC BC, built for Mausolus and one of the Seven Wonders of the Ancient World.

The smaller collection of Roman art begins in **Rms. 14 and 15** and continues upstairs in **Rm. 70** with the famous **Portland Vase** (c.1stC BC), a cameo glass production, with the top white layer carved to reveal the blue underneath. There are wall paintings from Pompeii, pleasant little architectural landscapes, and sculptures. Rooms above house smaller Greek and Roman antiquities, including fine figurines, busts, vases and household items. Particularly good are the representations of Greek and Roman life in **Rm. 69**, with a small fountain actually in operation and a Roman waterwheel from Spain.

One of two new galleries, **Rm. 70** contains "freedmen reliefs," stone portraits of freed slaves that were set into tomb walls, stunning sculptures, mosaics, coins, glassware, jewelry, including some delicate bronze animal brooches, and a remarkable crocodile-skin suit of armor from Egypt. Fascinating insights into daily Roman life are revealed by poll tax receipts and invitations.

The new **Rm. 71** covers the art of the 7th and 6thC BC Etruscan and Italian people, with some intricate filigree gold jewelry, engraved bronze mirrors, carved amber, and other rare objects, such as decorated ostrich eggs. There are also two sarcophagi, one of which is a magnificent example of painted terracotta. Cypriot antiquities dating from 4500BC to AD330 are in **Rm. 72**, and artifacts from the Greek colonies in Southern Italy and Sicily (founded in the second half of the 8thC BC) in **Rm. 73**.

Ancient Mesopotamia ★

The collections from the ancient cities of Assyria rival those of Greece, for Britain's close relations with Turkey in the mid-19thC made extensive excavations possible. Unlike the Greeks, the Assyrians seem to have been interested in a static, formal approach to representation, and the changes in style through the period are much less striking.

The Nimrud Gallery (**Rm. 19**) has huge **reliefs from the palace of Ashurnasirpal II** (9thC BC), showing highly ritualized hunting and military scenes. From a century later are two huge winged bulls with human heads (**Rm. 16**), from the entrance to the palace at Khorsabad. The best-observed and most enjoyable details among the Assyrian sculptures are not shown in the king and his countless soldiers but in the

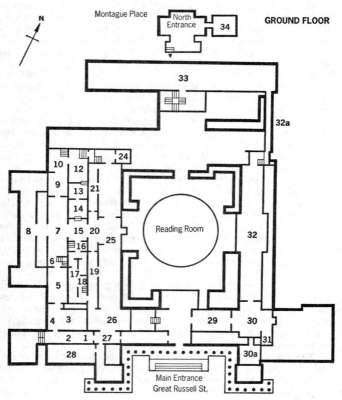

animals, particularly the lions depicted in the **relief series from Nineveh** (7thC BC), taken from Sennacherib's palace (**Rm. 17**).

Ancient Egypt ☆

The nucleus of this collection of 70,000 objects fell into British hands after Napoleon's defeat at the Battle of the Nile in 1798. The large **Egyptian Sculpture Gallery (Rm. 25)** gives an impressive indication of the overpowering scale and stern quality of Egyptian art with its ranks of massive, shiny, hard-edged statues, seemingly ageless.

At the s end is the famous inscribed **Rosetta Stone**, discovered in 1797; its text, in Greek as well as in Egyptian hieroglyphs, provided the key to a previously unreadable script. Among the huge **statues** are a pair of 3rdC BC granite lions found at Gebel Barkal, a colossus of **Rameses II** (c.1250BC) and a giant scarab beetle (c.200BC), an image of the sun god.

Upstairs, **Rms. 60-64** contain smaller Egyptian objects. The **mummies and mummy cases** have a macabre fascination — there are even mummies of animals. From the Roman period are mummy cases with unnervingly realistic portraits of the dead occupants. **Rm. 65** has an exhibition about Nubian society in Africa.

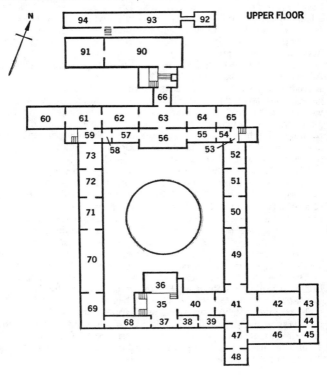

Oriental art

From **Rm. 66**, descend to the refurbished Edward VII Gallery (**Rm. 33**). Its superb collection of Oriental art includes the world's finest assembly of ancient **Chinese ceramics**, from flawless Ming plates to dramatic, expressive horses and camels. Even fiercer are bronze weapons and chariot fittings from 1500-1000BC and the impressive ritual vessels of the Shang period (1523-1027BC). A display of Buddhist material from all of Asia, including finds from the Silk Route, occupies the center of the gallery. Among other treasures are ancient bronzes, jades, and a collection of fine porcelain. There are also a number of good Indian sculptures, some with the characteristic eroticism of Hindu art, a famous garnet-encrusted gold reliquary from Afghanistan (c.1st-2ndC AD), and a life-sized bronze statue of Tara from Sri Lanka (c.950AD).

At the w end of the room, a large glass screen seals off a display area, the **Asahi Shimbun Gallery of Amaravati Sculpture** (★), where specially controlled atmospheric conditions enable the truly magnificent 2nd and 3rdC AD sculptures from the Indian monument of Amaravati to be displayed. Discovered in the ruins of a great religious center on the Krishna River, the sculptures were carved in panels of "Palnad marble," a local limestone, and depict scenes — full of vitality, movement, and fascinating detail — of the life of Buddha, and Buddhist symbols.

Temporary exhibitions of Japanese works are in **Rms. 92, 93** and **94**.

Books and manuscripts ★

Leaving the Edward VII Gallery at the E end, pass through to the **British Library Galleries** (**Rms. 29-32**), due to move to the new **British Library Building** at ST PANCRAS in the mid- to late 1990s. These galleries are devoted to regularly changed selections from the library's vast store of literary treasures around particular themes. The medieval manuscripts in particular are breathtaking, with their perfect miniature paintings and the unbelievably skillful calligraphy. On permanent display are the extraordinary **Lindisfarne Gospels**, made in an isolated monastery on England's NE coast in about 698.

The collection of holographs and annotated typescripts of many literary classics is supplemented by other treasures: Leonardo da Vinci's sketchbook, and one of Dürer's; two of the four originals of the Magna Carta; the last dying scribblings of Lord Nelson and Captain Scott of the Antarctic; the two 5thC manuscripts that were important in the compilation of the gospels; and chronicles, Bibles and legal documents from the Dark Ages. Among the printed books are Caxton's pioneering production of *Canterbury Tales*, the famous Gütenberg Bible and the Authorized Version of 1603, and the First Folio edition of Shakespeare's plays (1623).

The **British Library** receives a copy of every book published in Britain. The library's **Reading Room** (★ *open to the public only by guided tours Mon-Fri, check for times)* has attracted all the greatest scholars, most notably Karl Marx, who worked on *Das Kapital* in its hallowed calm. Opened in 1857, this spectacular room has a huge iron dome and massive windows, and a radial arrangement of reading tables around the circular bookcases containing the catalog. The dome is bigger than that of St Peter's in Rome.

Prehistory and early Britain

From the British Library Galleries, return to the main entrance hall. Upstairs to the E are the rooms devoted to prehistoric and Romano-British objects (**Rms. 36-40**). Stone Age products include carvings on mammoth and walrus tusks from France, and there is a rich collection of early metalwork. Lindow man, the 2,000-year-old remains of a Celt discovered in 1984 at Lindow Moss in Cheshire, is on display in **Rm. 37**. A hologram of the head affords a much closer examination of his red hair, mustache and features than was previously possible.

Look out for the superbly twisted electrum **torque** of the 1stC BC, found in Norfolk, and the exquisite Roman silver of the **Mildenhall Treasure (Rm. 40)**, including several superbly embossed platters.

Medieval and later

Rms. 41-7 are devoted to medieval (post-Roman) and later material, and **Rm. 48** to European and American decorative arts (1840-1940). Some rooms are darkened and their exhibits spotlighted, an effect that helps the visitor recognize the great quality of the items. The technique works very well with the **Waddesdon Bequest**, for example, in **Rm. 45**, which consists of elaborately wrought metal, glass and ceramic work from the Renaissance and Mannerist periods.

In **Rm. 41** is the famous **Sutton Hoo Treasure (★)**, a 7thC Angle burial ship unearthed in Suffolk in 1939. On display are finely wrought items of jewelry and weaponry, and a forbidding **helmet**, now reconstructed. Their craftsmanship speaks of a sophistication that belies the common image of the "Dark Ages," as they are usually called.

Famous objects in the medieval sections include the late Roman **Lycurgus Cup** and the **Franks Casket**, an Anglo-Saxon whalebone carving (both in **Rm. 41**). In **Rm. 42** is the Flemish parade shield of the 15thC showing a knight kneeling before a fairy-tale damsel; a skeleton looks over the knight's shoulder, and the inscription, representing the knight's words, can be translated as "You or death." Also in this room is the fabulous **14thC Royal Cup** of the kings of England and France, decorated with scenes from the life of St Agnes, in enamel.

The museum also possesses numerous important prints and drawings, including works by Michelangelo, Botticelli and other great masters. A periodically changed display can be found in **Rm. 90**, above the Edward VII Gallery.

BRITISH TELECOM TOWER ▥

Cleveland St., W1. Map 8E9. Not open to the public. Tube: Great Portland Street.
Still faithfully called the **Post Office Tower**, this 619-foot landmark, a jumble of transmitters and radio masts above an elongated cylinder, was erected in 1964 to achieve effective TV and radio telephone broadcasting above surrounding buildings.

BROMPTON ORATORY ▥

Brompton Rd., SW3 ☎(071) 589-4811. Open 7am-8pm. Map 15J6. Tube: South Kensington.
Converts are supposedly the most zealous adherents of any faith: cer-

tainly the Oxford Movement, a group of Victorian intellectuals turned Catholic, allowed no halfway measures when they created this church in 1884. All the drama of the Italian Baroque is here, in an interior dark with rich marbles, heavy with gilded detail. Some of the atmosphere is genuine: the huge marble *Apostles* (1680) by Mazzuoli come from Siena Cathedral.

BUCKINGHAM PALACE ⅲ ★
☎ *(071) 930-4832. Map 16|9. Not open to the public. Tube: Victoria, Hyde Park Corner.*
The royal standard flying signifies that the monarch is in residence, and then many an eye scans the windows of the palace hoping to catch a glimpse of a member of the Royal Family. But generally, visitors are satisfied by the splendors of the palace, with the Queen Victoria Memorial and THE MALL at their backs, and the solemn facade, guarded by soldiers in scarlet tunics and bearskins, behind railings to the front. (For the **Changing of the Guard** SEE CALENDAR OF EVENTS, page 56.)

Its familiarity and setting give it a certain grandeur, but in reality Buckingham Palace is an undistinguished example of early 20thC official architecture — it might be a rather large town hall. Behind, however, there is John Nash's older palace (pictured on page 25). In 1762, George III bought Buckingham House from the Duke of Buckingham, and Queen Charlotte moved in. In 1825 his son, the Regent, commissioned Nash to rebuild on a larger scale. The MARBLE ARCH was built as the entrance (later moved), but by 1850 the project was still incomplete, and Nash was sacked under suspicion of having squandered huge amounts of money and having bought building materials from his own companies. But the best parts of the palace are still his. To the right of the palace, there is a large arch leading to the gardens — the clearest part of Nash's work visible from outside.

When Queen Victoria came to the throne in 1837, the palace became the official residence, and it has been so ever since. It was her need for additional accommodation that led to the large side wings and front being built, although it was more humble until the facade was added in 1913.

To the left of the palace is Buckingham Gate and the **Queen's Gallery** (▨ *open during exhibitions only Tues-Sat 10am-5pm, Sun 2-5pm),* where exhibitions of treasures from the fabulous royal art collections are

mounted. Farther along, the road becomes Buckingham Palace Rd., and here can be found Nash's attractive **Royal Mews** (✉ *open Wed, Thurs noon to 4pm; times subject to change* ☎ *(071) 930-4832 before a visit)*, which can be visited when state processions are not taking place; on display are the Queen's beautiful carriages and harness. The state coaches are a great attraction; the star is the gilded and painted **Gold State Coach**, dating from 1762.

CABINET WAR ROOMS
Winston Churchill's wartime bunker in WHITEHALL.

CARLYLE'S HOUSE
24 Cheyne Row, SW3 ☎*(071) 352-7087. Map* **15L6** ✉ ✖ *Open Apr-Oct Wed-Sun, bank holiday Mon 11am-5pm. Tube: Sloane Square.*
The houses in Cheyne Row were built in 1708, making them some of the oldest surviving residences in CHELSEA, and when the Scottish writer Thomas Carlyle (1795-1881) was looking for a London home he was evidently impressed. He lived here from 1834 until his death, and the house can be seen today much as it was then, crammed with memorabilia and manuscripts of the famous, although now little-read, essayist and historian. It can also be enjoyed as a perfect example of a comfortable Victorian home. The **attic study**, with its double walls, was added in 1853 to provide a quiet working place.

CENTRAL CRIMINAL COURT
The imposing building is known universally as the OLD BAILEY after the street in which it stands.

CHARING CROSS
Map **9G11**. *Tube: Charing Cross.*
At the S end of TRAFALGAR SQUARE, a statue of Charles I looks down WHITEHALL to the place of his execution and occupies the site of the original Charing Cross, from where all distances to London are measured. This was the last of the Eleanor Crosses erected by Edward I in 1291 to mark the resting places of his queen's funeral cortège on its way to Westminster Abbey; Charing is a corruption of *chère reine* (dear queen).

The original was destroyed in the Civil War in 1647, but when E.M.

...ed Charing Cross Station Hotel nearby in 1863-64, he added ...h Gothic Eleanor Cross to the forecourt, where it still stands.

...SEA
...ny hold Chelsea to be London's quintessential "village," and it has ...ong been the most fashionable district in the capital. See LONDON'S DISTRICTS, page 66.

CHEYNE WALK ★
SW3. Map 14M5-15L6. Tube: Sloane Square.
There were grand houses here before the famous and beautiful terrace was built in the late 17thC. **Lindsey House** (subsequently subdivided into nos. 95-100), built about 1674, gives some idea of the detached stateliness of the even bigger Tudor mansions of CHELSEA, most notably the country estates of Henry VIII and Sir Thomas More. Once the red-brick Georgian terrace was built, Cheyne (pronounce the last "e") Walk's rural charm went largely unnoticed until the 19thC, when it suddenly became a haven for artists. Turner lived at **no. 119** from 1846 until his death in 1851, under the name of Puggy Booth, and D.G. Rossetti moved into **no. 16** in 1862. In 1880 the novelist George Eliot died in **no. 4**, a house dating from 1717. James McNeill Whistler lived at **no. 104** from 1863, and at **no. 96** from 1866-79, painting many of his most famous pictures here, including the series on the river itself, known as *Nocturnes*.

One of the most remarkable buildings, however, is earlier. **Crosby Hall** (☎ *(071) 352-9663* ☒ *open Mon-Sat 10am-noon, 2.15-5pm, Sun, bank hols 2.15-5pm)* was built between 1466 and 1475 by Sir John Crosby, a wool merchant, as his great hall residence in Bishopsgate in the City. It was moved to its present site in 1910 to save it from demolition. It has a superb **hammerbeam roof** and a 3-story **oriel window**, and displays a copy of Holbein's lost portrait of *Sir Thomas More and his Family.* Next to it, **Chelsea Old Church** contains a charming monument to Thomas Hungerford (1581), and Sir Thomas More's chapel (1528).

Between Crosby Hall and the church is Roper's Garden, next to an unusually ugly modern statue of Sir Thomas More, whose own gardens once occupied the site. There is a relief by Jacob Epstein in the garden. At the E end is Cheyne Row and CARLYLE'S HOUSE, and the gardens at the W end lead to **Albert Bridge** (1873), a decorative piece of Victorian suspension engineering.

CHISWICK
Pierced by the main W roads leading to Heathrow Airport and beyond, the Thameside village of Chiswick survives only in parts. See LONDON'S DISTRICTS, page 66.

CHISWICK HOUSE 🏛 ★
Burlington Lane, W4 ☎(081) 995-0508. Map 19C3 ☒ ✈ with flash ✗ by appt ▣ open in summer in grounds. Open mid-Mar to Sept daily 10am-1pm, 2-6pm; Oct to mid-Mar daily 9am-1pm, 2-4pm. Tube: Turnham Green, Chiswick Park.

The Palladian architecture so favored by 18thC English gentlemen, with its forms reduced to simple geometrical shapes and all detail ruthlessly contained, reached near-perfection in this ravishingly beautiful mansion in CHISWICK. Set in its own park, it retains the feel of a country house. The first Earl of Burlington bought the Jacobean mansion here in 1682. Little was changed until the third Earl of Burlington, an enthusiastic student of Classical art, added a villa to one end of the house, built to his own designs in 1725-29, with an interior by William Kent.

The villa's octagonal dome rises from a simple square block; a portico and stairs form the entrance. The link building and summer parlor survive at the E side, where the villa was joined to the main body of the old house. Through a low-ceilinged and severely Classical octagonal room, enter the three rooms that served as the earl's **library**. An interesting exhibition of engravings, plans and documents relating to the villa occupies the rooms on this floor. The upper rooms are reached by a spiral staircase, and immediately the style changes: these reception rooms, designed by Kent, are brighter in color, with richly patterned velvet wallpapers and heavily decorated cornices, architraves and fireplaces. At the rear is the 3-chambered gallery and, to the sides, the dramatic **Red and Green Velvet Rooms**. In the center, the impressive **dome** has elaborate coffering. The **garden** has grown to the modern, wilder taste.

THE CITY
London began here, with the fortified Roman settlement founded in the 1stC AD. But "the City" we know today is the one square mile forming the financial district of London, the most important of its kind in Europe. ST PAUL'S CATHEDRAL forms the centerpiece of an area rich in historical, architectural and social interest. See LONDON'S DISTRICTS, page 67.

CLEOPATRA'S NEEDLE
Victoria Embankment, WC2. Map 10G12. Tube: Embankment.
Now appropriately sited beside another symbol of timelessness, the Thames, this pink granite obelisk was made in Heliopolis in Egypt in 1500BC, predating Cleopatra by centuries. Presented to Britain by Egypt in 1819, it was finally towed by sea to its present site and erected in

1878. In that year, a little time capsule, in the form of everyday Victorian objects including hairpins and a railway timetable, was buried beneath the obelisk to be dug up and wondered at sometime in the far-off future. New York has a similar obelisk in Central Park, and there is one in both Paris and Istanbul.

THE COLLEGE OF ARMS 🏛

Queen Victoria St., EC4 ☎*(071) 248-2762. Map 11F15* 🖾 *Earl Marshall's Court only open Mon-Fri 10am-4pm. Tube: Mansion House, Blackfriars.*

The official body controlling the heraldry of the United Kingdom is housed in an interesting building constructed in 1671-88 following the Great Fire, which destroyed the older house given to the college by Mary I in 1555. The wrought-iron gates and railings, of uncertain date, are particularly splendid; the brick pilasters with carved stone capitals preserve some of its grandeur. As a professional body, the College of Arms will investigate queries relating to genealogy and heraldry — nobody knows more about argent chevrons, batons sinister or griffins rampant. Only the **Earl Marshall's Court**, also known as the Court of Chivalry, is open to the public.

COMMONWEALTH INSTITUTE 🏛

230 Kensington High St., W8 ☎*(071) 603-4535. Map 13I2* 🖾 ♿ 💺 ♣ *Open Mon-Sat 10am-5pm; Sun 2-5pm. Tube: Kensington High Street.*

With its extraordinary green copper roof, all peaks and elliptical curves, the Commonwealth Institute is an appropriately unusual tribute to a unique association, the Commonwealth. It was opened in 1962 as a study and display center, and houses a permanent exhibition representing its peoples, customs and economics. There is an excellent library, together with a cinema and restaurant. The exhibition area is open-plan, consisting of a large circle of galleries on different levels around a central concourse. Each country has a display, variously expressing the cultural traditions or economies of the nations.

There is always plenty going on at the Commonwealth Institute, particularly for schoolchildren, with temporary exhibitions, live performances, workshops and lectures year round.

THE CORAM FOUNDATION (Foundling Hospital Art Museum) ★

40 Brunswick Sq. WC1 ☎*(071) 278-2424. Map 4D12* 🖾 🖋 *Open Mon-Fri 10am-4pm (check first). Tube: Russell Square.*

In the 18thC, London was full of destitute children, and their plight moved nobody more than Thomas Coram, a retired sea captain who set up a foundling hospital in 1739. The original buildings were shamefully demolished in 1926, but the magnificent **Court Room** can be seen in the Foundation's modern offices, along with a model of the original complex. After its foundation, artists led by Hogarth tried to raise funds. It thus has a fine collection of pictures, of which the highlight is Hogarth's **portrait** of the sanguine philanthropist Coram (★). There are also works by Gainsborough and Reynolds, a study of Raphael, and a manuscript of Handel's *Messiah*.

Coram's Fields, a children's playground, is entered from Guildford St. through the hospital's original gateway.

COURTAULD INSTITUTE GALLERIES ★
Somerset House, Strand, WC2 ☎*(071) 873-2526. Map 10G12* 🔲 ⅆ. 🖳 *Open Mon-Sat 10am-6pm; Sun 2-6pm. Tube: Aldwych, Temple, Covent Garden.*

When the textile industrialist Samuel Courtauld helped found London University's main art history department, the Courtauld Institute, in 1931, he provided the nucleus of an important art collection. Swelled by several subsequent bequests, this has grown into an exceptional, broad-ranging group of pictures. The Institute is now in its new premises in the N block of William Chambers' Classical Portland-stone **Somerset House** (1776-78), original home of the Royal Academy and then the REGISTRY OF BIRTHS, DEATHS AND MARRIAGES. The move has enabled the Institute to exhibit a far greater number of its artworks, not previously displayed due to lack of space.

The galleries on the first floor begin with 15th and 16thC Renaissance art, and continue through the centuries to the Post-Impressionists and Modigliani. Highlights include the Morelli-Nerli *cassoni* (marriage chests) of 1472 (**Gallery 1**), Palma Vecchio's poetic and sensuous *Venus* (**Gallery 2**), Rubens' incomparable *Landscape by Moonlight,* famous for its eerie beauty (**Gallery 3**), and an important group of altarpiece *modelli* by Tiepolo (**Gallery 4**).

Samuel Courtauld's collection amounts to one of the best publicly accessible groups of both Impressionist and Post-Impressionist paintings (**Galleries 5 and 6**). Impressionist works include examples by Monet *(Fall at Argenteuil),* Sisley and Renoir, including the superbly colored *La Loge.* Manet is represented by a large oil sketch for the celebrated *Déjeuner sur l'Herbe* and by the sumptuous *A Bar at the Folies-Bergères.* Two large sketches by Degas show to perfection the artist's ability to fix an ordinary moment in time. The Post-Impressionists are represented by an exceptional collection of Cézannes, a Van Gogh self-portrait (with bandaged ear) and two haunting studies of Tahitian women by Gauguin, including the dreamy *Te Rerioa.*

The galleries on the second floor contain the Courtauld's silver collection (**Gallery 7**), and in **Gallery 8** riveting thematic exhibitions on subjects as diverse as *Stuart Portraiture, Woman and Modernity,* and *Roger Fry and the Omega Workshops.* Mainly British 20thC paintings and sculptures feature in **Galleries 9 and 10**; artists include Sickert, Duncan Grant and Ben Nicholson. Among the gems of 14th-16thC Italian and Netherlandish paintings in **Gallery 11** is a well-preserved triptych by Bernardo Daddi, *The Entombment,* a poignant masterpiece of Early Netherlandish painting; the brilliant, jewel-like *Madonna* by Quinten Massys; and Pieter Bruegel the Elder's rare and beautiful *Landscape with the Flight into Egypt.*

COVENT GARDEN
This neighborhood lost its *raison d'être* in 1974 when the fresh fruit and vegetable market moved across the river. But, conserving its archi-

tectural treasures, it has found a new one as a delightful area for wandering, shopping and eating. See LONDON'S DISTRICTS, page 74.

DESIGN MUSEUM 血

Butlers Wharf, Shad Thames, SE1 ☎*(071) 403-6933. Map 12H17* ▨ ◀€ ═▄
▨ *Open Tues-Sun 11.30am-6.30pm. Tube: Tower Hill, London Bridge.*

In a strikingly reconstructed 1950s warehouse, the Design Museum is the first of its kind in Britain. The brainchild of Sir Terence Conran and Stephen Bayley, it aims to show how and why objects that we may take for granted, from spoons to kettles to cars, are designed the way they are. It also shows that, when well designed, these objects can be very beautiful.

The theme of good design begins with the building itself, and more particularly its clean, clear, all-white interior. The museum is divided into three sections, which interact well. On the top floor is a permanent study collection, which may at first glance look like "Conran without the price tags" but does in fact do much to explain and evaluate design, particularly in the mass market. On the first floor is the **Boilerhouse**, where temporary exhibitions are held, and the **Design Review**, a fast-changing spotlight on current happenings in design, both new and speculative. This is an agreeable place to visit, not so much museum as resource center (with library and lecture theater), aided by its waterfront coffee shop and more serious **Blueprint Café**, a restaurant serving first-rate modern British food; both have wonderful views of the river. But the museum has a one-dimensional feeling. Quintessentially '80s, it is style-obsessed.

DICKENS' HOUSE ☆

48 Doughty St., WC1 ☎*(071) 405-2127. Map 4D12* ▨ *Open Mon-Sat 10am-5pm. Closed for 2 weeks mid-Dec to early Jan. Tube: Russell Square, Chancery Lane.*

When Charles Dickens lived at Doughty St. between 1837 and 1839, he was experiencing his first taste of success. The *Pickwick Papers,* which brought him sudden prosperity, was still being published, and he also worked on his first novels while in the house: *Oliver Twist, Barnaby Rudge* and *Nicholas Nickleby.*

In Dickens' time, Doughty St. had gates at either end, tended by liveried porters. It is still a handsome house but, unfortunately, the interior preserves almost nothing of its original appearance; instead, however, there is an extensive museum of Dickens memorabilia. There are pieces of furniture from later houses, numerous letters and manuscripts, portraits of the writer and his family, and contemporary illustrations of his famous characters. The drawing room has recently been reconstructed to look as it might have done in Dickens' day.

DOCKLANDS

Some 450 acres of derelict docks are being transformed into a 21stC river city, realizing at last some of the great potential of the Thames. The centerpiece of the whole show is CANARY WHARF. See LONDON'S DISTRICTS, page 75.

DOWNING STREET
SW1. Map 9H11. Tube: Westminster. Charing Cross.
Although overwhelmingly dominated by the massive buildings of WHITEHALL, Downing St., the Prime Minister's residence, is the power-house of the government. In fact, the interior of **"no. 10"** is more elegant and spacious than the unassuming facade might suggest, and from its Cabinet Room the country has been run since Sir Robert Walpole accepted the house ex officio from George II in 1735. **No. 11**, home of the Chancellor of the Exchequer, is the only other survivor of Sir George Downing's original terrace of 1683-86. Steps at the end of the street lead to ST JAMES'S PARK. At the Whitehall end, a simple barrier once kept the public out of Downing St.; now ceremonial gates have been erected.

DULWICH
Although considerably s of the city center, the village of Dulwich is well worth the short train ride from Victoria for its charm, the unique DULWICH COLLEGE and the **Horniman Museum**. See LONDON'S DISTRICTS, page 77.

DULWICH COLLEGE AND PICTURE GALLERY ▥ ☆
College Rd., SE21 ☎(081) 693-5254. Map 20D5 ▨ ▧ ✗ Sat, Sun 3pm. Open Tues-Fri 11am-1pm, 2-5pm; Sat 11am-5pm; Sun 2-5pm. Train to West Dulwich from Victoria.
In 1619, Edward Alleyn, a successful actor and colleague of Shakespeare, founded the "College of God's Gift" at Dulwich, and the large almshouses that were part of the original bequest have been added to, making Dulwich College today one of London's greatest schools.

Of particular interest is the remarkable **Picture Gallery**, in a severe Neoclassical building designed by Sir John Soane in 1811-14, which incorporates a mausoleum for its founders. The Dutch school of the 17thC is especially well represented: there are six Cuyps, for example, including some fine landscapes. Look out for the majestic *Landscape with Sportsmen* by Pynacker and important works by Poussin; also represented are Watteau, Claude and Canaletto. There are Rubens sketches, and English portraiture, including works by Gainsborough, and Reynolds' amusing portrait of his era's great actress, *Mrs Siddons as the Tragic Muse*. But pride of place goes to the awe-inspiring **Rembrandts**, including *Titus*, a moving portrait of his sick son.

ELTHAM PALACE ▥ ☆
Eltham ☎(081) 859-2112. Map 20D5 ▣ Open Nov-Mar Thurs, Sun 10am-4pm; Apr-Oct Thurs, Sun 10am-6pm. Train to Eltham from Charing Cross.
History has played some teasing games with this medieval palace near BLACKHEATH and GREENWICH. A favorite royal hunting retreat until the time of Henry VIII, it must have witnessed some huge banquets, such as when Henry IV received the Byzantine Emperor here in 1409. By the 1600s, it fell into ruins; only the Great Hall survived the Civil War, because it made a good barn. In the 1930s it was rescued by the Royal

Army Educational Corps, which now occupies the site. Past a lovely group of half-timbered houses in the outer court, known as the **Lord Chancellor's Lodgings** after Cardinal Wolsey, is a 15thC bridge over a moat with swans and geese. At the heart stands the **Great Hall** on the mound of the palace, with a superb **hammerbeam roof** and two great **oriel windows** at either side of the dais.

FENTON HOUSE ⌂ ☆

Hampstead Grove, NW3 ☎(071) 435-3471. Map 20C4 ▨ ✍ Open Mar Sat, Sun 2-5.30pm; Apr-Oct Mon-Wed 1-6.30pm, Sat, Sun, bank holiday Mon 11-5.30pm. Tube: Hampstead.

Although HAMPSTEAD is rich in fine houses, this is its jewel. Dating from 1693, Fenton House is a brick mansion of disarmingly simple design, hardly changed except for the benign addition of the Classical portico to the E front soon after 1800. The luxurious Regency decor of the interior reflects the changes made by James Fenton in about 1810. Among older items of furniture, look out for the charming little "grand-mother" clock of about 1695 on the stair landing. Meissen and Nymphenburg ware as well as English pieces are among a fine **porcelain collection**. Also kept in the house, and perhaps its crowning glory, is the **Benton Fletcher Collection of Musical Instruments**, which comprises mainly early keyboard instruments.

Concerts are performed in the house in summer. A Shakespeare play is staged in the delightful walled garden every July.

FLEET STREET

EC4. Map 10F13-14. Tube: Aldwych, Temple, Blackfriars, St Paul's.

Continuing from the STRAND toward the CITY, Fleet Street, named after the small river that now flows unseen beneath its sidewalks, is famous as the home of British journalism, although no major newspapers now have offices in the "street of shame" itself, having decamped to DOCK-LANDS and elsewhere.

Fleet Street begins at Temple Bar, the western limit of the City. Walking eastward, **Prince Henry's Room**, on the right opposite Chancery Lane, predates the Great Fire of 1666 and has a superb Jacobean enriched plaster ceiling. The gateways to the TEMPLE on the right date from the 17thC. On the left, **St Dunstan's in the West** is a fine example of an early Victorian church in the Gothic style; it incorporates an extraordinary clock with giants striking bells (1671) and a statue of Elizabeth (1586). **El Vino's** wine bar on the right (see NIGHTLIFE, page 252) is famous for providing newspapermen with liquid inspiration.

Farther along on the left (in Wine Office Court) is the **Cheshire Cheese**, an ancient pub frequented by Dr. Johnson and Boswell. Soon after comes the unusually ugly ex-*Daily Telegraph* building of 1928, followed by the ex-*Daily Express* building of 1931, aggressively modern with its entirely plain, shiny black facade and with a superb Art Deco entrance hall. Toward the end of Fleet Street, the wonderful wedding-cake spire of **St Bride's** is visible on the right. Built to Wren's design in 1701-3, it is the tallest and one of the most elaborate of his spires.

FLORENCE NIGHTINGALE MUSEUM
2 Lambeth Palace Rd., SE1 ☎*(071) 620-0374. Map 18I12* 🚆 ⚅ 🍴 *Open Tues-Sun 10am-4pm. Tube: Waterloo, Westminster.*

This museum (found beneath the Nightingale School, on the site of St Thomas' hospital), which celebrates the life and work of Britain's most famous nurse, "the Lady with the Lamp," is designed very much in the modern idiom. The museum displays Florence Nightingale's prized possessions as well as artifacts from the Crimea War and the early days of nursing. There is also an audiovisual program, plus the slightly pointless re-creation of a ward at Scutari and of Nightingale's living room, and a resource center, where people can see her own books and other archive material.

GEFFRYE MUSEUM 🏛
Kingsland Rd., E2 ☎*(071) 739-8368. Map 20C5* 📷 🍴 *Open Tues-Sat 10am-5pm; Sun, bank holiday Mon 2-5pm. Tube: Old Street.*

Shoreditch, in the East End, was traditionally the home of the furniture industry, and this museum was opened in 1914 not only to pay tribute to that past, but also to provide models for local craftsmen of the 20thC. The buildings are interesting enough, with a fine set of almshouses built in 1715 at the bequest of Sir Robert Geffrye, a former Lord Mayor whose statue stands over the door of the central block containing the chapel. The collection is imaginatively arranged as a series of rooms representing different periods, and household items and pictures give a lived-in feeling. Look out for the fine chimneypiece in the Elizabethan room and the splendidly fussy Victorian parlor.

GEOLOGICAL MUSEUM
Now renamed the **Earth Galleries** and subsumed into the NATURAL HISTORY MUSEUM.

GRAND UNION CANAL
Built during the late 18th and early 19thC, the canal linked London and the English Midlands. See REGENT'S CANAL.

GRAY'S INN 🏛
High Holborn, WC1 ☎*(071) 405-8164. Map 10E12. Tube: Chancery Lane.*

This ancient society of lawyers, one of the four INNS OF COURT, has occupied this site since the 14thC. **South Square**, the first quadrangle encountered, has one old set of chambers (no.1), dating from 1685. Opposite is the hall, badly burned but accurately restored. The fine carved late 16thC **screen** perhaps formed a backdrop to the first performance of Shakespeare's *Comedy of Errors* here in 1594. In the center of South Sq. is a modern **statue of Francis Bacon** (1561-1626), the great Elizabethan statesman and scholar, one of the Inn's most distinguished former members.

Beyond the hall is **Gray's Inn Square**, full of the calm grandeur of legal London; at the s end is the frequently restored and curiously characterless chapel. More appealing is **Field Court**, with no.2, a most attractive house of about 1780, and the dignified wrought-iron gates of 1723 that lead to the gardens. Designed in formal style by Francis Bacon himself, the **gardens** are the best of the Inns of Court, with a grand central walkway flanked by huge plane trees.

GREENWICH

Greenwich brings the ocean to London, even today when its role in the affairs of an island seafaring race is largely historic and commemorative. Wren, Hawksmoor and Vanbrugh all contributed to London's most spectacular architectural complex. See LONDON'S DISTRICTS, page 77; the entry includes a map.

GUILDHALL 血 ☆

Aldermanbury, EC2 ☎(071) 606-3030 ("Keeper's Office"). Map 11E15 🔲
& ✗ by appointment. Open Mon-Sat 10am-5pm; Sun May-Sept 10am-5pm (check first). Tube: Bank, St Paul's, Mansion House.

Although hidden away in its own yard in the CITY, the Guildhall has been parliament and palace for the Corporation of the City of London for almost 1,000 years. The present facade is not the one that would have greeted the powerful medieval Lord Mayors such as Dick Whittington; it was constructed in 1788-89 to the design of George Dance, an attractive but bizarre mélange of 18thC Gothic ideas. But the entrance porch dates from the 15thC building, as do parts of the **Great Hall**. The most entertaining of the statues inside are the giants Gog and Magog, new versions of old mythical figures. Below, in the large 15thC crypt, Purbeck marble columns support a vaulted roof.

The **Guildhall Library**, in an unremarkable new building on the w side, houses a sumptuous collection of books, leaflets and manuscripts giving an absorbing and unparalleled view of London. This building also houses the oldest **Clock Museum** in the world: the Collection of the Worshipful Company of Clockmakers. On show are many of the Company's 500 magnificent watches, 50 clocks and 30 marine chronometers. A French watch allegedly once owned by Mary Queen of Scots, with a large silver case in the shape of a skull, an astronomical clock said to have belonged to Sir Isaac Newton, a deck watch that accompanied Capt. George Vancouver aboard *Discovery,* and a recently acquired Earnshaw Chronometer, are also displayed.

GUINNESS WORLD OF RECORDS

Trocadero, Piccadilly Circus, W1 ☎(071) 439-7331. Map 9G10 🔲 💻 ✸
Open daily 10am-10pm. Tube: Piccadilly Circus.

From the first displays showing models of the tallest, heaviest and the shortest humans right through to the end, the visitor will be amazed by the superlatives displayed in this exhibition, which brings to life the world-famous *Guinness Book of Records*. Some of the more unusual achievements are shown on video or with models, and include sword-swallowing, stilt-walking, domino-toppling, and guzzling (a revolting sight). The animal world has its records too, and Noah is shown gathering animals for the ark, including the largest primate, tallest land animal, and bird with the largest wingspan. Scientific and structural records are shown by means of video screens and models. Farther on, an impressive array of computers enables the visitor to look up any sporting record, from grayhound racing to the long jump.

Downstairs the world of entertainment offers few surprises, with Bing Crosby, Elvis Presley and the Beatles still among the musical world's greatest stars. The final section unashamedly plugs Britain by showing great British achievements and occasions, ranging from the Spinning Jenny to the Trooping of the Colour.

HAM HOUSE 血 ☆

Ham St., Richmond ☎(081) 940-1950. Map 19D3. Closed for refurbishment until early 1994. Tube (or train from Waterloo) to Richmond.

One of several great mansions bordering the Thames to the W of London near HAMPTON COURT, this is unique in preserving virtually intact a grand Baroque interior of the 17thC. It was built in 1610 in conventional Jacobean style, but mostly its present appearance comes from the occupancy of Elizabeth Dysart, wife of the Duke of Lauderdale, a minister of Charles II. In the 1670s she remodeled the house in the grandest style of the period.

Behind the high-ceilinged entrance hall is the **Marble Dining Room**, perfectly proportioned and facing centrally down the formal garden. Upstairs were the grand reception rooms and state bedrooms, reached by a massive staircase, carved in the 1630s with pierced reliefs of trophies. One bedroom was originally decorated for Charles II's queen. You can also see the library, several closets (or private rooms) and the fine **North Drawing Room**, with marble fireplace, rich wall hangings and gilded chairs. Most spectacular is the **Long Gallery**, with rich dark and gilded paneling and superb furniture. There is a good collection of miniatures on display in one room, including works by the masters of the genre, Hilliard, Oliver and Cooper. Rabbits, strung up ready for the pot, and crusty pies can be glimpsed through a door in the restored period **kitchen**.

HAMPSTEAD

A meandering hill "village" adjoins a great wild heath just four miles N of Central London. Across Hampstead Heath is the neighboring "village" of HIGHGATE. See LONDON'S DISTRICTS, page 80.

HAMPTON COURT PALACE 血 ★

East Molesey, Surrey ☎(081) 977-8441. Map 19D3 ▨ ◀€ ዼ ⚑ Ⅹ May-Sept Mon-Sat 🍴 Open mid-Mar to mid-Oct Mon 10.15am-6pm, Tues-Sun 9.30am-6pm; mid-Oct to mid-Mar Mon 10.15am-4.30pm, Tues-Sun 9.30am-4.30pm. Train to Hampton Court from Waterloo.

This riverside palace, to the W of London, is not only the apotheosis of the great English Tudor style of architecture, but incorporates a grand Baroque palace designed by Wren. This dual character reflects its two periods of building, with only three patrons playing a significant part: Henry VIII's powerful Chancellor Cardinal Wolsey, the man who personified the zenith of Church and State power; Henry himself; and, over a century later, the joint monarchs William and Mary. Queen Victoria, who much preferred Windsor Castle as a Thameside home, opened it to the public in 1838. A tragic fire in 1986 devastated some private apartments, plus the King's Audience Chamber, the King's Drawing Room, Bedroom, Dressing Room and Writing Closet, and the Cartoon Gallery, all of which are now beautifully restored and reopened to the public.

The main entrance to the palace is through the mid-18thC **Trophy Gates** and along a walk that runs parallel to the river toward the West Front. The balancing projecting wings of Wolsey's magnificent gatehouse offer a regular and impressive aspect. Inset into the walls are roundels with relief busts of Roman emperors, bought as a set by Wolsey in 1521 from the Italian artist Giovanni da Maiano.

Henry VIII enriched the gatehouse with a superb oriel window with his coat of arms over the door, and also built the moat and bridge. The latter now has fine stone **heraldic beasts** along its parapet brought from the garden. Through the gate is **Base Court**, the first of Wolsey's quadrangles, a peaceful space surrounded by domestic buildings of mellow red brick decorated with diamond patterning.

At the far end is **Anne Boleyn's Gateway** (1540), built in Tudor red brick by Wolsey but later named after Henry's queen whose introduction, at the expense of Catherine of Aragon, Wolsey had to arrange with Rome. Her emblem, a falcon, is on the tracery decorating the vaulted roof beneath the arch, together with the monograms H and A. The arch leads through to **Clock Court**, with, above the belfried gate, a fabulously complex **astronomical clock** of 1540, by Nicholas Oursian. To the s side is a Classical colonnade, added by Wren.

Anne Boleyn's Gateway

To enter the **State Apartments** is to move on to a different age — the walls and ceilings of the King's Staircase are decorated with exuberant frescoes, with gods and heroes of the ancient world swirling illusionistically through Corinthian columns. They were painted after 1700 by an Italian artist, Antonio Verrio. Next comes a huge **Guard Chamber**, its walls decorated with 3,000 pistols, muskets and swords. A door from here leads into some of the rooms of Wolsey's palace, with 16thC linen-fold paneling.

The **Cumberland Suite** shows a different, 18thC, taste: regal pomp gives way to elegant comfort. An important collection of paintings, largely from the Italian High Renaissance, includes Titian, Tintoretto, Correggio, Raphael and Duccio; look out for the chilly gloss of Parmigianino's *Minerva*. Other schools of painting are also to be seen: Brueghel's *Massacre of the Innocents* and Cranach's lovely *Judgment of Paris* stand out. There are also works by Holbein, an artist associated closely with the Tudors. There are splendid views across the park and on to **Fountain Court**, a first glimpse of Wren's superb architecture in pink brick and white stone.

Before emerging, three rooms of special interest are encountered, all dating from the Tudor period. The small **Wolsey's Closet**, probably the cardinal's study, has paneled walls, a finely wrought ceiling of timber and plaster, and recently discovered paintings from the 16thC. The **chapel**, also built by Wolsey, is then seen from the Royal Pew; it has an elaborate ceiling added by Henry VIII, with pendants carved in the form of angels. The reredos was designed by Wren and its marvelously carved plant forms are the work of Grinling Gibbons. As a suitable climax, there is Henry VIII's **Great Hall** of 1531-36, hung with contemporary Flemish tapestries and boasting a superb **hammerbeam roof**.

Smaller rooms that help make the place come alive are the newly restored and authentically equipped **kitchens** and Henry VIII's **wine cellar**. In the **Great Kitchen** is the re-creation of the lavish feast of St John the Baptist, thrown by Henry VIII for his court on Midsummer's Day 1542. A fire burns in the fireplace, a wild boar turns slowly on a spit, and tables are piled high with delicacies such as red deer pasties and baked carp.

Emerging into Clock Court, an arch at the opposite end leads through to Fountain Court past the **Queen's Staircase**. Here Wren's bold but harmonious use of the contrast between stone and brick can be seen to dramatic effect from the cloister along the little courtyard. Another arch leads through to the center of the **East Front** and the lake, **Long Water**.

All around are spectacular **gardens** in various styles, some sunken and enclosed, other broad and open, some in the Tudor "knot" pattern, others with great avenues of trees. Note the 200-year-old **vine** in its special greenhouse (its stem is 78 inches thick), which produces 600 bunches of grapes yearly, and the famous **maze**, dating in its present form from 1714. The Chestnut Avenue, more than a mile long, flowers spectacularly in May.

HIGHGATE

North of Central London, the twin "village" of HAMPSTEAD lies across the Heath and enjoys spectacular views across the city. **Highgate Cemetery** strikes a romantic note. See LONDON'S DISTRICTS, page 81.

HOGARTH'S HOUSE

Hogarth Lane, W4 ☎(081) 994-6757. Map 20C4 ▣ Open Apr-Aug, last 2 weeks Sept, Mon, Wed-Sat 11am-6pm, Sun 2-6pm; Oct to early Dec, Jan-Mar Mon, Wed-Sat 11am-4pm, Sun 2-4pm. Closed first 2 weeks Sept, last 3 weeks Dec. Tube: Chiswick Park, Turnham Green.

The painter William Hogarth (1697-1764) was an urban artist, and only lived in the delightful riverside village of CHISWICK in the summer. The house that he occupied from 1749-64 is now stranded between industrial buildings on the noisy Great West Rd. Inside the pretty, old buildings, however, a quieter atmosphere prevails, providing an ironic background to the fine selection of Hogarth's bustling, sarcastic and sometimes scurrilous engravings. The house also contains some contemporary furniture, and the artist himself is buried in the nearby village churchyard.

HOLLAND HOUSE AND PARK
Map 5H1. Tube: Holland Park.
Although Holland House has hardly survived, its park retains the elegance of its prime. Narrow paths wind among mature woods; peacocks and other ornamental birds roam in a large enclosure; a formal flower garden, with a traditional pattern of box hedges, is decorated with statues; music drifts from the **Orangery** in summer; and the soothing sound of a waterfall heralds the park's most recent addition, a tranquil, well-designed **Japanese Garden**.

The bombs of 1941 destroyed most of the house and now only the E wing stands complete, with its attractive Dutch gabled roof line. There is also a marvelous arched **loggia**, with strangely checkered carvings and fleur-de-lys crenelations. The Classical **gateway** (1629) was designed by Inigo Jones.

HORSE GUARDS PARADE ⅏
Map 9H11. Tube: Westminster.
The Horse Guards of Whitehall is a curiously jumbled Classical building of the mid-18thC, all arches, pediments and separate wings. Troopers of the Household Cavalry will be seen mounting guard in resplendent uniforms astride their equally well-groomed horses (see CALENDAR OF EVENTS, page 56, for times of **Changing the Guard**). The large parade ground beyond the central arch sees the great **Trooping the Colour** ceremony in June (see ROYAL LONDON, page 32 and CALENDAR OF EVENTS, page 53); past the Guards' Memorial, it leads into ST JAMES'S PARK. State buildings surround the other three sides.

Looking back from the park, the **Old Admiralty** is on the left, an ugly brick and stone extravaganza of 1894-95; to the right of the Horse Guards is the more dignified **Scottish Office**, actually a fine mid-18thC house; and farther right are the **Treasury** and the rear of no.10 DOWNING STREET.

HYDE PARK
Map 6G-H ◄≡ *Tube: Marble Arch, Hyde Park Corner, Lancaster Gate.*
From the middle of the largest open space in London, formed by Hyde Park and Kensington Gardens, you see nothing but wooded, rolling grassland, punctuated only by the lake known as the **Serpentine**, made in 1730. **Rotten Row**, along the southern edge, was *the* place to parade in the 18th-19thC, and is still used by horseback riders, although sadly it has lost its trees to Dutch Elm disease.

In the SE, at Hyde Park Corner, is APSLEY HOUSE and a graceful screen that once formed an entrance to the park's carriageway. A little to the N, there is an absurd statue of Achilles, made in 1822 from captured French cannons. Much better is *Rima* by Jacob Epstein (1922), near the Hudson Bird Sanctuary in the center of the park. On the NE side is SPEAKERS' CORNER.

IMPERIAL WAR MUSEUM ☆

*Lambeth Rd., SE11 ☎(071) 416-5000. Map **18**J13 ▣ ♿ ✗ by appointment ▣ ✱ Open daily 10am-6pm. Tube: Lambeth North.*

"Lest we forget," the Imperial War Museum was established soon after the end of World War I to preserve the relics and memory of that terrible conflict. Since then its terms of reference have been expanded and today it is essentially the museum of 20thC British warfare (the period pre-1914 is covered by the ARMY MUSEUM).

The museum's Lambeth building used to be the central range of the Bethlem Royal Hospital, built in 1812-15, which was appropriately perhaps an asylum for the insane, successor to the notorious "Bedlam" in the City. The present building's large dome was added in 1846; the place was converted into a museum in 1936. In 1989 it reopened to widespread acclaim, after major redevelopment, and is now one of London's best presented museums.

The huge main exhibition hall (created by infilling a courtyard) houses machines of war, including a German V2 rocket, a Polaris nuclear missile, an extraordinary Italian human torpedo and the M3A3 Grant tank used by Montgomery at El Alamein. Suspended in the atrium are six famous aircraft, notably a Sopwith Camel and a Battle of Britain Spitfire. More exhibits, such as the cramped cockpit of a Handley Page Halifax bomber, which you can enter, are on show on upper-level viewing platforms. Up again are galleries devoted to the museum's important collection of 20thC war art. A gallery on the ground floor is dominated by John Singer Sargent's harrowing *Gassed;* another shows temporary exhibitions.

But the crux of this revitalized museum is its exhibition of **20thC warfare**, divided into First, Inter-, Second and Post-War. Thematically arranged, the exhibits have been brought to life by the use of audiovisual techniques, employing film and sound to add depth to the historic objects on display. Only the crowd-pulling yet mildly disappointing Blitz Experience is too much of a gimmick.

INNS OF COURT

All barristers must belong to one of these institutions (many work from their dignified ancient buildings): GRAY'S INN, LINCOLN'S INN, and the Middle and Inner TEMPLE.

THE IVEAGH BEQUEST

An important collection of paintings in KENWOOD HOUSE.

DR. JOHNSON'S HOUSE

*17 Gough Sq., EC4 ☎(071) 353-3745. Map **10**F13 ▣ Open Mon-Sat: May-Sept 11am-5.30pm; Oct-April 11am-5pm. Tube: Blackfriars, Temple, Chancery Lane.*

In this substantial terraced house, dating from about 1700, Dr. Samuel Johnson lived from 1748-59. This man of letters *par excellence* was the center of a whole literary world that flocked to see him here and in the nearby **Cheshire Cheese** (see PUBS, page 240) in FLEET STREET. In the large gabled attic, he and his six assistants worked on the celebrated *Dictionary.* Sadly, little can be seen of the house's original contents, but a few chairs and tables do give some idea of its historic atmosphere. Pictures and memorabilia give a picture of literary life in 18thC London. Look out for a first-edition copy of the *Dictionary*, and Johnson's will.

KEATS' HOUSE

Keats Grove, NW3 ☎*(071) 435-2062. Map 20C4* ▣ *✗ for groups by appointment. Open Apr-Oct: Mon-Fri 10am-1pm, 2-6pm (Nov-Mar Mon-Fri 1-5pm); Sat 10am-1pm, 2-5pm; Sun 2-5pm. Tube: Hampstead, Belsize Park.*

The Romantic poet John Keats (1795-1821) was already in the grip of tuberculosis when, in 1820, he left the house in HAMPSTEAD where he had spent his two most productive years to journey to Italy, where he died ten months later. Nevertheless, the house is a monument to his happiness and the rural seclusion that inspired *Ode to a Nightingale* and other poems. It was then split into two cottage homes sharing a garden; in the other lived Fanny Brawne, with whom Keats fell famously and poetically in love. The engagement ring she wore until her own death is part of the memorial collection, as are Keats' manuscripts and annotated books, and letters to and from such friends as Shelley.

KENSINGTON

Prosperous and predominantly residential, the inner district of Kensington incorporates South Kensington and its famous museums. See LONDON'S DISTRICTS, page 82.

KENSINGTON PALACE 🏛

Kensington Gdns., W8 ☎*(071) 937-9561. Map 5H3* ▣ ■ *in Orangery. Open Apr-Sept Mon-Sat 9am-4.45pm, Sun 11am-4.45pm; Oct-Mar Mon-Sat 9am-4.15pm, Sun 11am-4.15pm. Tube: High Street Kensington, Queensway.*

Kensington Palace was first made a royal residence when it was bought by William and Mary in 1689. The house had large grounds, which now form **Kensington Gardens** (see WALK 4, page 95), and was next to the expanse of HYDE PARK. Sir Christopher Wren was instructed to enlarge the palace and, apart from further work in the 1720s, most of what is seen was built under his supervision. It is a simple building, around three courts, and surprisingly unpretentious for a royal palace. Perhaps the most striking building is the **Orangery** of 1704, a little to the NE, probably designed by Nicholas Hawksmoor.

The interior is mostly private but the State Apartments can be visited. Some of the rooms are largely as Wren left them; others were made grander by William Kent in the 1720s. Kent's own Baroque paintings adorn several walls and ceilings, most notably in the **King's Staircase**, the **King's Gallery** and **King's Drawing Room**. One of the most attractive rooms is the **Queen's Bedroom**, sumptuously but intimately decorated, with fine 17thC furniture including the bed made for James II's queen. Look out particularly for the fine carving by Grinling Gibbons, Wren's carver, over the fireplace in the Presence Chamber, enhanced by Kent's "Etruscan" ceiling, and also the wind vane above the fire in the King's Gallery.

There is an interesting display of paintings of and exhibits from the Great Exhibition of 1851 in the **Council Chamber**. Several good paintings are on display in addition to the fine furniture: most notable is Van Dyck's seductive *Cupid and Psyche* (★), but look for Artemisia Gentileschi's powerful *Self-portrait,* an important work by a woman artist.

On the ground floor, the **Court Dress Collection** was opened in 1984. A unique display of court dress and army uniforms from 1750 to the 1950s, it also includes Princess Diana's wedding dress.

The royal tradition is kept up by the Prince and Princess of Wales, who have their London home here.

KENWOOD HOUSE (The Iveagh Bequest) 🏛 ★
Hampstead Lane, NW3 ☎*(081) 348-1286. Map* **20***C4* 🖭 ⛆ 🎑
✗ *by appointment* ◖ *Open daily mid-Mar to Sept 10am-6pm; Oct to mid-Mar 10am-4pm. Tube: Highgate.*

After a short walk through old and well-established woods, on HAMPSTEAD Heath, the exquisite 18thC mansion comes into view, with Robert Adam's superb Classical facade flanked harmoniously by wings containing the orangery and library. Adam was commissioned to adapt an old Stuart house in 1766 by the first Earl of Mansfield. The result was some of the Scottish architect's finest work, including the South Front, with its decorated pilasters and the stucco portico that forms the main entrance. Several Adam details survive; the **library** is outstanding. The room was intended for "receiving company" as well as housing books, and this explains its splendor.

Kenwood was saved from the hands of speculative builders in 1925 when the first Earl of Iveagh (Edward Cecil Guinness, of brewing fame) bought the house. He died only two years later, leaving the house, a sizeable bequest and a collection of pictures to the people of London. Apart from the library, the house is now laid out as an art gallery.

English 18thC painting is best represented, with excellent examples of Gainsborough and Reynolds; Gainsborough's sumptuous *Mary, Countess Howe* is a masterpiece of the artist's elegant later style. Kenwood's real stars, however, are Dutch paintings, with fine examples by Cuyp and Van de Velde. Linger over Vermeer's *Guitar Player* and, supreme, Rembrandt's *Self-portrait* of c.1663. Other notable artists represented include Van Dyck, Guardi, Boucher and Turner.

In summer, concerts are given by the lake (see PERFORMING ARTS, page 248). Dr. Johnson's summerhouse was moved here in 1968.

KEW
The village is grouped around Kew Green, the archetype of an English country village. But the main reason for an expedition is to visit the world-famous ROYAL BOTANIC GARDENS. See LONDON'S DISTRICTS, page 83.

LAMBETH PALACE 血
SE1 ☎*(071) 928-8282. Map **18**J12. Open only to organized groups reserving in advance: apply in writing to the Bursar. Tube: Lambeth North.*
In the possession of the Archbishops of Canterbury since 1197, Lambeth Palace grew into prominence as the Primate's residence in the later Middle Ages. In 1547, Thomas Cranmer wrote the English Prayer Book here, but caused great controversy by eating meat during Lent in the Great Hall. The superb red-brick **gatehouse** dates from 1495, and next to it stands the 15thC tower of the now deconsecrated church of St Mary-at-Lambeth. Beyond the walls can be seen the Classical stonework decorating the **hall**, rebuilt after the Civil War.

St Mary-at-Lambeth has been taken over by the **Museum of Garden History**, where a replica of a 17thC knot garden has been laid out in the former churchyard (▣ ▣ *open early Mar to mid-Dec Mon-Fri 11am-3pm, Sun 10.30am-5pm).*

LANCASTER HOUSE 血
Stable Yard, The Mall, SW1 ☎*(071) 839-3488. Map **8**H9. Closed to the public. Tube: Green Park.*
Previously known as York House and Stafford House, according to the aristocrat in residence, Lancaster House (begun in 1820) is the most westerly of the palaces of THE MALL, with its facades overlooking Green Park to the w and ST JAMES'S PARK to the s. Benjamin Wyatt designed the exterior in cool Bath stone with massive and severe Classical porticos similar to his APSLEY HOUSE, together with the imposing stairwell. Charles Barry, who took over in 1838, completed the interior in a much more grandiose and highly decorated Baroque style. Paintings by Veronese and Guercino, brought to the house to decorate ceilings of the antechamber and gallery, conform to this rich taste.

LAW COURTS
The popular name for the fine Victorian Gothic ROYAL COURTS OF JUSTICE on the STRAND.

LEIGHTON HOUSE 血
12 Holland Park Rd., W14 ☎*(071) 602-3316. Map **20**C4* ▣ *Open Mon-Sat 11am-5.30pm. Tube: High Street Kensington.*
Looking like one of several plain red-brick houses in a street once favored by successful artists, Leighton House contains a remarkable

surprise. Lord Leighton was the most famous of Victorian artists and, in building his house from 1865, he gave vent to his taste for the exotic, creating a rich interior in Moorish style. It is fantasy, a harem in London. The highlight is the **Arab Hall**, with its two stories culminating in a dome, and its walls covered with rich 13th-17thC Islamic tiles. Interesting Victorian paintings on show include works by Leighton himself and Edward Burne-Jones.

LINCOLN'S INN ▥ ★
☎(071) 405-1393. Map **10**E12 ▣ **Courtyards** open Mon-Fri 9am-8pm; **chapel** and **gardens** open Mon-Fri 12.30-2.30pm; to see **Old Hall** and **Great Hall** apply to the Treasury. Tube: Holborn, Chancery Lane.

This most unspoiled of the INNS OF COURT was founded in the 14thC. The best way in is from Chancery Lane, through a gatehouse (with the original gates) of 1518 and the Tudor red-brick **Old Buildings** (before 1520). Opposite the gate is the **Old Hall** (1490-92), which contains an uncharacteristically serious painting by Hogarth and a fine wooden roof. On the N side of the court is the **chapel**, dating from about 1619-23, standing on an open undercroft of Gothic vaulting with rich ribbing. Its high-backed boxed pews, and its stained-glass windows of numerous coats of arms of treasurers dating back to the 17thC, contribute to a deep serenity.

To the SW is **New Square**, not originally built as part of the Inn but a large and remarkably well-preserved square of about 1685-97; its dignified brick houses, with decoration restricted to the open pediments above the doors, enclose a splendid lawn. To the S is a gateway of 1697 leading into Carey St.

The northern part of the Inn includes the great bulk of **Stone Buildings** of 1774-80, with a severe Classical facade on the W side; the large sundial on this wall is dated 1794. Opposite are the Inn's attractive private gardens, together with the impressive Victorian brick Gothic **library** and **New Hall**. Beyond these lie the open spaces of **Lincoln's Inn Fields**, one of London's largest public squares.

LLOYD'S BUILDING
Richard Rogers' astonishing glass, steel and concrete insurance headquarters, in the CITY, is described in LONDON'S DISTRICTS, page 68.

LONDON BRIDGE
Map **12**G16. Tube: Monument, London Bridge.

London's *raison d'être*, one might call it — the Romans discovered that this was the farthest downstream they could easily cross the river, and built their town accordingly. In fact, their wooden bridge was almost certainly a little to the E of the present structure, but survived with periodic reconstructions until the medieval stone bridge appeared in 1176-1209. This stood for more than 500 years, encrusted with houses, shops, even chapels, and the famous iron spikes where traitors' heads were displayed. Eventually, all its buildings were removed and the bridge modernized in about 1749, at the same time as London's second bridge was built at Westminster. A new bridge, now moved to an amusement park in Arizona, was built in 1825-31. The present structure of three arches dates from 1967-73.

There are several attractions grouped around the vicinity of London Bridge. Collectively they are known as LONDON BRIDGE CITY.

LONDON BRIDGE CITY
London Bridge, SE1. Map 12G16. Tube: Monument, London Bridge.
You might arrive at this group of tourist attractions by tube, visit whichever sights you want, eat and shop in **Hay's Galleria**, with its giant kinetic sculpture, *Navigators*, and depart by River Bus from London Bridge Pier. Sights grouped between LONDON BRIDGE and TOWER BRIDGE include HMS BELFAST, SPACE ADVENTURE, the LONDON DUNGEON and SOUTHWARK CATHEDRAL. Just across London Bridge is Butlers Wharf and the DESIGN MUSEUM.

St Mary Overy Dock, in the shadow of London Bridge, is home to the *Schooner Kathleen and May*, the last surviving 3-masted topsail schooner (▨ *open Mon-Fri Apr-Oct 10am-5pm, Nov-Mar 10am-4pm*). Nearby is the **Clink Prison** *(1 Clink St., map 11 G15 ▨ open daily 10am-8pm)*, a permanent exhibition that tells the story of the original Clink Prison and bishops' licensed brothels, and includes an armory *(not for children)*. Well worth a visit, although not for the faint-hearted, is the fascinating but chilling early 19thC **Operating Theatre and Herb Garret** of St Thomas' and Guy's hospitals, discovered in the 1950s *(Old St Thomas' Hospital, 9a St Thomas' St., SE1 ☎ (071) 955-4791, map 12H16 ▨ open Mon, Wed, Fri 12.30-4pm; other times, by appointment)*.

LONDON CANAL MUSEUM
12-13 New Wharf Rd., N1 ☎(071) 713-0836. Map 4B12 ▨ Open Tues-Sun 10am-4.30pm. Tube: King's Cross.
In 1858 Carlo Gatti, an Italian Swiss restauranteur and ice-cream maker, established an ice business on this site, digging two huge wells beneath the building in which to store the ice. In the days before refrigeration, ice was imported in bulk from Norway, and then transported by barge along the Regent's Canal. The London Canal Museum, opened in 1992, looks at the old ice trade (one of the ice pits is still visible) and its demise around the turn of the century, when the pits fell into disuse, filling up with earth and rubbish, and at London canals in general. It focuses on the development of the canals, particularly REGENT'S CANAL, the people who lived and worked on them, wildlife, and canal boats. Barges were horse-drawn, and stables for the delivery horses still exist at the ice house.

LONDON DUNGEON
34 Tooley St., SE1 ☎(071) 403-0606. Map 12G16 ▨ & ▣ Open daily: Apr-Sept 10am-5.30pm; Oct-Mar 10am-4.30pm. Tube: London Bridge.
Enjoying the London Dungeon requires a special sense of humor — and a strong stomach. Its location in a series of dark, damp vaults under railway arches has been carefully chosen to foster discomfort,

and is ideally suited to its exhibits on the "darker side of British history." The vaults echo to the recorded sounds of screams and moans, and even the rumble of the occasional passing train. The ancient British heroine Boadicea, for example, is shown thrusting a blood-smeared spear into the throat of a gurgling victim, and in another set piece, *The Fire of London,* ingenious special effects create the illusion of being in Pudding Lane engulfed by flames. Robespierre sentences the nobility to death and heads roll at St-Lazare prison in the newest exhibition, a re-creation of the French Revolution, *The Theatre of the Guillotine.* Not for the faint-hearted.

LONDON, MUSEUM OF ★
150 London Wall, EC2 ☎(071) 600-3699. Map 11E15 ▧ & ■ ✦ Open Tues-Sat, bank holidays 10am-5.30pm; Sun noon-5.30pm. Tube: Barbican, Moorgate, St Paul's.

In a contemporary building on the corner of the BARBICAN, this museum traces the social history of London from prehistory to the present day in "social" manner. The museum possesses a substantial part of the stock of important archeological finds made in London, and is chronologically arranged so visitors follow a single winding course, with the two floors joined by a glass walkway.

Archeological finds from the **Stone, Bronze and Iron Ages**, most originating from sites in the Thames Valley to the w of London, are grouped in settings that show the purposes to which they were put by ancient people. Thus axe heads have been fitted with handles to show how they would have been used; and models and drawings reconstruct the appearance of prehistoric settlements and explain early hunting methods and agriculture.

Roman London is well represented in the museum and, as an added surprise, a carefully placed window looks down on one of the best-preserved parts of the Roman wall outside, with its medieval bastions. Inside, the display ranges from leather sandals to board games to the superb sculptures found buried in the floor of the Temple of Mithras discovered in 1954 during the construction of an office building in Queen Victoria St. The **head of Serapis** is particularly exquisite. A famous **mosaic floor** found in 1869 can be seen in a reconstructed room setting, with reproduction furniture showing the luxurious Roman way of life.

The displays of **Anglo-Saxon and medieval London** begin with the strange gravestone in the Viking Ringerike style, inscribed with runes dating from the 11thC. An excellent model of the original Tower of London shows it as a single stone tower surrounded by a wooden palisade. A model of old ST PAUL'S CATHEDRAL is even more impressive, and shows how the great Gothic cathedral must have been before its destruction in the Great Fire of 1666.

A Ming porcelain cup mounted on a silver-gilt stand and an exquisitely embroidered glove show the sophisticated tastes and superb workmanship of the **Tudor and Stuart** periods. Also noteworthy are a copper plate of c.1558, engraved with a contemporary map of London, and the Cheapside Hoard, a collection of 16thC jewelry.

In the Early Stuart Gallery, there is a striking new model of the **Rose Theatre** and a selection of artifacts found on the site. Politics now feature more prominently: the Civil War, Great Plague and Fire of London all receive ample attention. A darkened room with a large model graphically shows the progress of the fire; old London actually appears to disintegrate as you watch, with a commentary from Pepys' diary.

The exhibits from the 18th-20thC are even more varied, if more familiar, and the **Georgian** gallery has recently been completely renovated. **Shop fronts and interiors** are reconstructed, including a superb 18thC barber's, a 19thC pub, and an early broadcasting studio. There are some extraordinary barred doors from the notorious Newgate Gaol, an 1862 fire engine, and even an Art Deco elevator from Selfridges department store.

On a smaller scale, look out for some charming Victorian Christmas and Valentine cards and toys. But grandeur steals the show: the **Lord Mayor's Ceremonial Coach** (★) (1757), removed once a year for the Lord Mayor's Show, stands resplendent with its elaborate painted and gilt decoration.

LONDON TOY AND MODEL MUSEUM

21 Craven Hill, W2 ☎*(071) 262-7905. Map* **6F4** 🔄 ☮ ♣ *Open Mon-Sat 10am-4.30pm; Sun 11am-4pm. Tube: Paddington, Queensway.*

This remarkable museum appeals as much to adults as to the children for whom the exhibits were originally intended. Several of the toys on display can be activated by the touch of a button. Dolls, nursery toys, mechanical toys and a collection of model railway locomotives fill a warren of rooms. There is a double-decker bus, a carousel and a miniature railway, which children can ride on, in the small garden, and a "hands-on" video. Plans are afoot to redesign the museum to make it less cramped.

LONDON TRANSPORT MUSEUM

The Piazza, Covent Garden ☎*(071) 379-6344. Map* **9F11** 🔄 ♿ ♣ *Open daily 10am-5.15pm. Tube: Covent Garden.*

As part of the renovation of COVENT GARDEN, the Flower Market (1871-72) now houses a large number of historic public transport vehicles in its spacious galleries. This "hands-on" museum chronicles the history of the capital's transport, with illustrations, photographs, audiovisual displays, relics such as tickets and posters, and fine models of everything from the "wherries" that plied the river to electric trams. Children can press a button to operate an Underground elevator, sit in the driver's seat of a tram and a bus, and work the deadman's handle in a tube train.

The vehicles include a replica of the first omnibus of 1829, a development London copied from Paris, two late 19thC horse-drawn buses, with open-top decks, and early motor buses and trams, also with open tops and painted in the familiar fire-engine red of today. The tube engines and carriages go back to the 19thC, and there is a simulation of the Circle Line from the driver's point of view.

MADAME TUSSAUD'S ☆

Marylebone Rd., NW1 ☎*(071) 935-6861. Map 1D7* 📷 💺 ♣ *Open Mon-Fri 10am-5.30pm; Sat, Sun 9.30am-5.30pm. Tube: Baker Street.*

The redoubtable Madame Tussaud lived to be 89. Having begun her wax modeling in France with the aristocracy and royalty of the *ancien régime,* and having continued to work through the Revolution (the severed heads of king and queen as modeled by Madame can be seen in the museum's Chamber of Horrors), she came to England in 1802 and settled her waxwork museum in London in 1835. It is now linked to the PLANETARIUM.

The modern display combines the old and the new. A section at the start of the exhibition entitled *200 Years of Madame Tussaud's* displays the famous *Sleeping Beauty,* cast from one of Madame Tussaud's oldest molds, thought to have been made of Madame du Barry, Louis XV's mistress, with a mechanism that simulates breathing. The modern method of wax model-making is also explained here, showing how Jerry Hall was immortalized, and immortalizing her real-life model-maker in the process. To illustrate the technology of the 1990s, there is a small display showing how the animated figures now used in ROCK CIRCUS, Madame Tussaud's rock-and-pop outpost, are made, and there is promise of "walking" and "talking" figures in future exhibits.

Recent celebrities appear in the next room, the *Garden Party;* these range from Ian Botham and Luciano Pavarotti to Dame Edna Everage and Kylie Minogue. The following section features the supposedly less ephemeral "superstars" of the stage and screen, including Marilyn Monroe, Joan Collins and Michael Jackson. Downstairs, the *Grand Hall* features historical figures, ranging from Henry VIII and all his wives to Madame Tussaud herself. Contemporary figures include the present-day Royal Family and British Prime Minister and leaders of most countries, lined up with the more notable of their predecessors. Watch out for the occasional waxwork practical joke, such as the tourist asleep on a bench.

Nowhere are the visitors quieter than in the greatest draw of all, the **Chamber of Horrors**, which has among other terrors a reconstruction of the dark streets of Whitechapel where Jack the Ripper stalked.

THE MALL ☆

Map 9H10 ◀ *Tube: Charing Cross, Green Park.*

Whenever pomp and circumstance are on hand, the Mall is where the crowds gather. Originally laid out by Charles II in 1660-62 as a formal avenue through ST JAMES'S PARK, it is now a triumphal processional way leading from TRAFALGAR SQUARE to BUCKINGHAM PALACE. As such, it is largely the work of one man, Sir Aston Webb, between 1900-11.

Majestically lined with plane trees, it slopes gently but impressively down along the side of the park to the Victoria Memorial and Buckingham Palace facade, both also designed by Webb. Looking from Admiralty Arch, the first building on the right is **Carlton House Terrace**, built by John Nash in 1827-29 on the site of his earlier Carlton House, the great palace built for the Regent. Its two massive stucco facades are separated by the Duke of York Steps. The view is best from St James's Park — the balancing ranges, with their Corinthian colonnades, broad terraces at raised ground-floor level, and supporting dumpy Doric columns, are one of London's most exciting architectural views. On the s side of The Mall is the **Admiralty** of 1722-26 with the aggressively concrete Citadel next to it, a bold bombproof structure from World War II.

The rest of The Mall is surrounded by the park, but with the palaces that are scattered along its N side visible on the right. MARLBOROUGH HOUSE, of stone-dressed red brick, is followed by the complex making up ST JAMES'S PALACE and then the white stucco of **Clarence House**, built by Nash in 1825-27 for the Duke of Clarence, later William IV, and now the home of the Queen Mother. LANCASTER HOUSE follows, in more solemn yellow Bath stone.

The **Victoria Memorial** occupies a circus at the end of the avenue, a huge structure covered with elaborate sculpture of high quality in the florid Edwardian style. Queen Victoria's likeness faces up The Mall toward Admiralty Arch, topped by a gilded statue of *Victory*. The circus was laid out in 1900-1901 and the memorial built in 1911.

MANKIND, MUSEUM OF

6 Burlington Gdns., W1 ☎*(071) 437-2224. Map 8G9* 🔲 ♿ ♨ *Open Mon-Sat 10am-5pm; Sun 2.30-6pm. Tube: Piccadilly Circus, Green Park.*

The museum is the result of the recent upsurge of interest in non-European cultures. Since 1972 the British Museum's ethnographic collections have been based in this elaborate Victorian building, decorated with statues of British philosophers, built in 1866-67 as a part of London University. At present, the museum is organized as a series of temporary exhibitions on particular cultures or themes, but they achieve considerable depth of coverage.

The ethnographic collection is outstanding in African textiles, pottery and sculpture, American art from Plains Indians and those of the NW Coast, and Pre-Columbian Central and South America. From the Pacific Ocean, the collection has objects brought back in the 18thC by Captain Cook. From Indonesia come puppets, masks and other items collected by Sir Stamford Raffles in Java in the 19thC. A permanent exhibition of the museum's greatest treasures is kept in **Rm. 7**, including a life-sized skull carved from a solid piece of crystal from Mexico, a hauntingly beautiful object. **Rm. 5** provides an overview of the collection. Stunning Aztec turquoise mosaics in the forms of a skull-mask and double-headed serpent are shown in **Rm.1**.

MANSION HOUSE 🏛

Walbrook, EC4 ☎*(071) 626-2500. Map 12F16* 🔲 *Closed for refurbishment until late 1993. Tube: Bank.*

As if in reference to the ancient city-states, the residence of the Lord Mayor of London, symbol of the independence of the CITY, is Classical in character. It owes its Palladian simplicity to George Dance the Younger, who designed it in 1739-53. Its six giant columns support the only decoration, a pediment with sculptures representing the dignity and opulence of the City. But the interior is extremely ornate, with a series of state rooms leading back from the portico to the grand climax of the **Egyptian Hall** (Roman in style, despite its name).

The annual **Lord Mayor's Show**, which arrives here in November (see CALENDAR OF EVENTS, page 56), is the climax of a largely medieval system of government; during the year you can see here the liverymen, aldermen and sheriffs who choose the Lord Mayor, parading at various antiquated ceremonies. But their power is real — this is the only private residence in the kingdom with its own court and prison cells.

MARBLE ARCH
*Map **7**F7. Tube: Marble Arch.*
Now in the center of a major traffic island, the Marble Arch retains only part of the grandeur intended when John Nash built it in 1828 as the entrance to Buckingham Palace. Modeled on the Arch of Constantine in Rome, it was moved to its present site in 1851 when the palace was enlarged by Queen Victoria.

The traffic island was also the site of Tyburn Tree, London's traditional place of execution from the Middle Ages until 1783. A plaque marks the site of the permanent large triangular gallows where regular hangings, drawings and quarterings attracted big crowds. SPEAKERS' CORNER is close by on the corner of HYDE PARK.

MARBLE HILL HOUSE 血
*Richmond Rd., Twickenham ☎(081) 892-5115. Map **19**D3 ▣ ▣ in stable block. Open 10am-6pm Easter-Sept; 10am-4pm Sept-Easter. Tube: Richmond; or train to St Margarets from Waterloo.*
A house of elegant Palladian regularity, this fine riverside mansion w of London began life with some "irregular" occupants: it was built for George II's mistress, the Countess of Suffolk, in 1723-29, and then Mrs Fitzherbert, George IV's secret wife, lived here in the 1790s. Its stuccoed, pristinely white exterior has little decorative detail — the rear, garden side of the house is particularly impressive — and it stands in a fine open park.

The interior is quite beautiful, with a series of lovely rooms culminating in the splendid **Countess of Suffolk's Bedroom**, with Corinthian columns framing the alcove intended for the bed. Some attractive furniture has been put back into the house, together with a number of interesting paintings, including good copies of Van Dyck portraits. The **Lazenby Collection**, displayed on the second floor, includes Chinese paintings on mirrors, furniture and pottery. Flanking one side of the park is the exquisite **Montpelier Row**, a perfect terrace of 1720.

MARLBOROUGH HOUSE 血
*Pall Mall, SW1 ☎(071) 839-3411. Map **9**H10. Currently closed for restoration. Tube: Green Park, St James's.*
This red-brick house with bold stone dressings, the finest of the palaces bordering ST JAMES'S PARK, was built by Sir Christopher Wren for the Duke and Duchess of Marlborough in 1709-11, following the duke's series of victories over the French in the War of the Spanish

Succession, which also won him the enormous Blenheim Palace near Oxford (see EXCURSIONS, page 297).

Various additions were made in the 18th-19thC, notably the attic stories, but Wren's powerful conception can still be appreciated when viewed from the park. The entrance on the PALL MALL side is curiously unimpressive. Most of the present decoration is 19thC, but a series of original murals depicts Marlborough's battles, and the ceiling of the Blenheim Saloon is decorated with Gentileschi's series painted for the Queen's House at GREENWICH in 1636. The house now serves as the Commonwealth Centre.

MARYLEBONE

Although now somewhat anonymous in character, the former village of St Marylebone contains numerous historic points of interest and, on its northern perimeter on Marylebone Rd., MADAME TUSSAUD'S and the PLANETARIUM. See LONDON'S DISTRICTS, page 84.

MAYFAIR

Most exclusive of London's "villages," Mayfair smells of wealth, sometimes conspicuous, at other times (this being England, after all) discreet. But it also encompasses, in areas such as **Shepherd Market**, places of considerable charm. See LONDON'S DISTRICTS, page 84.

MOMI

An acronym: see MOVING IMAGE, MUSEUM OF THE.

THE MONUMENT 血 ☆

Monument St., EC3 ☎*(071) 626-2717. Map 12G16* 🔳 ◁€ *Open Apr-Sept Mon-Fri 9am-5.40pm, Sat, Sun 2-5.40pm; Oct-Mar Mon-Sat 9am-3.40pm. Tube: Monument.*

Deprived of its commanding appearance by the many modern buildings that surround it, the Monument, on its little hill close to the river, nevertheless retains the Baroque drama of its conception. Designed by Wren, and built in 1671, it commemorates the Great Fire of London that began on September 2, 1666 in the bakery in nearby Pudding Lane. A relief on the base plinth shows Charles II in Roman dress protecting the citizens of London; the original inscription unjustly blamed the disaster on a Catholic plot. A giant Doric column, 202 feet high, contains 311 steps up to a balcony and gilded urn. It is a stiff climb but worth it for the view.

MOVING IMAGE, MUSEUM OF THE (MOMI)

South Bank, Waterloo, SE1 ☎*(071) 928-3535. Map 10G12* 🔳 ⅙ 🖃 ✦ *Open daily 10am-5pm. Tube: Waterloo, Embankment.*

In a striking glass and steel building adjoining the National Film Theatre, MOMI traces the history of film, television and video from early Javanese shadow theater, by way of a magic lantern show, complete with sound effects, and exhibits such as the zoetrope or "wheel of life," and early cine cameras to the sophisticated techniques and special effects of today, used in movies like *Superman*. Expect lots of visitor participation, from operating a praxinoscope to reading the television news, a section devoted to animation, and a horde of fascinating memorabilia, including Charlie Chaplin's hat and cane, Fred Astaire's trousers, a towering model of Frankenstein's monster, and Kylie's wedding dress from *Neighbours*. There are also programs of special temporary exhibitions and of regular screenings in its own cinema.

NATIONAL ARMY MUSEUM
Royal Hospital Rd., SW3 ☎(071) 730-0717. Map 15L7 ☒ ◁€ ₺ ⊀ for groups only, by appointment through Education Dept ■ Open daily 10am-5.30pm. Tube: Sloane Square.

Opened in 1971 in a new building close to the ROYAL HOSPITAL, CHELSEA, the National Army Museum brings together objects from several older collections. The weapons gallery, called **Arms and the Army**, is a self-contained exhibition displaying a comprehensive collection of small arms used by the British Army from the 17thC to the present day; the use of both edged weapons and handguns, from muskets to self-loading rifles, is expertly explained. A new permanent exhibition called **The Road to Waterloo** covers the Peninsular Wars, leading up to the great battle, includes the skeleton of Napoleon's horse, Wellington's battlefield telescope, the saw used to amputate the Earl of Uxbridge's leg, and has as its centerpiece a huge model of the Battle of Waterloo (made shortly afterwards and never before displayed).

Flanders to Falklands tells the story from 1914 to the Falklands War, with life-sized displays, audiovisuals and dioramas. There is a fine **uniform gallery**, a picture gallery, a reading room, a small display on Baden-Powell, founder of the scouting movement, and another on the Gulf War, called **The Aftermath of Battle**. An exciting new exhibition on **Burma** features a life-like reconstruction of a POW camp with a walk-on booby-trap bridge.

NATIONAL GALLERY ★
Trafalgar Sq., WC2 ☎(071) 839-3321. Map 9G11 ☒ ₺ ✖ ⊀ ═ ■ Open Mon-Sat 10am-6pm; Sun 2-6pm. Tube: Charing Cross, Leicester Square.

Now possessing more than 2,200 pictures, the National Gallery is one of the world's finest collections of art. Few rivals can boast such a comprehensive account of Western art, and the way the paintings are shown provides a model for other great national collections: they are clean, clearly labeled, well-lit and given adequate space.

This freshness of approach accords with the National Gallery's relative youth. When most European capital cities already had public collections, in 1823, the threat of the sale of John Julius Angerstein's great collection to William of Orange forced a tight-fisted parliament to produce the money to found a national collection. Angerstein's pictures were bought for £57,000 and housed with other bequests in Angerstein's house in Pall Mall. By 1832, with the collection growing, a larger building was needed. It was designed by William Wilkins and completed in 1838, stretching the full length of the N side of TRAFALGAR SQUARE, but was never the imposing

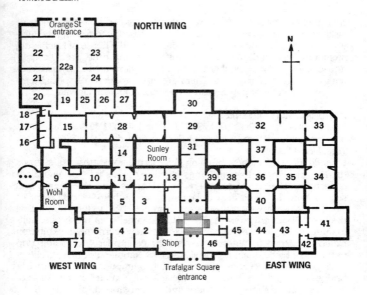

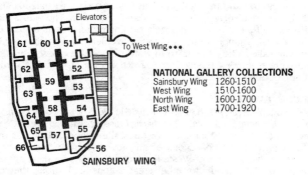

NATIONAL GALLERY COLLECTIONS

Sainsbury Wing	1260-1510
West Wing	1510-1600
North Wing	1600-1700
East Wing	1700-1920

building intended, and has been much expanded since. The northern extension (1975) is superbly functional, with excellent hanging space.

After much controversy over the choice of architect, Robert Venturi's **Sainsbury Wing**, an extension to the w of the gallery, finally opened in spring 1991, provides airy, well-designed new galleries to house the Early Renaissance collection of Italian and Northern works painted between 1260 and 1510, together with galleries for temporary exhibitions, a large auditorium for lectures, a computerized information room, conference rooms, and a shop and restaurant.

The collection of pictures has expanded steadily, its character changing in accordance with the taste of the different periods of acquisition. After some exploratory Italian forays in the 1840s, the pioneering director, Sir Charles Eastlake, purchased many early Italian works from 1855-65, when these pictures were little known. As a result the gallery has a collection of Italian art unequaled outside Italy. In 1861, Queen Victoria gave 20 German and Flemish pictures in memory of her husband Albert; this inspired a new round of acquisitions, resulting in a magnificent group of Dutch and Flemish works. In the 20thC, attempts have been made to strengthen the French collection.

British art is the specialty of the TATE GALLERY, as is modern art, but the National Gallery does have some fine 18thC British masterpieces. There are also outstanding Spanish works.

Since 1946, the National Gallery has had a conservation department and has been in the forefront in applying science to the care and restoration of paintings. Many National Gallery paintings can now be seen in the most beautiful condition, cleaned of dirt or past overpainting. Temporary exhibitions, usually in the **Sunley Rm.**, and now too in the Sainsbury Wing, bring in pictures on loan to develop particular themes.

The collection is exhibited chronologically starting in the Sainsbury Wing, where the first rooms contain Leonardo's famous and beautiful black-chalk *Cartoon* (★), restored after gunfire damage in 1987 and now beautifully displayed in a separate area off **Rm. 51**, and his mysterious *Virgin of the Rocks* (★). In the early Italian section is the *Wilton Diptych* (☆), actually not Italian but put here because of its early date (c. 1395). Probably French, it shows the English monarch Richard II being presented to the Virgin and Child, with saints and angels in attendance.

The other glowing medieval icons are further testimony to faith as well as artistic genius; Duccio's **Maestà altarpiece panels** (★) from Siena Cathedral are outstanding. Then comes the transition to a more realistic style. Lorenzo Monaco's *Coronation of the Virgin* is in the graceful International Gothic style, while Masaccio's innovative *Virgin and Child* (★) has the spiritual gravity and solid forms of the Renaissance, thrown into relief by Paolo Uccello's *Battle of San Romano* with its unsuccessful attempt at realistic perspective. The Renaissance can also be seen emerging in Botticelli's early *Adoration of the Magi* and his *Venus and Mars* (☆), admired for the purity of its line, and in Piero della Francesca's *Baptism of Christ*.

The Renaissance was not such an Italian monopoly as is sometimes supposed. The carefully observed naturalism of northern painters greatly influenced their Italian counterparts; the Dutch and Flemish collection illustrates this better than anywhere else in the world. The most famous work here is Jan Van Eyck's *Arnolfini Marriage* (★), full of realistic but symbolic detail. In the same room is a beautiful jewel-like altarpiece by Memlinc showing the *Virgin and Child with Saints and Donors* and a tiny but fine panel painting by Robert Campin, *The Virgin and Child in an Interior*.

Don't miss the **Micro Gallery** on the first floor, a room devoted to computers, from which you can glean information about any school of painting, individual work or artist you choose.

In the **West Wing** of the main building, the superb collection of Italian Renaissance art from 1510-1600 unfolds. Among too many highlights to list are: Michelangelo's unfinished *Entombment,* a rare easel picture; Raphael's *Pope Julius* (★), which was only recently discovered to be the original among several versions around the world; Correggio's charming *Mercury instructing Cupid before Venus* (☆) and Bronzino's *Allegory,* with its chilly eroticism and obscure subject. One of the original pictures bought from the Angerstein collection is Sebastiano del Piombo's huge *Raising of Lazarus,* for which the artist received guidance from Michelangelo. Of the Venetian works, Titian's breathtaking *Bacchus and Ariadne* (★) is ablaze with color and movement. Other important Venetian works include Tintoretto's dramatic *Origin of the Milky Way* and Veronese's *Family of Darius before Alexander.* All the greatest masters of the period are here.

As a reminder of the range of the northern painters, look out for a wonderfully grotesque *Adoration of the Kings* by Brueghel, and a weird rocky *Landscape with St Jerome* by Patenier. The German and Early Netherlandish pictures are less numerous, but include some important masterpieces such as Dürer's **portrait of his father**, the exquisite little Altdorfer *Landscape with a Footbridge* and Cranach's *Charity,* a charming early nude.

Holbein's *Ambassadors* (☆) was probably the most important picture painted in England in the Tudor period; as a reminder of frailty, the oblique shape in the bottom left corner shows itself to be a skull when viewed from the right angle. It hangs with the National Gallery's latest acquisition, *A Lady with a Squirrel and a Starling,* an arresting, well-preserved painting, where the sitter is shown against an intense blue background, pierced with fig branches. Holbein's skill is evident in the wicked gleam in the squirrel's eye and in the folds of the sitter's shawl.

Paintings of the 17thC are displayed in the **North Wing**, and the Dutch 17thC, the golden age of painting in the Netherlands, is strongly represented: there are several Rembrandts, including the extraordinary *Self-portrait* (★) of 1640, with its sad dignity, and the quietly powerful *Woman Bathing.* There are two Vermeers, of which the *Woman Standing at a Virginal* (☆) best demonstrates the sense of intimate silence that the artist generates. There are many fine landscapes, of which the most famous is the *Avenue at Middelharnis* (☆) by Hobbema, and also scenes of everyday life, with the restrained, precise style of the Dutch school.

The art of the 17thC in Flanders was altogether grander, dominated by Rubens and Van Dyck. Major works by both can be seen, including Van Dyck's *Equestrian Portrait of Charles I.* Rubens' joyous, colorful *Judgment of Paris* contrasts with the dignity of his landscape *Château de Steen* (☆).

French painting of the 17thC is shown with emphasis on Poussin and Claude, both of whom have been assiduously collected in Britain. Poussin's *Bacchanalian Revel* demonstrates his influential cool Classicism. Claude's mysterious and peaceful landscapes are altogether more approachable; the *Enchanted Castle* (☆) has an astonishing, dreamlike quality, achieved largely by superb mastery of light.

There are a small number of Spanish pictures of extraordinary quality. El Greco's *Christ driving the Traders from the Temple* (about 1600) is the finest of several paintings by this remarkable artist. From the later 17thC there is Velázquez's sensual tour-de-force, *The Rokeby Venus* (★), and a portrait of *Philip IV*, together with Zurbarán's *St Francis*, showing the dark religious passion so characteristic of Spanish art.

Rm 32 is occupied by 17thC Italian works. Caravaggio's *Supper at Emmaus* (★) shows the artist's revolutionary use of naturalism in religious art. The disciples are seen as real working people with coarse clothes — look at the drama even in the hands.

The **East Wing** is home to paintings from 1700-1920. The French 18thC is poorly represented by National Gallery standards; even so it offers Watteau's *La Gamme d'Amour*, Chardin's acute *Young Schoolmistress* (★), Boucher's *Landscape with a Watermill* and David's *Portrait of Jacobus Blauw*. A popular acquisition, found on the ceiling of a London house, is Tiepolo's *Allegory with Venus and Time*, full of light and air.

The gallery's strongest English period is the 18th-19thC. Outstanding works include Hogarth's satirical *Marriage à la Mode* paintings, the basis for the more famous series of engravings, and magnificent examples of that period's two best genres, Gainsborough's portrait of *Mr and Mrs Andrews* (★) and Constable's landscape *The Hay Wain* (★). Turner opens new vistas with this magical *Rain, Steam and Speed* (★) and *The Fighting Téméraire*.

The last rooms house the gallery's acquisitions charting the emergence of modern art. There are several good Goyas, including the famous portrait of the *Duke of Wellington*, and an impressive collection of Impressionist works, including Renoir's *Les Parapluies* (★) (periodically moved to Dublin) and Monet's stunning *Water-lilies* (☆), as well as Degas' *Beach Scene*. Van Gogh's intense, dynamic *Sunflowers* introduces a Post-Impressionist collection that also includes Seurat's *Bathers, Asnières* (★), works by Gauguin and Klimt's *Hermione Gallia*.

NATIONAL MARITIME MUSEUM
The Classical **Queen's House** at GREENWICH forms the greatest seafaring museum in the world. See LONDON'S DISTRICTS, pages 78-79.

NATIONAL PORTRAIT GALLERY ☆
2 St Martin's Pl., WC2 ☎*(071) 306-0055. Map 9G11* 🖼 &. 🖼 *with flash* ✗ *in Aug. Open Mon-Fri 10am-5pm; Sat 10am-6pm; Sun 2-6pm. Tube: Charing Cross.*
Opened in 1859 as a kind of "national pantheon," the emphasis from the start was on the *subjects* of the pictures rather than on artists or on art for art's sake. Nevertheless, the effort to obtain the best portraits has meant that the collection has acquired many fine paintings and drawings. Since 1968, photographs have been systematically included and caricatures are now also accepted. In fact, the emphasis on history gives great coherence to the exhibition, which is arranged chronologically with relevant background material, such as a pictorial essay on the Industrial Revolution. The excellent **temporary exhibitions** *(some 🖼)* also expand on themes or figures starting from the portraits.

The present buildings were constructed next to the NATIONAL GALLERY in 1896 and extended in the 1930s. The collection begins at the top (several flights of stairs have to be climbed), with a room devoted to **medieval** portraits. Portraits in a modern sense were not produced in the Middle Ages, so the images are few in number; a copy of the fine representation of *Richard II* in Westminster Abbey dominates.

Portraits became common from the **Tudor** period, and perhaps the most interesting examples in the whole collection come from this early section. There is an excellent version of *Henry VII* by Michel Sittow of 1505, painted for the Holy Roman Emperor when Henry was seeking his daughter's hand in marriage. Perhaps the finest work of all is Holbein's magnificent cartoon for a lost fresco at Whitehall Palace showing *Henry VIII with his Father Henry VII* (★). There is an exquisite full-length image of *Lady Jane Grey,* who was executed in 1554 after she had become queen at the age of 17. Several portraits of Elizabeth I are in the incredibly detailed style of the period, with the queen decked out in rich clothes and encrusted with jewelry. A portrait of *William Shakespeare,* dated about 1610, is the only one with any claim to authenticity.

The gallery continues through the **Jacobean and Stuart** periods, with the increasing formality of the court painters, giving way to the more lively images of the **18thC**. Figures from the arts and sciences increase gradually in proportion to the political and military leaders. This was another golden age of English portraiture; look for Hogarth's *Self-portrait,* several works by Gainsborough and Reynolds, and pictures of *Dr. Johnson* and *Charles James Fox.* A fine unfinished portrait of *Nelson* by Sir William Beechey and a romantic *Byron* in Greek costume show the greater concentration on the individual that becomes apparent in much of the **19thC** work. Royalty, however, is still shown in highly idealized fashion: *Victoria and Albert* sculpted in the costume of ancient Saxons is the most amusing example.

The portraits from the last years of the 19thC and later are varied in style. The **20thC** galleries are organized on two levels: the second covers the years 1914-45, is divided into areas such as politics, science and the theater, and includes portraits of the Bloomsbury Group, *James Joyce, Noel Streatfeild,* superb studies of *Edith Sitwell* by Wyndham Lewis, and some fine bronze busts by Epstein. Royalty, however, is still idealized with due deference.

Portraits painted between 1945 and the present day are displayed in the galleries on the first level. Among them are *Sir David Wester* by David Hockney, *Elizabeth Taylor* by Andy Warhol, *Richard Rogers* by Sir Eduardo Paolozzi, the double portrait of *Sir David and Sir Richard Attenborough* by Ivy Smith, *Paul McCartney* by Humphrey Ocean, and a new photograph of *John Major.* Other recent acquisitions include portraits of *John Wilkes and his daughter* and *John Mortimer.*

NATIONAL THEATRE

It was long held to be an anomaly that the National Theatre, throughout its days under the directorship of Sir Laurence Olivier and Sir Peter Hall, had not been granted the "Royal" prefix since its foundation, in pointed contrast with the Royal Shakespeare Company. Although Buckingham Palace finally rectified that situation, Londoners continue doggedly to call the ROYAL NATIONAL THEATRE "the National."

NATURAL HISTORY MUSEUM 🏛 ★
Cromwell Rd., SW7 ☎*(071) 938-9123. Map* **14J5** 🚇 ♿ 🅿 ⚒ *Open Mon-Sat 10am-5.50pm; Sun 11-5.50pm. Tube: South Kensington.*

When the BRITISH MUSEUM was formed from Sir Hans Sloane's collections in 1753, a high proportion of material consisted of plant, animal and geological specimens. Appropriately, these categories grew at enormous speed (they still do), and in 1860 it was decided to split off the natural history collections.

Between 1873 and 1880 the present building was erected in South Kensington, with Alfred Waterhouse as architect. His creation is a cathedral to nature, a vast Romanesque construction with a central porch opening onto a great iron-roofed nave. Unlike a cathedral, however, it has two immensely long side wings creating an impressive facade along the Cromwell Rd. Once criticized as austere and heavy, cleaning has revealed the bright colors of the cream and blue terracotta tiling, and the countless relief details that cover the exterior — a fitting showcase for the treasures housed within.

In the 1970s, a new policy was adopted by which the museum created a series of self-contained exhibitions, rather than continue attempting to show all of its millions of specimens in old-fashioned cabinets. As part of a recent reorientation of the museum, this long-established section was named the **Life Galleries**. In 1989 the former Geological Museum became part of the Natural History Museum and is now known as the **Earth Galleries**. This is linked at ground-floor level to the Life Galleries by a corridor signed as the **Waterhouse Way**, which gives access to all parts of the ground floor and to elevators and staircases to other floors. All exhibition galleries are clearly numbered and signposted, and uniformed members of staff are available to help you find your way around the enormous collection.

The Life Galleries
At the main entrance, parts of an older, dramatic display have survived all the upheavals: the giant **Central Hall**, where a huge dinosaur skeleton towers over the visitor, absurd, terrifying, and in marked contrast to the stunning new exhibition to the left of the entrance, called *Dinosaurs.* Approached in darkness along a suspended skeletal walkway, past dinosaur skeletons and skulls, the first scene, and centerpiece of the display, is a grisly, life-like episode, where three deinonychus tear at the flesh of a huge tenontosaurus, which twitches in its death throes. All are computerized robotic dinosaurs, brilliant examples of Japanese technology. Fossil skeletons and eggs, realistic life-sized models, serrated teeth, stomach stones and thigh bones that can be touched, plus "hands-on" computer graphics and videos that breathe life into these extinct creatures and show their relationship to living animals, comprise the rest of the exhibition.

To the right side of the Central Hall is another of the museum's most recent displays, *Creepy Crawlies*. Arachnophobes beware: this exhibition contains a full-sized house crawling with spiders, termites, carpet beetles and other insects. Nearby is an ambitious new exhibition on global ecology, housed in a vast glass structure. Also on the ground floor is an exhibition of British birds arranged by habitat, and an exceptionally lively presentation on every aspect of human biology.

One of the museum's most effective sections, *Discovering Mammals,* traces the life-cycle of whales and other mammals through fascinating dioramas and interactive models. It also contains the vast skeletons and jawbones of the great mammals and a life-sized model of a blue whale. A monumental staircase leads from the Central Hall to the upper floor, where an exhibition traces the evolution of man. Another, on the origin of the species, covers Darwin's work with admirable thoroughness.

The traditional hall, devoted to minerals, rocks and gems, serves as an effective contrast to the newer exhibition techniques, and is notable for the incredible diversity and beauty of its specimens. There is an exciting **Discovery Centre** *(open Mon-Sat 10.30am-5pm, Sun 1.30-5pm)* in the basement, where children can stroke a rock python's skin or try their hand at beachcombing.

The Earth Galleries

The traditional displays upstairs on the regional geology of Britain and world economic mineralogy are of limited interest compared with the stunning exhibitions on the ground floor. Here, the collection of **gem-stones** includes some beautiful specimens, both crude and cut. There are also two adventurous exhibitions entitled *The Story of the Earth* and *Treasures of the Earth,* and two smaller exhibitions, *Britain before Man* and *British Fossils*. On the first floor, displayed on a structure resembling a real offshore platform, *Britain's Offshore Oil and Gas* tells the full story of hydrocarbons, from both geological and operational viewpoints.

NELSON'S COLUMN

One of the most famous symbols of London, in TRAFALGAR SQUARE.

OLD BAILEY (Central Criminal Court)

Old Bailey, EC4 ☎*(071) 248-3277. Map* **11**F14 📷 🌂 💺 *Open Mon-Fri 10.30am-1pm, 2-4pm. Tube: St Paul's.*

The Old Bailey's famous gilt figure of *Justice,* complete with scales and sword, looks down on a site with a grim history. The Central Criminal Court replaced Newgate Gaol, dating from the Middle Ages, for many years a place of execution and eventually the 19thC reformers' ultimate symbol of penal squalor. The current Portland stone building dates from 1900-7. Inside its heavy Baroque frame, justice can be seen to be done from the public galleries, but you will have to line up early when a major criminal case is being heard — the crowds of the Newgate gallows have their modern counterparts.

ORLEANS HOUSE GALLERY 🏛

Orleans Rd., Twickenham ☎*(081) 892-0221. Map* **19**D3 📷 ⟁ 🌂 *Open Apr-*

Sept Tues-Sat 1-5.30pm; Sun and bank holiday Mon 2-5.30pm; Oct-Mar Tues-Sat 1-4.30pm, Sun 2-4.30pm. Tube: Richmond; or train to St Margarets from Waterloo.

Although it takes its name from the Duc d'Orléans, later King Louis Philippe of France, who lived here in the early 19thC, this house in Twickenham, near Strawberry Hill, dates from 1710. Regrettably, much of it was demolished in the 1920s, but the superb **Octagon** survives amid attractive woodland. It was designed by James Gibbs in 1720. The interior is richly decorated with Baroque stucco work: heads of George II and Queen Caroline can be seen on medallions. An adjacent gallery is used for a continuous program of temporary exhibitions covering a wide variety of subjects, sometimes including the **Ionides Collection** of 18th and 19thC topographical English paintings, but it is not on permanent display. Nearby is MARBLE HILL HOUSE and the grander HAM HOUSE (which can be reached by ferry).

OSTERLEY PARK ⑂ ☆

Isleworth, Middlesex ☎(081) 560-3918. Map 19C3 ⊠ ⚍ in summer. Open Apr-Oct: Wed-Sat 1-5pm; Sun, bank hols 11am-5pm (closed Good Fri). Tube: Osterley.

Already one of the finest country houses in the London area, Osterley gained more prestige after being completely refurbished between 1761 and 1782 by the great Scottish architect Robert Adam for the banker Francis Child, who was trying to emulate the other country houses nearby, such as SYON HOUSE. It still contains much of the furniture he designed for it, and is set in a large area of parkland, with lakes and woods, and an attractive brick stable block to one side, probably containing the buildings of the medieval manor house that originally stood on the site.

Adam's building is a large hollow square, with corner turrets and a great portico that opens to the central courtyard. This unusual scheme for the 18thC was dictated by the existing house, built on a magnificent scale by Sir Thomas Gresham (the wealthy founder of the Royal Exchange) in the 1570s. By Adam's time it had fallen into decay, and he completed the covering of the exterior with an entirely new skin of brick, and built the portico.

At the end of the courtyard the main door leads into the hall, the centerpiece to the whole design, beautifully decorated in Adam's Classical style, with white stucco reliefs on a gray background. At either end, copies of ancient Roman statues inhabit niches within apses. Note how the ceiling decoration is echoed in the marble floor pattern. Beyond the hall is the great **gallery**, a plainer room probably designed a few years earlier by Sir William Chambers.

The remaining rooms open to the public are by Adam, who even designed the door handles and friezes. The **Drawing Room** has a ceiling of extraordinary richness and contains fine original commodes. The **Tapestry Room** is hung with works from the French royal Gobelins workshop, in extravagant pink with Rococo designs from paintings by Boucher. The **State Bedchamber** has an absurdly elaborate four-poster bed. Plainer, but just as effective, is the **Etruscan Dressing Room**, with delicately painted walls.

PALL MALL
Map 9H9-G11. Tube: Charing Cross, Green Park.

When ST JAMES'S PALACE became the main royal residence in the 17thC, this avenue quickly became established as its main route into London and the site for the favorite Stuart game of palle-maille, resembling modern croquet. The street is now the most important in ST JAMES'S, famous for the traditional gentlemen's clubs that line its s side, a sequence of stern Classical buildings reflecting the importance of tradition in this most conservative of areas.

From the TRAFALGAR SQUARE end, Pall Mall becomes interesting beyond the soaring glass slab of **New Zealand House** (1957-63). This is at the bottom end of John Nash's great city planning scheme of the early 19thC that stretched up Regent St. and incorporated REGENT'S PARK. Just past New Zealand House will be found the delightful little **Opera House Arcade**, built by Nash in 1816-18 and the first in London; note the splendid wrought-iron lamps. At Waterloo Pl. the **Duke of York's Column**, built by Benjamin Wyatt in 1831-34, can be seen in front of the steps of **Carlton House Terrace**.

Back on Pall Mall, the gentlemen's clubs begin. These uniquely English and very exclusive institutions, designed to provide the gentleman with a "country house" haven to which he can retire in the city, thrive unchanged, still offering, in various mixes, snoozing, business talk and witty conversation, and hallowed peace. The corners with Waterloo Pl. are occupied by the impressive **Institute of Directors**, designed in 1827 by Nash (formerly the United Services Club), and the **Athenaeum** of 1828-30, traditionally the clergy's and academics' club. Farther along in a dignified terrace come the **Travellers' Club** (1829-32), a Victorian version of Italian Renaissance for those who have been more than 1,000 miles from London; the **Reform Club** (1837-41), a Liberal political grouping formed after the 1832 Reform Act; and then more modern buildings, including the **Royal Automobile Club** of 1908-11. Beyond comes **Schomberg House**, built in 1698, a tall brick structure with projecting wings.

Other clubs are the **Army and Navy** on the N side, jokingly known as "The Rag" after the toughness of its meat; the **Oxford and Cambridge** on the S; and the **Junior Carlton**, a stepping-stone for the famous senior Tory (Conservative) club. Pall Mall ends with the lower, brick buildings of ST JAMES'S PALACE, past the entrance to MARLBOROUGH HOUSE.

PARLIAMENT, HOUSES OF
See WESTMINSTER, PALACE OF for the home of the "mother of parliaments."

THE PERCIVAL DAVID FOUNDATION OF CHINESE ART
53 Gordon Sq., WC1 ☎*(071) 387-3909. Map 3D10* 🖾 ⚐ *with flash. Open Mon-Fri 10.30am-5pm. Tube: Euston.*

Gathered with scholarly precision by Sir Percival David and given by him to the University in 1951, this remarkably rich collection of Chinese ceramics of the 10th-19thC is aptly sited in BLOOMSBURY, surrounded by intellectual and artistic endeavor. Unfortunately, the presentation of the collection is rather too scholarly, and the great numbers of bowls, jars, vases and figurines grouped in display cabinets by classification tend to cancel each other out by their profusion. But the individual items are of great beauty, glazed in rich and subtle colors. Temporary exhibitions are displayed on the ground floor.

PICCADILLY
Map 8G8-9G10. Tube: Piccadilly Circus, Green Park.
As the famous "hub of Empire," **Piccadilly Circus** put on a pretty poor show a few years ago, with a motley collection of buildings covered in illuminated signs. But recently the TROCADERO, with its shops, restaurants and exhibitions, has brought a new sense of life, helped by the recently reopened **Criterion brasserie** (Victorian mosaics and tiles, next to the charming and newly restored **Criterion theater**), and the **London Pavilion,** a shopping and restaurant complex that includes ROCK CIRCUS.

The focus of the Circus is the **Shaftesbury Monument**, a statue and fountain of Eros (1893) around which international youth likes to gather while temporarily dropping out. Recently restored, it is now the center of a pedestrian mall, no longer marooned on its central island. It is always erroneously thought to be a statue to Love; in fact it was erected as a memorial to the great 19thC philanthropist Lord Shaftesbury.

Piccadilly itself, stretching W to Hyde Park Corner, is lined with imposing commercial buildings and famous shops: **Hatchard's** for books, **Simpson's** for clothes and **Fortnum and Mason** for anything expensive (see SHOPPING). And there are arcades of smart little shops, with the Piccadilly Arcade of 1909-10 to the S and the most attractive Burlington Arcade of 1815-19 to the N. Wren's ST JAMES'S, the **Ritz** (see HOTELS) and the hilly Green Park are of greatest interest on the S side; Burlington House (the ROYAL ACADEMY) on the N. By Hyde Park Corner is APSLEY HOUSE.

PLANETARIUM
Marylebone Rd., NW1 ☎(071) 486-1121. Map 1D7 ▦ ✗ ▣ ✦ "Starshows" every 40mins 10.40am-4.40pm. Tube: Baker Street.
Attached to MADAME TUSSAUD'S, the Planetarium's greater green copper dome is a striking landmark, providing convincing displays and "starshows" on astronomy. The highlight for all visitors is the moment they tip their heads back to gaze at the heavens projected on the dome above them.

To keep the crowds happy while they wait for the next show to start, a "space trail" has been created along the long ramp leading to the dome. Information about the planets is given by means of pictures from the Hubble Space Telescope, touch-sensitive video monitors and scale models. But it is the "starshow" — an interplanetary adventure narrated by well-known actors — that really counts.

POST OFFICE TOWER
What Londoners still tend to call the BRITISH TELECOM TOWER.

PUBLIC RECORD OFFICE MUSEUM Ⅲ
Chancery Lane, WC2 ☎*(081) 876-3444. Map 10F13* ⌷ *Open Mon-Fri 10am-5pm. Tube: Chancery Lane.*
Most of the public records are now kept at Kew, but in this successful example of Victorian Gothic official architecture, one room and a corridor are given over to a museum, boasting some remarkable treasures. Outstanding are the two volumes of the **Domesday Book**, the great survey of England carried out for William the Conqueror in 1086. Among later documents are a pipe roll of 1210-11, showing the account of the Sheriff of Nottingham, the enrolment of letters patent to William Penn, Collingwood's account of the death of Nelson, and the Assizes minute book, showing the conviction of the Tolpuddle Martyrs.

There is a display called the Human Dimension, documents and photographs relating to ordinary folk through the centuries, a small display of royal seals and an example of early Renaissance sculpture by Pietro Torrigiano: the recumbent figure of John Young, a Master of the Rolls (*d.* 1519), in a Classical architectural surround. It came from the Rolls Chapel, which once stood here. Note also the beautiful porcelain model of the chapel's original font, displayed in the corridor.

REGENT'S CANAL ★
Maps 1-6.
At the end of the 18thC, London was triumphantly linked to the industrial Midlands by canal, at the time the most efficient form of transport. The canal is still there, ignoring and largely hidden by the roads that have superseded it.

Its walks offer particularly interesting views of London not normally seen by visitors: the backs of houses, gardens rich and poor, crumbling industrial buildings of the 19thC, and the many details of the working canals themselves, such as brightly painted canal barges ("narrowboats"), locks, bridges, and tunnels. **Camden Lock**, with its restaurants, shops and craft studios and its brilliant weekend market (see SHOPPING, page 266), is a good place to start — you can take a boat trip (☎*(071) 482-2550)* or walk either to the W (REGENT'S PARK and **Little Venice**) or to the E (ST PANCRAS STATION and **Islington**). See also the LONDON CANAL MUSEUM.

REGENT'S PARK ★
Maps 1 & 2 ◈ *Tube: Regent's Park, Baker Street.*
Regency London was certainly sophisticated; and the legacy is one of the most impressive examples of town planning in the country. Marylebone Fields, a hunting preserve of Henry VIII's, reverted to the crown in 1809, and the Prince Regent's friend, John Nash, was put in charge of an ambitious scheme that would link it with Carlton House to the S via the new Regent St. Now Carlton House has gone, but the park retains much of the original plan.

It is approached from Portland Pl., leading into the elegant terraces of **Park Crescent** and **Park Square** (1812-23). To E and W around the flanks of the park stretch magnificent Classical terraces, mostly built in the 1820s;

Cumberland Terrace

to the w, the amazing length of **York Terrace** and, perhaps best of all, the imaginative, almost Oriental-looking **Sussex Place** with its octagonal domes. The dome motif is repeated in copper on the late 1970s **Mosque** nearby. On the E side of the park, **Chester Terrace** and **Cumberland Terrace** are ostentatiously grand, with their vast decorated porticos.

The park itself is attractively landscaped, with a massive straight **Broad Walk** continuing the line of Portland Pl. through the center. Two circular roads (the Inner and Outer Circles) carry road traffic; on the Inner Circle, **St John's Lodge** incorporates parts of a villa of about 1818. Here too is the marvelous **open-air theater** where superb productions of Shakespeare's plays can be enjoyed in summer months (see PERFORMING ARTS, page 251). There is a small lake in **Queen Mary's Gardens** within the Inner Circle, and a larger one with islands to the w. Across the N side is a branch of the GRAND UNION CANAL, nicely incorporated as part of Nash's plan, and the ZOO.

REGISTRY OF BIRTHS, DEATHS AND MARRIAGES
St Catherine's House, 10 Kingsway, WC2 ☎*(071) 242-0262. Map **10**F12* 🖂
🚻 *Open Mon-Fri 8.30am-4.30pm. Tube: Aldwych, Temple.*

With perseverance and a little money, it is possible to trace ancestry in England or Wales back to 1837, the date centralized registration of births, deaths and marriages began. To go further back, local records have to be consulted. The system is not difficult, but it is time-consuming, a factor that seems to discourage few people, for the offices are always busy. Simply look up the reference for yourself or an ancestor born in England or Wales (listed alphabetically by year) and order the birth certificates, which takes about two days. This will usually give the names, addresses and occupations of the parents. By searching for their marriage certificate or birth certificates it is possible to repeat the process back into history.

RICHMOND AND RICHMOND PARK
To the w of London, lying s of the Thames, this handsome riverside town is famed for its royal connections, most notably the adjoining 2,000 acres of rough, wooded heath that form **Richmond Park**. See LONDON'S DISTRICTS, pages 85-86.

ROCK CIRCUS
London Pavilion, Piccadilly Circus, W1 ☎*(071) 734-7203. Map **9**G10* 🖂 ✹
Open Sun, Mon, Wed, Thurs 11am-9pm; Tues noon-9pm; Fri, Sat 11am-10pm. Tube: Piccadilly.

Visitors don a headset and must prepare themselves for an onslaught of nostalgia at this outpost of Madame Tussaud's. Rock Circus presents the history of rock and pop music from Bill Haley to Michael Jackson through wax and "audio animatronic" figures, which move and perform golden oldies and more recent chart-toppers in an eerily lifelike way. The giants of rock and pop are all featured here, from Jerry Lee Lewis, Chuck Berry, Elvis, complete with a lip that really curls, the Beatles, Jimi Hendrix, the Rolling Stones, Eric Clapton, Elton John, Stevie Wonder and Tina Turner to Springsteen, Sting and Madonna.

ROYAL ACADEMY OF ARTS 🏛

Burlington House, Piccadilly, W1 ☎(071) 439-7438. Map 8G9 🚾 ⚑ 💺 Open daily 10am-5.30pm. Tube: Piccadilly Circus, Green Park.

Built as a mansion for the first Earl of Burlington in the newly developed Piccadilly area in about 1665, Burlington House was remodeled in 1717-20 in the elegant Palladian style. The third earl made this as celebrated a forum for the artists whose patron he became as his CHISWICK HOUSE; Pope, Arbuthnot, Gay, all often attended. Unfortunately, between 1868 and 1874 the profile of the Georgian house was obliterated by the rebuilding that marked its adoption by the Royal Academy of Arts. This new building is in the Victorian Renaissance style, with a screen along PICCADILLY opening onto a forecourt with a statue of Sir Joshua Reynolds in the center. Other learned societies occupy the buildings to the right and left.

The Royal Academy was founded in 1768, with Reynolds as its first and greatest president, to foster the arts of Britain. Except for a few decades after its foundation, however, the most interesting developments in British art have consistently taken place outside of, and even in opposition to, the dictates of the Royal Academy. This is still true: the Academy's free-for-all **Summer Exhibition** (see CALENDAR OF EVENTS, page 53) may be popular and enjoyable, but no one would claim that it does much to influence developments in art.

The modern academy consists of 70 academicians, the country's most successful establishment artists. Today, crucially, it hosts major loan exhibitions, always worth watching out for. In 1991 it held the phenomenally successful Monet exhibition, which attracted 7,000 visitors a day. In the same year the new **Sackler Galleries**, brilliantly designed by Sir Norman Foster to unite Burlington House with the Victorian building behind, opened to a colorful exhibition of Fauve paintings.

The academy has an important collection of works of art, many by academicians, who have always been obliged to donate one of their works to the academy. Paintings by Reynolds, Gainsborough, Constable and others are not on public display (except during special exhibitions). The decorative schemes of its grand interior include paintings by artists such as Benjamin West and Angelica Kauffmann (the entrance hall), and Marco Ricci. The academy's outstanding treasure is Michelangelo's beautiful relief tondo depicting the *Madonna and Child* (★).

ROYAL AIR FORCE MUSEUM, HENDON

Grahame Park Way, NW9 ☎(081) 205-2266. Map 20B4 🚾 ✦ 💺 Open daily 10am-6pm. Tube: Colindale.

The northern suburb of Hendon itself lays claim to the interest of aircraft enthusiasts: there was a pioneering flying school here before World War I, and it became one of the first aerodromes, staging regular air displays and becoming famous as the starting point for the first nonstop London-to-Paris flight in 1911.

The museum was opened in 1972 in an excellent modern building, which incorporates two historic World War I wooden hangars. Interesting displays trace the history of flight and show the development of the Royal Air Force, with its vital role in two world wars. But it is the aircraft themselves that take pride of place. They range from the Blériot XI, similar to that in which Louis Blériot made the first cross-channel flight in 1909, to the English Electric Lightning, capable of twice the speed of sound.

Famous World War I aircraft include a Sopwith Camel from Britain, a Caudron G3 of French design and a Hanriot HD1, which was used extensively by the Belgian Aviation Militaire. From World War II there is a Spitfire Mk1 that fought in the Battle of Britain, a Beaufighter, the only known Typhoon left in the world, and two new acquisitions, a Fairey Battle and a Focke Wulf Fw 190F-8/U1. Part of the museum's temporary exhibition in 1992 to mark the 50th anniversary of the USAAF in Britain has remained on permanent display. Postwar jet aircraft include the early Vampire and Gloster Meteor, the remarkable Canberra and, another addition, a Supermarine Swift, a mid-1950s jet fighter.

The splendid **Battle of Britain Hall** (▨) nearby contains a unique collection of British, German and Italian aircraft that fought in the great air battle of 1940. Also in the same complex is the vast new **Bomber Command Hall** (▨), with its impressive display of famous bomber aircraft including the Lancaster, Wellington, Mosquito and Vulcan.

ROYAL ALBERT HALL
See ALBERT MEMORIAL AND ROYAL ALBERT HALL.

ROYAL BOTANIC GARDENS (Kew Gardens) ★
Kew ☎(081) 940-1171. Map **19D3** ▨ Main **entrance** at Kew Green; entrance from tube station at Victoria Gate on Kew Rd.; entrance from riverside towpath at Brentford Gate ◀≡ ⚏ ♣ **Gardens** open daily early to late Jan, early Nov to Dec 9.30am-4pm; late Jan to early Mar, mid-Oct to early Nov 9.30am-5pm; early Mar to early Apr, early Sept to mid-Oct 9.30am-6pm; early Apr to early Sept, Mon-Sat 9.30am-6.30pm, Sun, bank hols 9.30am-8pm. **Glasshouses** open daily late Jan to early Nov 9.30am-4.30pm; early Nov to late Jan 9.30am-3.30pm (early Mar to mid-Oct Sun, bank hols 9.30am-5.30pm). **Galleries and museums** open daily late Jan to early Nov 9.30am-4.45pm; early Nov to late Jan 9.30am-3.45pm (early Mar to mid-Oct Sun, bank hols 9.30am-5.45pm). **Tube:** Kew Gardens. **Train** to Kew Bridge from Waterloo. **Exit** through Victoria Gate for tube; through Victoria Gate, Main Gate or Brentford Gate for British Rail; through Brentford Gate or Main Gate for Kew Pier; through Brentford Gate for car park. **Lavatories:** ladies and gents at Pavilion Restaurant, Woodland Glade, Cycad House, Cumberland Gate; ladies at Kew Palace; gents at the Orangery, Victoria Gate. **Distance** from Main Gate to Pagoda is 1 mile.
The full name of Kew Gardens — the Royal Botanic Gardens — comes

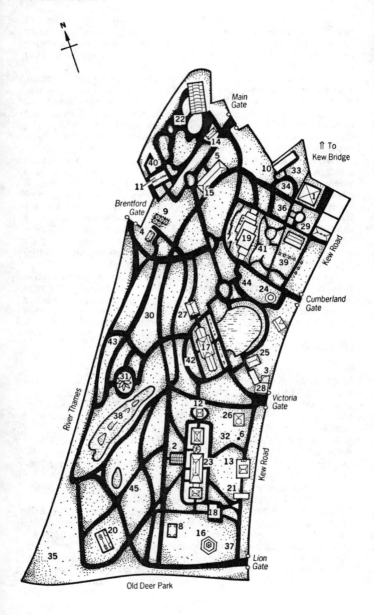

N

Main
Gate

⇑ To
Kew Bridge

22

14

5

40

10

33

34

11

15

Brentford
Gate

9

36

4

19

29

41

39

44

24

Cumberland
Gate

30

27

43

17

31

42

25

38

3

28

Victoria
Gate

12

26

32

6

2

23

13

45

21

18

20

8

16

37

35

Lion
Gate

Kew Road

River Thames

Old Deer Park

as a salutary reminder to those of us who are apt to be seduced by its supreme beauty and forget that it is a scientific institution. As such, it is unmatched, studying, classifying and cultivating a vast number of plants from all around the world.

Despite the devastation suffered in the storm that struck southern England in October 1987, and in a second in January 1990, Kew still boasts superb walks and dreamlike views. In spring it is sublime.

Kew Gardens was formed from the grounds of two royal residences: Richmond Lodge and the White House. George III united the two estates. From 1771-1820 Sir Joseph Banks, who had accompanied Captain Cook to the South Seas, extended the existing botanic garden (founded in 1759), sending young botanists all over the world in search of specimens.

With the help of Kew Gardens, breadfruit was introduced to the West Indies and rubber to the Malay Peninsula. In 1840, the gardens were handed over to the State and the first director was formally appointed in 1841. Further grants of land by the Crown in 1898 and 1904 took the total to more than 300 acres. Expansion continues even today, and as recently as 1990, a major exhibition area, housed in the **Sir Joseph Banks Building**, opened, using an innovative design that incorporates many energy-saving features.

KEW GARDENS: KEY TO NUMBERED PLAN

Buildings
1 Alpine House
2 Australian House
3 Campanile
4 Cycad House
5 Fern House
6 Flag Pole
7 Ice House
8 Japanese Gateway
9 Kew Bakery (refreshments)
10 Kew Gardens Gallery/Cambridge Cottage
11 Kew Palace
12 King William's Temple
13 Marianne North Gallery
14 Nash Conservatory
15 Orangery (shop/restaurant)
16 Pagoda
17 Palm House
18 Pavilion Restaurant
19 Princess of Wales Conservatory
20 Queen Charlotte's Cottage
21 Ruined Arch
22 Sir Joseph Banks Building

23 Temperate House
24 Temple of Aeolus
25 Temple of Arethusa
26 Temple of Bellona
27 Waterlily House
28 Visitor Centre

Garden features
29 Aquatic Garden
30 Azalea Garden
31 Bamboo Garden
32 Berberis Dell
33 Bulb Garden
34 Duke's Garden
35 Conservation Area
36 Grass Garden
37 Heather Garden
38 Lake
39 Order Beds and Rose Pergola
40 Queen's Garden
41 Rock Garden
42 Rose Garden
43 Rhododendron Dell
44 Woodland Garden
45 Woodland Glade

Begin at the main gates by Kew Green, and turn sharp left for the vast **Princess of Wales Conservatory**. It contains ten different habitats, from Namib Desert and mangrove swamp to cloud forest and tropical pools. Alternatively, proceed up the Broad Walk, which turns left at the Orangery, leading to the pond and Palm House, returning by smaller paths through flower-filled woodland, rock, grass and other gardens.

Not far from the main gates is the **Dutch House**, or **Kew Palace** (💀 *open Apr-Sept),* built in red brick with steep Dutch gables, by a wealthy merchant in 1631. To the rear is the **Queen's Garden**, an accurate reconstruction of a 17thC garden, with tightly-clipped hedges and aromatic herbs. Back at the Broad Walk, the refurbished **Orangery** (1761) contains a new carvery restaurant, cafeteria and shop.

Now bear right, away from the Broad Walk. The long Riverside Ave. here passes through cedar, plane and oak-planted woods. A detour left takes in the **rhododendron dell** (almost a crime to miss in late spring), the bamboo garden and azalea garden, with the beautiful lake to the s. Walk around the riverside for a fine view across the Thames to SYON HOUSE.

Farther sw are the grounds of **Queen Charlotte's Cottage** (💀), thatched in rustic style and built in the 1770s as a focal point for elaborate garden parties. It is now surrounded by an area left wild as natural habitat for native British plants and wildlife. To the e lies the **Japanese Gateway**, a fine replica erected in 1910 on a little hill, surrounded by pines and flowering azaleas. Farther e again is the 163-foot **Pagoda**, built in a more fanciful Oriental style in 1761-62, forming the focal point to one vista extending from the Palm House.

Pagoda Vista returns toward the entrance. On the way, take in the **Temperate House**, a large 19thC complex of greenhouses containing many fine specimens, with the **Marianne North Gallery** to the e, home of an extraordinary collection of 832 botanical paintings. A little farther N, mock temples and ruins survive from the 18thC garden layout.

The **Palm House** conservatorium (illustrated on page 26) then comes into view, a magnificent and graceful iron and glass construction of 1844-48 by Decimus Burton and Richard Turner. It contains a fabulous collection of tropical rainforest plants and, downstairs, a fascinating **Marine Display**, which has examples of seaweeds from all over the world. The recently refurbished **Waterlily House** is to the left as you emerge from the Palm House, and there is a brand-new visitor center and giftshop at the nearby Victoria Gate.

ROYAL COURTS OF JUSTICE 🏛

Strand, WC2 ☎*(071) 936-6000. Map 10F13* 🖾 ✍ ▬ *Open Mon-Fri 9.30am-4.30pm; courts open 10.30am-1pm, 2-4.30pm. Tube: Temple, Chancery Lane.*
Better known as the Law Courts, this extravagant complex in the STRAND, built by G.E. Street in 1874-82, houses the courts where important civil, as opposed to criminal, law cases are heard. Long despised as an example of Victorian plagiarism, the Early English Gothic buildings are now admired by many. Cleaning has helped, for the rich colors and intricate patterns in the stone can be appreciated. In addition, the Courts show a dignity suited to their purpose, and their complex ir-

regularity and inventive detail feast the eye. Inside too, the sheer scale of the **great hall** is quite as impressive.

ROYAL HOSPITAL, CHELSEA ▥ ☆

Royal Hospital Rd., SW3 ☎*(071) 730-0161. Map* **15L7** ▣ ◀€ ✗ **Grounds** *open Mon-Sat 10am-12.45pm and from 2pm; Sun open afternoons only. Closing times vary between 3.30pm and 8pm depending on time of year.* **Chapel and dining hall** *open Mon-Sat 10am-12pm, 2-4pm; Sun 2-4pm. Tube: Sloane Square.*
Amply surrounded by parkland and retaining all the dignity of its river-side setting, Wren's stately Royal Hospital, dating from 1682-92, is still a majestic sanctuary of calm, although now surrounded by CHELSEA. It was founded by Charles II in 1682 as a refuge for aged and disabled soldiers on the model of Louis XIV's Les Invalides in Paris. It now houses some 400 pensioners, including a dwindling number of World War I veterans, who can be seen around and about Chelsea in their old-fashioned scarlet or blue uniforms; and in May it hosts the **Chelsea Flower Show** (see CALENDAR OF EVENTS, page 53).

The best view is from the s, where an open courtyard looks down the extensive gardens toward the river. At the center of the courtyard is a statue of Charles II as a Roman emperor by Grinling Gibbons, Wren's master carver. The hospital is entirely symmetrical and quite plain, its red-brick facades embellished with minimal stonework. At the center of each block stands a tall white portico of four columns or pilasters, and the central block is capped by a graceful, spire-like lantern. The severely domed **vestibule**, lit by the lantern above, is entered through the portico in the courtyard.

To the right is the **chapel**, little altered since Wren's time. It has a fine carved reredos in dark wood, matching the organ gallery at the entrance end and, in the apse, a painting (about 1710-15) by Sebastiano and Marco Ricci, *Christ in Majesty,* a colorful burst of Baroque splendor.

The **Great Hall** occupies the corresponding space to the chapel on the other side of the vestibule. It is more solemn, with paneled walls and military standards hanging from the ceiling. At the far end, the dark and ponderous painting, *Charles II,* by Verrio and Cooke shows the king with mythological companions in front of the hospital buildings. A small **museum** in an eastern wing covers the hospital's history.

Tucked in between Royal Hospital and Chelsea Bridge Rds, **Royal Hospital Burial Ground** is an undiscovered treasure *(for admission ask at London Gate).* Among those buried here are William Hiseland, who lived to the ripe old age of 112, Fanny Burney's father, Charles, the hospital's organist, and two women who fought in the Crimean War and whose sex was only discovered when they were wounded.

For a tour by one of the charming and knowledgeable pensioners who act as guides, write to the Adjutant at the Royal Hospital, Chelsea. The address is Royal Hospital Bridge Rd., London SW1W 8PP.

ROYAL NATIONAL THEATRE ▥

Upper Ground, South Bank SE1 ☎*(071) 633-0880. Map* **10G13** ▧
✗ *backstage up to 5 times a day* ▣ ═ &. *Tube: Waterloo.*

It is a blessing that the institutionalization of the theater in London has not led to any stultifying subservience. The drama remains as true to its nature of subversiveness as when it was banished to the South Bank in the Middle Ages, and this component of the SOUTH BANK ARTS CENTRE created its own furor. The building itself, designed by Sir Denys Lasdun in 1970-75, is a prime example of the Brutal style, a lumpy abstract sculpture in concrete. But the interior is much more universally admired, with a superb intersection of horizontal and vertical planes creating a honeycomb of useful and interesting space. It has a decent restaurant, **Ovations** (☎ *(071) 928-3531* ▥).

See also THEATERS, page 250, where the building is illustrated.

ROYAL NAVAL COLLEGE

This masterpiece by Wren, Vanbrugh, Hawksmoor and other leading architects of their era dominates the Thames at GREENWICH. See LONDON'S DISTRICTS, pages 77-78.

ST BARTHOLOMEW-THE-GREAT ㎜ ★
Little Britain, EC1. Map 11E14. Tube: Barbican.
The churchyard through the 15thC gateway with the charming Tudor house on top used to be the nave of this, one of the oldest churches in London, founded in 1123. Now only the chancel and transepts remain with their 19thC refacing of flint and Portland stone. Inside, many original features survive. Huge columns in the **nave** support a Romanesque triforium, surmounted by a clerestory built in 1405 in Perpendicular Gothic style.

Beyond the altar is the much rebuilt **Lady Chapel**, dating back to 1335, where in 1725 Benjamin Franklin worked. At the w entrance, the massive crossing, which once supported a huge stone tower, can be seen. The present tower in brick is above the s aisle and dates from 1628. Five medieval bells are housed in the tower, making this one of the oldest peals in the country. On either side of the crossing are the much restored transepts.

There are a number of fine monuments, including the medieval tomb of the founder, Thomas Rahere, which has a delicate canopy of 15thC Gothic tracery. The monument to Edward Cooke (*d.*1652) actually weeps in damp weather as a result of condensation — a phenomenon referred to in the inscription.

ST GEORGE'S, BLOOMSBURY ㎜
Bloomsbury Way, WC1. Map 9E11. Tube: Holborn.
This splendid church compares well with the near contemporary but much more famous ST MARTIN-IN-THE-FIELDS. Built by Nicholas Hawksmoor in 1720-31, it is in some ways an even more dramatic design than Gibbs', with a huge portico of Corinthian columns and a layer-cake spire, topped with a statue of George I as St George, a typical piece of Baroque overstatement. The interior repeats the boldness of the exterior — simple shapes, plenty of light and more giant columns. Notice the fine patterned inlay of the wooden reredos.

ST JAMES'S

This is the most upper-class of London's neighborhoods, an area studded with gentlemen's clubs, grand 18thC and 19thC residences and superlative shops. See LONDON'S DISTRICTS, page 86.

ST JAMES'S PALACE   ▥ ★
Pall Mall, SW1. Map 8H9. Not open to the public. Tube: Green Park.

Despite its much greater antiquity, London has an architectural threshold formed by the plague and fire of 1665-66. This royal palace is unique in surviving intact, unadorned, and preserving a glimpse of Tudor London. There it sits, sandwiched by its larger offspring of ST JAMES'S and THE MALL, and yet dwarfing them, for all their grandeur and boldness, by its very antiquity and history. The official royal residence from 1698, when Whitehall Palace burned down, until BUCKINGHAM PALACE took over in 1837, its seniority is still recognized; the Queen's court is "the Court of St James" and new monarchs are still proclaimed from here. Today it provides "Grace and Favour" quarters for yeomen-at-arms, lords and ladies-in-waiting, and the Lord Chamberlain.

Henry VIII took over the site from a leper hospital in 1532, and had his palace built entirely in brick, with battlements and diapering (diagonal patterning in the brickwork). Even the State Rooms added by Wren in the 17thC, also with battlements, maintain the low, informal approach, echoing the domesticity of Tudor architecture. The best original feature, visible from PALL MALL, is the tall **gatehouse**, with octagonal corner towers.

The **Queen's Chapel**, across Marlborough Rd. but originally within the palace, is in style entirely different. Designed by Inigo Jones, it was built in 1623-27 in the Classical manner, with rendered white walls and Portland stone dressings. The beautiful interior boasts ornate Baroque work from the 1660s, including fine carving by Gibbons. To the w, attached to the palace, is **Clarence House**, built in 1825-27 by Nash and now the Queen Mother's home; when she is in residence, a piper plays the bagpipes in the garden at 9am. The palace is flanked by two grand mansions from later periods: MARLBOROUGH HOUSE to the E and LANCASTER HOUSE to the w, with ST JAMES'S PARK to the s.

ST JAMES'S PARK   ★
Map 9H10 ◁ Tube: St James's Park.

London's first royal park was always nearer to art than nature. In 1536 Henry VIII drained a marsh to make a park between ST JAMES'S and Whitehall Palaces, filled with deer (for ornament rather than hunting). In 1662, Charles II made it a public garden, laid out in the formal style of the period with avenues of trees, THE MALL as a carriageway, and a long straight canal. In 1828, it was remodeled on the present pattern by John Nash, who created the lovely complex of trees, flowerbeds and views across the natural-looking lake that we see today. The waterfowl, some of which breed on Duck Island at the E end, have always continued the contrivance — there are even pelicans.

The view from the bridge across the lake back toward WHITEHALL is one of the most beautiful in London.

ST JAMES'S, PICCADILLY 𝍐

Piccadilly, W1 ☎(071) 734-5244. Map 9G10. Tube: Piccadilly Circus, Green Park.

When ST JAMES'S was developed as a residential area after 1662, Sir Christopher Wren was commissioned to build the new church, completing it in 1674. It is basically one great room with plain galleries and a vaulted ceiling decorated with plaster moldings. Damaged by bombs in 1940, the church has been well restored and preserves some fine fittings. The organ is 17thC, moved from the old Whitehall Palace, topped by gilded figures carved by Grinling Gibbons, who also produced the marvelous marble **font**, with its virtuoso relief of Adam and Eve, and the rich floral arrangements carved on the wooden **reredos**.

ST KATHARINE'S DOCK ✰

Map 12G18. Tube: Tower Hill.

Next to the TOWER OF LONDON, St Katharine's was the first of the docks to be given an entirely new role (see also DOCKLANDS, page 75). Originally built in 1827-28 by the great engineer Thomas Telford, this was for many years one of the leading docks in the Pool of London, with the advantage of being closest to the City. Today, St Katharine's again profits from its proximity to the City, as a residential and tourist center and a yacht marina. The modern **World Trade Centre** looks down on the brick-brown sails of Thames sailing barges and gleaming hulls of luxury yachts moored in the docks. Telford's **Ivory House** (later modified) shows off 19thC industrial apartments, shops and an exhibition area. A timber-built warehouse is now the **Dickens Tavern**, and blocks of fashionable apartments sit between docks and river.

ST MARTIN-IN-THE-FIELDS 𝍐

Trafalgar Sq., WC2. Map 9G11. Tube: Charing Cross.

The first buildings in a new architectural style often seem oddities, and this church has maintained its nonconformity. Today it is the venue for concerts on Monday, Tuesday and Friday lunchtimes and a shelter for vagrants and drug addicts, as well as a church. The broad views allowed by TRAFALGAR SQUARE'S open spaces make enjoyment of this magnificent church's proportions possible, and it is now recognized for the seminal building it was. Designed in 1722-26 by James Gibbs (the foundation goes back to 1222) in a solemnly Classical style, it is very close to a Roman temple, except for the novel placing of a tower and spire above the Corinthian portico. The interior is similar to Wren's churches of a few decades earlier — spacious and light, with galleries to the sides and a splendidly molded ceiling. The crypt contains several interesting relics, including a whipping post dating back to the 18thC.

It also houses the **London Brass Rubbing Centre** (☎ *437-6023* ▨ *open Mon-Sat 10am-6pm, Sun noon-6pm ▣*), where rubbings can be made from replicas of medieval monumental brasses. Staff are on hand to teach the technique. The clothing, jewelry and souvenir **market** is open every day, as is the excellent **Café in the Crypt** for self-service meals underneath the arches.

ST MARY ABCHURCH 🏛

Abchurch Lane, EC4. Map 12F16. Tube: Cannon Street.

After its small cobbled churchyard, simple brick exterior and lead spire, the glories of St Mary Abchurch's interior are unexpected. Built by Sir Christopher Wren in 1681-86, it consists of little more than one huge dome on top of a square room, creating a sense of space with architectural detail kept to a minimum. The dome was painted in Baroque style by William Snow between 1708 and 1714, and shows the name of God in Hebrew surrounded by figures representing the virtues.

Although damaged in World War II, the church has been expertly restored; the **reredos** carved by Grinling Gibbons, for example, was rebuilt from fragments. Note the richly carved pulpit, the paneling and some original pews.

ST MARY-LE-BOW 🏛

Bow Lane, Cheapside, EC2. Map 11G15. Tube: Bank, St Paul's.

When Wren rebuilt London's churches after the Great Fire of 1666, he put particular emphasis on their steeples, and this is the most magnificent. A great tower capped by an intricate stone spire, it is still prominent among the larger modern buildings around it. The church was built in 1670-80, with the tower separated from the body of the church by a vestibule. The design and execution of the two doors to the tower that serve as the porch are particularly fine. The interior is large and simple, much restored after gutting during the war, and the crypt retains elements from the original Norman church.

St Mary's bells are of sentimental importance to Londoners: being born within range of their sound is traditionally the qualification for being a Cockney. The bells were destroyed in the Great Fire of 1666 and again in the Blitz; the current ones include recasts from remnants that were salvaged in 1941.

ST MARY-LE-STRAND 🏛 ☆

Strand, WC2. Map 10F12. Tube: Aldwych, Temple.

It is hard to imagine a more ironic fate for a jewel of the Baroque: the island in the middle of the STRAND is so small that the continuous traffic passes within inches of its walls, which over the years have needed drastic renovation. James Gibbs built this in 1714-18, fresh from the joys of Rome. The facade especially is a delight: from the portico, with its ornate capitals, the eye sweeps up to the triangular pediment and the bold layered spire.

The interior has a richly coffered ceiling with two tiers of columns and a pediment dramatically framing the apse. Notice the fine carving of the pulpit, originally on a taller base with a scallop-shell sounding board behind, all part of the grand theatrical effect.

ST PANCRAS STATION ⌂ ★
Euston Rd. NW1. Map 3C11. Tube: King's Cross, St Pancras.
That a railway station could be made into a Gothic fortress speaks much for the Victorians' confidence. St Pancras Station, with its accompanying hotel building (now used as offices), was the glory of Victorian London. It was designed by Sir George Gilbert Scott in 1868-74, freely using the northern Italian and French Gothic styles. Notice the harmony of its red bricks with the pink and gray stone, and the way the detail combines with complex shapes and angles to feast the eye (see the illustration on page 25, which gives some idea of the scale and mass of the structure, though of course none of its bold coloring). It was also a tremendous feat of engineering, with the great train shed covered by a single span of iron and glass.

The station's former goods yard is the site of the controversial new **British Library** building, opening in two phases in 1993 and 1996. London's deepest (75 feet) basement has been carved out of the ground to house the Library's collection of every book published in Britain, which is moving from the BRITISH MUSEUM.

ST PAUL'S, COVENT GARDEN ⌂
The Piazza, WC2. Map 9F11. Tube: Covent Garden.
As the Duke of Bedford neared completion of his COVENT GARDEN development, money became tight, and so he instructed Inigo Jones to build an economical church, suggesting as a model something like a barn. Jones declared that he would build "the handsomest barn in Europe," and today it stands as the sole surviving element of the piazza. In fact it cost a small fortune, but the barn analogy is not entirely inappropriate to the extreme simplicity of what was London's first entirely Classical parish church, completed in 1638.

The main features are the overhanging eaves and the superb Tuscan portico, ironically never used as an entrance because the altar was moved in 1636 and a smaller door made at the rear in Bedford St. Today it is the "actors' church," and every so often a grand theaterland funeral adds another monument to the collection.

ST PAUL'S CATHEDRAL ⌂ ★
Map 11F14 ▨ except Sun and for worshippers. Entrance and movement restricted during services ◁€ Tube: St Paul's.
There are a very few great churches in the world that strike all visitors, whatever their religious convictions, as a sublime witness to man's ability to reach toward the infinite. St Paul's was built as both a religious and secular statement of London's faith and self-confidence after the devastating Great Fire of 1666, and almost 300 years later it was to soar alone amid the total destruction of the surrounding buildings in the Blitz, preserved miraculously to breath fresh hope into the beleaguered Londoners.

No building so clearly demonstrates Sir Christopher Wren's prodigious skill and energetic inventiveness. In this, his greatest work, detail is used with characteristic Baroque exuberance but always subordinated to the highly controlled overall scheme. Even today, the dome still dominates the encroaching modern buildings.

The current cathedral is the third to stand on this site, and not the largest. The first was founded in 604 and periodically enlarged until destruction by fire in 1087. A medieval cathedral was constructed in the 11th-12thC; in the 13thC it was enlarged, and in 1315 a huge spire was completed. It was one of the great churches of medieval Europe, with a spire that reached 489 feet from the ground, taller and longer than the present St Paul's. (For a fine model, see LONDON, MUSEUM OF.)

Decline set in as the Middle Ages waned, however. The spire burned down in 1561 and was not replaced. The building fell into disrepair and was used more as a marketplace than a place of worship. The central aisle, "Paul's Walk," was a famous social forum. In 1634, Inigo Jones carried out substantial repairs, but the medieval structure continued to deteriorate, and in 1666 Christopher Wren came up with his first scheme for drastic renovations. That year, the Great Fire destroyed most of London, raging in St Paul's for several days and reducing it to ruins.

Given the task of reconstructing the cathedral, Wren proposed sweeping away what remained of the medieval building and starting afresh. He began with daringly modern designs that were rejected by the ecclesiastical authorities. In the end, he was forced to return to the basic plan for a Gothic cathedral, even if not in appearance, and his design of 1675 was just that — with a nave, aisles, a crossing, transepts and a chancel, all forming a Latin cross. But the crossing was to be covered by a dome rather than a tower or spire, the first in England, following the example of the great Renaissance churches of Italy. Wren also fought for, and won, the freedom to alter the "ornamentation" of the cathedral, which in effect left him able to design the building's appearance as he went along.

Wren's **exterior** owes much to Inigo Jones' BANQUETING HOUSE. There are two stories, with pilasters that decorate rusticated walls and a balustrade at the top — a first stroke of sophisticated ingenuity, for the aisles behind the exterior side walls are only one story high, just as in a Gothic cathedral. The upper is therefore a false wall (hence the blank niches instead of windows) connected to and supporting the walls of the nave by means of flying buttresses inside — an entirely Gothic device, but quite out of sight.

The E end of the cathedral, containing the chancel, was built first. It has a rounded end, thus forming an apse as in a medieval church, but with a curved roofline giving a Baroque flourish. This effect is echoed in the curved porches to the N and S transept facades, but these have more solidly Classical pediments at the roofline. The W end, the ceremonial entrance (illustrated on page 24), was built later (1706-8), with massive towers at either side — the ornate tops to these are the most complex elements in the whole building: architecture handled as sculpture. The central portico is on two stories with pairs of Corinthian columns — another emphatically Baroque motif.

All this serves to balance the solemnity of the **dome**, suitably weighty and dignified as the dominant element of the composition. It is arguably the most beautiful dome in the world, 365 feet high to the tip of the lantern

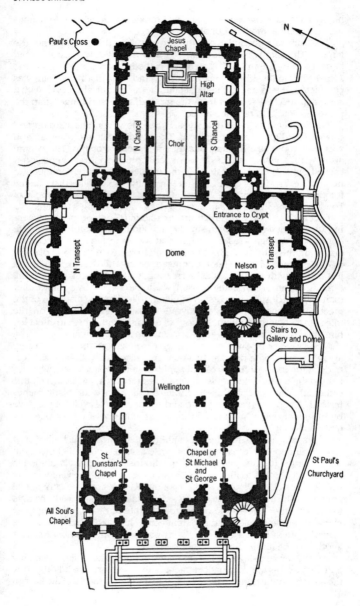

Paul's Cross ●

N

Jesus Chapel

High Altar

N Chancel

Choir

S Chancel

Entrance to Crypt

N Transept

Dome

Nelson

S Transept

Stairs to Gallery and Dome

Wellington

St Dunstan's Chapel

Chapel of St Michael and St George

St Paul's Churchyard

All Soul's Chapel

and 100 feet across inside. The quality of the carving of such elements as the garlands just below the frieze, or the capitals to the columns and pilasters, is superb. The sculptures, too, are well executed. The reliefs in the transept pediments are by G.B. Cibber and Grinling Gibbons, the statues by Francis Bird, who also carved the relief in the W pediment showing the *Conversion of St Paul.*

Although the area around St Paul's was spoiled by modern developments, conceived in the mid-1950s and built in the 1960s, plans are now afoot to redevelop the Paternoster Square area more sympathetically. At present, traffic whistles around alarmingly close to the walls. There remain, however, the fine **railings** that surround the churchyard, made in 1714 and an early example of the use of cast iron. In front of the portico stands a statue of Queen Anne, made in 1866 to replace the original of 1709-11 by Bird (but did the original look so like Queen Victoria?).

In the churchyard gardens to the NE is **St Paul's Cross**, a bronze structure of 1910. Two of the old cathedral buildings survive, both designed by Wren: to the S is the little **Deanery** of 1670, and to the N the larger red-brick **Chapter House** of 1712-14. To the E, still inside the road, is the tower and elongated onion spire of the ruined church of St Augustine designed by Wren in 1680-83, now attached to the new buildings of the celebrated St Paul's Choir School.

The **interior** gives an impression of the great bulk of the structure, but this is offset by the height of the nave and by the vast open space at the very center beneath the dome. The roofs are supported on a series of shallow cupolas, and the decorative elements are richly and finely carved, but limited in extent to the capitals of the pilasters, with garlands between, and geometrically patterned bands around the cupolas. The emphasis is on the sweeping drama of the Baroque. The eye is led along the nave or aisles, or across the transepts, and there seems to be a calculated attempt to create vistas with a sense of distance, focusing on the open space beneath the dome but leading ultimately toward the long chancel beyond the crossing. A great deal of light enters the cathedral from the clerestory windows of the nave, windows that are invisible from the outside because of the false upper story of the external wall.

Walk to the left from the main W entrance. The small **All Soul's Chapel** contains **Lord Kitchener's monument** of 1925, one of the more effective of the cluster of memorials to national heroes introduced since about 1790, with an effigy of the soldier in deathly white marble. Then comes **St Dunstan's Chapel**, behind a superbly carved wooden screen of 1698. Outstanding monuments are to Lord Leighton, the leading Victorian painter, and to General Gordon of the Sudan. In one of the arches farther along this N aisle is the great **monument to the Duke of Wellington**, erected in the mid-19thC and the most elaborate in St Paul's, with an equestrian statue of the duke on top of the canopy. The N transept, reserved for private prayer, contains monuments to the fallen heroes of the Napoleonic Wars, and the marble font, carved in 1727 by Francis Bird.

At this point the **crossing** can be admired, the focal point of the entire design. It is a huge space, with the circle of the **dome** supported on eight massive arches. The mosaics in the spandrels are Victorian, in the style of Michelangelo's Sistine Chapel frescoes, and there are Victorian statues in the niches above the Whispering Gallery. The breathtaking dome itself actually consists of three layers: an outer skin, a cone supporting the masonry of the lantern, and a shallow domed ceiling. This is painted with illusionistic architectural frescoes in monochrome, depicting scenes from the life of St Paul, by Sir James Thornhill, dating from 1716-19. Monuments in the crossing include those to Dr. Johnson (in an unlikely toga) and Sir Joshua Reynolds, first president of the ROYAL ACADEMY. The lectern was made in 1720, but the pulpit is modern.

The **chancel**, stretching off toward the high altar, makes a sumptuous display, although it is not at all as Wren left it: the gaudy and fussy mosaics that decorate the ceiling date from the 1890s and are really not in keeping. The modern baldacchino, attempting to follow Wren's original scheme for a high altar canopy as a focal point, is only partly successful, in an unhappy marriage with the ceiling decorations. However, the **choir stalls and organ case**, which originally closed the chancel off from the crossing, are quite magnificent, with exquisite carving by Grinling Gibbons, made in the 1690s. The chancel aisles can be visited, giving a fine close-up view of the rear of the stalls and of Jean Tijou's extraordinarily fine **wrought-iron gates**, again of the 1690s but moved to their present site in 1890. Behind the altar is the **Jesus Chapel**, now a memorial to the American dead of World War II.

Returning along the s chancel aisle, **John Donne's monument** shows the poet, who was Dean of St Paul's (1620-31), wrapped in his shroud, just as he posed during the (soon justified) bouts of melancholy before his death in 1631. It is the only monument to survive from the medieval cathedral. Returning back toward the crossing, the s transept includes several military monuments, of which Sir John Moore's (1851) is the most moving, although Lord Nelson's includes a fine portrait. In the s aisle is a striking example of high Victorian religiosity, a late version of Holman Hunt's painting *Light of the World*, and a fine wooden screen of 1706 in front of the **Chapel of St Michael and St George**.

Crypt
Entrance from s transept ☎ *Open Mon-Fri 10am-4.15pm; Sat 11am-4.15pm.*
The piers and columns support a crypt the size of the whole cathedral, a quiet and dignified place crammed with monuments to national figures. A few battered remains of monuments survive from before the 1666 Great Fire, but the majority are from the 19th to 20thC. By far the most impressive are the tombs of **Wellington**, a massive porphyry block on a granite slab, and **Nelson**, an elegant black sarcophagus originally made for Cardinal Wolsey in 1524-29 but denied him after his fall from royal favor. Other monuments include numerous generals and admirals, and, in "Painter's Corner," the tombs of Turner and Reynolds and monuments to Van Dyck, Constable and William Blake. Wren himself is buried nearby.

The **Treasury of the Diocese of London** also has an exhibition in the crypt, containing elaborate vestments, illuminated medieval manuscripts from the cathedral library, and some fine plate from London churches of the 16th-20thC.

Whispering Gallery and Dome
Stairs in s transept 🔳 *Hours as crypt.*
The stiff climb to the gallery inside the dome is repaid with stupendous views of the concourse below and the painted inner dome. The acoustics that give it its name enable the slightest sounds to be heard across the span; the traditional trick, much loved by children, is to whisper against the wall and wait for the sound to travel around to the next auditor. The next section of the ascent is not for the fainthearted, with steps winding up throughout the struts supporting the outer dome. The stunning views from the **Golden Gallery** at the base of the lantern make the 542-step climb worthwhile.

ST STEPHEN WALBROOK 🏛 ☆
Walbrook, EC4. Map ***12****F16. Tube: Bank.*
Although a parish church, its position behind the MANSION HOUSE means that St Stephen Walbrook is also the Lord Mayor's church. It is appropriately grand for this ceremonial function, with a simple exterior giving way to a magnificent structure inside, with Corinthian columns, and eight richly molded arches supporting a coffered dome. Wren built the church in 1672-79: it is thought that he was trying out some ideas for ST PAUL'S CATHEDRAL. The contrast with his ST MARY ABCHURCH is illuminating, for here the dome is not used to create a simple, large space but to contribute to the series of constantly changing views as the visitor moves through the columns. The tower is slightly later, 1717, and the crypt survives from the 15thC.

SCIENCE MUSEUM ★
Exhibition Rd., SW7 ☎*(071) 938-8000. Map* ***14****J5* 🔳 💺 ♿ *Open Mon-Sat 10am-6pm; Sun 11am-6pm. Tube: South Kensington.*
The Science Museum originated in 1857 within the great South Kensington museum complex conceived by Prince Albert. It was separated from the VICTORIA & ALBERT MUSEUM, housing the products of art rather than science, in 1909. Its present building, solemn and functional, was constructed in 1913.

On the ground floor, the **East Hall**, a large room with galleries above on three levels and a glass roof, is devoted to the development of motive power. Industrial machinery, vast and now seemingly crude in its construction, shows the development of steam power in the 18thC. By contrast, a huge mill engine of 1903, with a great gleaming flywheel, shows the continuing use of steam into the 20thC. The following section on transport is a great favorite, with famous steam locomotives such as Stephenson's *Rocket* of 1829 and the magnificent *Caerphilly Castle* of 1923 outstanding; the fascination with the visible working parts explains why something as messy and noisy as a steam train should have such romantic appeal. There are also horse-drawn carriages, automobiles and fire engines.

An excitingly topical gallery called **Food for Thought**, on the first floor, sponsored by the Sainsbury Family Charitable Trust, explores how we buy, prepare and eat food. The displays on the upper floors (the galleries around the central East Hall and a few separate rooms) cover a great many aspects of science in turn. On reaching the first floor, children make an immediate break for the **Launch Pad**, a marvelous hands-on exhibit where everyone can get down to working the machines themselves. Industrial processes, such as iron, steel and glass manufacture, and agriculture are here too.

On the second floor, subjects range from chemistry to nuclear physics to computers, and there are superb **models of ships**. There are also more theoretical areas such as biochemistry, where attractive models comprehensibly explain the structure of molecules. Fascinating exhibitions on the third floor cover photography, cinematography and optics.

Here too is the **Aeronautics Gallery**: see the Vickers Vimy in which Alcock and Brown made their pioneering flight across the Atlantic, Amy Johnson's *Jason* in which she flew to Australia, a Spitfire and the first-ever jet engine. In the adjacent **Flight Lab** you can test the principles of flight by experimenting with the 24 hands-on exhibits. Stairs lead up to the excellent **Wellcome Medical Museum**, where the history of medicine and its most up-to-date manifestations are shown in spirited dioramas.

The Science Museum succeeds well in balancing the interests of both children and adults, and is a favorite destination for families, particularly on a rainy weekend.

SHAKESPEARE GLOBE MUSEUM
1 Bear Gdns, Bankside, SE1 ☎*(071) 928-6342. Map* **11**G15 ▨ *Open winter Mon-Sat 10am-5pm, Sun 2-5pm; summer Mon-Sat 10am-6pm, Sun 2-6pm. Tube: London Bridge.*
Until the 18thC, Southwark acted as London's pleasure center, an area of taverns, brothels and theaters. The museum houses exhibitions on this area of Shakespeare's London and the discovery and excavation of the **Rose Theatre** and the original **Globe Theatre**, as well as a model of the proposed **International Shakespeare Globe Centre** *(due to open whenever funding becomes available* ☎ *620-0202 for information)*. The center is reconstructing the famous polygonal theater, burned down in 1613 during a performance of *Henry VIII.* Both the Globe and Rose sites are near to the museum.

SHERLOCK HOLMES MUSEUM
221b Baker St., NW1 ☎*(071) 935-8866. Map* **7**E7 ▨ *Open 10am-6pm. Tube: Baker Street.*
Devotees of Sir Arthur Conan Doyle's creation, Sherlock Holmes, and his puzzled partner, Dr. Watson, can visit their fictional address, 221b Baker St., which has been realized in the style of their Victorian apartment, complete with letters and trophies from their adventures. A case of fiction becoming fact . . . . There is also a souvenir shop.

SIR JOHN SOANE'S MUSEUM ★
13 Lincoln's Inn Fields, WC2 ☎*(071) 405-2107; information (071) 430-0175. Map* **10**E12 ▣ ✗ *Sat 2.30pm, tickets available at 2pm. Open Tues-Sat 10am-5pm; first Tues of the month 6-9pm. Tube: Holborn.*

Nothing could be further from modern ideas of museum display than Soane's Museum, for the great architect left his house as a museum on his death in 1837 on the condition that nothing be changed. His enormous collection of pictures, architectural fragments, books, sculptures and miscellaneous antiquities is crammed into every available space, giving some idea of his idiosyncracy as well as his tastes.

Born in 1753, Soane lived at no. 12 Lincoln's Inn Fields from 1792, in a plain Georgian house he designed himself. In 1812-14 he added the much more elaborate no. 13 with its grand facade, rebuilding no. 14 to complete a balanced design in 1824. The interior, joined between the three houses, is the most ingeniously complex layout, offering numerous vistas through the houses, both laterally and vertically, as several of the rooms and yards extend through two or more stories. Mirrors create additional illusory space. Most exciting are the paired **Dining Room** and **Library**, and the lovely domed **Breakfast Room**.

The fascination of the great number of objects on display from fossils to furniture is only increased by the capricious, even humorous, way in which they are jumbled together. Among them are several important works of art, as well as Soane's own architectural models. In the **Picture Room** are Hogarth's original paintings for two series, *The Rake's Progress* and *The Election*, comprising 12 paintings in all. In the **New Picture Room** are three Canalettos, and elsewhere are three Turners. Outstanding is the beautiful alabaster **sarcophagus**, covered with hieroglyphics, of Seti I, a pharaoh who died in 1290BC, for which Soane paid the then princely sum of £2,000.

SOHO

The name evokes low-life, but in fact this is among London's most authentic villages, in its energetic mix of local "characters" (Cockney, Italian, Chinese and others), trendy media folk, small cosmopolitan shops, exotic street markets and affordable restaurants. See LONDON'S DISTRICTS, page 86.

SOUTH BANK ARTS CENTRE

Map 10G12 ⟨⟨ *Tube: Waterloo.*

The plans for a national arts center were formulated in the years after World War II, and crystallized when this derelict South Bank site was developed for the Festival of Britain in 1951, with the first stages of the Festival Hall and National Film Theatre.

The **Festival Hall**, one of Britain's outstanding postwar buildings, was not finally completed until 1956. Its impressive glass facade makes full use of its panoramic riverside location. Like later South Bank buildings, however, the exterior is more massive and monumental than appealing, and it is the interior that is most successful. This has a complex arrangement of spaces, efficiently and attractively laid out, with public areas offering views across the river, bars, restaurants and the great concert hall itself, seating almost 3,000, with near-perfect acoustics. For smaller concerts, the **Queen Elizabeth Hall** and **Purcell Room**, seating 1,100 and 372 respectively, were completed next to the Festival Hall in 1967.

The **National Film Theatre**, under Waterloo Bridge, which now has two cinemas, shows an always interesting program of historic and contemporary movies. The **Hayward Gallery**, next to the bridge, was opened in 1968, and presents a program of major art exhibitions organized by the Arts Council of Great Britain. Its design, however, has been much criticized, and it has little natural light.

The ROYAL NATIONAL THEATRE continues the Brutalist theme. Newest addition to the South Bank complex is **MOMI**, the MUSEUM OF THE MOVING IMAGE, in a striking glass and steel building adjoining the Film Theatre.

Although some elements of the South Bank Centre are architecturally praiseworthy, and its arts output is second to none, it is seen by many Londoners as a hostile, unfriendly place that is isolated from life in the rest of the capital. It should be captivating; instead, with its windy, threatening walkways and harsh concrete walls, it alienates. Now, major plans, masterminded by architect Terry Farrell, are underway to improve the site. They include the reconstruction of the Hayward Gallery, the demolition of the walkways and the relandscaping of the whole area, with provision for shops, restaurants and arts-related entertainments.

See also PERFORMING ARTS.

SOUTHWARK CATHEDRAL ▥ ☆
Map 12G16. Tube: London Bridge.
This Gothic church is under siege from the encroaching railway viaducts, covered market and approaches to LONDON BRIDGE that crowd up to its walls, but it is still one of the most important medieval buildings in London. The tower is the best feature, dating from the 14th to 15thC, with pinnacles of 1689.

It was founded as the Augustinian priory of St Mary Overie (meaning "over the water") in 1106, becoming the parish church of St Saviour after the Reformation, and a cathedral only in 1905. The priory burned down in about 1212 and was replaced with a Gothic structure, of which the present chancel and retro-choir were complete by 1220. Since then, restoration has been periodically necessary, the chancel of 1890-97, in a medieval style, being the latest major reworking.

Interesting features include the **ceiling bosses** from the 15thC, opposite the present main entrance, graphically carved with heraldic devices or grotesque figures. The rebuilt **chancel** actually shows very well the beauty and purity of early Gothic architecture, with its layers of perfectly proportioned arches. Behind the high altar, a superbly rich **reredos** dates from 1520.

The monuments are of great interest, although several have been crudely painted in restoration. Look out for John Gower, a medieval poet and friend of Chaucer, who died in 1408, a wooden effigy of a knight of about 1275, and Richard Humber (died 1616) with his fashionably dressed wives. Next to the N transept is a chapel (rebuilt in 1907) devoted to John Harvard, founder of the great American college, who was baptized here in 1607. The **Nonesuch Chest**, in the retro-choir, is an outstanding example of 16thC furniture in the Classical Renaissance style. In the S aisle, there is a memorial of 1912 to William Shakespeare.

SPEAKERS' CORNER

Map 7G7. Tube: Marble Arch.

Speakers' Corner in the NE tip of HYDE PARK offers the dubious spectacle of numerous wild-eyed eccentrics haranguing small groups of spectators on everything from hellfire to Utopia. Established as late as 1872 as a place where such holding-forth could be tolerated without arrest, it has in recent years begun to attract more serious attention thanks to exiles from countries where free speech is denied. It is at its busiest on Sunday.

SPENCER HOUSE ⅏

27 St James's Pl., SW1 ☎(071) 409-0526; (071) 499-8620 for advance reservations. Map 8H9 ▣ ✖ ✗ compulsory, every 15mins: maximum 15 visitors. No children under age 10. Open Sun 10.30am-4.45pm. Closed Jan, Aug. Tube: Green Park.

A five-year restoration has returned Spencer House to the full splendor of its late 18thC appearance. It was built for Earl Spencer, ancestor of the Princess of Wales, in 1756-66, and the magnificent Neoclassical interiors were designed by John Vardy and James "Athenian" Stuart.

Vardy's **Palm Room**, with its spectacular screen of gilded palm trees, is a unique Palladian set piece, while the elegant murals of Stuart's **Painted Room** reflect the 18thC passion for all things Classical. Original gilded furniture, by Stuart, has been returned to the house from the VICTORIA AND ALBERT MUSEUM, and the Queen has lent five paintings by Benjamin West.

STAPLE INN ⅏

Holborn, EC1. Map 10E13. Tube: Chancery Lane.

Close to the entrance to GRAY'S INN is a remarkable survivor of Elizabethan London: a pair of timber houses dating from 1586 forming the facade to Staple Inn, a former Inn of Chancery. Together they look like a quaint jumble of haphazardly placed beams and gables, with charming overhanging stories and oriel windows.

Through the gateway on the left, the courtyards of the Inn (now housing the Society of Actuaries) can be entered. Dr. Johnson lived at no. 2 in 1759-60, where he supposedly wrote *Rasselas* in a week in a bid to pay for his mother's funeral.

STRAND

Maps 9G11-10F13. Tube: Charing Cross.

"Strand" means river bank, and that is what this street was until the embankment was built in 1864-70; the old **watergate** still stands in Victoria Embankment Gardens. Once the main route from Westminster to the City, it was lined with great houses, and is today a motley collection of theaters, shops and hotels.

Its E end begins at Temple Bar, on the edge of the City, continuing the direction set by FLEET STREET. On the N side are the splendid Victorian Gothic ROYAL COURTS OF JUSTICE, with an attractive tangle of buildings opposite. The church of **St Clement Danes** occupies an island in the middle of the road, built by Sir Christopher Wren in 1680-82, with the stone tower completed by James Gibbs in 1719. Entirely wrecked by a bomb in 1941, the church has been restored with exceptional skill and is now the church of the Royal Air Force. Behind is a statue to Samuel Johnson erected in 1910, and to the front is a more pompous monument to Gladstone (1905).

The **Aldwych** follows on the N side of the street, an ambitious planning scheme begun in 1900. Its crescent shape is made up of massive, somber buildings in heavy Edwardian style, including Australia House and the BBC's Bush House. The exquisite church of ST MARY-LE-STRAND occupies another island in the middle of the road at this point, with the 1971 concrete facade of King's College almost opposite. **Somerset House** (now home to the COURTAULD INSTITUTE GALLERIES) comes next on the S side, just a little farther along from the Aldwych.

Two large hotels are farther W: the Art Deco-ish **Strand Palace** (**Simpson's** ultra-traditional restaurant opposite: see VENERABLE INSTITU-TIONS, page 236) and the famous **Savoy** (see HOTELS). Several theaters are to be found along the N side of the Strand from here, in a section largely given over to bustling shoppers. The W end, opening onto TRAFALGAR SQUARE, is marked by CHARING CROSS, with the remarkable **Coutts' Bank building** opposite.

SYON HOUSE 🏛

Brentford, Middlesex ☎*(081) 560-0881. Map **19**C3* 🚌 🚗 ✗ 🅿 *Open Apr-Sept Sat-Thurs noon-4.15pm; gardens daily 10am-6pm, or till sunset if earlier. Tube: Gunnersbury.*

Syon House was originally a convent, founded by Henry V in 1415 and exceptionally rich until suppressed by Henry VIII in 1534. In 1547, it was taken over by the Lord Protector, the Duke of Somerset, who transformed it into a large mansion on the pattern of a hollow square. Somerset went to the scaffold in 1552, as did his successor to Syon, John Dudley, and also Lady Jane Grey, who set out from the house to be Queen of England for eight days in 1553. Since 1594, the Percy family, Dukes of Northumberland, have held the house.

In 1762, Robert Adam was brought in to "modernize" the Tudor house, thus creating the extraordinary contrast between the plain square exterior with battlements and corner towers, and the incomparable interior. As at OSTERLEY PARK nearby, the centerpiece of Adam's planning is the **Great Hall**, a cool and elegant room with restrained Classical decoration in stucco, including Doric columns, giving the house a dramatic entrance. To complete the scholarly effect, there are genuine Roman statues and some copies of famous antique models, including a fine bronze version of the *Dying Gaul*.

Adam's intention was to create a sequence of pleasurable contrasts: the next room, **The Ante Room**, is altogether more lavish, with rich gilding, dark green marble columns and a brightly patterned floor in colored artificial stone. The suite of state rooms continues the contrast, with **Dining Room, Red Drawing Room** and **Long Gallery** all in different, variously elaborate styles; some furniture is gilded, some in beautifully inlaid wood. In the Red Drawing Room there is a fine carpet designed by Adam, and in the Long Gallery, landscape panels by Zucca- relli. Paintings in the house include works by Van Dyck, Lely and Gainsborough.

The gardens, remodeled in the late 18thC by the great Capability Brown, have many rare botanical specimens and carefully planned vistas. The **Great Conservatory** was added in 1830, with its large, almost Oriental, glass dome, and now contains an aquarium. In the park there is also a huge garden center, a Koi carp center, a **butterfly house** (🔯), where British and tropical specimens can be seen all year round flying free, and the **British Heritage Motor Museum** (☎ *(081) 560-1378* 🔯 *open Mar-Oct 10am-5pm, Nov-Apr 10am-3.30pm)*, which boasts a col- lection of 90 cars, including an 1895 Wolseley and several prototypes, and a small display of Dinky Cars.

TATE GALLERY ★

Millbank, SW1 ☎*(071) 821-1313, recorded info* ☎*(071) 821-7128. Map* ***17K11*** 🔯 *𝄞* 🎥 *Open Mon-Sat 10am-5.50pm; Sun 2-5.50pm. Tube: Pimlico.*
Appropriately for a gallery famous for modern art, the Tate was founded by the modern type of patron, a businessman, when in 1892 the sugar millionaire Sir Henry Tate gave his collection of British paint- ings to the nation, together with funds to build a special gallery, offi- cially opened in 1897. In fact, only later, in 1917, was the decision taken to add modern foreign art, largely because at the time the Tate was seen as an adjunct to the NATIONAL GALLERY.

Several extensions have increased the available space many times over, most recently in the large galleries opened in 1979, and the Clore Gallery extension opened in 1987. With the exception of the Turner galleries, the collection has recently undergone a complete rearrange- ment. Displays now change annually to explore the wealth and variety of the Collection. Each annual display traces the development of British art chronologically from the mid-16thC to the present, linking it with foreign art in the 20thC. Regular special displays from the permanent collection present themes through different generations of art as well as works of individual artists.

Throughout the year the Tate may rehang individual rooms, and works of art mentioned in the following description may not always be on view.

New displays start at the rear of the building on the left. The first room covers the 16th-17thC, when foreign artists working in England ruled the roost. A few works, such as the superb portraits by William Dobson, show the influence of European painting on British artists of this period.

In the 18thC, a truly national school appeared, particularly with William Hogarth, whose eye for contemporary life was unrivaled. His *Study of the Heads of Six Servants* shows a great and original under- standing of the ordinary people making up his household, whereas *Calais Gate* reveals his biting satire. In the 18thC, with Reynolds and Gainsborough, two contradictory approaches to portraiture emerged, but in the end both artists concentrated on pleasing their sitters. Reynolds favored a grand, Classicizing manner (as in *Three Ladies Adorning a Term of Hymen*); Gainsborough concentrated on charm and prettiness with his extraordinarily fluent technique.

The Tate has good examples of the development of landscape painting in the 18thC: Richard Wilson's *Cader Idris* demonstrates an emerging naturalism. Two other important 18thC artists were George Stubbs (sporting and animal scenes, including the finest horses ever painted) and Joseph Wright of Derby (highly individual night scenes closely bound up with advances in science and industrialization). By contrast, the eccentric mysticism of William Blake and his followers is effectively shown in a semi-lit room.

In studies and finished works such as *Flatford Mill,* Constable showed an appreciation of the real appearance of the countryside, which was revolutionary in his time. The Pre-Raphaelites are well represented at the Tate, and Millais' *Ophelia* and Rossetti's *Beata Beatrix* are among the most famous examples. Victorian painting is now admired and the Tate has a remarkable selection, from John Martin's apocalyptic *The Great Day of His Wrath* to Frith's *Derby Day,* with its unbelievably complex story-telling detail. From the later 19thC, Whistler stands out. This American painter working in England placed great emphasis on abstract pictorial qualities such as color harmony.

Next come the French and British Impressionists and Post-Impressionists, with all the major figures represented with works of varying quality. Degas' bronze *Little Dancer* and Gaugin's *Faa Iheihe* are notable. An important masterpiece by the pioneering artist of the Fauve group, Matisse, is the late collage *The Snail.* Cubism, short-lived but vitally important, is demonstrated with a few works of high quality by Picasso and Braque. Stanley Spencer and his circle are also well represented.

The move to complete abstraction is shown by Kandinsky and Mondrian. Important works by Picasso, the giant of modern art, include the famous *Tree Dancers* in his unique version of the Surrealist style. The Surrealists themselves, Miró, Ernst, Magritte and Dalí, are well represented, as are the American Abstract Expressionists.

There is a room devoted to Henry Moore as well as one to Francis Bacon, Lucian Freud, Kossoff, Auerbach and Hodgkin. A high point of the gallery is the room devoted to Mark Rothko's powerful murals for the Seagram Building in New York, a potent reminder of the achievements of modern art.

The three central **Duveen Sculpture Galleries** display the work of Auguste Rodin, Matisse, Epstein and minimal artists. To the right of the North Duveen is the exhibition area where three major loan exhibitions are held each year. Displays of works on paper are held in the Lower Galleries.

The **Clore Gallery for the Turner Collection** (James Stirling, architect — beautifully proportioned and lit) houses Turner's bequest of his works to the nation, a dazzling display of light and color, revealing an unmatched understanding of nature in all its moods and prefiguring the Impressionists' innovations by several decades. The late works, such as the studies of *Norham Castle,* are outstanding.

TEMPLE 🏛 ☆

Map 10F13. Tube: Temple.

It can be easy to miss the gateway to the Inner and Middle Temples amid the bustle of FLEET STREET, yet behind them lies a large and relatively peaceful enclave of historic buildings and gardens down toward the Thames. The Temple is named after the Knights Templar, a religious order founded in the Middle Ages to further the Crusades, who came to this site — then outside the City walls — in about 1160. They constructed a great complex of monastic buildings, of which the chapel survives. Some time in the 14thC, the buildings were taken over by lawyers, and there they have remained, today organized into two of the four INNS OF COURT.

The red-brick **Middle Temple Gateway** was built in 1684 to a design using Classical motifs, and leads through to Middle Temple Lane, lined with chambers and courtyards. Much was destroyed by wartime bombing, although some buildings date back to the 17thC and beyond. Outstanding is the **Middle Temple Hall** of 1562-70 *(* 🔲 *open Mon-Fri 10-11.30am, 3-4pm)*, expertly restored and retaining a superb Elizabethan **hammerbeam roof** and **oak screen**, with Doric columns and arches, and finely carved figures. It is likely that Shakespeare himself appeared in the performance of *Twelfth Night* given here in 1602.

> There are still worse places than the Temple, on a sultry day,
> for basking in the sun, or resting idly in the shade.
> There is yet a drowsiness in its courts, and a dreamy dullness
> in its trees and gardens.
> (Charles Dickens, *Barnaby Rudge,* 1841)

To the E, narrow alleys lead through to the **Inner Temple**. Here, the most important building is the **Templar church**, a fascinating medieval structure. It is one of five circular churches in England, based on the Church of the Holy Sepulcher in Jerusalem. The round nave was begun in about 1160 and completed by 1185, one of the earliest Gothic structures in England. The chancel is from about 1220-40, in a more openly airy Gothic style. On the floor of the nave are nine 13thC effigies of knights in Purbeck marble.

The **Inner Temple Gateway**, leading back to FLEET ST., is an attractive half-timbered house of 1610-11, restored in 1906. Upstairs is Prince Henry's Room, with an elaborately decorated plaster ceiling. The Prince of Wales Feathers and the initials "PH" suggest the link with James I's son.

THEATRE MUSEUM

1E Tavistock St., WC2 ☎*(071) 836-7891. Map 10F12* 📷 *✗ by arrangement* 📽 *Open Tues-Sun 11am-6pm. Tube: Covent Garden.*

Opened in 1987, this is an outpost of the VICTORIA AND ALBERT MUSEUM appropriately sited in COVENT GARDEN, close to theaterland and the Royal Opera House. It is rich in theatrical history and memorabilia. In the lobby, a giant gilt angel, rescued from the Gaiety Theatre, Aldwych, beckons. All aspects of the performing arts are included: models, costumes, playbills, posters, puppets, props and much more besides. Here are the box office from the Duke of York's, Noël Coward's mono-grammed dressing gown and slippers, original models for the opera by master designer Oliver Messel, Elton John's platform boots and Mick Jagger's jumpsuit. There is also a box office for all London shows and concerts, and a theatrical reference library.

TOWER BRIDGE
SE1 ☎(071) 403-3761. Map **12**H17-G17 ☒ ✱ ◀ *Open Apr-Oct 10am-5.45pm; Nov-Mar 10am-4pm. Tube: Tower Hill.*
With its towers and drawbridges, this landmark, adjacent to the TOWER OF LONDON, has become a symbol for London. Built in 1886-94, it is the most easterly bridge across the Thames, and though designed so that large ships can pass beneath its easily raised roadway, it is deceptively graceful when viewed from a distance.

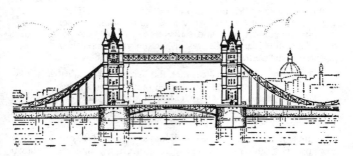

Enter by the N tower to visit the glass-enclosed walkway, which has splendid views: Butler's Wharf downstream, HMS BELFAST to the W and ST KATHARINE'S DOCK on the N bank. The **Tower Bridge Museum**, located to the S of the bridge, contains the original steam-driven machinery used to lift the bridge. Closed for the first half of 1993 for modernization, the museum reopens with an impressively expanded, hands-on audiovisual display, which includes animatronic figures who recount Tower Bridge's history, and interactive CD technology capable of showing changing views of the river through the ages. There are further exhibitions in the NW and S towers.

Superbly lit at night, Tower Bridge is one of London's most memorable sights after dark.

TOWER HILL PAGEANT
Tower Hill Terrace, Tower Hill, EC3 ☎(071) 709-0081. Map **12**G17 ☒ ⚕ ✱ *Open Apr-Oct 9.30am-5.30pm; Nov-Mar 9.30am-4.30pm. Tube: Tower Hill.*
Devised in conjunction with the Museum of London (see LONDON, MU-SEUM OF), this is a "dark ride" where computer-controlled cars (one of them is specially adapted for wheelchairs) take visitors past tableaux depicting scenes of waterfront London from Roman times to the Blitz.

The pageant was inspired by the Museum of London's archeological work along the waterfront, and finds from that long-running project are displayed in the second-level museum.

TOWER OF LONDON 🏛 ★

EC3 ☎(071) 709-0765. Map 12G17 🔲 🖾 *in Jewel House* ✗ *last about 1hr, starting at Middle Tower: last tour 3.30pm summer, 2.30pm winter* ♣ ✖ *except guide dogs. Open Mar-Oct Mon-Sat 9.30am-5pm, Sun 10am-5pm; Nov-Feb Mon-Sat 9.30am-4pm. Tube: Tower Hill.*

The Tower's great keep rises from its complex accretion of massively fortified walls, moats, towers and bastions, and today its forbidding but thrilling appearance is often used as a symbol for London. The best views are from Tower Hill to the N and w, by All Hallows church, from TOWER BRIDGE, or perhaps from the river itself, on a boat trip from Tower Pier. The Tower is London's most substantial medieval monument, steeped in a bloody past and containing a superb collection of arms and armor, and the priceless Crown Jewels. As a result, it is a prime tourist attraction and is often crowded; a visit near opening time is therefore recommended.

It was founded by William the Conqueror just inside the Roman wall at the E end of London following his arrival in 1066, to encourage the loyalty of the townspeople as much as to defend them. William's castle was initially a wooden structure, but from about 1077 the great stone White Tower, first of the square Norman keeps, began to rise, to be completed by 1097 in the reign of the Conqueror's son, William Rufus. At this time, the White Tower stood alone, joined to the river by an enclosed bailey, but Richard the Lion Heart began to build a curtain wall in the late 12thC, a process continued under Henry III. Edward I (1272-1307) completed the transformation of the Norman stronghold into a fully-fledged medieval castle; the White Tower was now surrounded by a continuous curtain wall with 12 towers. The moat surrounding the whole was up to 12 feet wide, with a barbican on the far side guarding the drawbridges. This is substantially the Tower we see today.

Until the reign of James I (1603-25), the Tower was a leading royal residence. Its strength meant that it was also used as a principal armory and house for royal treasure. These functions have continued, and the Tower still holds the Crown Jewels and weaponry that have been amassed over the ages. The Tower's security also commended it as a prison, and kings and queens have kept many of their most notable enemies within its walls: Anne Boleyn, Sir Thomas More, Elizabeth I (while a princess), Sir Walter Raleigh and, most recently, Rudolf Hess in World War II.

The continuous traditions of the Tower have cloaked it in rich ceremony. It is guarded still by the Yeomen Warders, or the "Beefeaters," a company founded by Henry VII in 1485, who still wear Tudor

THE TOWER OF LONDON

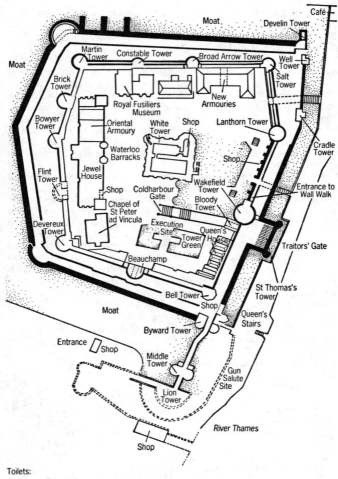

Toilets:
Ladies: at Beauchamp, Brick and Cradle Towers
Gentlemen: at Brick and Cradle Towers
Disabled/Nursing Mothers: at Brick Tower

costume, with blue tunics carrying the sovereign's monogram on the chest, and broad, flat caps. On ceremonial occasions, a more elaborate scarlet version of the same dress is worn. Together with guardsmen from the Regular Army, Yeomen Warders participate in the **Ceremony of the Keys** at 9.50pm each day, formally locking up the Tower for the night (see CALENDAR OF EVENTS, page 56).

Another tradition hangs around the six ravens that live inside the Tower's walls. These are kept jealously, with a meat allowance: there is a legend that the Tower will fall when the ravens leave.

The easiest way to see the inner walls and to grasp the overall layout of the Tower is by following the **Wall Walk**, a 500-yard stroll along the elevated battlements, passing through six towers. It starts with the Wakefield Tower and ends with the Martin Tower. Children under 16 must be accompanied by a responsible adult.

The outer fortifications

The main entrance to the Tower, as in the Middle Ages, is to the w, near the river. Evidence can be seen of the medieval causeway that led up to the vanished Lion Tower, so called because it housed the royal menagerie — lions and leopards included — until 1834. The whole entrance defense work, or barbican, was originally surrounded by water and reached by drawbridge.

Another drawbridge led to the **Middle Tower**, the present outer gateway, an 18thC reconstruction. From here, a causeway leads across the broad moat (once with another drawbridge) to the gate in **Byward Tower**, built by Edward I. The moat was drained in 1843 and is now grassed over. Byward Tower leads into the corridor between the curtain walls, with the angled **Bell Tower** on the left, probably built soon after 1200 by King John, one of the oldest surviving parts. Farther along on the right is the notorious **Traitors' Gate**, through which royal barges and boats bearing prisoners (or provisions) could enter the castle.

The inner buildings

The inner precincts of the Tower can be entered through the gate in the **Bloody Tower** opposite, overlooked by the heavily fortified round structure of the **Wakefield Tower** to the side. The Bloody Tower is by tradition the site of the murder of the young princes by their uncle, Richard III, in 1485, hoping to secure his succession to the throne, although modern historians are less certain about the event than was Shakespeare.

Inside the tower, a winch used to raise the portcullis can be seen, and two rooms are furnished as they might have been when Sir Walter Raleigh was imprisoned here. Other notable prisoners included Thomas Cranmer, Archbishop Laud and the notorious Judge Jeffreys.

The great open space enclosed by the fortification of the curtain walls can now be appreciated. On the right is a portion of 12thC wall, surviving from the Norman bailey, only exposed in 1940 when a bomb destroyed a 19thC building. When the top of the steps ahead is reached, the **Queen's House** *(not open to the public),* a pretty half-timbered structure begun in about 1540, is on the left. In its rooms, Guy Fawkes was tortured following the 1605 Gunpowder Plot.

To the N is the entrance to the **Beauchamp Tower**, used again and again as a prison. The interior is covered with carved graffiti, giving witness to the suffering of prisoners. Nearby is the **Chapel of St Peter ad Vincula**, built in the early 16thC on a 12thC foundation, in Perpendicular Gothic style. It retains some late medieval monuments. Beyond the chapel, the **Bowyer Tower** contains a display of torture instruments.

The Crown Jewels ★

Nearby begin the long lines for the Crown Jewels, the Tower's greatest single attraction. The lines move quickly, so you cannot expect more than a brief look.

Kept below the 19thC Waterloo Barracks, the jewels are reached through a suitably dramatic pair of polished steel doors, and are the Tower's best-guarded prisoners ever. The fire and brilliance of the stones are even more spectacular than their reputation or their worth. Almost all the royal regalia was melted down or sold off by Cromwell, so most of what is left dates from after the 1660 Restoration. The display begins with a selection of plate, massive and ornate pieces in silver-gilt; look out for the fabulous **wine cooler** of 1829, gilded state maces and bejeweled swords. The rich vestments of the knightly orders are on display, but overshadowed by the coronation robes of the sovereign, elaborately covered in gold embroidery.

The **Crown Jewels** themselves are in the next room. Two items of coronation regalia survive from the Middle Ages: an exquisite **spoon**, probably made for King John's coronation in 1199, and a much restored early 15thC **ampulla** in the form of an eagle (from which the anointing oil is poured).

The **Royal Sceptre** contains the largest diamond ever cut (530 carats), one of the "Stars of Africa" from the Cullinan diamond found in 1905. Another piece was added to the **Imperial State Crown**, originally made in 1838, which also incorporates an immense and beautiful ruby, probably the one given to the Black Prince by Pedro the Cruel after the Battle of Najara in 1367 and worn by Henry V at the Battle of Agincourt. The oldest crown is "King Edward's," made for Charles II's coronation in 1660. It weighs 5lbs and is worn by the sovereign at coronations. The **Queen Mother's Crown**, made for her coronation in 1937, contains the famous 109-carat Kohinoor diamond, bought by the British Crown in 1849.

The White Tower and armories

The dominant White Tower (pictured on page 23) is the oldest and largest of the Tower's buildings; its massive walls, built of Caen stone, are up to 15 feet thick, supported by external buttresses and carrying square or curved turrets at the corners. The large semicircular protuberance at the SE contains the apse of the chapel; the round turret on the NE corner contains a spiral staircase. The medieval facade was even starker — since then the decorative cones have been added, and Wren enlarged the windows.

Inside are displays from the superb collections of arms and armor. On the first floor, the **Sporting and Tournament Galleries** contain crossbows, muskets, lances, swords and the specialized armor made for jousting, already in the late Middle Ages a leisurely exercise in archaism.

The **Chapel of St John** on the second floor is the finest example of early Norman architecture in England, almost totally without ornament, massive and severe. More armor is displayed in the other two rooms; notice the awesome bulk of a suit made for a giant almost 7 feet tall.

The 3rd-floor rooms contain outstanding examples of Tudor and later armor, with several suits that belonged to Henry VIII, growing progressively larger as their owner grew older and fatter. The ceremonial armor of the 17thC is decorated to a high degree; a suit belonging to Charles I from 1630 is chased and gilded over its entire surface.

Stairs descend to ground level where a fine selection of handguns, uniforms and cannons from various periods can be seen. The Oriental armor, including fine examples from India, China, Japan, even Africa, is housed in the **Waterloo Barracks**, worth visiting in particular for the elaborate elephant armor captured at the Battle of Plassey in 1757. Of many interesting artillery pieces scattered throughout the Tower's enclosures, note a Turkish bronze cannon of 1530-31.

TRAFALGAR SQUARE
Map 9G11. Tube: Charing Cross.

Trafalgar Square is known as a rallying point for political demonstrations and New Year's Eve revelries, and even as a sanctuary for pigeons. When Nash began its redevelopment in the 1820s, it already had the fine equestrian statue of Charles I on the site of CHARING CROSS, and the superb church of ST MARTIN-IN-THE-FIELDS. Since then, the surrounding architecture has rather let down Nash's vision: the NATIONAL GALLERY, added on the high N side in 1832-38, is too small in scale to make the triumphant statement that its site demands, and Admiralty Arch (1911), a monument to Queen Victoria that saves its best face for THE MALL, is equally uninspired.

All this, however, does allow **Nelson's Column** to steal the show, as Nash intended. The 170-foot granite column was erected in 1842. Its base is decorated by spirited reliefs made from the guns of ships captured at Trafalgar and other battles, and the deservedly famous lions were added by Landseer in 1858-67.

Two recent changes to the vista at Trafalgar Square caused a stir. Prince Charles's "monstrous carbuncle on the face of an old friend" (in the words of his heartfelt and potent attack on an earlier, Modernist design for an extension to the National Gallery) was never built, but its replacement design for the **Sainsbury Wing**, by Robert Venturi and Denise Scott-Brown, has nevertheless caused controversy and was received with mixed reactions. Meanwhile **Grand Buildings**, on the corner of Northumberland Ave., were reconstructed as an exact replica of the former structure and have helped to smarten up Trafalgar Square.

TROCADERO
Piccadilly Circus, W1. Map 9G10 ♣ Open daily 10am-10pm. Tube: Piccadilly Circus.

A host of activities jostle for attention in this shop-and-restaurant complex on the corner of Shaftesbury Ave. Built as a dance hall at the turn of the century, it became a popular Lyons restaurant between the wars. Today it is worth a visit for the GUINNESS WORLD OF RECORDS exhibition alone. Alternatively you can make a video of yourself, miming to the latest chart-topper at **Star Tracks**, dress in period costume and have a sepia photograph taken at **Old Time Portraits**, or immortalize your face on a poster or T-shirt at **Amazing Pictures**.

Teenagers will enjoy **Funland**, with its blaring music, dodgem cars and hi-tech simulators, including the all-too-realistic **Virtual Reality Centre**, where a screen incorporated in a driving helmet gives the impression of 365° vision. They will also head for **Quasar**, the bad-taste war game where you can have "serious fun with a laser gun."

VICTORIA & ALBERT MUSEUM ★

Cromwell Rd., SW7 ☎(071) 938-8500. Map **14J5** ▣ *voluntary contributions invited* ✗ *start from information desk at main entrance: Mon-Sat at 11am, noon, 2pm, 3pm; Sun at 3pm only* ▣ ✦ *Open Mon-Sat 10am-5.50pm; Sun 2.30pm-5.50pm. Tube: South Kensington.*

Probably the world's greatest museum of the decorative arts, it is a vast storehouse of extraordinarily varied treasures. While fine art is emphatically included, the reverence of the art gallery is absent. The "V&A" is thus a lively, informal place, and one of London's most popular museums. The range of the exhibits is overwhelming, including everything from entire furnished rooms, brought from the great houses of Britain and the Continent, to spoons, shoes and locks.

The museum, one of the largest in the world, is a labyrinth of galleries and passages in which it is easy to become lost, and around which it is almost impossible to plan a coherent or comprehensive tour. But, to an extent, this drawback contributes to the museum's appeal, for even regular visitors know that no matter how often they come, there are still new treasures to be discovered.

The initial impetus and financing for the Victoria & Albert came from the Great Exhibition of 1851, the profits of which were used to purchase the large site in South Kensington on which it stands. Under the enthusiastic direction of Prince Albert's friend Sir Henry Cole, it first opened as the Museum of Ornamental Art in 1852, temporarily at MARLBOROUGH HOUSE, dedicated to fostering the "application of fine art to objects of utility," but in 1857 the museum moved to its iron and glass construction at South Kensington.

Almost from the first, Cole's ideals became diluted by the desire to fill the museum with great works of art. In 1865 Raphael's tapestry cartoons arrived from the Royal Collection. In 1888, the Constable Collection was bequeathed by a member of the great painter's family, adding another fine-art element of the greatest importance but having little to do with the museum's intention. Before long, the museum felt free to acquire any item of esthetic or historical interest.

Similar uncertainties have dogged the museum's building programs, contributing to the sense of confusion. After 1863, the red-brick buildings were constructed around the gardens in a northern Italian Romanesque style with terracotta and mosaic ornament. The leading artist, Lord

Leighton, and the firm of William Morris contributed to the decoration of the interior, but shortage of funds prevented the scheme's completion. The library, especially attractive and now called the **National Art Library**, was completed by 1882. But all this was haphazard and without any underlying plan. The final phase came in 1899-1909 with Sir Aston Webb as architect. The museum was renamed the Victoria & Albert in 1899. From this time date the great facades along Cromwell Rd.

Finding your way

It is not possible to suggest a complete route through the 7 miles of galleries in the V&A — the result would be both difficult to follow and exhausting. Instead, two particularly well-displayed but contrasting departments are proposed as the starting and ending points — the Jones Collection and Constable Collection — and suggestions are made below for sections to be visited in between. Visitors should stay alert on their travels for the countless minor surprises that the museum has to offer. Good large plans for the galleries are available at the main entrance.

Note that the collection is arranged into "art and design" collections, cutting across the arts of a given culture or period, and "study collections," grouped by material and techniques.

The suggested route

Begin from the main entrance by turning left and following the signs for the **Jones Collection**, a dazzling display of French interior decoration, painting, furniture, ceramics and other decorative arts. Elaborate furniture, some of which belonged to Marie-Antoinette, is inlaid with brass or with finely-grained woods, or covered with enameled panels. The rich, aristocratic mood is complemented by paintings such as Boucher's *Portrait of Madame de Pompadour.* German, Dutch and Italian decorative arts on display echo the French Rococo of the 18thC. The 17thC follows, just as elaborate but more solemn in mood. Several Dutch cabinets, inlaid with complex floral designs, are outstanding, as are German metalwork and Venetian glass.

At the end of these splendidly laid-out galleries steps lead up to the section devoted to the Renaissance, a series of rooms grouped around the court containing the gardens. In a less organized collection, some superb works stand out. There is a statue, for example, by Giovanni Bologna of *Samson and a Philistine,* a full-sized marble composition of Mannerist complexity. From the High Renaissance, there is the famous elegantly gilded **Antico miniature bronze** of Meleanger (*c.*1500), and from the 15thC several important **reliefs by Donatello**, the greatest sculptor of the early Renaissance, including an exquisite and moving *Dead Christ Tended by Angels.* Rooms on the side of the gallery opposite the garden have been restored to their original decoration; one was carried out by William Morris' workshops. Another has tiles by Minton and stained glass designed by James Gamble.

The northern Renaissance is also well covered. Particularly beautiful are two late Gothic carved limewood angels made as candlesticks by Tilman Reimenschneider in the early 16thC. At the end of the gallery of Gothic art is a vast and gruesome Spanish altarpiece of the early 15thC, showing scenes from the life of St George, which, according to this account, consisted almost entirely of hideous torture. Be sure to study the **Syon Cope** closely — this early 14thC example of *opus anglicanum* needlework is one of the finest embroidered pieces ever.

Also on the ground floor is the large and stunning **Dress Collection** (✰), with one of the world's great clothing collections of everyday garments and high fashion. We relate to this instantly, of course, but it is notable that some outfits of even a decade or two ago seem as strange as an 18thC ball gown or Jacobean court dress. Above is the collection of **musical instruments**, especially strong in the 16thC keyboards such as virginals and the first harpsichords, many with exquisite carving and inlaid work.

A huge gallery nearby exhibits the seven **Raphael cartoons** (★), on permanent loan from the Royal Collection. These vastly influential designs of the *Acts of the Apostles* were carried out in 1516-19 as designs for tapestries for the Sistine Chapel in the Vatican. Next to this room is the main museum shop, housed in a gallery containing part of the **woodwork collection**.

Oriental arts are also represented on the ground floor, although even the large galleries allow room for only a small part of the V&A's great holdings. In the **Nehru Gallery** of Indian Art and the gallery of Indian sculpture nearby are several beautiful temple sculptures. More unusual is **Tipoo's Tiger**, a large wooden model of a tiger mauling a European, identified as British by his red coat; made in about 1790 for an anti-British sultan, it has organ pipes that simulate the groans of the victim. Outstanding is the exquisite **jade wine cup** made for Shah Jahan in 1657, with a lotus flower base and a graceful antelope head as the handle.

The **Islamic gallery** is dominated by the vast **Ardabil Carpet** of 1540 from a Persian mosque, and some superb lacquered pottery. Outstanding in the new **Tsui Gallery** of Chinese Art is an incredibly elaborate carved lacquer throne of the mid-18thC, ceramic and jade horses from more than 1,000 years earlier, and finely embroidered court costumes, all testifying to the unchanging sophistication of Chinese art. The **Toshiba Gallery** of Japanese art, opened in 1986, contains exquisite collections of *netsuke,* kimonos, armor and ceramics.

The important **British Collection** stretches through sizable galleries on two upper floors to the left (or w) of the main entrance. First encountered is the furniture, especially beautiful but generally simpler than the Continental equivalents, often relying more on shape and the quality of the wood than on elaborate decoration. Several complete rooms transplanted into the museum include the massively Baroque gold and white **Music Room from Norfolk House** (mid-18thC) and Robert Adam's much more delicate **Glass Drawing Room from Northumberland House** (1773-74).

Two beds dominate the furniture: the huge Elizabethan **Great Bed of Ware**, which became instantly legendary for its size and was mentioned by Shakespeare; and a chinoiserie fantasy by Chippendale of 1750-55. Quite outstanding are several **miniatures**, a form of painting that reached its peak in 16th-17thC England, including Nicholas Hilliard's famous *Young Man Amongst Roses*. The same artist is thought to have produced the miniature on the **Armada Jewel**, produced for Elizabeth I in 1589 to celebrate the destruction of the Spanish Armada, and the highlight of a fine jewelry collection. British decorative arts are brought up to 1960, and there are several important examples of the work of William Morris and the Arts and Crafts Movement that had so much influence on modern British design.

Before leaving, be sure to visit the **Henry Cole Wing**, opened in 1984 at the rear of the museum to the w. Here is found the **Ionides Bequest**, consisting largely but not exclusively of 19thC paintings, with several important works: outstanding are a Degas ballet scene, Millet's *Wood Sawyers,* Burne-Jones' *Day Dream*, Gainsborough's portrait of his two young daughters, and works by Turner.

Here also is the **Constable Collection**, the finest anywhere of the work of the most English of painters, providing a refreshing, open-air view for even the most jaded visitor. The fleeting effects of the changing weather of the English countryside are here shown utterly convincingly. Clouds rush over Hampstead Heath, rainbows hover over Salisbury Cathedral, and the trees of Suffolk rustle in gentle breezes. There are also some superb small oil and watercolor "sketches" by the master.

The Henry Cole Wing also houses the new **Gallery of European Ornament**, a study in design, decoration and style in Europe from 1450 to the present. Objects as diverse as a customized leather jacket, a 1960s Op Art tie, 16thC tableware and William Morris wallpapers are brought together to illustrate the development of design, geometry and figurative patterns over a variety of materials, functions and geographical regions.

Next door, in the main body of the museum, is the **20thC exhibitions gallery**. It mounts temporary exhibitions, often imaginative, on leading figures and aspects of 20thC design production.

WALLACE COLLECTION ★

Hertford House, Manchester Sq., W1 ☎*(071) 935-0687. Map 8E8* 🖾 ✉ *Open Mon-Sat 10am-5pm; Sun 2-5pm. Tube: Bond Street.*

Flying in the face of the renowned English insularity, this magnificent monument to Francophilia is arguably the finest selection of French art to be found outside France, together with many other paintings and objets d'art of exceptional quality. It is a great private art collection of the 19thC "frozen" in the grand house equipped by its wealthy owner to contain it.

Hertford House in Manchester Sq. was built for the Duke of Manchester in 1776-88 and acquired by the Second Marquess of Hertford in 1797. After some years as the French Embassy, it was used to store pictures by the Fourth Marquess, who did most to build up the fabulous collection while living in Paris, adding to that of his father. He bequeathed both house and works of art to his natural son, Sir Richard Wallace, who returned to London and transformed Hertford House in the 1870s into a showcase for the collection. In 1897, his widow left it to the nation, and it was opened as a public gallery in 1900. It thus reflects the tastes of five generations of the Hertford family.

The finest objects are on the first floor, which should be seen first. Large paintings by Boucher are on the walls of the top landing, full of the frivolous eroticism of the Rococo court style. Turning to the left, **Rm. XIII** contains several scenes of Venice by Guardi and Canaletto. **Rms. XV-XVIII** are devoted to Flemish and Dutch art, including fine studies by Rubens. Look out for Potter's animal scenes: even the cows have personality. Caspar Netscher's *Lace-Maker,* quietly realistic, is serenely haunting; the landscapes include marvelous works by Hobbema, and Flinck's eerie *Landscape with a Coach,* formerly attributed to his master, Rembrandt.

Rm. XIX is a large picture gallery built by Sir Richard Wallace, containing many outstanding works: Titian's *Perseus and Andromeda,* Rubens' magical *Rainbow Landscape* and Velázquez's cool *Lady with a Fan* are the most important. Also noteworthy are Rembrandt's deeply sympathetic *Portrait of Titus,* his son, Reynolds' famous portrait of the courtesan *Nelly O'Brien* and Frans Hals' *Laughing Cavalier.*

Among superb, richly ornate Rococo furniture is a roll-top desk made by J.J. Riesener for Count d'Orsay in the 1760s (**Rm. XXV**), and a chest of drawers made for Louis XV's bedroom at Versailles by Antoine Gaudreaus in 1739 (**Rm. XXI**). In the corridor between Rms. XXIII and XXIV an impressive collection of gold snuffboxes is displayed, mostly elaborate French 18thC work.

Some of the best French Rococo pictures are in **Rms. XXI-XXV,** leading in an unparalleled procession through Watteau, Lancret, Pater, Boucher and Fragonard and complemented by richly decorated furniture in the same style, much of it from French royal palaces. Watteau's *Lady at her Toilet* and Fragonard's *Swing* sum up the leisured mood, and Boucher's *Portrait of Madame Pompadour* shows unexpected candor. **Rm. XIV** contains a superb display of Sèvres porcelain.

On the ground floor, **Rm. X** and the adjoining corridor contain the best public collection of works by R.P. Bonington, an English artist working in France in the early 19thC. The clear light of his seascapes is exquisite.

The rest of the ground floor is more an Aladdin's cave of miscellaneous treasures, many grouped into specialist collections of great merit — of armor, miniatures or pottery, for example. There is a splendid collection of terracotta statuettes, mostly from the Italian Renaissance, and a unique cabinet of wax portraits.

Furniture, including works attributed to the great A. C. Boulle, and more Sèvres porcelain, continue the French bias of the collection. Italian majolica pottery and Limoges enamels of the Renaissance are as well represented here as anywhere in the world. Paintings include works by Murillo, Reynolds, Memlinc, Lawrence and Luini. And if anything, the remarkable collection of elaborately wrought and decorated **arms and armor** stands out. Look out for the northern Italian body armor and helmet of about 1620-35.

THE WELLINGTON MUSEUM

APSLEY HOUSE, the former home in Piccadilly of the "Iron Duke," the Duke of Wellington, is now a museum.

WESTMINSTER

Home of Britain's government, Westminster was once a city in its own right rivaling what is now the CITY. See LONDON'S DISTRICTS, pages 87-88.

WESTMINSTER ABBEY 🏛 ★

Broad Sanctuary, SW1 ☎*(071) 222-5152. Map 17I11* 🖾 *to royal chapels*
🖾 *except Wed 6-7.45pm* ✗ *Open Mon-Fri 9am-4pm; Sat 9am-2pm, 3.45-5pm.*
Tube: Westminster.

Since William the Conqueror chose the new, incomplete Westminster Abbey for his coronation as king of his new subjects on Christmas Day, 1066, it has been the scene of the coronation, marriage and burial of British monarchs, a place of tribute to Britain's heroes, and in every way Britain's mother church. While St Paul's Cathedral belongs to London, Westminster Abbey belongs to the nation. It is also, of course, one of Britain's finest Gothic buildings, a soaring and graceful offering to God, with a strikingly unified interior.

The date of Westminster Abbey's foundation is uncertain. Legend takes it back to the 7thC; in any case, there was certainly a religious foundation here by the 9thC. In 1050 Edward the Confessor began work on a large new abbey church, in the Norman style, and it became a Benedictine monastery attached to the new Palace of Westminster.

Work continued on the Norman buildings well into the 12thC, and remains can be seen in the ruined infirmary chapel of St Catherine to the s of the present abbey church. In 1245, Henry III began a vast new building program in the latest French Gothic style of the cathedrals of Amiens and Reims. Work proceeded quickly. The chancel, transepts, part of the nave and the chapter house were completed by 1259. The great speed of the construction gave the building a remarkable unity of style and, when work was resumed more than a century later in 1375, the existing style was imitated in the rest of the nave.

The mid-16thC was a time of religious upheaval, which first threatened and then confirmed the abbey's role. The royal connection preserved it from destruction at the dissolution of the monasteries and, in 1540, Henry VIII made it a cathedral, with its own bishop. Queen Mary, briefly restoring Catholicism, turned it back into a monastery in 1556. The permanent establishment of the protestant Church of England came under Elizabeth I, who in 1560 gave the abbey the status of a collegiate church independent of both the Bishop of London and the Archbishop of Canterbury. It thus became a Royal Peculiar, a great church serving Crown and State.

The building of Westminster Abbey did not end with the Middle Ages, although what has come since has tended to detract from its beauty. In 1698, Sir Christopher Wren began the designs for the w towers and facade. These were continued by Nicholas Hawksmoor and completed in 1745 — in pseudo-Gothic style but sitting uneasily all the same with the existing structure. In the 19thC, restoration work was carried out on a substantial scale, much of it destroying the medieval detail. Thankfully, the restoration work currently under way concentrates on conservation rather than improvement.

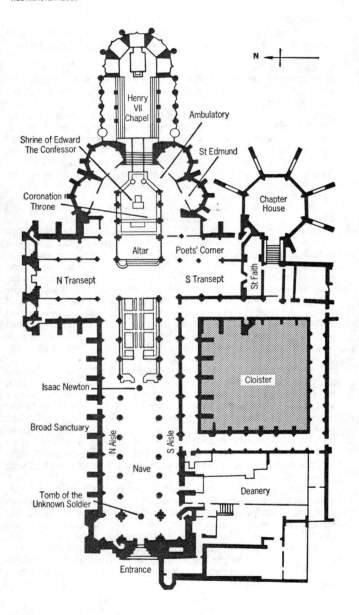

N

Henry VII Chapel

Ambulatory

Shrine of Edward The Confessor

St Edmund

Coronation Throne

Chapter House

Altar

Poets' Corner

N Transept

S Transept

St Faith

Isaac Newton

Cloister

Broad Sanctuary

N Aisle

S Aisle

Nave

Deanery

Tomb of the Unknown Soldier

Entrance

The exterior

A huge program of restoration is under way, begun in the mid-1970s and due to be completed by the mid-1990s. Cleaning has revealed the beauty of the abbey's soft Reigate stone (although where replacement is necessary Portland stone is being used, which will better stand the test of time). The w facade, with the main entrance, is perhaps the most dramatic approach, although Hawksmoor's towers are insubstantial — just too narrow and too high to suit the medieval facade — and their provenance can be detected in the Baroque stonework above the clock face and matching round windows in the opposite tower.

The abbey looks best from the N; the N transept forms a tremendous centerpiece, with its great triple porch and huge rose window, framed by a superb series of flying buttresses. Alas, all the stonework is a product of 19thC restoration and only indicates in a general way the detail that was there before.

To the E lies the far more elaborate exterior of Henry VII's chapel, entirely covered with dense late Gothic tracery. The outer walls have turrets capped by "pepperpots" and connected to the chapel's nave by delicately pierced flying buttresses. The nave is topped by a pierced balustrade and narrow pinnacles. The whole effect is wonderfully decorative. To the s of the chapel can be seen the earlier, much plainer chapter house. The pointed roof is 19thC.

The area around Westminster Abbey once formed a part of it and was densely covered with buildings. The open space to the NW was the Sanctuary, where anyone could seek the Church's protection in medieval times; as a result it became packed with timber buildings inhabited by felons on the run. The s of the abbey was made up of the monastic buildings, and the cloister remains, but this is best visited from within the abbey, as is the Chapel of St Faith.

Other monastic buildings to the s of these are now incorporated in Westminster School, the leading public school that has evolved from the monastery's teaching function. To the N is **Dean's Yard**, now an open space, which can be entered through a 19thC arch to the w of the abbey. Until the 18thC it was covered over by monastic buildings.

The interior

The abbey is entered from the w, immediately presenting the visitor with a stunning view along the nave. Sweeping exaltedly upward, it is very like a French Gothic cathedral, much higher and narrower than other English churches, supported on piers of dark Purbeck marble. Above the main arches is the triforium, containing a gallery (unlike the French style); then the clerestory containing the windows, beneath the gracefully vaulted ceiling, completing the majesty. The western end of the nave was built last to match the style of the 13thC work to the E; the huge, plain window above the w door is late 15thC.

Set in the floor ahead of the entrance is a memorial to Winston Churchill with the **Tomb of the Unknown Warrior** beyond; the brass lettering is made from cartridges brought back with the body from the World War I trenches. On the first pier of the nave to the right hangs a famous and rare medieval **portrait of Richard II**, probably painted in

1398. Both the aisles are filled with monuments, jumbles of marble statuary, both good and bad. In the s aisle, that to Colonel Townshend, killed at the Battle of Ticonderoga in the American War of Independence, is of particular merit. It was designed by Robert Adam and made soon after 1759.

The N aisle is even more crowded with monuments. Most notable is that to Charles James Fox of 1823. Look out also for the small kneeling wall effigy of Mrs Jane Hill of 1631, with *Death in a Shroud* and the *Tree of Life* above. Buried in the nave are David Livingstone, the explorer, and the engineers Thomas Telford and Robert Stephenson, among many national figures. The E end of the nave is closed by a brightly colored Neo-Gothic choir screen of 1848. On the left in one of its arches is a fine monument of 1731 to Isaac Newton, designed by William Kent and carved by J.M. Rysbrack.

The rest of the abbey is reached through a gate in the N aisle. Memorials to scientists cluster near Newton's tomb: Lister, Darwin, Faraday, Rutherford; musicians including Elgar, Vaughan-Williams and Benjamin Britten are commemorated by plaques in the floor near Purcell's monument. In the N transept the monuments come thick and heavy, and include those to 19thC statesmen. The architecture is of Henry III's time (1216-72), but the great rose window was substantially restored in the 19thC.

In the E of the transept, among several older monuments, is one of the most impressively carved and imaginatively conceived of all — that to Mrs J.G. Nightingale, made by Roubiliac in 1761. It shows a grim figure of Death pointing a lance at the unfortunate lady, who died after being struck by lightning. The fine monument to Sir Francis Vere from 1609 is also remarkable.

At this point, notice the **crossing**, where Wren intended that a spire should rise that was never built. The wooden pulpit is early 17thC. To the w, the choir stalls are overdone Victorian Gothic, and to the E is the sanctuary, with an elaborately gilded reredos of 1867. To its right are rare and important early 14thC wall hangings, together with an early Renaissance Italian altarpiece. The medieval monuments to either side of the sanctuary are best seen from the ambulatory. Particularly fine is that to the Earl of Lancaster of 1296.

Before approaching the centerpiece of the whole abbey — the chapel and shrine to Edward the Confessor — visit the superb **Henry VII's chapel** at the E end of the abbey. Begun in 1503 and completed in 1512 by Henry VIII, it is in the much more richly elaborate Gothic style of the late Middle Ages, a mature, sophisticated farewell flourish. The whole surface is adorned with carvings — there are more than 100 statues, and the ceiling is a marvel of delicate tracery. The choir stalls are equally finely carved in wood — be sure to inspect the misericords, carvings that are visible when the seats are folded up. Henry VII's tomb in the chapel was started in 1506 in the same rich Gothic style, with a bronze screen. For the monument within, however, the Italian Pietro Torrigiano produced the first Renaissance sculpture in England in 1512-18; the heads of the corner angels are specially beautiful.

Henry VII's chapel is dedicated to the Knights of the Order of Bath —

the helmets decorated with coats of arms and the standards above each seat in the choir belong to the current Grand Knights, usually high-ranking members of the Armed Forces. The chapel has its own subsidiary chapels and aisles. In the N aisle is the joint tomb of Elizabeth I, completed in 1606 with a suitably stern effigy, and her hated rival Mary Queen of Scots. Beyond are two monuments to daughters of James I. The S aisle contains several Tudor monuments rather grander than that to Queen Elizabeth herself. The easternmost chapel is dedicated to the Royal Air Force.

From Henry VII's chapel, **Edward the Confessor's shrine**, located just behind the main altar of the abbey, is reached by a bridge, and entered past the wooden effigy and chantry chapel of Henry V, a Gothic structure of the early 15thC. Only the base remains from the magnificent tomb built by Henry III to contain the remains of the Confessor, but enough remains of the gold mosaic to indicate its former splendor. It was made by an Italian artist in about 1270, as was the fine mosaic floor and Henry III's own similar tomb.

Also in the chapel is the **coronation throne** of 1300-1, where almost every monarch since William I has been crowned. The graffiti on it, now part of history, was carved by 17thC schoolboys from nearby Westminster School who were allowed to roam unchecked around the abbey. It contains, under the seat, the **Stone of Scone**, the mystical coronation stone of the Scottish kings, captured by Edward I in 1297. Legends identify it with Jacob's pillow when he dreamed at Bethel, and also as a holy stone in Ireland. It was certainly in use as a coronation stone for Macbeth and other Scottish kings from the 9thC. Its symbolic value persists: in 1950 it was stolen by Scottish nationalists but was recovered a year later. Beside the throne are the state sword and shield of Edward III, and all around are the tombs of the medieval monarchs, some of the finest sculpture surviving from this period in England.

After this holy of holies, the chapels of the S ambulatory are an anticlimax. In the ambulatory itself are the remains of a 13thC painted retable, with a well-preserved figure of St Peter on the extreme left. St Edmund's Chapel contains a fine effigy of William of Valence, Henry III's half-brother, from 1296. Look for the lovely miniature alabaster effigies of a knight and his lady.

The S transept has two beautiful carved angels from the mid-13thC in the spandrels of the main arch, but is more famous as **Poet's Corner**. Here are buried, or commemorated, many of the greatest writers in the English language. The best monument, to Geoffrey Chaucer, was placed here in 1555, but probably includes older elements.

More recent poets commemorated include Ben Jonson, Milton, Blake, Longfellow and Shakespeare (a most undistinguished statue). Browning, Byron, Tennyson, Henry James and Dylan Thomas have plaques in the floor. Artists other than writers are also commemorated; Noël Coward is one, while the last ashes to be interred in Poet's Corner were those of Lord Olivier, the actor, who died in 1990. On the S wall are two fine late 13thC wall paintings, discovered in 1936.

In the S choir aisle a doorway leads through to the cloister, as dignified as a monastic cloister should be. The earliest part is to the E and N, dating from the 13thC and among the oldest remnants of Henry III's work on the abbey; the cloister was finished in the 14thC, and much restored in the 19thC. It now contains a **brass-rubbing center** *(open 9am-5pm, Mon-Sat)*, where copies can be made from replicas of medieval brass monuments. On the E side, a passageway leads through to the **chapter house** *(▥ ✰ open Apr-Sept 10am-6pm, Oct-Mar 10am-4pm)*, an exquisitely symmetrical octagon, with its vaulted roof supported on a slender Purbeck marble pier. It was built c.1250 and has been well restored to its medieval state, with beautiful red and gold tiles decorating the floor, and wall paintings. The chapter house was used throughout the Middle Ages for the occasional meetings of Parliament. To the N of the entrance is the small chapel of St Faith, with a high vaulted roof and, behind the altar, a well-preserved painting, probably late 13thC.

Beyond the chapter house is the **Norman Undercroft**, where the **Abbey Museum** *(▨ open daily 10.30am-4pm)* houses a display of the abbey's history. There are examples of carving and a number of royal funeral effigies. Those of the Middle Ages are wood; later ones are wax, clothed in contemporary costume. Armor from Henry V's funeral is particularly interesting.

WESTMINSTER CATHEDRAL ▥ ✰
Ashley Pl., SW1 ☎(071) 834-7452. Map 16J9 ▨ to campanile, open Easter-Oct 10am-5pm ◄€ Tube: Westminster, Victoria.

When designs were being considered in the late 19thC for the Roman Catholic Cathedral of Westminster, intended to be London's most important Catholic church, a Neo-Gothic structure at first seemed the inevitable choice. In the end, however, an early Christian approach was courageously adopted, against all the prevalent dictates of the era. The result of this far-sighted decision is a building of great originality, a strange Byzantine basilica unique in London and cleverly avoiding a false comparison with nearby WESTMINSTER ABBEY.

The cathedral was built under the direction of J.F. Bentley between 1895 and 1903, using as a model Santa Sophia in Istanbul, together with some Italian Renaissance ideas, the most striking of which is the huge campanile, similar to that of Siena Cathedral but in red brick with lighter stone striping. The top of the tower, 273 feet high, can be visited *(by ✿)* in summer, and affords marvelous views.

The interior is deeply impressive, with a massive open space created by the great nave, supporting a roof of four shallow domes, purely Byzantine in inspiration. The decoration is still incomplete, with rough brick exposed above the lower levels contributing to the solemn effect. The piers of the nave are giant columns of dark green marble, supposedly from the same quarry as those in Santa Sophia. Other marbles, dramatically patterned in gray and black, cover the walls, and over the altar is a great baldachin of even more brightly colored marble, but again to a restrained design. Eventually the whole interior should be covered with mosaics, although those parts completed so far fail to reflect the grandeur of the overall conception. The outstanding works of art in the cathedral are the **Stations of the Cross**, reliefs carried out by Eric Gill in 1913-18.

WESTMINSTER, PALACE OF 🏛 ★

Parliament Sq., SW1 ☎ (071) 219-4272 (House of Commons), (071) 219-3107
*(House of Lords). Map 17|11 ▣ ✖ ✗ To listen to **debates**, UK residents*
should apply to an MP or Peer, foreign residents to their Embassy or High
Commission, both well in advance, or come at off-peak times without prior
*arrangements (☎ for details). For a **tour** of the building, UK residents should*
apply to an MP or Peer, foreign residents in writing to the Commons Public
Information Office, both well in advance. During parliamentary sittings,
admittance** to public galleries is from St Stephen's entrance. **Tube:
Westminster.

The effect is stunning: sheer size combines with immense variety and
inventive detail to create an architectural triumph so instantly recogniz-
able that it has come to symbolize the very system of government,
representative democracy, housed within. In fact, this riverside complex of buildings, often known simply as the Houses of Parliament, is
only the "new" home of the mother of parliaments, a high Victorian
exercise in medievalism.

A royal palace was probably moved from Winchester to Westminster
in about 1000, being established on the Island of Thorney in the marshes
next to an existing monastery, and Edward the Confessor began an
ambitious building program in 1050-65, the monastery becoming WEST-
MINSTER ABBEY. The Norman kings followed his lead, and William Rufus,
the Conqueror's son, built Westminster Hall in 1097-99, at the time almost
certainly the largest hall in Europe. When in residence, medieval kings
would call their councils of noblemen to meet at Westminster, a forerun-
ner of the House of Lords.

In 1265, a powerful baron called Simon de Montfort began the practice
of calling additional councils of knights and burghers to represent the
shires and towns. Meeting together from 1332, these subsequently became the House of Commons. A medieval king was not obliged to call a
parliament, and only did so when he needed the cooperation of his lords
and knights. In theory, they came to advise him, but, in practice, he
needed their assistance in the raising of taxes. From this grew the fact,
unpalatable to medieval monarchs, that the country could not be governed without the consent of lords and commons.

In the 16thC, when Henry VIII moved his residence to the nearby Whitehall Palace, the Palace of Westminster became the permanent and more exclusive base of Parliament, the Commons using from 1550 the abandoned royal chapel of St Stephen. Westminster Hall was not used for Parliament, however, but retained for the royal courts until 1882.

The 17thC saw the long struggle that would eventually lead to the constitutional pre-eminence of Parliament. In 1640-49, Charles I attempted to assert the royal power and crush the Commons, losing both crown and head in the process. Since his last desperate entry in 1642 to arrest parliamentary opponents, no monarch has entered the Commons. In 1660 Charles II was recalled to the throne and the struggle between King and Parliament was renewed. During the 18thC, the monarchy lost ground steadily and parliamentary government became a reality, with a prime minister appointed by the monarch according to the electoral wishes of the country.

In constitutional terms, Parliament consists of Monarch, Lords and Commons, all of whom have to assent to the laws by which the country is governed. But, by a process of recurring struggle, members of the Commons have acquired the dominant role: the Lords can now only delay legislation by one year, and royal assent is never refused. The Lords is still the highest Court of Appeal in the land. A much criticized anachronism is that the Lords is still largely composed of hereditary peers, although increasingly they are now created for life only. The British system has developed slowly, through reforms and bitter struggles, and uniquely combines traditional ritual with democratic practice. The palace is still a web of ancient regulations: for example, in the Commons, the hatless must take opera hats provided for them in boxes.

Tightened security limits public access to the interior of the palace. The medieval royal palace, with its 17th to 18thC additions, was largely destroyed by fire in 1834. In 1840, rebuilding began, with only the old cloister, Westminster Hall and the crypt of St Stephen's Chapel being preserved. The architect was Sir Charles Barry, with the younger A.W.N. Pugin as his assistant. Barry was essentially a Classicist, forced by his brief to work in the Gothic idiom. Pugin, on the other hand, was a passionate medievalist — indeed, it was his meticulous drawings that won the commission. The House of Lords chamber was complete by 1847, the Commons by 1850. Both men died in 1852, and the work was not completed overall until 1860.

The exterior

The most splendid views of the palace are from Westminster Bridge or across the river, taking in the great regular facade Barry constructed along the riverside, with large asymmetrical towers at either end: the huge square **Victoria Tower** to the s and the more slender and original **Clock Tower** to the N, the superb clock of which is Britain's most authoritative. Although this tower is often known as **Big Ben**, that name actually applies to the huge bell inside the clock itself, supposedly named after Benjamin Hall, the then Commissioner of Works.

From the landward side are seen several different facades and views of the towers, spreading to N and s behind the central bulk of medieval

Westminster Hall. Golden-brown Yorkshire limestone was chosen, but it was badly quarried and has needed constant repairs; it also needs regular cleaning to remove the blackened grime and reveal its original mellow color. The exterior is covered with tracery, statues and pinnacles, with a dominant pattern that echoes Henry VII's chapel across the road.

Of the few remaining medieval elements of the palace, **Westminster Hall** (★) is outstanding. The lower walls are the oldest part, dating from the late 11thC. In 1394-99, Richard II replaced the upper walls and roof with the remarkable structure that is seen today. It is one of the world's greatest timber constructions, and the very apogee of English Gothic, a huge and beautiful oak **hammerbeam roof**, with wonderfully carved tracery and angels on the ends of the beams. Statues of early kings, also dating from Richard II's reign, can be seen in niches.

The other medieval survivor is the 1365 **Jewel Tower** *(open Apr-Sept 10am-6pm, Oct-Mar 10am-4pm* 🔳*)* across Abingdon St. and actually closer to the abbey. Strongly fortified and moated, it was first used as a royal treasure house, and then to store records. It now houses an exhibition on the history of Parliament on the first two floors, with a video about "Parliament today" on the top floor, useful for those visitors unable to see inside the Palace of Westminster itself.

The interior

There are two public entrances to the Victorian parts of the palace. For those wishing to "lobby" their members of parliament (a practice whereby constituents can ask their representative to come to the lobby to discuss a particular issue), there is St Stephen's Porch beside the hall. This entrance leads above the medieval crypt, now the Parliament chapel, and to the great lobby beneath an elaborate, spiral lantern that can be seen from outside. This entrance also gives access to the public galleries of the two debating chambers.

Tours of the palace are sometimes allowed: entrance is by the Norman Porch next to the Victoria Tower. The gate beneath the tower itself is used by the Queen only, for official ceremonies such as the **State Opening of Parliament** (see ROYAL LONDON, page 32 and CALENDAR OF EVENTS, page 55). The porch leads through to the **Robing Room**, a spectacular paneled chamber that amply demonstrates Pugin's effective use of Gothic and Tudor motifs; note especially the ornate fireplace. The **Royal Gallery** beyond is more spectacular still, with a colorful ceramic floor and statues of monarchs.

Through the Prince's Chamber is the **House of Lords**, a quite stunning chamber surrounded by sumptuous red leather benches. The leather and wood, the rich colors, and the deep calm make it feel like a monumental clubland lounge, an analogy not altogether inappropriate for the more detached, learned deliberations of the upper house. The Lord Chancellor, who chairs the debates, sits on a red-covered woolsack, and behind him is the royal throne the Lords still maintain (the State Opening takes place in this chamber) beneath an extraordinarily fine gilded canopy, held to be Pugin's masterpiece.

Beyond the Peers' Lobby, Central Lobby and Commons' Lobby is the **House of Commons** itself. It was burned during an air raid in 1941 and the entrance arch has been rebuilt, using some of the damaged stones, between statues of Winston Churchill and Lloyd George. The chamber itself was built in 1945-50 in plainer style, neither Pugin-elaborated nor obviously modern. The governing party occupies the benches on one side, the opposition the other. Neither side is supposed to cross the red lines in the carpet, traditionally two drawn swords apart in distance.

The rest of the Houses of Parliament, consisting of more than 1,000 rooms and two miles of corridor, is not open to the public. It is a place of work: committees struggling over the details of legislation and MPs taking care of their constituency business. Restaurants and terraces for the MPs look out across the river, as does Pugin's magnificent **House of Lords Library**.

WHITECHAPEL ART GALLERY ▥

80 Whitechapel High St., E1 ☎ *377-0107. Map* **12***F18* ▣ *(for nearly all exhibitions)* ▨ *with flash* ▦ *Open Tues-Sun 11am-5pm (8pm on Wed). Tube: Aldgate East.*

A scruffy row of shops in the East End is an unlikely place to find one of England's most celebrated Art Nouveau buildings, but there it is, with a large arched doorway in a plain facade topped by a delightful foliage relief. It was built in 1897-99 by C. Harrison Townsend, a follower of the influential Arts and Crafts Movement, who also designed the Horniman Museum in DULWICH. The gallery enjoys a high reputation for staging important temporary exhibitions of contemporary art.

WHITEHALL

Map **9***G11-H11. Tube: Charing Cross, Westminster.*

The word Whitehall is so firmly embedded in English that it is applied to people, institutions and buildings quite irrespective of whether they belong to the street of that name. Nevertheless, Whitehall has not changed — it is still lined by large government offices, and it is still Britain's administrative center. Running S from TRAFALGAR SQUARE toward WESTMINSTER, it took on this character in the late 17thC, as government departments began building around the Royal Palace of Whitehall.

Before 1514, Whitehall Palace was called York Place, a house belonging to the Archbishop of York. Henry VIII took it over from Cardinal Wolsey in 1530 and turned it into a huge rambling palace, and in 1619-25 Inigo Jones' magnificent BANQUETING HOUSE was added, the only building that survives.

The northern end of Whitehall resembles any other commercial street in Central London until the **Admiralty** is encountered on the W side, a brick building (1722-26) with a large Ionic portico. In front is a handsome screen designed by Robert Adam in 1759-61 with winged sea horses surmounting the gates. Government buildings from about 1900 are followed by the Banqueting House, with the attractive **Welsh Office**, occupying a private residence from 1772, soon after.

On the w side, opposite, is the HORSE GUARDS PARADE, built in 1750-60 to William Kent's designs. Next to it is **Dover House** (the Scottish Office) with an elegant facade of 1787. Whitehall at this point is dominated by the great bulk of the **Ministry of Defence** building, a Portland stone monster finished as late as 1959. Somewhere beneath it are Henry VIII's **wine cellars**, surviving from the old palace. Looking tiny, the modern statues in front depict Sir Walter Raleigh and Field-Marshal Montgomery. Opposite is DOWNING STREET.

From here, Whitehall becomes Parliament St., with massive 19thC government buildings in Italian Renaissance style. At **no. 79**, William Whitfield's bold new government office complex echoes the adjacent Norman Shaw buildings in its banded stone and brick: a stunning example of modern architecture, which blends beautifully with its surroundings. The **Cenotaph** of 1919, the national monument to Britain's war dead, is opposite in the center of Parliament St.

Beneath the offices, with a public entrance in King Charles St., are the fascinating **Cabinet War Rooms** (⛨ *open 10am-5.15pm*). This fortified bunker, deep in the bowels of the earth, housed Churchill's emergency center of operations during the war. It can now be seen as it was, with maps, telephones and even the great man's cigars on display.

WILLIAM MORRIS GALLERY ⛨

Lloyd Park, Forest Rd., E17 ☎*(081) 527-3782. Map* **20**B5 ⛨ ✗ *by appointment. Open Tues-Sat 10am-1pm, 2-5pm; first Sun in every month 10am-noon, 2-5pm. Tube: Walthamstow Central.*
Off the beaten track, in a part of East London that has little else to attract visitors, this is well worth a visit for anyone interested in the development of William Morris' design ideas. The gallery is housed in the lovely 18thC **Water House**, which was Morris' home during his school and student days, from 1848-56. The house, set in attractive grounds, has been beautifully preserved, and contains Morris wallpapers, printed and woven textiles, embroideries, carpets, printing blocks, furniture, stained glass and ceramics.

The collection of works by Morris is complemented by Pre-Raphaelite paintings, a Rodin sculpture, decorative and applied work by Sir Frank Brangwyn, and furniture by important designers of the period, such as Walter Crane, Ernest Gimson and William De Morgan. Highlights include the "medieval" helmet and sword designed by Morris in the 1850s as props for the Oxford Union murals, his *Woodpecker tapestry,* and his masterpiece in fine printing, the *Kelmscott Chaucer.*

WIMBLEDON

This sw suburb of London is famous chiefly for the tennis championships that transform its leafy streets in mid-summer. See LONDON'S DISTRICTS, page 88.

THE ZOO 🏛 ☆
Regent's Park, NW1 ☎*(071) 722-3333. Map 1B7* 🔲 💺 ✈ *Open daily*
10am-5.30pm, 4pm in winter. Tube: Regent's Park, Mornington Crescent,
Camden Town.

More properly named the gardens of the Zoological Society of London,
the zoo occupies an attractive portion of REGENT'S PARK bisected by the
GRAND UNION CANAL. Founded in 1826, it is the oldest such institution in
the world, and one of the most important. Together with Whipsnade
Wild Animal Park in Bedfordshire, where the animals are kept in large
open paddocks in the countryside, London Zoo has more than 600
species and more than 12,000 animals, and as well as showing animals
to the public, it enjoys worldwide repute in the fields of conservation
and animal medicine.

Innovation has changed the ways of showing animals, and bold
architectural experiments have displaced the old iron cage approach. In
many cases the animals are in larger compounds, designed to reflect their
natural habitats and separated from the public by moats rather than bars.
Giraffes, camels and okapi can be seen only a moat's width away, for
example, on the **Cotton Terraces**. (The celebrated Mappin Terraces, an
artificial mountain divided into layers and opened as long ago as 1914,
are closed, and are likely to remain so for some time, victim of the Zoo's
enormous financial troubles of recent years, which now appear to have
been resolved.)

The **African Aviary**, opened in 1990, was a revolutionary design of
nearly invisible "piano wires," intended to keep vultures, eagles and
spoonbills separated from visitors. Similarly, the big cats can be seen at
close range in their dens through glass, or watched as they roam paddocks stocked with suitable vegetation. These animals do not have that
bored, lethargic appearance that can make zoos so depressing. Precisely
because they are so active, the monkeys and apes in the **Michael Sobell
Pavilion** (opened in 1972) are perhaps the most enjoyable of the zoo's
creatures. More morbidly alluring is one of the world's most extensive
collections of reptiles and insects, poisonous snakes and giant spiders.

Two special features are the newly refurbished **Moonlight World**,
where nocturnal animals can be seen behaving as if in the dead of night,
and the **children's zoo and farm**, with tame animals which will give
children rides or can be handled.

There are important examples of modern architecture. The **Penguin
Pool** of the 1930s pioneered the use of prestressed concrete, and still
looks contemporary. The **Snowdon Aviary**, opened in 1965 and containing a variety of birds in a large open space, is superbly functional
even if criticized for looking rather like a collapsed radio mast.

For a period in 1992 it seemed that London Zoo was doomed, and
although its future seems now assured, the direction it should take is the
subject of continuing debate.

Where to stay

Making your choice

Among the most expensive in the world, London's large luxury hotels have had to work hard to weather the recession of recent years. To maintain their competitive standing and attract international business travelers, they have improved their facilities, by installing business centers and providing secretaries, portable telephones, fax machines and word processors, as well as fitness centers, gyms, saunas and swimming pools.

The city's smaller, more intimate hotels are less vulnerable. What appeals to tourists is frequently their charm and lower cost, rather than the extent of their services.

A CHOICE OF STYLES

At the most expensive end of the spectrum, the grand old hotels of London — the **Savoy**, **Ritz**, **Dorchester**, **Connaught**, **Brown's** and their ilk — bear witness to the Englishman's notion of style as something that murmurs rather than shouts. They know that a gentleman does not have to prove anything, and neither do they. They assume that quality, although hideously expensive these days, is timeless, and so they can seem old-fashioned to some. They were built for people with ancient country estates who needed a home-away-from-home in town. The traveler with the resources to understand this will enjoy them. Others may prefer something less English.

Most of the international chains have at least one establishment in London, offering the style of accommodation and service to which their regular patrons are accustomed, although at rather cosmopolitan prices. Examples are the **Hyatt Carlton Tower**, **Sheraton Park Tower** and **Hilton**. As most of them offer conference facilities, and are popular with business travelers, advance reservations are essential.

Of the British chains, Trust House Forte is the largest, with the **Grosvenor House** as its flagship. Inter-Continental has a stronghold in London with several top hotels including the **Inter-Continental**, **Britannia** and **May Fair** under its aegis. The deluxe Savoy group includes the **Savoy**, **Berkeley**, **Connaught** and **Claridge's**. Thistle (now part of the Mount Charlotte Group) is a good chain of mainly business hotels concentrated in and around London, as are Ladbroke's hotels.

In the middle price range, "house hotels" are becoming increasingly popular. They usually only have a few rooms and are often converted from attractive terraced houses. They range from the designer-decorated, such as **Dorset Square** and **L'Hôtel**, to the quaint, such as **Ebury Court**.

BED-AND-BREAKFAST
The cheaper type of British hotel is often known as a boarding house, or a "bed-and-breakfast" (or simply "B & B"). At their best, such as the **Claverly** and **Collin House**, they are clean, comfortable and friendly. But currently, with good "B & B's" in London in short supply, they are rarely to be trusted unless you have a recommendation. The **British Tourist Authority** is promoting a pleasant alternative — staying with a British family. The booklet *Stay in a British Home* is available from overseas **British Tourist Authority** offices.

APARTMENTS
Staying in a serviced apartment is a real alternative to a hotel, especially if you wish to entertain privately, or if you are bringing your family. Business travelers, perhaps seeking complete privacy, can also find them preferable to the glare of a large hotel.

They are also very competitively priced compared to hotels: a three-bedroom apartment in **Beaufort House** *(45 Beaufort Gdns., SW3* ☎ *(071) 584-2600* ⓕⓧ *(071) 584-6532, map15 I6)* costs significantly less per day than one room in one of London's grand or deluxe hotels. The apartments are split-level, elegantly furnished and fully equipped, and situated in the heart of Knightsbridge. Among the services provided are a regular maid and 24-hour porter, plus plenty of extras, such as a full secretarial service, baby-sitting, and help with tourist itineraries. A less expensive alternative to Beaufort House, **Bolton Studios** *(Gilston Rd., SW10* ☎ *(071) 937-4376/7978* ⓕⓧ *(071) 938-2340, map14 L4)* provide maids, a porter, burglar alarm, laundry and dry-cleaning, fax machines and a telephone message service.

Agents for both short- and long-stay serviced apartments include **Harrods Estates** *(* ☎ *(071) 584-6600* ⓕⓧ *(071) 581-1287)* and **Barnard Marcus** *(* ☎ *(071) 584-2014* ⓕⓧ *(071) 584-2072)*.

If the idea of a self-catering (efficiency) apartment appeals to you, look for the list in the booklet *Self Catering Apartments and Accommodation Agencies in London,* available from BTA offices or from the **London Tourist Board** (whose postal address is given on the opposite page).

EXECUTIVE ACCOMMODATION
Business travelers will find an extensive choice of accommodation, and many of the larger hotels have conference facilities. Two leading examples with several floors dedicated to executive accommodation are the **Hilton** and **Sheraton Park Tower**; and **Thistle** (now Mount Charlotte) and **Halkin** hotels are substantially oriented toward visiting businessmen.

Other notable choices include the **Churchill** and **Hyatt Carlton Tower**, both with very fully equipped business centers; the superb **Howard**, near the City; and the luxurious **Montcalm**, **Fortyseven Park Street** and **Dorchester**. More modestly priced but also offering excellent accommodation and office-from-office facilities are the **White House** and **John Howard Hotel**.

All these and many others are described in the following pages.

RESERVATIONS

If you want to be able to choose the particular hotel you stay in, advance reservation is essential, preferably at least a month ahead. Depending on the time of year, you might be lucky with short-notice reservations, but be prepared to be flexible.

Advance reservation of an inexpensive to medium-priced hotel can be arranged by writing to the **London Tourist Board** *(Accommodation Services, 26 Grosvenor Gardens, London SW1W 0DU)*. Write at least six weeks in advance, suggesting the price level you wish to consider and any general preference for location, and the organization will then make a provisional reservation before writing to you to confirm it. A telephone reservation service is also now available *(☎ (071) 824-8844)*, using Visa or MasterCard to pay a deposit on the reservation.

Given some flexibility, it is possible to make instant reservations at London Tourist Board and Convention Bureau Information Centres at Heathrow Airport or Victoria Station.

PRICE

London hotels usually charge by the person, rather than by the room, and sometimes include breakfast in the price — increasingly only a "Continental breakfast" of toast or croissants and coffee, with a supplement for the fried "English breakfast." Check whether VAT (Value Added Tax) is included.

Service is usually included. If you are very pleased with the service, give a small tip to the chambermaid or receptionist.

Our price categories are based on the approximate cost of a double room with bathroom, including the cost of breakfast. Single rooms are somewhat cheaper.

Symbol	Category	Current price
▥	very expensive	over £170
▨	expensive	£130–170
▧	moderate	£100–130
▫	inexpensive	£70–100
▢	cheap	under £70

As a guideline at the time of printing, these prices are based on actual costs quoted across these price categories in fall 1992. Naturally, prices tend to rise, but, in general, hotels stay in the same price category.

MEALS

The dining facilities range from some of the best restaurants in London to those that do not expect to attract most of their guests. What they nearly all offer, at extra cost, is the great British breakfast of bacon and eggs or kippers. Residential terms, with an evening meal included in the price, are rare.

HOTELS CLASSIFIED BY AREA

BAYSWATER/PADDINGTON
Royal Lancaster ▥ ♣

BELGRAVIA/KNIGHTSBRIDGE
Basil Street Hotel ▥
Beaufort ▥ to ▥
Berkeley ▥ ▩
Capital ▥ ▩
Claverly ▥ ♣
Halkin ▥
L'Hôtel ▥
Hyatt Carlton Tower ▥ ▩
Hyde Park ▥ ▩
Knightsbridge ▥
Knightsbridge Green ▥
Lanesborough ▥ ▩
Sheraton Park Tower ▥

BLACKHEATH
Bardon Lodge ▥ ♣

BLOOMSBURY
Academy ▥
Imperial ▥
Kingsley ▥ ♣

CHELSEA
Draycott ▥
Eleven Cadogan Gardens ▥
Fenja ▥ to ▥
Franklin ▥
Sloane ▥
Wilbraham ▥

CITY
Great Eastern ▥
Howard ▥ ▩

**SOHO/COVENT GARDEN/
STRAND**
Hazlitt's ▥ ♣
Savoy ▥ ▩
Strand Palace ▥
Waldorf ▥

KENSINGTON
Alexander ▥ to ▥
Blakes ▥
Gore ▥ ♣

Halcyon ▥
John Howard Hotel ▥
Kensington Palace ▥
Observatory House ▥
One Cranley Place ▥ to ▥
Pembridge Court ▥ to ▥ ♣
Portobello ▥ to ▥

LITTLE VENICE
Colonnade ▥ to ▥

MARYLEBONE/WEST END
Berners ▥ to ▥
Churchill ▥ ▩
Dorset Square ▥ ♣
Durrants Hotel ▥
Montcalm ▥ ♣
White House ▥ ♣

MAYFAIR
Britannia ▥
Brown's ▥
Chesterfield ▥
Claridge's ▥ ▩
Connaught ▥ ▩
Dorchester ▥ ▩
Fortyseven Park Street ▥
Grosvenor House ▥
Hilton ▥
Inn on the Park ▥ ▩
Inter-Continental ▥
May Fair ▥
Westbury ▥ ♣

PICCADILLY
Athenaeum ▥ ▩
Le Meridien London ▥ ▩
Park Lane ▥
Ritz ▥ ▩

ST JAMES'S
Dukes Hotel ▥
Stafford ▥

VICTORIA
Collin House ▥ ▤
Ebury Court ▥
Elizabeth ▥
Goring ▥

See HOW TO USE THIS BOOK on page 7 for the full list of symbols.

London's hotels A to Z

ALEXANDER
9 Sumner Pl., SW7 ☎*(071) 581-1591/5*
📠*(071) 581-0824. Map* **14**K5 ▥ *to* ▥
39 rms, all with bathrm 🆎 ⊕ 🆎 📷 ⌕
✳ ☐ 🖼 ☙ ✍ ❖ *Tube: South*
Kensington.

*Location: In the South Kensington
heartland.* S.J. Perelman once issued
the entreaty, "Please don't give me
nothing to remember you by," but they
haven't forgotten his stays at the Alexander; they named a room after him. If
he observed the strangeness of a hotel
in a street so attractive that it is not
allowed to hang a sign, he didn't say so.
The Alexander is announced only by a
brass plate outside, and maintains a
similar note of restful discretion inside.
It is a Victorian house, done up in English country-house style, in which all
bedrooms have been impeccably modernized, and a number have four-poster
beds. There is a lovely, high-walled garden for the use of guests, and those with
a bar at home will feel comfortable in
the serve-yourself lounge, operating on
an honesty system.

ATHENAEUM 🏨
116 Piccadilly, W1 ☎*(071) 499-3464*
📠*(071) 493-1860. Map* **8**H8 ▥ *112 rms,
all with bathrm* ▤▤ ⇉ 🆎 ⊕ ⊕ 📷 ✳ ☐
🖼 ▤ ✍ 🏨 ❖ *Tube: Green Park.*

*Location: West End, between Mayfair
and Green Park.* Although it is especially well known for its unrivaled selection of malt whiskies, this smallish,
pristine 1940s hotel is impeccably run
and full of good ideas. Guests are
warmly welcomed on arrival by the ge-
nial head porter; those who want to jog
in the park are loaned track suits. Attention to detail is the keynote. If you have
an afternoon nap, your sheets will be
changed again before bedtime. Unlike
so many present-day hotels, the Athenaeum doesn't stint on towels — there
are mounds of them, and luxury bathrooms too. The next-door house contains 30 self-catering (efficiency)
apartments, which are run by the Athenaeum.

BARDON LODGE ♣
Stratheden Rd., Blackheath, SE3 ☎*(081)
853-4051* 📠*(081) 858-7387* ▥ *37 rms,
2 with bathrm* ⇉ 🆎 ⊕ ⊕ 📷 ☐ 🖼 ✍
🏨 ❖

*Location: In South London, between
Greenwich and Blackheath.* Good inexpensive hotels are hard to come by in
London at present, and it may be
necessary to look farther afield for a fair
deal. Blackheath is on the edge of the
city, an impressive place with its vast
common and fine Georgian houses;
close by is Greenwich. Bardon Lodge,
owned and run with some pride by
Donald Nott, is a beautifully kept hotel
with spacious rooms (two with private
bathrooms, the rest with a shower
cubicle) and a pleasant dining room.

BASIL STREET HOTEL
8 Basil St., SW3 ☎*(071) 581-3311*
📠*(071) 581-3693. Map* **15**I7 ▥ *96 rms,
86 with bathrm* ⇉ 🆎 ⊕ ⊕ 📷 ✳ ☐
🖼 🏨 ❖ *Tube: Kensington.*

*Location: Knightsbridge, behind Har-
rods.* Much loved not only for the high
standard of service it provides, but also
for its depth of personality. A woman's
hotel in the days when ladies came from
the country to do their shopping in
Knightsbridge (it is a convenient "91
steps" from Harrods), it still runs the
female counterpart to a gentlemen's
club. In the hotel, however, guests of
both sexes are offered what the Basil
describes with some accuracy as "an
island of hospitality in our brusque,
modern world." Decorated with British
and Oriental antiques, in an Edwardian
building, part of which was once the
reservation hall of a rail station, the Basil
has a coziness that belies its size; it
remains small enough to offer the personal touch, but sufficiently large to
provide the services of a first-class
hotel.

BERKELEY 🏨
Wilton Pl., SW1 ☎*(071) 235-6000*
📠*(071) 235-4330. Map* **15**I7 ▥ *160
rms, all with bathrm* ▤▤ 🖼 ⇉ 🆎 ⊕ ⊕

▥ ⚓ ♿ ☐ 🖾 ⚏ ♈ ⚓ ♈ 𝄞 ☞ *Tube:*
Knightsbridge.
*Location: Knightsbridge, opposite Hyde
Park.* Noël Coward's old Berkeley is
gone, yet much of its character has re-
emerged in the new one, built by the
same management in 1972. "The last
really deluxe hotel to be built in Europe," they claim. Deluxe rather than
grand because, by today's standards, it
is small for a hotel of this style. The hotel
is known for its service, organized separately on every floor, has a rooftop
swimming pool, a gymnasium, sauna,
movie theater, beauty parlor, one of
London's better French restaurants, the
Le Perroquet bar, and the **Buttery**.

BERNERS

Berners St., W1 ☎*(071) 636-1629*
🖾*(071) 580-3972. Map* **9E10** ▥▥ *to* ▥▥
235 rms, all with bathrm ⚏ ♿ ☐ 🖾 🍴 ⚓ ♈ *Tube: Tottenham
Court Road.*
Location: Off Oxford St. A grand old
hotel with a splendid interior, which
seems at odds with its never having
been famous or fashionable. The location is wrong for that, yet right for shopping, and near to theaterland.
Bedrooms round the central well are
very quiet. Ten rooms are specially designed for the benefit of handicapped
people. There is a carvery-type restaurant.

BLAKES

33-35 Roland Gdns., SW7 ☎*(071)
370-6701* 🖾*(071) 373-0442. Map* **14K4**
▥▥ *52 rms, all with bathrm* ⚏ 🆎 ☐ ☐
▥ ⌂ ☐ 🖾 🍴 ☐ *Tube: South
Kensington.*
*Location: South Kensington, off Old
Brompton Rd.* Mandatory for media
folk, who are suitably at home in a hotel
owned by a designer. It shows, too,
with that beautiful birdcage, the black
and white dining room, a sunken bed
in one suite, pristine white-tiled or
plush marble bathrooms. And which
other small London hotel serves pastrami on rye? Also one of the best hotel
restaurants in town, and what the
management describes as "all the best

services to be expected from a first-class
hotel," all in a prim Victorian street.

BRITANNIA

Grosvenor Sq. (entrance Adam's Row), W1
☎*(071) 629-9400* 🖾*(071) 629-7736.*
Map **8G8** ▥▥ *317 rms, all with bathrm* 📺
⌂ ⚏ 🆎 ☐ ☐ ▥ 🍴 ☐ 🖾 🍴 ⚓ ♈
Tube: Bond Street.
*Location: Mayfair, near Oxford St. and
Hyde Park.* This very large Georgian
square, lined with embassies, has
largely been rebuilt and restored, and
there is little to suggest that behind its
facades lies a large hotel. Even more
surprisingly, the Britannia was built
only in 1970, and its well-decorated interior is a successful blend of original
and reproduction Georgiana. Nonetheless, its built-in "pub" can claim to stand
on the site where a Cabinet meeting
learned from a horse-borne messenger
that Wellington had beaten Napoleon at
Waterloo. It has an Anglo-American
café, and two restaurants, one Japanese.

BROWN'S

22-24 Dover St., W1 ☎*(071) 493-6020*
🖾*(071) 493-9381. Map* **8G9** ▥▥ *120 rms,
all with bathrm* ⚏ 🆎 ☐ ☐ ▥ ⌂ ⚓ 🍴 ☐
☐ ☐ 🍴 ⚓ ♈ *Tube: Green Park.*
*Location: Mayfair, near Bond St. and
Piccadilly.* The original Mr Brown was
butler to Lord Byron, and the hotel he
founded became the most renowned
among those intended to be a London
home-away-from-home for the gentry.
It still retains this character in the charm,
individuality and style of its rooms, although many are, by modern standards,
rather small and gloomy. Wood-paneling, oil paintings and leather sofas char-
acterize the public rooms, and it is still
the place in which to take afternoon
tea. Theodore Roosevelt was married
from Brown's, and FDR and Eleanor
honeymooned there; the Dutch Government in exile declared war on Japan,
and Queen Wilhelmina and Princess
Juliana stayed here. Brown's still takes
pride in maintaining the privacy of its
guests, but life is inevitably less serene
in the late 20thC. Now owned by the
Trust House Forte chain.

CAPITAL 🏨

Basil St., SW3 ☎*(071) 589-5171* 🖷*(071) 225-0011. Map* **15**/7 🛏 *48 rms, all with bathrm* 🔲 🔲 ⇌ 🔲 ⊙ 🔲 🔲 ✦ ⬤ 🔲 🔲 ♈ 🔲 *Tube: Knightsbridge.*

Location: Knightsbridge, behind Harrods. So friendly and informal that the designation "luxury hotel" seems unfairly intimidating. Yet this sophisticated little modern hotel is the sort of place that provides each guest with a toothbrush and bathrobe, leaves a rose for every lady, and has a *concierge* who attends to every need. Public rooms and reception areas decorated by Nina Campbell highlight the feeling of intimate luxury. Upper floors have been decorated in Ralph Lauren fabrics by the owner's wife Margaret Levin, responsible also for their bed-and-breakfast establishment next door, L'HÔTEL. The Capital Hotel has a good French restaurant (SEE RESTAURANTS).

CHURCHILL 🏨

30 Portman Sq., W1 ☎*(071) 486-5800* 🖷*(071) 486-1255. Map* **7**F7 🛏 *448 rms, all with bathrm* 🔲 🔲 ⇌ 🔲 ⊙ 🔲 🔲 ✦ ⬤ 🔲 🔲 ♈ 🛎 *Tube: Marble Arch.*

Location: Off Oxford St. The glittering, marbled lobby is a suitably impressive introduction to this modern luxury hotel, owned by Park Lane Hotels International, which sits in a busy elegant square behind Selfridges store. The public rooms and the thickly-carpeted bedrooms are in a more relaxed, but equally sumptuous, Regency style. The Churchill has an international restaurant and a newly refurbished bar, with a clubby feel, for drinks and snacks. A fully-equipped business center can provide secretaries, portable telephones and word processors. Service is efficient and unobtrusive.

CLARIDGE'S 🏨

Brook St., W1 ☎*(071) 629-8860* 🖷*(071) 499-2210. Map* **8**F8 🛏 *190 rms, 56 suites, all with bathrm* 🔲 ⇌ 🔲 🔲 ⊙ 🔲 🔲 ✦ 🔲 🔲 ♈ 🛎 *Tube: Bond Street.*

Location: Mayfair, near Oxford St. Visiting royals and statesmen are inclined to choose Claridge's, which, despite its fame, is imperturbably discreet. No bar, because such trappings don't fit a country house, even if it is in the middle of London. Drink in the living room (not "lounge" — it isn't an airport), where a small orchestra plays at lunchtime and in the evening. Nor would it be very dignified to publish a tariff, so they don't. Lots of Art Deco, but the tone is better set by log fires in the suites. A guest who has been shopping returns with a brace of pheasants; without batting an eyelid, the porter carries them for her as if they were Gucci suitcases. **The Causerie** provides an excellent value-for-money smorgasbord lunch.

CLAVERLY ♣

14 Beaufort Gdns., SW3 ☎*(071) 589-8541* 🖷*(071) 584-3410. Map* **15**/6 🛏 *32 rms, 29 with bathrm* 🔲 ⊙ 🔲 ✦ 🔲 🔲 ✻ *Tube: Knightsbridge.*

Location: Close to Harrods. In a quiet enclave off busy Brompton Rd., this privately-owned upmarket bed-and-breakfast hotel has won a British Tourist Award for its general friendliness, cleanliness and comfort.

COLLIN HOUSE 🏨

104 Ebury St., SW1 ☎*(071) 730-8031. Map* **16**J8 🛏 *13 rms. No charge/credit cards* ✻ *Tube: Victoria.*

Location: Belgravia, close to Victoria Station. One of the very few reliable, relatively inexpensive bed-and-breakfast hotels in central London, run with care by Welshman Mr D.L. Thomas. Eight of the 13 bedrooms have en-suite showers. Ebury St. is an excellent location that has spawned many small hotels such as Collin House, many of them not to be recommended, although see EBURY COURT for another commendable example of the genre.

CONNAUGHT 🏨

16 Carlos Pl., W1 ☎*(071) 499-7070* 🖷*(071) 495-3262. Map* **8**G8 🛏 *90 rms, 24 suites, all with bathrm* ⇌ 🔲 🔲 ✦ 🔲 🔲 ✻ ♈ *Tube: Bond Street.*

Location: Mayfair, near Hyde Park and Oxford St. The finest of London's grand old hotels, according to its devoted following, the Connaught is smaller than other hotels in its peer group, and accordingly offers a little less in the way of facilities and services. But that kind of expansiveness isn't its style; the luxury is more personal. Likewise, the cozy public rooms make a virtue of their intimacy. The clubby atmosphere perfectly fits this part of Mayfair. (See also RESTAURANTS.)

DORCHESTER 🏨
Park Lane, W1 ☎*(071) 629-8888*
🖷*(071) 409-0114. Map 8G8* ▥ *197 rms, 55 suites, all with bathrm* ▤ ▣ ☰ ▣
◑ ◉ ▩ ✻ 🕭 ⬜ ◿ ▤ ⛛ ☛ ☷ ☗
▰ Tube: Hyde Park Corner.
Location: Overlooking Hyde Park. With its stately terraces, the Dorchester looks like an ocean liner that has somehow been moored on Park Lane. Bought in 1985 by the world's richest man, the Sultan of Brunei, the hotel closed in late 1988 for a £70 million refit and reopened in spring 1990. The elegant and spacious public rooms were sumptuously renovated, from the marble-floored lobby to the gold leaf moldings in the splendid **Promenade**, where guests can take afternoon tea. The furniture has been reupholstered, the bedrooms redecorated in country chintzes, and the famous Oliver Messel suites painstakingly restored to their original condition. The pastel-decorated **Terrace Restaurant** and traditional English **Grill** remain much the same, but there is a brand-new **Oriental Restaurant**, offering a choice of Far Eastern cuisines. Other recently added facilities include a health club and business center.

DORSET SQUARE ✿
39 Dorset Sq., NW1 ☎*(071) 723-7874*
🖷*(071) 724-3328. Map 7D7* ▥ *37 rms, all with bathrm* ☰ ▣ ◉ ▩ ✻ 🕭 ☙ ⬜
▤ ◿ ⛛ Tube: Marylebone.
Location: Close to Marylebone Station, s of Regent's Park. Situated in a lovely Regency square (guests have the use of the central garden), this is one of London's best and more stylish "house hotels." One is immediately struck by the

carefully contrived decoration, which is almost alarming in its perfection, but nevertheless a charming evocation of the country house style. All the bedrooms are impressive, with marble bathrooms. Service is intelligent and efficient. The bar is run on an honesty system and, if reserved in advance, a chauffeur-driven Bentley is at the disposal of guests.

DUKES HOTEL
34-36 St James's Pl., SW1 ☎*(071) 491-4840* 🖷*(071) 493-1264. Map 8H9* ▥ *36 rms, 24 suites, all with bathrm* ☰
▣ ◑ ◉ ▩ ☙ ✻ ⬜ ◿ ☗ ☷ Tube: Green Park.
Location: St James's, near Green Park and St James's Palace. In a gas-lit courtyard, a small but rather grand hotel opened in 1906, occupying what was once presumably someone's Upstairs-Downstairs town house. Dukes was pleased when an enthusiastic guest described it as "the smallest castle in England." Only in London could a location be so pretty and tranquil yet so close to the throbbing heart of the city. Despite its being almost claustrophobically small, Dukes offers full hotel facilities, to the highest standard, including 24-hour service, and a cozy, well-patronized dining room, serving French-inclined cuisine.

DURRANTS HOTEL
George St., W1 ☎*(071) 935-8131*
🖷*(071) 487-3510. Map 8F9* ▥ *100 rms, 70 with bathrm* ☰ ▣ ◉ ▩ ✻ ⬜ *in rooms with bathrm* ◿ ☷ ☗ Tube: Bond Street.
Location: Near Oxford St. In a street which is, as its name suggests, Georgian, this attractive small hotel is perennially popular, although rooms are rather small. A portrait of a Durrant patriarch, dating back to 1782, hangs among the delightful collection of oils and prints. There are leather chairs and pretty desks in the writing room, antiques on sale to guests, an open fire in the bar, Ruddles beer in the bottle, pheasant for dinner when it's in season, and brass bedsteads.

EBURY COURT
26 Ebury St., SW1 ☎*(071) 730-8147*
🖷*(071) 823-5966. Map* **16***J8* ▥▯ *45 rms,*
22 with bathrm ⇥ 🎛 🎛 📺 ✱ ☐ 🖭
Tube: Victoria, Sloane Square.
Location: Victoria/Pimlico. Cottagey,
quaint and under the proud eye of the
owners, Mr and Mrs Kingsford, who live
on the premises. The hotel has been in
the family since the 1930s, and to be a
guest is thus to stay in the Kingsfords'
home. Their excellent full English
breakfast includes haddock and kippers.

ELEVEN CADOGAN GARDENS
11 Cadogan Gdns., SW3 ☎*(071)*
730-3426 🖷*(071) 730-5217. Map* **15***J7*
▥▯ *60 rms, all with bathrm* 🝙 🎛 📺 🖭
✱ ☐ 🖭 🍴 🛥 *Tube: Sloane Square.*
Location: Chelsea, near Sloane Square.
So discreet that it has no sign even on
the door, which is kept locked. No wonder it is favored by diplomats. Late Victorian exterior, with decor to match: a
glorious marble fireplace in one room;
a drawing room with open fire. Full
English breakfast in bed, and they'll
send out for a bottle of champagne (the
establishment has no liquor license);
what's more, they'll even deliver you to
the airport in a Rolls-Royce.

GORE ♣
189 Queen's Gate, SW7 ☎*(071)*
584-6601 🖷*(071) 589-8127. Map* **14***I4*
▥▯ *54 rms, all with bathrm* ⇥ 🝙 🎛 🎛
📺 ✱ ☐ 🖭 🖃 ⅄ *Tube: South*
Kensington.
*Location: Kensington, near the Albert
Hall and Hyde Park.* The recent sale of
the Gore to the owners of **Hazlitt's** has
given this already warm and welcoming
hotel an extra fillip. They decorated
where necessary, piled up the pot
plants, and put 5,000 pictures on the
walls. They also invited Anthony Worrall-Thompson, owner of the adjoining
One Ninety Queen's Gate (see RES-
TAURANTS), to take over the hotel's existing restaurant, so becoming the hugely
popular **Bistro 190**. Bedrooms, some
small, are individually and prettily decorated. Of the honeymoonish deluxe

rooms, one, in Italian style, has a bed
that belonged to Judy Garland, stained-
glass windows, and a magnificent tiled
bathroom. A happy hotel (save the rear
lounge, which has a sobering effect),
with some illustrious names in its register, particularly among musicians.

GORING
15 Beeston Pl., Grosvenor Gdns., SW1
☎*(071) 834-8211* 🖷*(071) 834-4393.*
Map **16***I9* ▥▯ *82 rms, all with bathrm* 🝙
⇥ 🝙 🎛 🎛 📺 ✱ ☐ 🖭 🍴 🛎 ⅄
Tube: Victoria.
*Location: Victoria, near Buckingham
Palace.* A book on Buckingham Palace
written by the hotel's founder is provided for each guest along with the
Bible, and royal carriages may occasionally be seen calling at the Goring to
collect diplomat guests. The thorough-
minded Mr Goring was the first hotelier
in the world to fit all of his rooms with
central heating and baths, and he would
undoubtedly be pleased to know that
the hotel is still in the family three
generations later — the current Mr Goring, born in Room 114, was recently
awarded the OBE for his services to the
hotel trade. There are, after all, few
full-service hotels of this size still in
private hands. Some of the original furniture, including brass bedsteads, is still
in use, and the policy has clearly been
to renovate rather than replace, although all the rooms have now been
given thorough face-lifts, complete
with marble bathrooms, and there is
now 24-hour room service. The public
rooms are elegant and inviting (although the color scheme in the front
hall excited some controversy), with an
excellent writing room, a small bar and
a good restaurant that is certainly worth
sampling.

GREAT EASTERN
Liverpool St., EC2 ☎*(071) 283-4363*
🖷*(071) 283-4897. Map* **12***E17* ▥▯
161 rms, 126 with bathrm ⇥ 🝙 🎛 🎛
📺 ✱ ☐ 🖭 🖃 🛎 ⅄ *Closed Christmas.*
Tube: Liverpool Street.
Location: The City. Away from the West
End (although only a few stops on the

tube), and in the heart of old London. Handy, too, for those wishing to travel on to the eastern counties of England or to Continental Europe. There is a genuinely traditional quality about railway hotels like this one. Spacious, high-ceilinged bedrooms, although with twin beds more available than doubles, and simple fittings. Some bedrooms have wash basins, but the majority also have bathrooms, usually with big, deep tubs, although often without showers. High ceilings in the public rooms, too, with ornate moldings. A magnificent stained-glass dome hangs over **Bowlers** (one of three restaurants in the building).

GROSVENOR HOUSE

Park Lane, W1 ☎*(071) 499-6363*
☒*(071) 493-3341. Map 7G7* ▥ *466 rms, 70 suites, 160 apartments, all with bathrm*
▤ ▣ ⇌ ▣ ⊙ ⊚ ▨ ⚡ ⚅ ▢ ▨ ▤
⟪ ⇜ ♈ ↝ ⛾ ⛾ ♌ ⚓ *Tube: Marble Arch.*

Location: Mayfair, overlooking Hyde Park. The flagship of the Forte Group is something of a modern-day grand hotel in its scale and in the extent of its service and facilities, which was one of the first to include a pool, solarium, gymnasium and Jacuzzi. Built in 1928 as apartments, a social center during World War II when it accommodated American officers, it is famous for its huge banqueting room. In the newly refurbished **Park Terrace** lounge, a pianist accompanies afternoon tea at which, despite the grandeur of the place, the atmosphere is relaxing and children are made to feel welcome. There is more musical accompaniment each evening in the **Pavilion** restaurant, or you could choose the pompous **Ninety Park Lane** in which to dine. A well-run hotel.

HALCYON

81 Holland Park, W11 ☎*(071) 727-7288*
☒*(071) 229-8516. Map 5H1* ▥ *44 rms, all with bathrm* ▤ ⇌ ▣ ⊙ ⊚ ⚡ ⚅
▢ ▨ ▤ ♆ ♈ ▨ *Tube: Holland Park.*
Location: Close to Kensington High St. Expensive and very *à la mode,* the Halcyon is ideally placed for the visitor:

away from the hurly-burly in gracious and exclusive Holland Park, but just a short taxi ride from the city center. The interior is a kind of modern rendition of the *belle époque,* luxurious and very soothing. There's a classy, pastel-shaded restaurant opening onto a small garden where drinks can be taken in the summer. 24-hour room service is another feature.

HALKIN

5 Halkin St., SW1 ☎*(071) 333-1000*
☒*(071) 333-1100. Map 16I8* ▥ *41 rms, all with bathrm* ▤ ⇌ ▣ ⊙ ⊚ ▨ ⚡ ▢
▨ ♆ ▤ *Tube: Hyde Park Corner.*
Location: Belgravia, in a side street off Belgrave Sq. One of London's new breed of small luxury hotels, the Halkin opened in 1990 to great acclaim. The hotel oozes Italian style from the light, airy lobby, with a marble terrazzo and mosaic floor, based on a Michelangelo piazza in Rome, down to the Giorgio Armani-designed staff uniforms. The bedrooms are equally chic, with exquisite wood-veneer Deco furniture, curved walls, clever concealed lighting and use of mirrors, and plush marble bathrooms in co-ordinating colors. Business executives are well catered to with two-line telephones, private fax machines and video recorders. Appropriately, the restaurant, overseen by Gualtiero Marchesi, serves modern Italian food.

HAZLITT'S ♣

6 Frith St., W1 ☎*(071) 434-1771*
☒*(071) 439-1524. Map 9F10* ▢ *22 rms, 1 suite, all with bathrm* ▣ ⊙ ⊚ ▨ ▢
▨ *Tube: Tottenham Court Road.*
Location: Soho. There are precious few hotels of character at this price range in central London, certainly no others in Soho; a pity, for it makes an amusing and convenient location. Hazlitt's, named after the essayist William Hazlitt who resided and died here in 1830, is unpretentious and refreshingly simple — even puritanical — in appearance; it has cream-painted walls, plain antique furniture and wobbly, uneven floors and staircases. Bedrooms are spotless

and comfortable: bathrooms are great fun, with free-standing Victorian baths and matching loos and basins, antique prints on the walls and stone busts balancing on window sills. Ambience and a pleasant professional young staff together make up for the lack of luxury and extras.

HILTON

22 Park Lane, W1 ☎*(071) 493-8000*
🖬*(071) 493-4957. Map 8H8* 📖 *395 rms,
53 suites, all with bathrm* 🖃 🖵 ⇌ 🖃
🖸 🖸 📖 ✿ 🗆 🖾 🖃 ⇌ & 🖃 ● *Tube:
Hyde Park Corner.*

Location: Mayfair, overlooking Hyde Park. There was great excitement when the 28-story new Hilton presented itself in Park Lane in the early 1960s, and some controversy about its modern style and proportions. Today, it is part of the scenery, with its **Trader Vic's** restaurant and bar almost an institution. Recently, improvements have been carried out. On the ground floor are the **Brasserie**, which has the atmosphere and quality of an airport restaurant, and **St George's Bar**, which serves pub food. **Windows on the World** is the roof restaurant, with its marvelous views. Room service still offers Middle Eastern gastronomic specialties. The rooms have very large beds but are otherwise quite simple. One whole floor is devoted to nonsmokers, and there are now six executive floors.

L'HÔTEL

28 Basil St., SW3 ☎*(071) 589-6286*
🖬*(071) 225-0011. Map 15I7* 📖 *11 rms,
1 suite, all with bathrm* ⇌ 🖃 🖸 📖 🖂
✿ 🗆 🖾 *Tube: Knightsbridge.*

Location: Next to Harrods. A very upmarket version of the big-city B & B, whose well-heeled clientele feel that it's a relief to get away from the relentless pace of a large, bustling full-service hotel once in a while. Rooms are fairly small, attractive without being glamorous; breakfast, both "full English" and Continental, is taken in the smart basement **Métro** wine bar, which is also open to nonresidents for light French lunches and dinners. As befits an establishment owned by the same couple as the CAPITAL next door, the staff is professional and courteous. Families are welcomed.

HOWARD 🏨

Temple Pl., WC2 ☎*(071) 836-3555*
🖬*(071) 379-4547. Map 10F13* 📖
117 rms, 24 suites, all with bathrm 🖃 🖂
⇌ 🖃 🖸 🖸 📖 🖂 ✿ 🗆 🖾 ⚒ 🖢 🖴
�></ *Tube: Temple.*

Location: Overlooking the Thames, on the edge of the City. Annoyingly for visiting businessmen with little time on their hands, the City was until recently deprived of hotels. Then came the **Tower Thistle** *(* ☎*(071) 481-2575* 📖*)* at St Katharine's Dock, which is now joined further upstream by the Howard. Exorbitant prices are evident from the over-the-top decor in the public rooms, although the bedrooms are more understated and luxurious. Business facilities are legion and service is appropriately smooth. Recently opened in Docklands, and therefore also convenient for the City, is the **Britannia International** *(Marsh Wall, E14* ☎*(071) 515-1551* 📖*).*

HYATT CARLTON TOWER 🏨

2 Cadogan Pl., SW1 ☎*(071) 235-5411*
🖬*(071) 245-6570. Map 15J7* 📖 *224
rms, all with bathrm* 🖃 🖂 ⇌ 🖃 🖸 🖸
📖 🖂 ✿ 🗆 🖾 🖢 ⟨⟨ ⌖ 🖴 🌢 🍴 🍷
Tube: Knightsbridge, Sloane Square.

Location: Between Knightsbridge and Chelsea, off Sloane St. Whether your requirement is for enormous breakfasts or a kosher dinner (and guests here range from rock stars to foreign politicians), American-cut beef or contemporary French cuisine, the Carlton Tower can meet your wishes, and you can always make your penances in the health club, the **Peak**. The hotel has always had an individuality, perhaps because the very building itself is distinctive: a handsome rectangular structure with a matching 15-floor tower that looks more 1930s than 1960s (which it actually is). Under the Hyatt banner it underwent major cosmetic surgery a few years back. Now, with a well-equipped business center, it can vie as one of the best business hotels in London. The location, in a quiet square, has a character of its own.

HYDE PARK 🏨

Knightsbridge, SW1 ☎*(071) 235-2000* ⊠*(071) 235-4552. Map* **15**|**7** ▥ *166 rms, 19 suites, all with bathrm* ▦ 𝔸𝔼 ⬤ ⬤ ▥ ✱ & ▢ 🖾 ≪ 🜚 ♈ ⏃ ♈
Tube: Knightsbridge.

Location: Overlooking Knightsbridge at Sloane St. to the front and Hyde Park to the rear. Although the Hyde Park has recently created a fitness center "which very few guests will actually use" (in its own disarming words) and has all the other extras now expected of top hotels, its appeal lies in the steady, old-fashioned values that have made it famous since 1892. Exiled royalty have often made it their home away from home, and more recently Pavarotti, almost royalty, stayed here for his open-air concert in Hyde Park (an especially large shower had to be built for him). Rooms are luxurious but personal rather than glitzy, and the public rooms have the same air of unshowy comfort. The excellent **Park Room** restaurant, with its stunning views (particularly when the Cavalry trot by), serves Italian food with a creative twist, while the **Cavalry Grill** opts for simple English dishes. Bedrooms overlooking the Park, including the Royal Suite, are at a premium, but worth the extra.

IMPERIAL

Russell Sq., WC1 ☎*(071) 837-3655, reservations (071) 278-7871* ⊠*(071) 837-4653. Map* **3**E**11** ▥▢ *447 rms, all with bathrm* 🖾 ≕ 𝔸𝔼 ⬤ ⬤ ▥ ✱ ▢ 🖾 ⚱
Tube: Russell Square.

Location: Bloomsbury, near the British Museum. This modern, custom-built hotel is the flagship of a small group owned by one family. It stands on the site of a previous Imperial hotel, which was famed for its Turkish baths. The present Imperial is much more functional, but nevertheless provides well-equipped accommodation in a convenient location.

INN ON THE PARK 🏨

Hamilton Pl., Park Lane, W1 ☎*(071) 499-0888* ⊠*(071) 493-1895/6629. Map* **8**H**8** ▥ *187 rms, 27 suites, 14 conservatory rms, all with bathrm* ▦ 🖾 ≕ 𝔸𝔼 ⬤ ⬤ ▥ ✱ ▢ 🖾 ⚱ ⏃ ♈
Tube: Hyde Park Corner.

Location: Mayfair, overlooking Hyde Park. The only European hotel in the Four Seasons group, built in 1970, is kept in superb condition. Although favored by stars, it is better known as the home of Howard Hughes during one of his most demanding years. Despite its being such a recent building, the architecture of the Inn On The Park has a look of the 1950s, and some of its suites are in a 1930s style, although each is individually appointed, and the hotel is lavishly furnished with antiques. In the Queen Anne-style lounge, ten different variations on the theme of tea are offered, to the soothing accompaniment of a pianist or harpist. Service in the hotel is outstanding, and it boasts two superb restaurants, **Four Seasons** (see RESTAURANTS) and **Lanes**. There are many people who speak of this as London's best hotel.

INTER-CONTINENTAL

1 Hamilton Pl., Hyde Park Corner, W1 ☎*(071) 409-3131* ⊠*(071) 409-7460. Map* **8**H**8** ▥ *490 rms, all with bathrm* ▦ 🖾 ≕ 𝔸𝔼 ⬤ ⬤ ▥ ✱ & ▢ 🖾 ≪ ⚱ ♈ ⦿ 🞐 *Tube: Hyde Park Corner.*

Location: Hyde Park Corner, overlooking Hyde Park. Very much the American style of luxury hotel, despite now being jointly owned by the SAS airline and a Japanese corporation: spacious rooms, often with separate sitting areas; individual heating and air-conditioning controls; dual-voltage and doorbell; telephone extension in the bathroom, free in-house movies, not to mention scales and a clothesline. A coffee house with sufficient privacy for breakfast conferences, and no wonder female executives seem to favor this hotel, with its Aquascutum and Cartier shops. Excellent cocktail barman, and excellent restaurant, **Le Soufflé**. Rolls-Royces are available for rental.

KENSINGTON PALACE
De Vere Gdns., W8 ☎*(071) 937-8121*
🖷*(071) 937-2816. Map 14I4* ⬚
298 rms, all with bathrm ⬚ 🆎 ⬚ ⬚ 🈂
⬚ ⬚ ⬚ ⇚ ⬚ ♫ *Tube: Kensington High Street.*

Location: Opposite Kensington Gardens. Beautifully and lavishly refurbished a few years back as one of the London showpieces of the Scottish group Thistle Hotels, now part of Mount Charlotte Hotels. In true Scottish style, kippers and black pudding are proudly featured on the breakfast buffet menu, and they can be enjoyed in an elegant restaurant overlooking the park. Rooms are attractive and comfortable. The hotel is much used by airline staff and executives. Another excellent middle-market Thistle hotel is the **Royal Horseguards** (*Whitehall Court, SW1* ☎ *(071) 839-3400, map 9H11*), with splendid views from its river-facing rooms from the 4th to 9th floors. Another is **Cannizaro House**, set in lovely public gardens on the edge of London (*West Side, Wimbledon Common, SW19* ☎*(081) 879-1464*).

KINGSLEY ♣
Bloomsbury Way, WC1 ☎*(071) 242-5881*
🖷*(071) 831-0225. Map 9E11* ⬚
146 rms, all with bathrm ⬚ 🆎 ⬚ ⬚ 🈂
⬚ ⬚ ⬚ ⬚ 🍸 *Tube: Tottenham Court Road.*

Location: Bloomsbury, near the British Museum. A member of the Mount Charlotte Thistle Group (SEE KENSINGTON PALACE, above), this warm, inviting hotel is ideal for families, offering accommodation at good-value prices in a convenient spot. The Kingsley is a full-scale hotel, with bar and carvery restaurant.

LANESBOROUGH
I Lanesborough Pl., SW1 ☎*(071) 259-5599* 🖷*(071) 259-5606. Map 8H8*
⬚ *49 rms, 49 suites, all with bathrm* ⬚
⬚ ⬚ 🆎 ⬚ ⬚ 🈂 ⬚ ⬚ ⬚ ⬚ ⬚ ⇚
⬚ ⬚ 🍸 ♫ *Tube: Hyde Park Corner.*

Location: Overlooking Hyde Park Corner. Triple glazing ensures that the roar of traffic struggling round Hyde Park Corner is totally eliminated; instead a rather somber hush pervades this latest addition to London's deluxe hotels. Owned by the Texan Rosewood group, it occupies the entirely rebuilt former St George's Hospital, a landmark building designed by William Wilkins in 1829, and was opened in the teeth of the recession in 1992. The hotel is decorated in quasi-Regency style, with bold use of color in the two restaurants, but the reliance on reproduction furniture and such devices as false bookends give a deadening effect. In the bedrooms, 24-hour butler service, computer-controlled lighting, state-of-the-art audio and video equipment, personal fax and telephone lines and personalized stationary are all provided, yet each room is a mirror of the next, down to the same pink and blue striped wallpaper. Time alone will tell whether or not this is a luxury hotel with all the trappings but without a heart.

MAY FAIR
Stratton St., W1 ☎*(071) 629-7777*
🖷*(071) 629-1459. Map 8G9* ⬚ *237 rms, 50 suites, all with bathrm* ⬚ ⬚ 🆎 ⬚
⬚ 🈂 ⬚ ⬚ ⬚ ⬚ ⬚ ⬚ ⬚ 🍸 ⬚ ⬚
⬚ *Tube: Green Park.*

Location: Mayfair, just off Piccadilly. The most entertaining hotel in London. With its own in-built theater, the May Fair continues to pursue the performing arts, although in a lower key than it did during the big band era, with its long-gone Candlelight Room. Indeed, its cinema has recently transformed into the **Spa** health club, complete with swimming pool. The rooms are well decorated, with huge beds and attractive bathrooms — you can even have a spa bath if that is what turns you on. An Inter-Continental hotel.

LE MERIDIEN LONDON ⬚
Piccadilly, W1 ☎*(071) 734-8000* 🖷*(071) 437-3574. Map 9G10* ⬚ *222 rms, 41 suites, all with bathrm* ⬚ ⬚ 🆎 ⬚ ⬚
🈂 ⬚ ⬚ ⬚ ⬚ ⬚ ⬚ ⬚ 🍸 ⬚ ♫ ⬚ ⬚
⬚ *Tube: Piccadilly Circus.*

Location: Near Piccadilly Circus. The once-famous Piccadilly hotel was transformed in 1985 into Le Meridien, a hotel very much in the modern idiom, but retaining all the Piccadilly's architectural glories. The Edwardian extravagance of the interior, protected by preservation orders, has been restored, with the **Oak Room** as its superb *pièce de résistance* (see RESTAURANTS), while the pillared roof terrace has been glassed-in to create a stunning conservatory-style brasserie. Executives in particular will be lured by the extensive conference facilities, and the luxurious basement health club, **Champneys**, which includes a pool, a gym, squash courts and Turkish baths. Recent reorganization on the upper floors has led to previously small bedrooms being enlarged to become "studio suites."

MONTCALM ♣

Great Cumberland Pl., W1 ☎*(071) 402-4288* ☒*(071) 724-9180. Map* **7F7** ▥ *104 rms, 12 suites, all with bathrm* ▤ ☴ 🗚 ⊙ ⊙ 🖾 ⌂ ✦ ☐ ⌻ ☷ ⅄ *Tube: Marble Arch.*

Location: Near Marble Arch and Oxford St. Behind its dignified Georgian facade, a hotel that quietly evinces all the pampering luxury and style required by the international businessman or his wife. The antique gilt reception desk, lavish leather sofas and military chests set the tone, and suites have spiral staircases.

PARK LANE

Piccadilly, W1 ☎*(071) 499-6321* ☒*(071) 499-1965. Map* **8H8** ▥ *271 rms, 14 suites, all with bathrm* ▤ *partial* ▤ ☴ 🗚 ⊙ ⊙ 🖾 ✦ ☐ ⌻ ☷ ⬛ ⅄ ⚘ ⍦ *Tube: Green Park.*

Location: Piccadilly, overlooking Green Park. This lovely old establishment is still privately-owned, one of the largest in London. From its needlessly misleading name (Piccadilly is every bit as grand as Park Lane), the hotel is full of quirkiness and character. The French restaurant is decorated with carved paneling from J.P. Morgan's home, and the ballroom is a magnificent consummation of the Art Deco themes that pervade the hotel. Rooms are spacious, with walk-in closets and

often with mahogany, 1920s-style beds. The beauty parlor offers aromatherapy, and there is a gymnasium.

PEMBRIDGE COURT ♣

34 Pembridge Gdns., W2 ☎*(071) 229-9977* ☒*(071) 727-4982. Map* **5G2** ▥ *to* ▥ *21 rms, all with bathrm* ☴ 🗚 ⊙ ⊙ 🖾 ⌂ ✦ ☐ ⌻ ⅄ *Tube: Notting Hill Gate.*

Location: Notting Hill, 1 mile w of the center. The Notting Hill locals who enjoy the French cooking and countrified ambience of **Caps** restaurant aren't always aware that this is part of a hotel. Caps in fact doubles as a breakfast room, apart from which there is a comfortable, newly enlarged lounge and bar. The rooms, many of them also recently enlarged, are impeccably kept and welcoming. All now have bathrooms. There is 24-hour bar service. The hotel's walls are adorned with a collection of Victorian fans and lacework, and the place exudes a strong family feel. Loyal clients include antique dealers visiting Portobello Road market.

PORTOBELLO

22 Stanley Gdns., W11 ☎*(071) 727-2777* ☒*(071) 792-9641. Map* **5G1** ▥ *to* ▥ *25 rms, 7 with bathrm* ☴ 🗚 ⊙ ⊙ 🖾 ⌂ ✦ ☐ ⌻ ⅄ *Tube: Notting Hill Gate.*

Location: Just n of Holland Park. An idiosyncratic small hotel, which people tend to love or hate. Rooms vary greatly in style, quality and size and are priced accordingly; ones termed "cabins" are tiny. Only suites and "special rooms" have bathrooms (all others have showers) and these are spacious and fun — a good choice for a romantic weekend. An added bonus for escapees is the 24-hour food and drink service, although it can be erratic. Porterage and daytime room service have recently been introduced. Meals are taken in the small restaurant, under the same management as nearby **Julie's Bar**.

RITZ ▩

Piccadilly, W1 ☎*(071) 493-8181* ☒*(071) 493-2687. Map* **8G9** ▥ *116 rms, 14*

suites, all with bathrm 🚭 🖭 🔘 🖭 🖾 ☀
🔲 🖾 🖃 🐾 ⚘ ⚑ 🍴 ♫ *Tube: Green Park.*

Location: Near St James's and Green Park. The first hotel to bear the name of César Ritz was in Paris, and he brought with him the architectural style of the Rue de Rivoli when he opened this London establishment at the beginning of the 1900s. He even imported French craftsmen to work on the Louis XVI interior. In the early days of the Ritz, the Prince of Wales used to dance there; later it became a favored lunch place for Noël Coward, and postwar residents included millionaires such as Getty and Gulbenkian. With the disappearance of such grandiosity, the Ritz has faced the difficult task of adapting itself to a less richly textured world. Sadly, one of its two famous bars has long gone, but other features are happily immovable, such as the staircase and rotunda, the restaurant (see RESTAURANTS), with its stunning view and *trompe-l'oeil* ceiling, and the spectacular **Palm Court**, with its ornate marble fountain. The decor and furnishings in the Palm Court have been restored, and afternoon tea is served there, while on Friday and Saturday nights there is dancing to a 1920s-style big band orchestra.

ROYAL LANCASTER ♣

Lancaster Terrace, W2 ☎(071) 262-6737 🖾(071) 724-3191. *Map* 6G5 🖿 418 rms, all with bathrm 🖭 🖾 🚭 🖭 🔘 🖭 🖾 ☀ 🔲 🖾 🖃 ◁ ⚑ ☿ *Tube: Lancaster Gate.*

Location: Bayswater, opposite Kensington Gardens. A comfortable and well-maintained modern hotel in the Rank group, in an excellent location, from which some rooms have lovely views of the park. The rooms are well-appointed, and the hotel has an informal café serving pasta dishes and grills, as well as its Anglo-French restaurant. The recently modernized conference and banqueting facilities can now accommodate up to 1,500 people.

SAVOY 🛏

Strand, WC2 ☎(071) 836-4343 🖾(071) 240-6040. *Map* 10G12 🖿 152 rms, 48

suites, all with bathrm 🖾 partial 🖾 🚭 🖭 🔘 🖭 🖾 ☀ 🔲 🖾 🖃 🐾 ⚘ ◁ ⚑ 🍴 ☿ ♫ ♪ *Tube: Charing Cross.*

Location: Strand, near Covent Garden and South Bank. The Earl of Savoy built a palace on this site in 1245, and the present hotel was opened in 1869 by Richard D'Oyly Carte. He first staged the operettas of Gilbert and Sullivan in the adjoining **Savoy Theatre**, which was severely damaged by fire in early 1990. It has been restored with the addition of a "relaxation center" complete with rooftop swimming pool. With its tucked-away entrance at the front, and gardens facing the Thames at the back, the Savoy is full of extravagant treats. An open fire greets guests, afternoon tea, with piano accompaniment, is served in a garden setting with a gazebo, and recent renovation has uncovered yet more 1920s features. The emphasis is on thorough hotel-keeping and comfort, with Irish linen sheets on the beds, and mattresses made by the Savoy's own workshop. Most bathrooms have marble floors and satisfyingly deep tubs. Service from waiters is patchy, however: exemplary from some, distinctly slapdash and offhand from others, which is not as it should be, and the hotel's peerless reputation is perhaps a little tarnished now. There are three restaurants to choose from: the famous **Savoy Grill**, where the rich and powerful do much of their business entertaining, some at regular tables; the **River Restaurant**; and the more recent **Upstairs** "chablis and seafood" bar, beautifully decorated, where you can choose anything from a cup of coffee (the hotel has its own blend) to a meal.

SHERATON PARK TOWER

101 Knightsbridge, SW1 ☎(071) 235-8050 🖾(071) 235-8231. *Map* 15I7 🖿 295 rms, all with bathrm 🖭 🖾 🚭 🖭 🔘 🖭 🖾 ☀ ⚙ 🔲 🖭 🖾 ⚘ ◁ ☿ *Tube: Knightsbridge.*

Location: Knightsbridge/Belgravia, near Hyde Park. European flagship of the group, and very much the metropolitan, luxury type of Sheraton, as opposed to some of the smaller ones in American provincial cities. The hotel towers above Knightsbridge in an outwardly ugly cylindrical shape. All the rooms have a view and are spacious and luxurious, decorated in English traditional style, with lots of pale wood fittings. Floors 10-17 are handsomely devoted to "executive rooms" that provide accommodation for groups of visitors from blue-chip corporations. Other treats for guests include superb marble bathrooms, a beauty parlor, a barbershop, and valeting service to keep guests well-groomed.

STAFFORD

St James's Pl., SW1 ☎*(071) 493-0111* ⊠*(071) 493-7121. Map* **8***H9* ▥ *62 rms, all with bathrm* ▭ AE ◉ ◎ ▭ ♣ ☐ ▭ ✿ ▲ ▭ *Tube: Green Park.*

Location: St James's, near Green Park. Elegant and discreet hotel in gentlemanly St James's, where almost every house is of historical interest. The Stafford's 300-year-old wine cellars once belonged to St James's Palace. Much of the interior is in the style of Adam, although the brickwork facade is much later. The building once housed the Public Schools Club, and during World War II accommodated American officers and French resistance workers. A beautifully kept hotel, with four comfortable salons that are rented for business meetings.

STRAND PALACE

369 Strand, WC2 ☎*(071) 836-8080* ⊠*(071) 836-2077. Map* **10***G12* ▥ *777 rms, all with bathrm* ▭ AE ◉ ◎ ▭ ♣ ☐ ▭ ▲ ☑ *Tube: Covent Garden.*

Location: Strand, near Covent Garden. When it was built in the early part of this century, a 900-bedroom hotel was by definition a palace (its palatial original entrance is now in the Victoria and Albert Museum, an Art Deco masterpiece). Now, the Strand has slimmed a little, been extensively modernized, and turned its attention to a different business: that of providing straightforward, middle-of-the-road accommodation. It does so from a vantage point

right opposite the **Savoy**, in a location handy for many theaters and for city sightseeing. The Strand Palace has most of the facilities to be expected in a large hotel, although there is no room service. Tea and coffee-making facilities in each room, an 18-hour coffee shop, Neapolitan chefs in the Italian restaurant, and an American-style cocktail bar. A Trust House Forte hotel.

WALDORF

Aldwych, WC2 ☎*(071) 836-2400* ⊠*(071) 836-7244. Map* **10***F12* ▥ *291 rms, 19 suites, all with bathrm* ▭ AE ◉ ◎ ▭ ♣ ♿ ☐ ▭ ▭ ▲ ▭ *Tube: Aldwych.*

Location: N side of the Aldwych. Exemplifying the Edwardian era with its crystal chandeliers, marble floors and vast pot plants, the Waldorf is a comfortable hotel, offering both old-world charm and excellent service and facilities. These include mini-bars in the bedrooms, a video channel for in-house movies, a hairdresser and valet service. There is a *thé dansant* on Friday, Saturday and Sunday.

WESTBURY ✿

Conduit St., W1 ☎*(071) 629-7755* ⊠*(071) 495-1163. Map* **8***G9* ▥ *224 rms, 19 suites, all with bathrm* ▭ AE ◉ ◎ ▭ ♣ ♿ ☐ ▭ ▭ ▲ ☑ *Tube: Bond Street.*

Location: Mayfair, near Bond St. and Oxford St. The first Westbury Hotel, on Madison Avenue, New York, was named by a polo buff after the ground on Long Island. Like its New York counterpart, the London Westbury still has a bar called the **Polo**, and its martinis are of American dryness. When it opened in 1955, the London Westbury was the first hotel in Britain to be operated by an American chain, but since 1977 it has been owned by Trust House Forte. Its library-style lounge, with an open fire in winter, and its comfortable rooms nonetheless sustain the feel of a 1950s American hotel.

WHITE HOUSE ✿

Albany St., NW1 ☎*(071) 387-1200* ⊠*(071) 388-0091. Map* **2***D9* ▥ *575 rms,* *all with bathrm* 🚬 🖾 ⊙ ⊠ 🖾 ‡ ⑤ ☐ 🖾 🛥 ☥ 🖙 ☥ *Tube: Great Portland Street.*

Location: Near Regent's Park. A handy location for sightseeing, shopping, and taking relaxing walks in the park, although this is not a hotel area. The White House is well appointed, offering 24-hour room service and all the other amenities of a first-rate hotel (including leisure and business centers) at more modest prices. Despite its name, the White House is a British hotel (the building is actually shaped like the Union Jack), and is owned by the Rank group. The block is large enough to shrug off the traffic that swarms all around it.

Further recommendations

The hotels listed and described in the preceding pages represent our personal choice across the very broad range of prices, styles, fashions and locations currently on offer in the capital. Some very nice establishments did not quite make it onto our short list for this edition, but they might make it onto yours. Here are short descriptions.

ACADEMY
17-21 Gower St., WC1 ☎*(071) 631-4115* 🖾*(071) 636-3442. Map* **3E10** 🖾
A delightful, peaceful Georgian hotel, only a stone's throw from the British Museum.

BEAUFORT
33 Beaufort Gdns., SW3 ☎*(071) 584-5252* 🖾*(071) 589-2834. Map* **15I6** 🖾 *to* 🖾
This is a small, friendly Knightsbridge hotel in two Victorian town houses with an attractive "country house"-style decor.

CHESTERFIELD
35 Charles St., W1 ☎*(071) 491-2622* 🖾*(071) 491-4793. Map* **8G8** 🖾
In the heart of Mayfair, this is designed to feel more like an exclusive club than a hotel.

COLONNADE
2 Warrington Crescent, W9 ☎*(071) 286-1052* 🖾 *to* 🖾
Family-run since 1948, it is situated in attractive Little Venice. Some rooms have four-poster beds and coronets.

DRAYCOTT
24 Cadogan Gdns., SW3 ☎*(071) 730-*
6466 🖾*(071) 730-0236. Map* **15J7** 🖾 *to* 🖾
A romantic and stylish small hotel with no dining room but friendly personal service.

ELIZABETH
37 Eccleston Sq., SW1 ☎*(071) 828-6812/3. Map* **16J9** 🖾
A small, simple hotel in a tranquil setting, overlooking the square's gardens.

FENJA
69 Cadogan Gdns., SW3 ☎*(071) 589-7333* 🖾*(071) 581-4958. Map* **15J7** 🖾 *to* 🖾
Between Harrods and Peter Jones, this is another private house turned into an elegant hotel, decorated with original paintings and marble busts.

FORTYSEVEN PARK STREET
47 Park St., W1 ☎*(071) 491-7282* 🖾*(071) 491-7281. Map* **7G7** 🖾
No less than 52 luxury suites with kitchens and every imaginable service for business people, created by Albert Roux, owner of Le Gavroche, to which the hotel is linked by private entrance.

FRANKLIN
24 Egerton Gdns., SW3 ☎*(071) 584-5533*

📠*(071) 584-5449. Map **15J6** 🕮*
Sumptuous air-conditioned town-house hotel opened in 1992.

JOHN HOWARD HOTEL

*4 Queen's Gate, SW7 ☎(071) 581-3011 📠(071) 589-8403. Map **14J4** 🕮*
All mod cons for the business executive, from conference room to 12 efficiency apartments, in a well-restored Regency building.

KNIGHTSBRIDGE

*10 Beaufort Gdns., SW3 ☎(071) 589-9271 📠(071) 823-9692. Map **15I6** 🕮*
An inexpensive hotel in the same leafy enclave as the CLAVERLY and BEAUFORT. Guests are issued with a front-door key on arrival.

KNIGHTSBRIDGE GREEN

*159 Knightsbridge, SW1 ☎(071) 584-6274 📠(071) 225-1635. Map **15I7** 🕮*
A well-located, family-run hotel, this is unusual in that it consists mostly of suites. Recently it underwent a major face-lift.

OBSERVATORY HOUSE

*Observatory Gdns., 37 Hornton St., W8 ☎(071) 937-1577 📠(071) 938-3585. Map **5H2** 🕮*
A demure family-oriented hotel on the quiet Kensington site of the old Observatory.

ONE CRANLEY PLACE

*1 Cranley Pl., SW7 ☎(071) 589-7944 📠(071) 225-3931. Map **14K5** 🕮 to 🕮*
Cozy, with gingham tablecloths and blue and white china in the dining room, antiques throughout and a pretty patio garden.

SLOANE

*29 Draycott Pl., SW3 ☎(071) 581-5757 📠(071) 584-1348. Map **15K7** 🕮*
Twelve individually designed bedrooms ranging from the contemporary to the Neoclassical to the traditional. A discreet and intimate small hotel.

WILBRAHAM

*Wilbraham Pl., Sloane St., SW1 ☎(071) 730-8296 📠(071) 730-6815. Map **15J7** 🕮*
Slightly faded gentility, between Chelsea and Knightsbridge.

Eating and drinking

Dining out in London

Recent years have seen something of a revival of English cooking, blighted two centuries ago by the disruption of the world's first industrial revolution. The invasion by foreign cuisines, with the French leading, was thorough, but now the ethnic diversity of London's restaurant world is being tempered by the resurgence of the native table. Just as *nouvelle cuisine* brought French cooking up to date, so English cooking is now being reworked by many chefs — often under the loose term of Modern British Cookery. There is a whole new breed of English chefs now operating who look as much to Britain as to France for their inspiration. They look farther afield, too, particularly to Italy, California and the Orient. Modern European Cookery is another commonly used term, which perhaps best describes the breadth of influence.

There are, of course, some excellent French restaurants of unimpeachable authenticity in London, and equally notable standard-bearers of many another national cuisine. Even local cooking illustrates London's propensity for absorbing outside influences. Those who can muster the appetite to begin the day with the great British breakfast might find that the kippers come from Scotland, the bacon from Ireland (or, more lately, Denmark), and the tea from India. This is a meal that draws upon the tradition of home cooking, like that other British speciality, high tea (see CAFÉS AND TEAROOMS, page 237); to sample either, the visitor should go to one of the grand old hotels rather than a restaurant.

The English are traditionally eager carnivores, and feast day dishes are still usually some sort of roast meat. The South Downs of Kent and Sussex produce the finest English lamb and mutton. It's odd that Sussex also claims to have invented the steak-and-kidney pudding, when the most famous beef is produced far away in Hereford or Scotland. Presumably it was the time taken to transport the beef that led, in the days before refrigeration, to its being preserved by pickling — hence the Londoners' beloved boiled beef. There seems to be less doubt about the origins of sweet puddings and pies, filled with the apples, cherries and soft fruits of Kent and Essex.

Among geographical influences on London's own specialities, the Thames is paramount. Cockles, mussels and whelks are sold for immediate consumption by vendors in many open markets (see SHOPPING). Shellfish from the estuary and beyond are very much the capital's own love, and the well-heeled diners of Mayfair throng to oyster bars such as

Bentley's or **Green's**; City folk have **Sweetings**. Fish specialities such as whitebait and eel were originally pulled from the river itself. Street sellers still offer jellied eels, while the stewed version is the stock in trade of the pie-and-mash shop, one of London's own "ethnic" eating places, usually to be found near a street market.

Whisper it not, but that other tradition, fried fish and chips, was brought to Britain by immigrants from Italy and Belgium respectively, and they seem to have met in the North of England. Still, Londoners do make good fish and chips; apart from fashionable places such as **Geale's** or **Sea Shell**, the capital is well endowed with fish-and-chip shops of varied quality.

CHOOSING A RESTAURANT

London has at least 2,000 restaurants. Like most things in the city, their keynote is diversity, and they are widely dispersed. The recession of the early 1990s proved a testing time for many of them, and they coped with varying degrees of success. Some closed — Burt's, Columbus and Keats, for example, which all featured in our last edition. Others staggered on, half empty, waiting for the good times to return. Still more tried to woo customers with new gimmicks and bargain prices. Londoners' favorite restaurants, however, remained impervious, some fully booked for days, sometimes weeks in advance. Stalwarts — places which are fashionable and fun, and serve good food — include **Bibendum**, **Le Caprice**, **Kensington Place**, **Langan's**, **Orso**, **Museum Street Café**, **Bistrot 190** and **River Café**.

Restaurateurs are nothing if not optimistic, and there have lately been more notable openings than closures. Themes are popular, and often the themed menu is devised long before the chef is hired or the premises are designer-decorated (which is equally *de rigueur*). Thus **Chutney Mary**, with its "Anglo-Indian" food, **Tall Orders** with its dishes served in superfluous bamboo baskets, **Christopher's**, with jet-setters for backers and models for waitresses, which styles itself an "American Grill," and **Bellgo**, which takes its inspiration from a Belgian beer hall.

As a great city not only of its old empire but also of Western Europe, London is richly cosmopolitan. Recently Italian restaurants have seen a resurgence, moving away from the trattoria style popularized in the 1960s. Gone are the *mozzarella in carozza* and *vitello marsala* of the old days; nowadays flavors are strong, dishes are simple, and olive oil, *polenta* and *ciabatta* bread feature often. **River Café**, **Riva**, **Cibo**, **Orso** and **Osteria Antica Bologna** are proponents of this style. French restaurants are represented at every level, from the *haute* (**Le Gavroche**, **La Tante Claire**) to the bistro (**Le Bouchon**, **Café du Marché**) and the brasserie (**La Brasserie**, **Grill St Quentin**).

From farther afield are the various cuisines of which Chinese and Indian are the most obvious. As in many cities, "ethnic" eating can be remarkably good and excellent value. Chinese and Indian restaurants in particular have also become known for producing good take-out foods, and late at night a Londoner might simply declare that he is going "for an Indian" or "for a Chinese." These two and other ethnicities are manifest in dozens of inexpensive restaurants, and a few grander ones: go to **Gerrard St.** (W1) for Chinese; the **British Telecom Tower** area (W1), **Westbourne Grove** (W2) or **Hammersmith** (W6) for Indian; and **Charlotte St.** (W1) for Greek. The explosion of new Thai restaurants, many markedly similar in food and decor, has ensured that Far Eastern food is now, deservedly, as popular as that of China and India.

London also boasts humbler eating places, many doing their trade mostly by day. The pub is certainly more likely to serve meals at lunchtime, and is usually cheap; the fare will range from French bread and cheese to, typically, steak-and-kidney pie or shepherd's pie. Wine bars also offer inexpensive eating, some of them content to serve quiche and pâté, others stretching to full meals. At a pace more agreeable than fast food, and in a restaurant ambience, such chains as **Pizza Express**, **Bistro Bistingo**, **Bistro Vino** and **Spaghetti House** offer good value. The carvery types of dining room in some hotels are also a good value, providing a selection of roast meats, often for a set price.

If you need further help in choosing a suitable restaurant in the right location, or you want to make a group reservation, try calling the free advisory service, **Restaurant Switchboard** (☎ *(081) 888-8080).*

WHEN TO EAT

Restaurants in the West End and the City are busy at lunchtime, with a largely business clientele, but those dining for pleasure tend to come out at night, usually 8 or 9pm. Most restaurants close after lunchtime, reopen at 6 or 7pm, and wind down after 10 or 11pm. It is usually possible to find somewhere good to eat on the spur of the moment, but the careful diner will always reserve a table first.

PRICE

By the start of the decade the cost of eating out in London had never been higher, but the onset of the recession made restaurateurs cautious, and prices have largely held since then. The cost can vary considerably; some very good establishments make a conscious effort to keep prices down, while others charge for every little extra thing.

One sticking point on prices is the wine list: too many first-rate restaurants assume that their reputations will be prejudiced if they have nothing but expensive bottles on their lists. Of course mark-ups are inevitably large; but surely a good list will produce outstanding wines in every price range.

Set-price menus were relatively uncommon in London, but now appear much more often. Many of the best restaurants have excellent-value set-lunch menus, which bring them within range of the less affluent. They include **La Tante Claire**, **Le Gavroche**, **Chez Nico**, **L'Arlequin**, the **Oak Room**, **Mijanou**, the **Bombay Brasserie**, and among hotels, the **Savoy** and the **Berkeley**. On all menus look out for items that might bump up the quoted or apparent price: check whether VAT (Value Added Tax) and service are included, and whether salads and vegetables are going to be expensive.

Pre- and after-dinner drinks can also prove costly — don't be afraid to ask. If service is not included, and you are happy with your treatment, give a tip of 10-15 percent.

Our price categories are based on the approximate cost of a meal for one, with service, Value Added Tax (VAT) and house wine.

Symbol	Category	Current price
▦	very expensive	over £45
▦	expensive	£30–45
▥	moderate	£20–30
▤	inexpensive	£15–20
▢	cheap	under £15

As a guideline at the time of printing, these prices are based on actual costs quoted by restaurants across these price categories in summer 1992. Naturally, prices tend to rise, but in general restaurants stay in the same price category.

See HOW TO USE THIS BOOK on page 7 for the full list of symbols.

WINE AND FOOD

Wine is one area where French dominance continues. Italian and German white wines are also almost universally available, and a well-chosen selection of "New World" wines is to be found on the list of any self-respecting trend-setting newcomer. The term denotes bottles from non-European countries, principally California and Australia, but also New Zealand, Chile and so on. There is a small, and growing, English wine industry, producing mainly white wine, but it is regrettably rare to find it on offer in London.

Away from the mainstream of Anglo-French-Italian cooking, wine might not always be the best bet; beer goes well with Indian and much Oriental food, and jasmine tea can be ordered with a Chinese meal.

APERITIFS AND AFTER-DINNER DRINKS

The English have long been leading consumers of fortified wines, and have played a leading part in the sherry and port trade. If there is a traditional aperitif in England, it is dry sherry, which whets the appetite perfectly. However, London restaurants will generally be able to cater to most tastes.

After dinner, the English gentleman traditionally "takes" port. It is one of the longest-lived wines, and develops great complexity — do not dismiss it as a "sweet" drink. Usually available also are brandy, liqueurs, or perhaps malt whisky.

RESTAURANTS CLASSIFIED BY AREA

BATTERSEA/WANDSWORTH
L'Arlequin ▦
Harvey's ▦
BAYSWATER
Baba Bhelpoori House ▢ ♣ ☗
Kahns ▢ ♣

BELGRAVIA/KNIGHTSBRIDGE
Capital Hotel ▦ ⌂
Grill St Quentin (*see* St Quentin) ▥
Pizza on the Park (*see* Kettners)
　　▢ to ▤
St Quentin ▥

Salloos 🎟🎟🎟

San Lorenzo 🎟🎟🎟 to 🎟🎟🎟🎟

Les Spécialités St Quentin (*see*
  St Quentin) 🎟 🎟🎟🎟

BLOOMSBURY

Museum Street Café 🎟 to 🎟🎟🎟

CAMDEN TOWN/EUSTON

Nontas 🎟 to 🎟🎟🎟

CHELSEA/SOUTH KENSINGTON

Bibendum 🎟🎟🎟🎟

The Canteen (*see* Harveys) 🎟🎟🎟

Daquise 🎟 ☕

Deal's 🎟🎟🎟

Ed's Easy Diner 🎟

English Garden (*see* English House)
  🎟🎟🎟🎟

English House 🎟🎟🎟🎟

Gavvers 🎟🎟🎟 ♣

Ognisko Polskie 🎟 ♣

Star of India 🎟🎟🎟

La Tante Claire 🎟🎟🎟🎟 ⌂

Tui 🎟🎟🎟

CITY

Le Poulbot 🎟🎟🎟

CLAPHAM

Osteria Antica Bologna 🎟 to 🎟🎟🎟

CLERKENWELL

Café du Marché 🎟🎟🎟 ♣

Quality Chop House 🎟🎟🎟 to 🎟🎟🎟

COVENT GARDEN/STRAND

Ajimura (*see* Ikkyu) 🎟🎟🎟

Andrew Edmunds 🎟🎟🎟

Christopher's 🎟🎟🎟 to 🎟🎟🎟🎟

Deals West 🎟🎟🎟

Joe Allen 🎟 to 🎟🎟🎟

The Ivy 🎟🎟🎟🎟

Luigi's 🎟🎟🎟

Mon Plaisir 🎟🎟🎟 to 🎟🎟🎟

Now and Zen 🎟🎟🎟🎟

Orso 🎟🎟🎟

Smollensky's on the Strand (*see*
  Smollensky's Balloon) 🎟🎟🎟

EAST END

Bloom's 🎟🎟🎟

HAMMERSMITH/FULHAM

Blue Elephant 🎟🎟🎟🎟

Pagu Dinai 🎟🎟🎟

River Café 🎟🎟🎟 to 🎟🎟🎟🎟

HAMPSTEAD

Café Flo 🎟 to 🎟🎟🎟 ♣

Ed's Easy Diner 🎟

Flo's Bar and Grill (*see* Café Flo)
  🎟 to 🎟🎟🎟

Nautilus (*see* Sea Shell) 🎟

ISLINGTON/KINGS CROSS

Ganpath 🎟🎟

Mon Plaisir du Nord 🎟🎟🎟

Upper Street Fish Shop (*see* Sea Shell)
  🎟🎟

KENSINGTON/NOTTING HILL

L'Altro 🎟🎟🎟🎟

Belvedere in Holland Park 🎟🎟🎟

Bistrot 190 (*see* One Ninety Queen's
  Gate) 🎟🎟🎟

Bombay Brasserie 🎟🎟🎟

Cibo 🎟🎟🎟

Clarke's 🎟🎟🎟 to 🎟🎟🎟🎟

Galicia 🎟🎟 ☕

Geale's 🎟🎟 ☕

Kensington Place 🎟🎟🎟 to 🎟🎟🎟 ♣

Launceston Place (*see* Kensington
  Place) 🎟🎟🎟

Leith's 🎟🎟🎟🎟

Mon Petit Plaisir 🎟🎟🎟

Malabar 🎟🎟 to 🎟🎟🎟

192 🎟🎟🎟

One Ninety Queen's Gate 🎟🎟🎟 to 🎟🎟🎟🎟

Phoenicia 🎟🎟🎟 to 🎟🎟🎟 ♣

MARYLEBONE/WEST END

Chez Gérard 🎟🎟🎟

Chez Nico 🎟🎟🎟🎟

Gaylord 🎟🎟🎟

Ikkyu 🎟 to 🎟🎟🎟 ♣ ☕

Lal Qila (*see* Red Fort) 🎟🎟🎟

Odins 🎟🎟🎟🎟

Sea Shell 🎟🎟 ♣ ☕

MAYFAIR

Al Hamra 🎟🎟🎟 ♣

Connaught Hotel 🎟🎟🎟🎟 ⌂

Four Seasons 🎟🎟🎟🎟 ⌂

Le Gavroche 🎟🎟🎟🎟 ⌂

Greenhouse 🎟🎟🎟 to 🎟🎟🎟

Hard Rock Café 🎟

ST JAMES'S/PICCADILLY

Le Caprice 🎟🎟🎟 ♣

Chez Gérard 🎟🎟🎟

Green's 🎟🎟🎟🎟 to 🎟🎟🎟🎟

Langan's Brasserie 🎟🎟🎟

Oak Room 🎟🎟🎟🎟 ⌂

Ritz 🎟🎟🎟🎟 ⌂

Smollensky's Balloon 🎟🎟🎟 to 🎟🎟🎟

Suntory 🎟🎟🎟🎟

SOHO

Alastair Little 🎟🎟🎟🎟

Bahn Thai 🎟🎟🎟 to 🎟🎟🎟

La Bastide 🎟🎟🎟🎟

La Capannina 🎟🎟🎟 ♣

Chuen Cheng Ku (*see* Fung Shing) 🎟🎟🎟

Ed's Easy Diner ▢ ♣
L'Escargot ▨ to ▨
Fung Shing ▨ to ▨
Gay Hussar ▨
Au Jardin des Gourmets ▨ to ▨
Kettners ▢ to ▨
The Lindsay House (*see* English House) ▨
Manzi's ▨ ♣ It
Melati ▢ 🍴
Mr Kong (*see* Fung Shing) ▢

New World (*see* Fung Shing) ▢
Pizza Express (*see* Kettners) ▢ to ▨
Poons ▢ to ▨ ♣ 🍴
Red Fort ▨
SOUTHWARK
Le Pont de la Tour ▨ to ▨
VICTORIA/PIMLICO
Mijanou ▨ to ▨ ♣
Tate Gallery Restaurant ▨ to ▨
Very Simply Nico (*see* Chez Nico) ▨ to ▨

London's restaurants A to Z

ALASTAIR LITTLE *English/French*
49 Frith St., W1 (Soho) ☎*(071) 734-5183.*
Map 9F10 ▨ ▢ 🆔 📷 *Closed Sat lunch;*
Sun; Christmas. Tube: Leicester Square.
Much-vaunted media hang-out with an equally high profile chef/proprietor, the eponymous Mr Little. His dining room, with the kitchen in view, is tiny, and uncomfortably stark: Venetian blinds, bare floorboards, curly tube lighting on the ceiling, black tables set with paper napkins, hard black chairs. "Designer setting for designer food," says one disparaging critic.

Whatever label you give the food, it is generally very good, reminiscent of Californian cuisine but notably more vigorous (although Little's constant experimentation and daring combinations can sometimes fail). He is a talented, instinctive cook, able to change his menu twice daily according to what he finds in the market. Meat and fish are simply cooked — grilled, stir-fried, steamed — and served with vivid sauces and excellent vegetables and salads. The evening clientele is usually less uncompromisingly trendy than at lunchtime.

AL HAMRA *Lebanese*
31-33 Shepherd Market, W1 (Mayfair)
☎*(071) 493-1954. Map 8H8* ▨ ▢ 🍴
🆔 📷 🆔 📷 *Closed Christmas Day; Jan 1.*
Tube: Green Park.
Even the most jaded palates will buck up at the sharp, fresh tastes of Leba-non's superb cuisine. An excellent example is to be found at this comfortable, mainly business-oriented restaurant in Mayfair. Make a selection from the list of 65 hot and cold hors d'oeuvres (more properly called *mezze*), possibly baulking at the grilled lambs' testicles, but including perfect renditions of well-known Lebanese dishes, such as *tabouleh, hommos* and stuffed vine leaves, as well as *montabel, loubeih, foul moulaka, sujuk, makdous batinjan* and mixed fresh vegetables with herbs and Lebanese bread, all quite delicious. Main courses are more perfunctory, mostly char-grilled but well flavored. Try to avoid the waiters making a selection of *mezze* for you, as they tend to over-order.

ANDREW EDMUNDS *English/French*
46 Lexington St., W1 (Soho) ☎*(071)*
437-5708. Map 9F10 ▢ *to* ▨ ▢ 🆔 📷
Tube: Leicester Square.
Bottle-green walls and plain wood tables give a puritanical look to this Soho wine bar, belying its relaxed and convivial atmosphere. The food is always pleasing, with some interesting touches: venison and juniper berry stew; parmesan, rocket and aubergine salad. If you want to be in Soho, but don't want a fully fledged restaurant, this is a good choice, although its popularity can make it uncomfortably crowded. The owner's fusty antiquarian bookstore is next door.

L'ARLEQUIN *French*

123 Queenstown Rd., SW8 (Battersea)
☎*(071) 622-0555. Off map* **16**M8 ▥ ▭
◼ *lunch* ▦ ▲ ▣ ▣ ▨ *Closed Sat;*
Sun; 3 weeks in Aug; 1 week at Christmas.
Tube: Clapham Common.

In the unlikely setting of this dingy Battersea street, top-class restaurateurs Christian and Geneviève Delteil have established one of London's most impressive restaurants, one of the few to have been awarded two Michelin stars. The soberly pretty, rather formal dining room is beautifully run by Mme. Delteil and her team, while her husband creates light and inventive delicacies with more than a passing reference to his native southwest France. The wine list is short and very expensive, though the house wine is reliable.

BABA BHELPOORI HOUSE ◉ ♣ *Indian*

29-31 Porchester Rd., W2 (Bayswater)
☎*(071) 221-7502. Map* **5**F3 ▭ ▭ ▣
▨ *Closed Mon; Christmas. Tube:*
Bayswater, Royal Oak.

An open-armed welcome awaits diners at this very simple, quietly decorated restaurant, which specializes in South Indian vegetarian cooking. Specialities on the short menu include *thali, pani poori, masala dosai* and *aloo papri chat,* all home-cooked and deliciously spicy. The *bhel pooris* are irresistible, consisting of crisp whole-wheat Indian bread, filled with puffed rice, *vermicelli,* potatoes, onions and fresh coriander, served with chili sauce, garlic and a variety of chutneys. The restaurant is run by a charming husband and wife, and is exceptionally good value.

BAHN THAI *Thai*

21a Frith St., W1 (Soho) ☎*(071)*
437-8504. Map **9**F10 ▥ *to* ▥ ▭ ◼ ▦
▲ ▣ ▨ *Closed Christmas; Easter. Tube:*
Leicester Square.

One of the first of London's Thai restaurants and still one of the best. The menu features all the standard dishes and many unusual ones, some very spicy — hot dishes are indicated by a symbol on the menu. Among starters, look for satay, boned stuffed chicken wings, and squid in batter, among soups for hot and sour seafood with lemon grass. Drink Thai beer or a balancing white wine such as Gewürztraminer or Sauvignon. For devotees of dear departed Bianchi's, a visit here is somewhat unnerving, for it's the same premises, still creaking, but now with Oriental touches. After complaints about its shabbiness, it was recently given a much needed face-lift. The tables are crammed in, and the pace is relaxed and leisurely, in authentic Thai tradition.

LA BASTIDE *French*

50 Greek St., W1 (Soho) ☎*(071)*
734-3300. Map **9**F10 ▥ ▭ ◼ ➤ ⬛
▦ ▲ ▣ ▣ ▨ *Closed Sat lunch; Sun.*
Tube: Tottenham Court Rd.

Nicholas Blacklock's restaurant is one of those places it feels good to be in: comfortable and elegant, with the sedate feel of a French country-hotel dining room. The cuisine is styled *bônnete,* and there are three menus to choose from: an excellent set menu devoted to a particular region of France, which changes monthly; a small *carte* of traditional French dishes; and the brasserie-style Soho menu. The wine list is regional too, featuring country wines from all over France; the Côtes de Gasgogne are inexpensive and good. Pre- and post-theater menus make this a good choice for opera or theater-goers.

BELVEDERE IN HOLLAND PARK
French/English

Holland House, off Abbotsbury Rd., W14
☎*(071) 602-1238* ▥ ▭ ▦ ▲ ▣ ▣
▨ *Closed Sun eve.*

An elegant modern restaurant with blue-edged wooden tables, upholstered chairs, dapper waistcoated staff and an attractive location, in HOLLAND PARK, which looks particularly stunning when floodlit at night. The Modern British cooking shows a strong Mediterranean influence, and dishes such as ravioli of lobster in chicken bouillon with red pepper, fillet of sea bass on a warm salad of rocket and poupier, and grilled calves' liver, leek tartlet, fried sage and celery leaves, are full of flavor and temptingly presented.

BIBENDUM English/French

Michelin House, 81 Fulham Rd., SW3 (South Kensington) ☎*(071) 581-5817. Map* **15J6**
▦ ▭ *dinner* ▬ *lunch* ▬ ▤ ▣ ▨
Closed bank hols. Tube: South Kensington.
Lunch is a particular delight here, as light streams through huge windows into the 1st-floor dining room, brilliantly designed by Sir Terence Conran, and graced at either end by two splendidly jolly Michelin men in stained glass. Seating is spacious and supremely comfortable, and the food, by Simon Hopkinson, is just right: definite, appealing and carefully presented. The menu may reveal delicate risotto with wild mushrooms, clear fish soup, sweetbreads, spiced beef with Oriental salad, or chocolate soufflé. The wine list is catholic in taste and unimpeachable in quality, though there are almost no inexpensive bottles. Reserve weeks in advance — this is the place to be, and it feels just right. The ground floor of the famous Michelin building houses the Conran shop and an **oyster bar** *(open 10am-11pm).*

BLOOM'S Jewish

90 Whitechapel High St., E1 (East End)
☎*(071) 247-6001/6835. Map* **12F18** ▭
▤ ▭ ▨ ▣ ▣ ▨ *Closed Fri eve; Sat; Jewish holidays; Christmas Day. Tube: Whitechapel.*
While Manhattan's Jewish families were migrating from Lower East to Upper West Side, London's were making an almost identical journey. Even Bloom's restaurant opened a branch in Golders Green, NW11, but its soul remains in Whitechapel, where the nostalgia is thicker than the *borscht* and noisier than the *matzos,* and the waiters as crotchety as any on Lower East Side. Eat here on Sunday after visiting **Petticoat Lane** and **Brick Lane** markets (see SHOPPING, page 266).

BLUE ELEPHANT Thai

4-6 Fulham Broadway, SW6 (Fulham)
☎*(071) 385-6595* ▦ ▭ ▬ ▤ ⵙ ▨

▣ ▣ ▨ *Closed Sat lunch; Christmas. Tube: Fulham Broadway.*
The surroundings of this leading Thai restaurant (a scruffy corner on Fulham Broadway) are no match for its eye-opening interior: a veritable garden of greenery, complete with bridge, stream and waterfall. Tables are set in several pagoda-style areas, each on a different level; the banks of plants afford plenty of privacy. On leaving, every lady is presented with an orchid — it's that sort of place. Perhaps Londoners have become more discerning about Thai food since the Blue Elephant opened, but it no longer seems the best, although it will by no means displease. Most popular is the banquet menu, where the choosing is done for you, but you should try the deliciously spicy seafood soup and an interesting hot chicken salad.

BOMBAY BRASSERIE Indian

Courtfield Close, Courtfield Rd., SW7 (Kensington) ☎*(071) 370-4040. Map* **14J4**
▦ *to* ▦ ▭ ▬ *lunch* ▤ ⵙ ⵣ ▣ ▨
Tube: Gloucester Rd.
Housed in a huge conservatorium leading off the palatial 1920s main dining room, this European vanguard of India's thoroughbred Taj Hotels group ranked for years as one of London's most impressive Indian restaurants. Today, both the colonial decoration and the regional home cooking look frayed at the edges. Although the varied menu features specialities from all over India (Goa, Bombay, Punjab), criticism has been leveled at tired, overcooked dishes. The restaurant is open every day of the year, with last orders at midnight. The staff is cosmopolitan and friendly, and although Bombay Brasserie is generally expensive for an Indian restaurant, the set-price buffet lunch is a good value. Despite the critics' reservations, this remains a good choice for entertaining.

CAFÉ FLO ♣ French

205 Haverstock Hill, NW3 (Hampstead)
☎*(071) 435-6744* ▭ *to* ▦ ▭ ▬ ⵗ
▣ ▨ *Tube: Belsize Park.*

Jazz music throbs in the background of this comfortable bistro, where the easy ambience attracts the North London intelligentsia. The simple menu is characterized by robust French regional favorites, such as fish soup, baked chicken, lamb steak and veal scallop in breadcrumbs with ham and cheese, with a few more serious dishes, such as haddock tart with spinach sauce and salmon with a tomato and shallot sauce. The set menu, *L'idée Flo*, is exceptionally good value. Sunday lunch is particularly popular here. Across the road, **Flo's Bar and Grill** *(216 Haverstock Hill* ☎ *(071) 794-4125* ▭ *to* ▭*)* is an offshoot of Café Flo, with tables set outside in summer and brasserie-type food. Other branches of Café Flo have sprung up in Islington, Richmond, Camden and St Martin's Lane.

LE CAFÉ DU MARCHÉ ♣ *French*
22 Charterhouse Sq., Charterhouse Mews, EC1 (Clerkenwell) ☎ *(071) 608-1609. Map* **11E14** ▥ ▭ ■■ ▦ ▣ ▨ *Closed Sat lunch; Sun; Easter; 2 weeks at Christmas. Tube: Barbican, Farringdon.*
The *marché* is Smithfield, the meat market, but this café could easily be in Paris, with the convivial ambience of a Left Bank bistro. It occupies a converted warehouse, where the original open-plan space has been retained and the bare brick walls are decorated with posters. On the set-price menu, you will find deliciously garlicky fish soup, *rumpsteak de boeuf dijonnaise, andouillette grillée à la mode* and *brandade de morue.* It's simple fare, but satisfying and carefully cooked. For grills, eat upstairs at **Le Grenier.**

LA CAPANNINA *Italian*
24 Romilly St., W1 (Soho) ☎ *(071) 437-2473. Map* **9F10** ▥ ▭ ▦ ▣ ▣ ▨ *Closed Sat lunch; Sun. Tube: Leicester Square, Piccadilly Circus.*
A good example of the type of unpretentious, friendly Italian restaurant in which Soho specializes, and the longest lasting of them all. Well-prepared basic Italian dishes such as *gnocchi, raviolini, crespolini,* sea-bass with fen-

nel, beef braised in Barolo, rabbit in white wine. The somewhat cramped interior is decorated in an endearingly dated Alpine style.

CAPITAL HOTEL ⌂ *English*
22 Basil St., SW3 (Knightsbridge) ☎ *(071) 589-5171. Map* **15I7** ▥ ▭ ■■ *lunch* ⚌ ▦ ▣ ▣ ▨ *Tube: Knightsbridge.*
Under the guidance of chef Philip Britten, this extremely small, very grand, slightly intimidating hotel dining room, all pink, festooned and candlelit, is in perfect order and lends itself especially well to business entertaining. Britten's classically based cooking pays more attention to flavor than unnecessary decoration; dishes are simple, light and perfectly judged. The service is attentive and the wine list excellent, although pricey.

LE CAPRICE ♣ *English/French*
Arlington House, Arlington St., SW1 (Piccadilly) ☎ *(071) 629-2239. Map* **8G9** ▥ ▭ ⚌ ▦ ▦ ▣ ▣ ▨ *Tube: Piccadilly Circus.*
Ten years into its reincarnation (it was one of London's most celebrated prewar society restaurants), the Caprice has lost none of its edge and remains one of the few consistently fashionable rendezvous for West End glitterati. Beneath the black-and-white Bailey photographs, famous faces abound, although ordinary mortals are made to feel entirely welcome. The hardest part is getting a table. The food is surprisingly good and just right for the ambience: steak tartare, salmon fishcakes, bang-bang chicken (with peanut and hot and sweet chili sauce), imaginative salads, white and dark chocolate mousse. And it's perhaps the best place in London for Sunday brunch. If you fail to get in at the Caprice, try its owners' more recent venture, THE IVY.

CHEZ GÉRARD ♣ *French*
8 Charlotte St., W1 (West End) ☎ *(071) 636-4975. Map* **9E10** ▥ *to* ▥ ▭ ■■ ▦ ▣ ▣ ▨ *Closed Sat lunch; bank holidays. Tube: Goodge Street.*
The punters flock to Chez Gérard for its

speciality, because when it comes to steak and chips, nobody cooks them quite like the French. There is also an array of French cheeses on offer. The wood floors, paper tablecloths and French waiters give the impression of a genuine, if somewhat sloppy Left Bank bistro. The straightforward four-course set menu is excellent value. Service is fairly peremptory. *(Branches at 31 Dover St., W1* ☎ *(071) 499-8171, map 8G9, and 119 Chancery Lane, WC2* ☎ *(071) 405-0290, map 10E13)*

CHEZ NICO *French*
35 Great Portland St., W1 (Marylebone)
☎*(071) 436-8846. Map 8E9* ▥ ▭ ▰
▰ ▦ ▣ ▣ ▨ *Closed Sat; Sun, 3 weeks in summer; 10 days at Christmas. Tube: Oxford Circus.*
In his small, brightly-lit, L-shaped dining room, decorated in elegant beige, with striking Tiffany glass skylights and large mirrors, Nico Ladenis performs the culinary miracles that have earned him two Michelin stars. Having its origins in Provence, the food is sensational. Flavors are combined with supreme skill to create such delicacies as *ravioli de champignons au fumet de champignons sauvage, rognons de veau au cassis, blanc de poulet farci de foie gras aux nouilles fraîches* or *glace caramel au coulis d'abricot*, all exquisitely prepared and presented. In the opinion of many hard-nosed critics, Chez Nico produces the best French food to be found in the city. The wine list excels, and the service is faultless.

Nico Ladenis has also converted his old premises into a bistro-style restaurant, called **Very Simply Nico** *(48a Rochester Row, SW1* ☎*(071) 630-8061, map 17J10* ▥*)*, where graduates of the Chez Nico kitchen continue to interpret the master's recipes at a fraction of the price.

CHRISTOPHER'S ♣ *American*
18 Wellington St., WC2 ☎*(071) 240-4222. Map 10F12* ▥ *to* ▥ ▭ ▣ ▣ ▣ ▨
Tube: Aldwych, Covent Garden.
Opened in the teeth of the recession by man-about-town Christopher Gilmour

plus a bevy of influential backers, this sophisticated "American Grill" has nevertheless proved an instant success. The premises are former offices, with a beautiful Italianate staircase winding from the downstairs bar to the upstairs restaurant, and even more beautiful young women fronting the startlingly trendy reception desk at its foot. The clientele is suave, and not infrequently famous, but the atmosphere is pleasantly relaxed and informal. The food is just right, and also affordable: perfect steaks, excellent Caesar salad, crab cakes, grilled swordfish and the like, and great chips. Excellent for a light post-theater meal in the downstairs bar.

CIBO *Italian*
3 Russell Gdns., W14 (Kensington)
☎*(071) 371-6271* ▥ *to* ▥ ▭ ▣ ▣
▣ ▨ *Closed Sun eve; bank holidays. Tube: Kensington (Olympia).*
Behind an unprepossessing exterior this is an unexpectedly sophisticated little restaurant, very *à la mode*. The stippled green walls are hung with exotic contemporary art works, all for sale. Light and airy with a profusion of plants and twig arrangements, a marble bar and cane furniture, it serves robust northern Italian cuisine, in similar vein to the pioneering ORSO and RIVER CAFÉ. When it opened, Cibo was greeted with noisy approval by the celebrity foodies; their affections have now transferred to its recently opened sister restaurant, **L'Altro** *(210 Kensington Park Rd., W11* ☎ *792-1066, map 5G1* ▥*)*, serving Italian fish dishes in designer surroundings.

If you enjoy the Italian food produced by the likes of Cibo, River Café, and **Riva** (in Barnes), but not the overheated prices, you might want to try **Osteria Antica Bologna** *(23 Northcote Rd., SW11* ☎*(071) 978-4771* ▭ *to* ▥*)*, a simple but deservedly popular Clapham café.

CLARKE'S ♣ *American/English*
124 Kensington Church St., W8
(Kensington) ☎*(071) 221-9225. Map 5H2*
▥ *to* ▥ ▰ ▰ ▦ ▣ ▨ *Closed 4 days*

at Easter; 2 weeks in Aug; 10 days at Christmas; bank holidays. Tube: Notting Hill Gate.

In her bright, airy restaurant, with lots of pale wood and cane chairs, Sally Clarke has quickly established a reputation for inspired Californian-based cooking. At lunchtime, there is a choice of three courses on the menu; there is no choice for the 4-course dinner (but alternatives for vegetarians). Menus are changed daily and hardly ever repeated, but salads, dressed with the purest olive oil, are popular starters, and char-grilling is favored for meat and fish, served with subtle sauces. The various unusual breads are outstanding (and on sale at their shop next door). There is a very good selection of Californian wines. From the basement, so cleverly lit that it feels as light as the upstairs room, the spotless, efficient kitchen is on view. Everything feels fresh, from the crisp linen napkins and pretty china to the flowers on the tables and excellent unobtrusive service.

CONNAUGHT HOTEL ♨ **French/English**
Carlos Pl., W1 (Mayfair) ☎(071) 499-7070. *Map* **8G8** ▦ ▦ *restaurant* ▢ *Grill Room* ☰ ▦ ▣ ▦ *Grill Room closed Sat; Sun; bank holidays. Tube: Bond Street.*

Perhaps the Connaught should more properly feature in our list of VENERABLE INSTITUTIONS, since it is rapidly becoming a splendid anachronism among the capital's fashion-led top restaurants. Michel Bourdin's faith in his menu — *oeufs de caille Maintenon*, salmon *quenelles* in a pink champagne sauce, kidneys and bacon, Irish stew — has never wavered, nor has the balletic service performed by fleets of hovering white-coated waiters. With the understated grandeur of its paneled Edwardian dining room, the Connaught epitomizes all that is — or was — traditionally English.

DAQUISE ♨ ♥ *Polish*
20 Thurloe St., SW7 (South Kensington) ☎(071) 589-6117. *Map* **14J5** ▢ ▢ ▦ *lunch. Tube: South Kensington.*

A home-away-from-home for the Polish community, and a welcome refuge for hungry students. This is a little corner of Eastern Europe in Central London. There's 1950s decor, much nostalgia, and huge helpings of Polish fodder such as borscht *(barszcs)*, goulash, and steamed buckwheat *(kasza)*. The ground-floor room is more informal than the neat, wood-paneled basement dining room.

DEAL'S *American*
Chelsea Harbour, SW10 (Chelsea/Fulham) ☎(071) 376-3232 ▢ ▢ ▦ ▦ ▣ ▣ ▦ *Tube: Fulham Broadway/Sloane Square.*

Although equally popular with adults, Deal's is a good place to take the kids: there's hamburger and fries on the menu, a relaxed atmosphere and plenty of space. Outside, in the largely deserted Chelsea Harbour complex, they can ride the glass elevator and admire the yachts in the marina. Apart from standard American fare, there are also Far Eastern dishes on offer, such as *satay* and Oriental chicken salad.

Deals West is the sister restaurant if you're in the NW corner of Soho *(14-16 Foubert's Pl., W1* ☎ *(071) 287-1001, map 8F9* ▢*)*.

ED'S EASY DINER ♨ ♥ *American*
12 Moor St., W1 (Soho) ☎(071) 439-1955. *Map* **9F10** ▢ ▢ ▦ *Closed Christmas; Jan 1. Tube: Leicester Square.*

Chili con carne, hot dogs, burgers and fries are the staple at this meticulous replica of a 1950s American diner. It has been perfectly reconstructed by young restaurateur Bruce Isaacs down to the last detail, from the sleek chrome counter to the ten original juke boxes, which throb to the beat of Buddy Holly or Jerry Lee Lewis. Even the phone number is a 1950s one. It's hard to find better burgers anywhere else in the city, and they should be accompanied by a choice from the eclectic selection of beers, Rolling Rock for example. Staff are brisk but helpful, often funny and particularly good with children. *(Other branches include 362 King's Rd., SW3* ☎ *(071) 352-1956, map 14L5, and 16 Hampstead High Rd., NW3* ☎ *(071) 431-1958.)*

ENGLISH HOUSE *English*

3 Milner St., SW3 (Chelsea) ☎*(071) 584-3002. Map* **15**J6 ▥ ▭ ◼ *lunch* ▣ ◙ ◙ ▨ *Tube: Sloane Square.*

In intimate chintzy rooms in a Chelsea town house, old English recipes have been adapted and modernized to provide one of the capital's few interesting British menus. Mouthwatering specialities include *ragout* of wild mushrooms tossed with cream and Madeira and topped with toasted breadcrumbs, potted venison with juniper berries and Cumberland jelly, pheasant, apricot and chestnut pie topped with flaky pastry, stew of salmon and scallops marinated with spring onions, root ginger and sorrel, brown bread and ginger ice cream and honey cheesecake with cinnamon custard. Other restaurants in this small chain, with the same culinary style, are **The English Garden** *(10 Lincoln St., SW3* ☎*(071) 584-7272, map* **15**K7 ▥), with a conservatory dining room awash with plants, cozy with an open fire in winter, and **The Lindsay House** *(21 Romilly St., W1* ☎ *(071) 439-0450, map* **9**F10 ▥), where the pretty upstairs dining room is decked out in pastel shades and elegant antique furniture.

L'ESCARGOT *English/French*

48 Greek St., W1 (Soho) ☎*(071) 437-2679. Map* **9**F10 ▥ *to* ▥ ▭ ▬ ▤ ▣ ◙ ◙ ▨ *Closed Sat lunch; Sun. Tube: Tottenham Court Road.*

One of Soho's venerable institutions. After a period of closure, L'Escargot was revamped and given a new lease on life ten years ago. The downstairs brasserie-type menu is a lighter version of the Modern British food on offer to the media-folk in the upstairs dining rooms. The global selection of wines was created by wine-writer Jancis Robinson. Graphically-arresting snail-trails wind around the carpets, and marbled *eau-de-nil* walls rise to lofty skylights. The life-force is *maîtresse d'* Elena Salvoni, enticed from the much-loved, now defunct Bianchi's. Local competition is provided by the **Groucho Club** *(44 Dean St.* ☎*(071) 439-4685, map*

9 *F10)*, another media hot-spot, open to members and guests only.

FOUR SEASONS △ *French*

Inn on the Park, Hamilton Pl., W1 (Mayfair) ☎*(071) 499-0888. Map* **8**H8 ▥ ▭ ◼ ▬ ▤ ▬ ▣ ▣ ◙ ▨ *Tube: Hyde Park Corner.*

Raymond Blanc's young and brilliant protégé Bruno Loubet is currently doing spectacular and imaginative things at this hotel restaurant. In ostentatious palm-fringed surroundings, Loubet presents his innovative *cuisine de terroir* (food of the earth), which originates from his native southwest France. Every component is original: the lightly smoked salmon and beef, caramelized vegetables, sublime sauces, some fragrant, others piquant, and perfect mousses. The wine list is strong, but exorbitantly priced.

FUNG SHING *Chinese*

15 Lisle St., WC2 (Soho) ☎*(071) 437-1539. Map* **9**G10 ▥ *to* ▥ ▭ ◼ ▤ ▤ ▣ ◙ ◙ ▨ *Tube: Leicester Square.*

Chinatown presents a bewildering choice of restaurants to the newcomer, perhaps wandering through after the theater (no need to reserve, although you might have to wait for a table). Most are perfectly reasonable, but POONS, for lunch or a quick supper, **Chuen Cheng Ku** *(17 Wardour St., W1* ☎ *(071) 437-1398, map* **9**F10 ▥*)* and **New World** *(Gerrard Pl., W1* ☎*(071) 734-0677, map* **9**F10 ▥*)*, for good *dim-sum* and an amusing venue, **Mr Kong** *(21 Lisle St., W1* ☎ *(071) 437-7341, map* **9**G10 ▥*)*, for excellent Cantonese food, and Fung Shing stand out. Fung Shing is small and rather cramped, with bland un-Oriental decor. But its Cantonese food is the very best in Chinatown: one delicious meal for two consisted of state-of-the-art *wun-tun* soup, crunchy quail baked with salt and chili, green vegetables with slivers of garlic, and slices of duck with lemon sauce.

GALICIA ▤ *Spanish*

323 Portobello Rd., W10 (Notting Hill) ☎*(071) 969-3539. Map* **5**G2 ▭ ▭

■■ lunch Tues-Fri 🎫 💳 🆔 🎫 Closed Mon. Tube: Ladbroke Grove.

One of a crop of Spanish *tapas* bars that have sprung up throughout London recently, Galicia is probably the most down-to-earth and authentic. It serves hearty Galician specialities, such as hake, octopus, squid and paella, all fresh, tender and simply but well cooked. The unfussy decoration (plain walls and dark wood) matches the cuisine. Linger over coffee and a liqueur at the long bar, favored by the Spanish habitués for lengthy animated conversations.

GANPATH *Indian*
372 Grays Inn Rd., WC1 (King's Cross) ☎(071) 278-1938. Map **4**C12 🔲 🔲 ■■ lunch 💳 🆔 🎫 Tube: King's Cross St Pancras.

South Indian food is very different from that of the northern part of the subcontinent, which is more commonly found in Britain. Southern cooking is usually (although not always) hotter, and this particular restaurant also gives it a vegetarian emphasis, although fish and meat dishes are available on a menu that is authentic, interesting and varied. Try spiced green bananas, *avial* (vegetables in coconut and yogurt) and *masala dosa*. The service is gracious too.

LE GAVROCHE ⌂ *French*
43 Upper Brook St., W1 (Mayfair) ☎(071) 408-0881. Map **7**F7 🎫 🔲 ■■ ≡ 🎫 💳 🆔 🎫 Closed Sat; Sun. Tube: Bond Street.

For the money you could fly to Paris, but even there you wouldn't get the wonderful creations of Michel Roux, son of Albert and nephew of Michel senior, the famous brothers from Charolles, in Burgundy, who created Le Gavroche. Theirs is widely regarded as one of the two or three best French restaurants in London. The menu is sufficiently varied to meet most requirements, and it does list a few popular classics among the heavenly sauces and soufflés, mousses and *mousselines*. Although Le Gavroche doesn't specialize in fish, its *mousseline* of lobster and

turbotin au Chardonnay are notable delights. Burgundian the Roux family may be, but the lengthy wine list pays equal homage to Bordeaux. Service is attentive, courteous and helpful, and the ambience formal but unstuffy. The set lunch is almost a bargain.

GAVVERS ✿ *French*
61-63 Lower Sloane St., SW1 (Chelsea) ☎(071) 730-5983. Map **15**K7 🎫 ■■ 🎫 💳 🆔 🎫 Closed Sat lunch; Sun; 1 week at Christmas. Tube: Sloane Square.

There are few restaurants where fixed-price means what it says, but this young relation of LE GAVROCHE is one of them. From the crisp vegetable canapés to the final cup of coffee not a single extra creeps onto the bill. Included in the price is a half bottle per person from a small but excellent selection of house wines. But be warned: veering off this list and onto the impressive main wine list can make a dramatic difference to what you end up paying. Bruno Valette, the talented chef, who has his vegetables brought by truck from France, changes his imaginative menu regularly. Service is efficient yet discreet and the atmosphere lively, although the tables are too cramped.

GAY HUSSAR *Hungarian*
2 Greek St., W1 (Soho), ☎(071) 437-0973. Map **9**F10 🎫 🔲 ■■ lunch ≡ 🎫 Closed Sun. Tube: Tottenham Court Road.

The name predates any sexual connotation, and persuasions are more obviously political in this famous plotting place. It is an irony that a Hungarian emigré establishment should be so well patronized by leading socialist politicians, but they obviously enjoy such Central European sustainers as cherry soup, pressed boar's head, goose, mallard, dumplings and lemon cheese pancakes. There is a considerable choice at modest prices on the lunch menu. Although it has changed hands, care has been taken to keep the restaurant exactly as it was — clubby, with paneled walls and velvet seats — in the famous Mr Sassie's day.

225

GAYLORD *Indian*
79 Mortimer St., W1 (West End) ☎*(071) 580-3615. Map 8E9* 🔲 ⏺ ■■ 🎴 🆎 🔘 🔘 📠 *Tube: Oxford Circus.*

The first Gaylord was in Delhi, but the London branch, which opened in 1966, has probably done most to spread the name of this family of restaurants, with their own delicate style of Indian *haute cuisine.* The Gaylords boast that they open for lunch and dinner "365 days a year." The *pilaus, tandoori* chicken, lamb *pasanda* and *korma* dishes are an impressive introduction to Indian cooking. There is a take-out service too.

GEALE'S 🍽 *English*
2 Farmer St., W8 (Notting Hill) ☎*(071) 727-7969. Map 5G2* 🔲 ⏺ ■■ *lunch* 🔘 📠 *Closed Mon; Sun; 10 days at Easter; 2 weeks in Aug and at Christmas. Tube: Notting Hill Gate.*

Fish and chips should be eaten out of a newspaper held hotly in the hand, in the course of a winter's evening stroll; every true Briton knows that, in much the way that all Americans prefer their franks to be served at a ball-game. The notion of a fish-and-chip restaurant is heresy enough to the purist, and a fashionable one defies the logic of the world's greatest take-out food. Geale's became fashionable when it was patronized by media heroes in search of simple pleasures. Success hasn't spoiled the place, which remains very basic, with excellent fish, despite such nonsense as a wine-list. No reservations, but be prepared to stand in line.

GREENHOUSE *English*
27a Hays Mews, W1 (Mayfair) ☎*(071) 499-3331. Map 8G8* 🔳 ⏺ 🎴 🆎 🔘 🔘 📠 *Closed Sat lunch; Sun eve; bank holidays. Tube: Green Park.*

The newest, brightest star in the culinary firmament, chef Gary Rhodes is pulling in the crowds at this unfussy country-style Mayfair restaurant, where the walls are appropriately decorated with vegetable prints. Rhodes' revolutionary talent is for transforming solid, traditional British favorites, such as faggots, Lancashire hotpot, oxtail, sponge

and bread and butter puddings into refined, melt-in-the-mouth specialities, where flavors are subtly combined. Starters in particular — carpaccio and fettucine, for example — reveal a Continental influence. Advance reservations are essential.

GREEN'S *English*
36 Duke St., SW1 (St James's) ☎*(071) 930-4566. Map 8G9* 🔳 *to* 🔳 ⏺ 🎴 🆎 🔘 🔘 📠 *Closed Sun eve; bank holidays. Tube: Green Park.*

In the heart of St James's, this refined wood-paneled restaurant has all the exclusivity of a gentlemen's club. Although it only opened a few years ago, Green's feels as though it has been here for centuries. The cooking is traditional too. Oysters are the speciality and the Champagne list is distinguished, if you can stand the expense. Perfect for plotting or secret assignations, the **Bar**, with its private booths, serves good-quality cold food, such as salmon, lobster and dressed crab.

HARD ROCK CAFÉ *American*
150 Old Park Lane, W1 (Mayfair) ☎*(071) 629-0382. Map 8H8* 🔲 ⏺ 🆎 🔘 📠 *Tube: Hyde Park Corner.*

The legendary line outside the Hard Rock is as long as ever as hordes wait to sample indifferent hamburgers, steaks, sandwiches, chili in winter, American beer, and good ice cream plus wonderful pop memorabilia. Not a place for conversation, though; it might better be called the Loud Rock Café. No reservations.

HARVEY'S *English/French*
2 Bellevue Rd., SW17 (Wandsworth) ☎*(081) 672-0114* 🔳 ⏺ ■■ 🎴 🔘 📠 *Closed Sun. Train to Wandsworth Common.*

This pretty pastiche of a 1930s dining room in a gentrified backwater overlooking Wandsworth Common is an unlikely setting for some of the most creative cooking currently on offer in Britain. But this is where Marco Pierre White, an explosive, driven young Yorkshireman, has decided to unleash his considerable talents, and he has been rewarded with his second Michelin star. His commitment to the culinary art and his fresh approach are evident in every beautifully presented dish, whether it be tagliatelle with oysters, *ragôut* of shellfish or pigeon *en crepinette* with thyme. Cheese and desserts stand up well. The young French staff are courteous and professional, belying the tumult presumably going on unseen in the kitchens. **The Canteen** (⬛), Marco Pierre White's latest venture, opened in Chelsea Harbour in the fall of 1992.

IKKYU 🍴 ♣ *Japanese*

Basement, 67 Tottenham Court Rd., W1 (West End) ☎(071) 636-9280. Map **9**E10 ⬛ to ⬛ ⬛ ■ ⬛ ⬛ ⬛ Closed Sat; Sun lunch. Tube: Goodge Street.

A world away from SUNTORY with its serious, expense-account clientele, Ikkyu is one of the cheapest and most humble Japanese restaurants in town; it is also one of the jolliest, with some of the best food. The entrance, down steep steps beneath an electronics store, is easy to miss and positively tacky. The room itself is not much of an improvement, but it's a relaxed and amusing place to dig into big portions of *sushi, sashimi* or *yakitori*, or *roba-tayaki*, the country cooking of Japan, which might include stewed meat with potato, or rolled conger in seaweed. The set menus are incredibly cheap. Drink whisky (sold by the bottle), sake or lager, or free green tea. Service can be confused, but persevere. **Ajimura** (*51-53 Shelton St., WC2* ☎ *(071) 240-9424, map 9F11* ⬛), in Covent Garden, is a similarly informal Japanese restaurant.

THE IVY *English*

1 West St., WC2 (Covent Garden) ☎(071) 836-4751. Map **9**F11 ⬛ ⬛ ⬛ ⬛ ⬛ ⬛ ⬛ Tube: Leicester Square.

When the owners of LE CAPRICE took over and revamped the Ivy, they re-created the successful, stylish restaurant that it had been in the 1930s. With its wood-paneling, starched linen tablecloths, stained-glass windows and impeccable

waiters, it exudes old-fashioned charm, and is packed nightly with theater-goers and the stars themselves, some of whose photographs adorn the walls. The Ivy poached talented chef Nigel Davis from the now defunct Sud Ouest, and his menu of delectable Modern British specialities (bang bang chicken, salmon fishcakes with sorrel sauce, lobster salad with celeriac chips) equals that of LE CAPRICE.

AU JARDIN DES GOURMETS *French*

5 Greek St., W1 (Soho) ☎(071) 437-1816. Map **9**F10 ⬛ to ⬛ ⬛ ■ ⬛ ⬛ ⬛ ⬛ ⬛ ⬛ Closed Sat lunch; Sun. Tube: Tottenham Court Road.

Although it is especially noted for its fine wines — one of the best lists in London, acquired with great care and served with love — this elegant, discreet classical French restaurant has for many years been a firm Soho favorite. Theater-goers can split their meal: starter and main course before curtain-up, dessert and coffee after. The restaurant has recently been expanded and revamped, with an area set aside for non-smokers.

JOE ALLEN *American*

13 Exeter St., WC2 (Covent Garden) ☎(071) 836-0651. Map **10**F13 ⬛ to ⬛ ⬛ ⬛ ♈ No charge/credit cards. Tube: Covent Garden.

Branch of the New York restaurant, and very similar in style and decor, although somehow less intimate and more bustling. Very popular with journalists and actors, more for its social ambience than its food. Sizeable menu on a chalkboard, with salads, burgers (called "chopped steak"), etc., and American desserts. Cocktails at the bar. Open late, until 1am.

KENSINGTON PLACE ♣ *English/French*

201-5 Kensington Church St., W8 (Kensington) ☎(071) 727-3184. Map **5**G2 ⬛ to ⬛ ⬛ ■ lunch ⬛ ⬛ ⬛ Tube: Notting Hill Gate.

A great brasserie, more Manhattan than Paris, which packs in the crowds for its glamorous feel and its uncomplicated, inexpensive food. It's not to everyone's taste: some people complain that it's like eating in a goldfish bowl, since the street side is a huge wall of glass. But most people enjoy the exposure: the use of expensive wood for floor, table tops and (uncomfortable) chairs, the mass of bright spotlights, and the long, buzzing bar at one end all add to the glitzy effect. This isn't the place for a lingering meal; the idea is to eat, talk loudly (a necessity), and go: they need your table. The food sometimes misses, mostly hits. The menu changes often, although the choice is limited, particularly among main courses. Highlights include the delectable chicken and goat's cheese mousse with olives, with a texture like *crême caramel,* and baked tamarillos with vanilla ice cream. The more expensive items, such as *foie gras* and oysters (poached with chanterelles and cucumber), are done very well indeed.

Under the same management and on the other side of the Royal Borough, **Launceston Place** (*1a Launceston Place, W8* ☎ *(071) 937-6912, map 14I4* ▥ *closed Sat lunch, Sun eve)* has a cozier feel, more like a private dining room than a restaurant. Here, accomplished chef Charles Mumford produces fine Modern English cuisine (salt cod fishcakes with aioli, vegetable strudel, warm chicken liver with chives), but does not exclude stalwart favorites like sirloin of beef for Sunday lunch.

KETTNERS *Italian/American*
29 Romilly St., W1 (Soho) ☎ *(071) 437-6437/734-6112. Map 9F10* ▢ *to* ▥ ▢ ☙ ♪ ▥ ▣ ▣ ▥ *Tube: Leicester Square, Tottenham Court Road.*

A famous London restaurant in days gone by, Kettners is nowadays home to yet another Pizza Express. This is all to the good, since it means that those with only a few pounds to spend can enjoy their tasty pizzas and hamburgers in splendidly plush surroundings (avoid the modern, tiled dining room if you can: it's attractive enough, but irrelevant). There is also a champagne bar and a pianist in the restaurant, where on

Thursday and Friday at lunchtime and every evening you will be serenaded by Alfredo, the singing *maître d'.*

There are more than 20 Pizza Express branches in London, at two of which, **Pizza on the Park** (*11 Knightsbridge, SW1* ☎ *(071) 235-5550, map 8H8* ▢ *to* ▥) and **Pizza Express** (*10 Dean St., W1* ☎ *(071) 437-9595, map 9 F10* ▢ *to* ▥), live jazz can be heard nightly.

KHANS ✿ *Indian*
13-15 Westbourne Grove, W2 (Bayswater) ☎*(071) 727-5420. Map 5F3* ▢ ▢ ▥ ▥ ▣ ▣ ▥ *Tube: Bayswater.*

A feeling of light and spaciousness created by the palm tree pillars and *trompe l'oeil* floating clouds does much to counteract the hustle and bustle of this thriving, well-established Indian restaurant. The authentic and extremely reasonably priced menu makes it highly popular, particularly with Indian families. Tables should be reserved in the evening, and do request the main room rather than the less appealing basement or back room.

LANGAN'S BRASSERIE *French*
Stratton St., W1 (Piccadilly) ☎*(071) 493-6437. Map 8G9* ▥ ▢ ▣ ♪ ▥ ▣ ▣ ▥ *Closed Sat lunch; Sun. Tube: Green Park.*

Michael Caine, the archetypal knowing Cockney, was one of the founding members of this headquarters of London's café society, where the famous are not only sketched on the menu but also seated at the tables. Londoners have always enjoyed the various watering-holes, such as **Odins** (*27 Devonshire St., W1* ☎ *(071) 935-7296, map 2 E8* ▥ *closed Sat lunch, Sun),* established by extrovert Irish restaurateur Peter Langan. Despite Langan's sad death, his buzzing and crowded brasserie has retained its pizazz, even if more tourists and soccer stars than moguls and movie stars have crept in of late. The food, under the control of roving chef Richard Shepherd, has lost some of its edge, but it remains surprisingly superior (try the spinach soufflé, *croustade d'oeufs de caille*, profiteroles with chocolate sauce). Langan's may not be at its zenith, but this is still the most exciting dining room in London, a huge space, wonderfully lit, filled with white-covered tables, black-aproned waiters, beautiful modern paintings, and above all, people.

LEITH'S *English*
92 Kensington Park Rd., W11 (Notting Hill)
☎*(071) 229-4481. Map 5G2* 🖩 ▆ ▆
🖽 🆎 ⬥ ⬥ 🖩 *Closed lunch; Aug holiday weekend; 4 days at Christmas. Tube: Notting Hill Gate.*

A school of food and wine, a catering company, a farm growing produce for the restaurant, and an impressive *oeuvre* as a cookery writer, all underpin the work of Prue Leith and her partners in this Victorian building, with a now slightly dated interior by expatriate American architect Nathan Silver. The result is an ambience of discreet, glittering comfort, of respect for food by the kitchen and diners alike. Leith's is a temple of the very best English food and an especially inventive style, served from a very short menu. The restaurant is well known for its trolley of cold starters, on which a typical item might be smoked trout pâté parcels wrapped in smoked salmon. Dishes from the kitchen are usually even better: stilton soup is a favorite, perhaps followed by traditional roast duckling served with a light orange *jus*. There is an equally varied menu of delectable vegetarian dishes, an excellent, if expensive, wine list, and a choice of superb vegetables, cheeses and delicious desserts served from a groaning trolley.

LUIGI'S *Italian*
15 Tavistock St., WC2 (Covent Garden)
☎*(071) 240-1795. Map 9G10* 🖩 🖩 🖩
⬥ ⬥ 🖩 *Closed Sun. Tube: Covent Garden.*

Theater-goers who exit stage east, in the Strand/Covent Garden/Drury Lane area, flock to Luigi's, a bustling old favorite on several floors. It offers a typical Italian menu, with reasonable pastas and *zabaglione*.

MALABAR *Indian*
27 Uxbridge St., W8 (Notting Hill Gate)
☎*(071) 727-8800. Map 5G2* 🖩 *to* 🖩
🖵 ▆ 🖽 ⬥ 🖩 *Closed Christmas; 1 week in Aug. Tube: Notting Hill Gate.*

A friendly Indian restaurant with attractive European decor in a quaint area of Notting Hill Gate known as "Hillgate Village." The menu is quite short, but inspired, and includes such tempting specialities as shashlik kebab, venison marinated in tamarind, and chicken with cloves and ginger, served authentically on stainless-steel plates.

MANZI'S ✿ *Italian*
1 Leicester St., WC2 (Soho) ☎*(071) 734-0224. Map 9G10* 🖩 🖵 🆎 ⬥ ⬥
🖩 *Closed Sun lunch. Tube: Leicester Square.*

This family-run Italian fish restaurant, now owned by the fourth generation of Manzis, has been a much-loved London institution for many years. Its atmosphere is less overtly Italian than generalized between-the-wars "Continental." Downstairs, Manzi's is all bustle and rush-rush lunchtime or pre-theater dining. Upstairs, however, the Cabin Room is calmer, for post-theater dinners or romantic assignations. Commendable starters, excellent scallops, sole, crab, lobster, all simply prepared, are characteristic. Custardy strawberry flan is an essential dessert. Unpretentious and good fun.

MELATI 🍲 *Indonesian*
31 Peter St., W1 (Soho) ☎*(071) 437-2011. Map 9F10* 🖵 🖵 ▆ 🆎 ⬥
⬥ 🖩 *Closed Sun. Tube: Piccadilly Circus.*

Fair Indonesian food, with some Malaysian/Singaporean dishes, in a little Soho spot, more café than restaurant, just behind Berwick St. market. *Satay*, of course, with the distinctive flavor of lemon grass, but also a wide variety of soups, noodle dishes, seafood and vegetarian specialities.

Another larger restaurant, also called **Melati** *(21 Great Windmill St., W1* ☎*(071) 437-2745, map 9G10* 🖵*)*, but unconnected with the one in Peter St., is found nearby.

MIJANOU ♣ French

143 Ebury St., SW1 (Pimlico) ☎*(071)*
730-4099. Map 16J8 ▥□ *to* ▥▥ ■■ 国 🚬
🚗 ▣▣ ▨▨ *Closed Sat; Sun. Tube: Victoria.*
Here is a timeless little restaurant, per-
sonally run, recently refurbished with
colorful murals, and excellent for a
quiet *diner à deux* where you can be
assured of good food and wine and
helpful service. Sonia Blech cooks; her
husband Neville oversees and is responsible for one of the best wine lists
in town. The menu consists of several
set-price meals that reflect Mrs Blech's
impressively wide repertoire. It makes
a pleasant change from some of London's higher-profile quality restaurants.
Smoking is only allowed in the downstairs sitting room.

MON PLAISIR *French*

21 Monmouth St., WC2 (Covent Garden)
☎*(071) 836-7243. Map 9F11* ▥□ *to* ▥□
□ ■■ ▣ ▣ ▣ ▨▨ *Closed Sat lunch;*
Sun. Tube: Covent Garden.
The cheese board at Mon Plaisir is so
good that one day a diner will order it
for all four courses. The notion has been
discussed, but no one has yet dared risk
the wrath of the staff, who can at times
be very Parisian. The cuisine is more
tuned to country cooking such as *coq
au vin* and *escargots Bourguignons,*
than complex dishes, and the atmosphere is appropriately bistro-like. Mon
Plaisir is on the edge of the Covent
Garden area in something of a no-man's
land, but by no means inconvenient,
and it has for years been everyone's
favorite secret. It is small, intimate, and
pleasantly busy.

Its success has spawned two sibling
restaurants, the cozy **Mon Petit Plaisir**
(33c Holland St., W8 ☎ *(071) 937-
3224, map5 H2* ▥□*), and in North London,* **Mon Plaisir du Nord** *(1st floor,
The Mall Antiques Arcade, 359 Upper
St., N1* ☎ *(071) 359-1932, map4B13*
▥□*).* Both adhere to the same bistro
formula.

MUSEUM STREET CAFÉ *English*

47 Museum St., WC1 (Bloomsbury)
☎*(071) 405-3211. Map 9E11* ▥□ □ ■■

*No charge/credit cards. Closed Sat; Sun.
Tube: Tottenham Court Road.*
Some of the best Modern British cuisine
in the least pretentious of surroundings,
a stone's throw from the British Museum. Chefs Gail Koerber and Mark Nathan have combined their talents to
produce some exquisite dishes, using
the freshest ingredients, simply cooked
and artistically presented. In this tiny
basic café, with white walls, contemporary watercolors, wood tables and
hard chairs, the menu is chalked up on
a blackboard. To start with, it might
include a light leek and saffron tart, a
more robust black bean soup or *porcini
risotto,* accompanied by deliciously
crusty home-baked bread. Most of the
main courses are wonderfully succulent
char-grilled fish or meat, served with a
crisp, fragrantly dressed salad. Try and
save space for one of the mouthwatering desserts. Apparently the search is on
for much-needed larger premises, but
in the meantime it is essential to reserve
a table. There is no license, so bring
your own wine.

NONTAS *Greek*

16 Camden High St., NW1 (Camden Town)
☎*(071) 387-4579* □ *to* ▥□ □ 🚗 ▣
▣ ▣▣ ▨▨ *Closed Sun. Tube: Camden Town.*
The Greek Cypriot ethnic neighborhoods of London are Camden and
Kentish Towns and points NW, and so
throughout this area there are inexpensive local restaurants of greatly varying quality. In Camden Town, Nontas
is a popular local Greek restaurant, full
of life, with flavorsome cooking, including good lamb and fish dishes, varied
mezze and delicious Hymettus honey
and yogurt to finish what should be a
most pleasant meal.

NOW & ZEN *Chinese/Thai/Japanese*

*4a Upper St Martin's Lane, WC2 (Covent
Garden)* ☎*(071) 497-0376/7/8. Map
9F11* ▥▥ □ 国 ▣ ▣ ▣ ▨▨ ♫ *Tube:
Leicester Square.*
Water cascades down the height of this
three-tiered restaurant in an elaborate
system of half-filled glass bowls and
tubes: just one soothing element in a

cool, sparse, yet elegant, lemon-painted addition to the Zen chain. The furniture is hi-tech, and the menu offers a range of unusual but authentic Chinese, Thai and Japanese dishes. There is a *sushi* bar on the ground floor.

OAK ROOM ⌂ *French*
Le Meridien London Hotel, Piccadilly, W1 (Piccadilly) ☎*(071) 734-8000. Map* **9**G10 ▥ ▭ ◼ ⇶ ▦ Ⓐ ⊕ ⓒ ⓥ *Closed Sat lunch; Sun. Tube: Piccadilly Circus.*

One of a handful of luxury restaurants (**L'Auberge de Provence** and **Ninety Park Lane** are others) guided from afar by a luminary French chef, in this case Michel Lorain from A La Côte St-Jacques at Joigny. Together with chef David Chambers he has won a Michelin star for this sumptuous hotel dining room (see LE MERIDIEN LONDON in WHERE TO STAY), second only to the RITZ in Edwardian splendor. The food is creative and complex, spectacularly garnished (only the desserts can disappoint); the selection of cheeses formidable; the wine list all-embracing; the service polished; the prices sky-high. *The* place for a money-no-object celebration.

OGNISKO POLSKIE ♧ *Polish*
55 Princes Gate, Exhibition Rd., SW7 (South Kensington) ☎*(071) 589-4635. Map* **14**J5 ▭ *to* ▥ ▭ ◼ Ⓐ ⊕ ⓒ ⓥ *Tube: South Kensington.*

The elegant, slightly faded dining room of the Polish Hearth Club, with its portraits, gilt mirrors and yellow drapes, has a particular charm. Here, for next to nothing, you can tuck into simple, hearty Polish fare (go feeling hungry) such as *bigos* (hunter's stew) or *pierogi z miesem* (meat dumplings) accompanied by a flavored vodka or two. Fellow diners are a distinctive mix of penniless students, Solidarity dignitaries, family groups and the odd frock-coated priest.

192 *French/English*
192 Kensington Park Rd., W11 (Notting Hill) ☎*(071) 229-0482. Map* **5**G1 ▥ ▭ ⇶ ▦ Ⓐ ⓒ ⓥ *Closed Mon lunch. Tube: Ladbroke Grove.*

Although it's probably meant to be stunning, the all-glass front of this restaurant-cum-wine bar is somehow rather uninviting, as is the self-consciously stylish Post-Modern/1950s interior, with its mainly blank *eau-de-nil* walls and tightly packed seating. Often crowded, it continues to be the local canteen for Notting Hill's media crowd. And the food and wine continue to be pretty good value. In the Modern European manner, warm salads, grilled fish, goat's cheese and lentils all feature on the menu. The wine list is excellent and not over-priced.

ONE NINETY QUEEN'S GATE (DOWNSTAIRS) ♧ *English/French*
190 Queen's Gate, SW7 (Kensington) ☎*(071) 581-5666. Map* **14**I4 ▥ ▭ ◼ ⇶ ▦ Ⓐ ⊕ ⓒ ⓥ *Closed lunch; Sun; 2 weeks in Aug; Christmas. Tube: Kensington High Street.*

Antony Worrall-Thompson is a chef-proprietor whose ventures always attract attention. His particular talent is for spotting a culinary trend or fad and stylishly turning it to his advantage. Witness a previous highly successful venture (now sold), **Ménage à Trois**, where eating nothing but delectable starters and puddings became, for a time, highly fashionable. Worrall-Thompson's latest stroke is to transform his basement premises from *haute* French restaurant to "fish brasserie" (his description). The place is lighter, whiter, less clubby than before. Bright, bold paintings adorn the walls and a pianist soothes unobtrusively while you dine. The prices are lower (exceptionally low, given the raw materials on offer). The food — there are game dishes and brilliant *steak frites* as well as fish — is versatile and inventive: try the steamed mussels in a broth of lentils and coriander, or the roast scallops with carrot juices and Thai spices. One Ninety Queen's Gate is now aligned to the adjoining hotel, the GORE (see WHERE TO STAY). The Gore's own dining room has also been entrusted to Worrall-Thompson and, like **Bistrot 190** (☎*(071) 581-5666* ▥*),* has become an instant success. In the pretty fin-de-siècle room, always buzzing, you will find marvelous brasserie food — with a strong Italian streak — at very reasonable prices.

ORSO *Italian*

27 Wellington St., WC2 (Covent Garden) ☎*(071) 240-5269. Map 10F12* ▨ ▭ ▦ ▰ *No charge/credit cards. Tube: Covent Garden.*

Under the same ownership as JOE ALLEN around the corner, and just as fashionable, perhaps more so, but quieter. The food is certainly better. This was the first of the new breed of Italian restaurants in which the cooking is truly praiseworthy, rather than merely passable. The shortish menu features good meat and offal dishes and excellent vegetables, as well as crispy pizzas and the usual crop of homemade pastas. The wine list has been thoughtfully chosen and priced. Open from noon to midnight, and with two evening sittings and crisp service, this is an excellent spot either for a pre- or post-theater supper.

PAGU DINAI *Italian (Sardinian)*

690 Fulham Rd., SW6 (Fulham) ☎*(071) 736-1195* ▨ ▰ ▣ AE ▣ ▣ VISA *Tube: Parsons Green.*

The name may sound faintly Oriental — *another* Thai restaurant? — but in fact it's Sardinian dialect for "good value," which isn't far off the truth. And it is the Sardinian cooking that saves Pagu Dinai from being just another Italian *"trat"* — albeit a well-lit and comfortable one. So go for the Sardinian specialities such as a strongly flavored fish stew, melting semolina *gnocchi* or clam soup. The Italian wine list includes a fresh Sardinian house wine. The waiters still flash their giant peppermills here, but only briefly.

PHOENICIA ♣ *Lebanese*

11-13 Abingdon Rd., W8 (Kensington) ☎*(071) 937-0120. Map 13I2* ▨ *to* ▨ ▭ ▰ ▦ AE ▣ ▣ VISA *Tube: Kensington High Street.*

AL HAMRA may be London's most suave Lebanese restaurant, but Phoenicia, although much simpler, is every bit as enjoyable. Those who already know and love Lebanese dishes will find everything here as delicious as they would expect. Those who don't will have a first-class introduction, in pleasant surroundings, neither artificially ethnic nor self-consciously smart, with smiling, helpful service. Avoid the obvious temptation to have a (chargrilled) main course and stick to a selection of the *mezze* (the waiter will advise); it's fun to pick at all the different dishes (you should eat straight from the plates they are served on), and it livens up anything from a *tête-à-tête* to a family gathering. A meal here is never expensive, and the serve-yourself lunch *(Mon-Sat)* is a notable bargain.

LE PONT DE LA TOUR *English/French*

Butler's Wharf, Shad Thames, SE1 (Southwark) ☎*(071) 403-8403. Map 12H17* ▨ *to* ▨ ▭ ▰ ▦ ▣ ▣ VISA *Tube: Tower Hill, London Bridge.*

Sir Terence Conran has a sure touch when it comes to restaurants — not surprisingly since his two great passions are good food and good design. At BIBENDUM, the **Blueprint Café** (see DESIGN MUSEUM) and now at Le Pont de la Tour, he has created the sort of restaurants that people love to be in and the sort of food that people love to eat. The latter forms part of his converted warehouse complex, Butler's Wharf, and has exceptional views of Tower Bridge and the Thames. The long, glossy dining room, with its mirrors, pillars, partitions and black-framed picture windows, is especially stylish at night. The food is in Bibendum style, though not as accomplished. A typical meal might be fish soup with *rouille, tête de veau, sauce ravigote* and *crème brulée,* or alternatively beef consommé with Madeira, followed by lemon sole and chips. The wine list is long, strong on Burgundy and dessert wines.

POONS ♣ ♣ *Chinese*

4 Leicester St., WC2 (Soho) ☎*(071) 437-1528. Map 9G10* ▭ *to* ▨ ▭ ▰ ▦ *No charge/credit cards. Closed Sun. Tube: Leicester Square.*

Here is one of Chinatown's best establishments: good, tasty Cantonese dishes; clean cafeteria-style surroundings; efficient service. Poons' speciality is wind-dried food — salty but addictive sausages, pork and duck — as well as excellent Singapore-style noodles, steamed scallops, eel with pork and garlic, or sweet and sour *wun-tun*, all perfectly accompanied by delicious Jasmine tea. Reservations recommended. Around the corner is the original **Poons** *(27 Lisle St., WC2* ☎ *(071) 437-4549, map 9 G10* ☐ *to* ☐☐*)*, which is smaller and scruffier than its offspring, but with an equally good kitchen.

LE POULBOT *French*
45 Cheapside, EC2 (City) ☎*(071)* *236-4379. Map 11F15* ▥ ■■ ▤ ▨ ▣ ▣ ▨ *Closed evenings; Sat; Sun. Tube: St Paul's.*

Haute cuisine's only outpost in the City, and inevitably a popular place in which to plot or consummate a big business deal. Very discreet, and excellent, as might be expected from one of the Roux brothers' establishments (see LE GAVROCHE). Lunch only, with a short menu that changes daily. Superb cheese board. Upstairs, **Le Pub** serves brasserie-style food.

QUALITY CHOP HOUSE ♣ *English*
94 Farringdon Rd., EC1 (Clerkenwell) ☎*(071) 837-5093. Map 4D13* ▨ *to* ▥ ☐ *No charge/credit cards. Closed Sat lunch. Tube: Farringdon.*

This delightful restaurant is well worth the short taxi ride from the West End, or an excellent choice after a visit to nearby Sadler's Wells (see PERFORMING ARTS, page 246). Although the Quality Chop House, "Progressive Working Class Caterer," has been in existence since 1862, when Frenchman Charles Fontaine, formerly head chef at LE CAPRICE, found the tiny premises in 1990, the original decor had been obscured by formica. Behind it he found a fragment of the old embossed wallpaper and had it faithfully restored. The wooden pews, which at first seem too narrow to bear, but soon become quite comfy, are original too, as is the splendid shop-front. The Chop House promises now, as then, "quality and civility," and that is what you will get from M. Fontaine and his dedicated staff. You might start with crab soup or eggs benedict, followed by a perfect steak and chips or salmon fishcake, washed down by a fine English ale, or house wine if you prefer. A terrific find.

RED FORT *Indian*
77 Dean St., W1 (Soho) ☎*(071)* *437-2525. Map 9F10* ▥ ☐ ■■ ▾ ▤ ▨ ▣ ▣ ▨ *Tube: Leicester Square.*

The Red Fort, along with BOMBAY BRASSERIE and **Lal Qila** *(117 Tottenham Court Rd., W1* ☎ *(071) 387-4570, map 2 D9* ▥*)*, was a vanguard of the new-wave "Indian" that banished flock wallpaper and piped "snake-charmer" music in favor of pastel prints, palm fronds, cane chairs and cocktail bars. In neutral, soothing surroundings, on two floors, the Red Fort dispenses above-average if not outstanding North Indian cooking. Good starters, prawn dishes, quails marinated in yogurt, Goan-style fish and vegetable dishes. To drink, stick to lager if you can; the wine list is unadventurous and pricey.

RITZ ⌂ *English/French*
Piccadilly, W1 (Piccadilly) ☎*(071)* *493-8181. Map 8G9* ▥ ☐ ■■ ▤ ♨ ▨ ▣ ▣ ▨ *Tube: Green Park.*

London's prettiest dining room continues to produce food that doesn't quite live up to the ravishing pink and marbled Empire surroundings. Keith Stanley, originally from the Savoy Grill, is the third successive English chef to try his luck here, and reviews are mixed. Best to stick to the plainer dishes such as lobster salad *américaine*, whole Dover sole or tournedos Rossini. Service is back to its former balletic self. Prices are high, but a meal here is still worth every penny for the sheer thrill of being in this legendary room.

RIVER CAFÉ *Italian*
Thames Wharf, Rainville Rd., W6

(Hammersmith) ☎*(071) 381-8824* ▥▥ *to* ▥▥ ☐ ▬ ▲ ▣ ▨ *Closed Mon lunch; Sat and Sun eve. Last orders 9pm. Tube: Hammersmith.*

Currently London's least accessible, but most trendy restaurant, the River Café was started by its chef/proprietors Rose Gray and Ruth Rogers to serve as a staff canteen for the workers in high-profile architect Richard Rogers' Thames Wharf office development. Word soon got out, and they have never looked back. Theirs is real Italian home cooking, and what a change it makes from the bland fare we are used to in Italian restaurants. Dishes are pungent and robust, starring top-quality olive oil, basil, *polenta*, peppers, *cavolo nero*, truffles, char-grilled fish and other such earthy ingredients, simply served. The menu changes constantly (there are a few dud dishes, notably desserts), and there is a short, skillfully chosen wine list.

It's a real oddity, this River Café, a small, spartan, faintly scruffy room kitted out in run-of-the-mill Modernist garb, filled with famous people wolfing down rough peasant food. But it works, and you must reserve well in advance.

ST QUENTIN *French*
243 Brompton Rd., SW3 (Knightsbridge)
☎*(071) 581-5131. Map 15J6* ▥▥ ☐ ▬ ▬ ▣ ▣ ▣ ▨ *Tube: Knightsbridge, South Kensington.*

Open a helpful seven days a week, St Quentin has the atmosphere of a bustling, upmarket Parisian bistro: all mahogany, mirrors and starched white table cloths. The food is typical too, and of fairly high standard, although there are mistakes (such as dishes arriving tepid rather than hot). Choose upstairs for the people, downstairs for the calm.

If St Quentin models itself on a *rive gauche* bistro, **Grill St Quentin**, around the corner *(Yeoman's Row, SW3* ☎*(071) 581-8377, map 15J6* ▥▥ *closed Sun)*, is imitation La Coupole. It's huge and jolly, and the food is first-rate. The St Quentin group have also spawned *pâtisserie-traiteur* **Les Spécialités St Quentin** *(256 Brompton Rd., SW3, map 15J6* ☐*)*.

SALLOOS *Pakistani*
62-64 Kinnerton St., SW1 (Belgravia)
☎*(071) 235-4444. Map 15I7* ▥▥ ☐ ▤▤ ▣ ▣ ▣ ▨ *Closed Sun; bank holidays. Tube: Knightsbridge.*

A rare, very smart Pakistani restaurant. The ethnicity is a matter of some pride to patron "Salloo" Salahuddin, who also has a restaurant in Lahore. What it really indicates is the food of the NW corner of the subcontinent, with an emphasis on kebabs and other roasted meats. Specialities include lamb in wheat germ, chicken *jalfrezi* and tandoori quails.

SAN LORENZO *Italian*
22 Beauchamp Pl., SW3 (Knightsbridge)
☎*(071) 584-1074. Map 15I6* ▥▥ ☐ *No charge/credit cards. Closed Sun. Tube: Knightsbridge.*

Despite the success of fashionable Italian restaurants like the RIVER CAFÉ, old-style establishments such as San Lorenzo have not been eclipsed, and comfortingly little has changed here. It is still the favorite of royalty and high society, and owner Mara Berni still circles the tables, greeting her gold-plated customers. Much loved for its conservatory-like interior, and roof which opens in summer. Favored dishes include *crudités* with *bagna cauda* and veal San Lorenzo, although the quality of the cooking does not quite justify the excessively high prices charged.

SEA SHELL ⚓ ♣ *English*
49-51 Lisson Grove, NW1 (Marylebone)
☎*(071) 723-8703. Map 7E6* ☐ ☐ ▬ *lunch* ▤▤ ♣ ▣ ▣ ▨ *Closed Sun. Tube: Marylebone.*

Once it was a humble fish-and-chip shop, then people started coming in Rolls-Royces, and now it is a restaurant. The Sea Shell offers a notably wide variety of excellent quality fried fish in generous helpings — not only the traditional cod and haddock but also skate, plaice, sole, and others — followed by better apple pie than might be expected. There is also a take-out service. Two other good fish-and-chip shops are **Upper Street Fish Shop** *(324*

Upper St., N1 ☎ *(071) 359-1401, map* **4**B13 ▭*) and* **Nautilus** *(27-29 Fortune Green Rd., NW6* ☎ *(071) 435-2532 ▭).*

SMOLLENSKY'S BALLOON *American*
1 Dover St., W1 (Piccadilly) ☎*(071) 491-1199. Map* **8**G9 ▭ *to* ▥ ▭ ▤ ▼ ♪ ♣ ▣ ◉ ◐ ▨ *Tube: Green Park.*

Open all day, this is a lively, busy restaurant-plus, very much in the American mold, successful because what it does, it does well. Getting down to basics, the steaks are properly charcoal-grilled, and they are big. On top of that, the service is notably friendly and prompt, there's an abundance of un-funny jokes on the walls, live music, marvelous entertainment for the children on weekends *(reserve well in advance)*, a crowded cocktail bar, heart-shaped steaks on St Valentine's Day, and more in the same style. The formula works, and owner Michael Gottlieb has an even bigger branch nearby, **Smollensky's on the Strand** *(105 Strand, WC2* ☎ *(071) 497-2101, map* **10**G12 ▥*).*

STAR OF INDIA *Indian*
154 Old Brompton Rd., SW5 (South Kensington) ☎*(071) 373-2901. Map* **14**K4 ▥ ▭ ▣ ◉ ◐ ▨ *Tube: South Kensington.*

Never content to take a back seat, the 35-year-old Star of India has transformed itself into a sort of Hollywood pastiche of a Roman palace, even making the pages of *Interiors* magazine. The food, however, remains comfortingly Indian, and though it may lack the panache of the decor, it is always reliable. Good fun.

SUNTORY *Japanese*
72 St James's St., SW1 (St James's) ☎*(071) 409-0201. Map* **8**H9 ▥ ▭ ▬ ▤ ▣ ◉ ◐ ▨ *Closed Sun. Tube: Green Park.*

In surroundings of simple elegance, with cool Japanese screens, Suntory dispenses Shabu-Shabu dishes in one room, and Teppan cooking in another. The restaurant is owned by the Japan-

ese vineyard, distilling and brewing company Suntory, and is something of a showpiece of the country's cuisine, in preparation, presentation and service. On the menu, all dishes are described in detail in English, and service is helpful. Prices are geared to Japanese expense accounts.

LA TANTE CLAIRE ⌂ *French*
68 Royal Hospital Rd., SW3 (Chelsea) ☎*(071) 352-6045. Map* **15**L6 ▥ ▭ ▬ *lunch* ▬ ▤ ▣ ◉ ◐ ▨ *Closed Sat; Sun; 2 weeks at Christmas. Tube: Sloane Square.*

It was the Roux brothers' LE GAVROCHE that gave birth to Pierre Koffman's La Tante Claire, and after vying for supremacy for some years, both are now happily settled as the stately *grand dames* of London's *haute cuisine* restaurants. Both are noted, as *haute cuisine* surely should be, for their exquisite and complex sauces. Tante Claire, once cramped and tiny, is now spacious, comfortable and sunny, yet still delightfully unpretentious. It can be reserved weeks in advance, evenings especially. Excellent sommelier.

TATE GALLERY RESTAURANT *English*
Millbank, SW1 (Pimlico) ☎*(071) 834-6754.* Map **17**K11 ▥ *to* ▥ ▭ ▬ ▤ ▣ ◉ ◐ ▨ *Closed evenings; Sun. Tube: Pimlico.*

Not a museum snack bar but a full-scale restaurant whose reputation was founded on its excellent wine list and the beauty and wit of its Rex Whistler mural. The food, once dull, is at last catching up with the wine, and always includes tempting vegetarian dishes. Try to leave room for one of the excellent puddings.

TUI *Thai*
19 Exhibition Rd., SW7 (South Kensington) ☎*(071) 584-8359. Map* **14**J5 ▥ ▭ ▣ ◉ ◐ ▨ *Closed Christmas; bank holidays. Tube: South Kensington.*

Tui, on two floors, is a tiny wedge of a place. Its stark black and cream interior is meant to be chic, but feels uninviting unless the restaurant is full, which it mostly is. Tui's strong suit is its exceptionally fragrant and delicate Thai cooking: state-of-the-art *tom yam* soup, for example, is served with either prawns, seafood or chicken, deliciously spicy *mee grob* and *gai yarng*. Unfortunately the prices are pretty chic too, but they are certainly worth it for the delicious tastes.

Venerable institutions

London has a wonderful stock of restaurants that go on and on, unflinchingly ignoring current fads and fashions, and serving up, with dignity and style, exactly what they have always served up.

B.J. ATKINS
140 Wandsworth Bridge Rd., SW6 ☎*(071) 731-1232* □
First-rate example of a traditional cockney eel pie and mash shop.

BENTLEY'S
11-15 Swallow St., W1 ☎*(071) 734-4756. Map* **9**G10 ▨
Excellent oysters and plain seafood dishes in unchanged postwar premises. Owner/chef Kevin Kennedy has breathed new vitality into BOULESTIN (see below).

BOULESTIN
Garden Entrance, 1a Henrietta St., WC2 ☎*(071) 836-7061. Map* **9**G11 ▨
London's foremost French restaurant during the 1930s and '40s, now producing *grande cuisine* in splendid surroundings, with all its original flair.

L'EPICURE
28 Frith St., W1 ☎*(071) 437-2829. Map* **9**F10 ▨ *to* ▨
Memorable for the flaming torches that flank its entrance: a restaurant that has never bowed to fashion, either in its endearingly faded 1950s decor or in its high-cholesterol cooking. Service is notoriously relaxed.

L'ETOILE
30 Charlotte St., W1 ☎*(071) 636-7189. Map* **9**E10 ▨
Old-fashioned bourgeois French restaurant, where a fleet of waiters guide their trolleys deftly around the tables.

FORTNUM AND MASON'S, ST JAMES'S RESTAURANT
181 Piccadilly, W1 ☎*(071) 734-8040. Map* **9**G10 ▨ *to* ▨
Grandest of Fortnum's three restaurants and a lovely setting in which to sample real English food. Noted for its game pies.

RULES
35 Maiden Lane, WC2 ☎*(071) 836-5314. Map* **9**G11 ▨
Founded in 1798 and still serving simple English food, true, traditional and robust, as well as some imaginative new dishes.

SAVOY GRILL
Strand, WC2 ☎*(071) 836-4343. Map* **10**G12 ▨
Bastion of the country's richest and most influential business people; a favorite place for power lunches.

SCOTTS
20 Mount St., W1 ☎*(071) 629-5248. Map* **8**G8 ▨
Here, in discreet alcoves at this plush 135-year-old London institution, succulent seafood is served at exorbitant prices.

SIMPSON'S-IN-THE-STRAND
100 Strand, WC2 ☎*(071) 836-9112. Map* **9**G11 ▨
Unquestionably the most famous home of roast beef and nursery puddings (spotted dick, treacle roll); very male, very British.

SWEETINGS
39 Queen Victoria St., EC4 ☎*(071)*
248-3062. Map 11F15 ▢ *to* ▢
First-rate but no-frills seafood is served
to pin-striped City workers, who jostle
for a place in this timeless 150-year-old
establishment.

VEERASWAMY
99-101 Regent St., W1 ☎*(071) 734-1401.*
Map 8G9 ▢
London's oldest Indian restaurant, dating back to 1927 and, although quite
recently redecorated, retaining something of its colonial feel. The vegetarian
dishes are particularly recommended

from the authentic regional menu.

WHITE TOWER
1 Percy St., W1 ☎*(071) 636-8141. Map*
9E10 ▢ *to* ▢
Founded in 1938, the fanciest and least
ethnic of Fitzrovia's Greek restaurants,
famous for the florid language of its
menu.

WILTONS
55 Jermyn St., SW1 ☎*(071) 629-9955.*
Map 8G9 ▢
Clubby and masculine, with a traditional English menu that relies on fresh
ingredients simply prepared.

Cafés and tearooms

Britain's colonial adventures made her controller of the world's tea
trade. United with a rich tradition of cakes, biscuits and breads, this
resulted in an institution nobody has copied: afternoon tea. The traditional meal is a substantial affair, with cakes, toasted teacakes or crum-
pets, perhaps even fish or cold meat. Eternally popular is the "cream
tea": scones, jam and whipped cream. More than mere refreshment, it
is a graceful, sometimes even formal, social occasion.

AFTERNOON TEA
Most of the better hotels offer a traditional afternoon tea between
about 3.30 and 5.30pm. Taking tea there is a uniquely metropolitan
experience. A choice of India or China tea, or Earl Grey, camomile or
even tilleul (linden or lime-blossom) if you care to ask is offered at the
Ritz Hotel, W1 *(essential to reserve);* and there is a *thé dansant* at the
Waldorf, WC2, on Friday, Saturday and Sunday. Those who enjoy the
full gastronomic delights favor **Brown's Hotel**, W1, and the Park
Room at the **Hyde Park Hotel**, W1; but those more concerned with
the drink itself incline to the Ritz and to the **Savoy** group (which
includes **Claridge's** and the **Connaught**, both W1, and the **Berkeley**,
SW1), which has its own blend. There is a harpist at La Chinoiserie in
the **Hyatt Carlton Tower**, SW1; and piano accompaniment is on hand
at most grand hotels.

One of the most stylish locations in which to take afternoon tea is
Fortnum & Mason, Piccadilly, either in the St James's or Fountain
restaurant, which serve sandwiches and cakes, as well as salads and "high
tea" specialities, such as Welsh rarebit. Of the other department stores
that offer afternoon tea, **Heal's** boasts an excellent choice of sandwiches,
cakes, fruit salad and cheesecake. The Terrace Bar in **Harrods**, enlarged
a few years ago with an attractive conservatory, has a fairly expensive set

price, but you can eat as much as you like. Tea is also served in the more formal Georgian Restaurant. Opposite Harrods, on Brompton Rd., SW3, is a branch of **Richoux**, at which rather high prices are matched by an expensive ambience.

Modeled on the good old-fashioned tea shops of the 1930s and '40s, **Tea-Time** *(21 The Pavement, SW4)* is particularly agreeable in summer when tables are set outside, overlooking Clapham Common. Unfortunately, the City, where the tea trade has its roots, now has only countless anonymous snack bars.

CAFÉS AND PÂTISSERIES

London has long been sufficiently cosmopolitan to have a number of good pâtisseries. For gossipy ambience, try **Valerie** *(44 Old Compton St., Soho, W1, map 9 F10)*; for privacy and good pastries, visit nearby **Maison Bertaux** *(28 Greek St., W1, map 9 F10)*; for sheer elegance and delicious brioches, the 70-year-old **Maison Sagne** *(105 Marylebone High St., W1, map 2 E8)*; for excellent pastries, **Maison Bouquillon** *(45 Moscow Rd., W2, map 5 G3)*.

Rivals for the best coffee served in London are **Gambarti** *(38 Lamb's Conduit St., WC1, map 4 D12)*, a good place for breakfast, and the stylish café/restaurant in **Emporio Armani** *(191 Brompton Rd., SW3, map 15 I6)*, which also serves superior Italian food, now much in vogue: a good lunch stop for Knightsbridge shoppers. Equally chic and convenient for lunch is **Joe's Café** *(126 Draycott Ave., SW3, map 15 J6)*, another, all black and chrome, part of Joseph Ettedgui's empire; other branches are **L'Express** *(126 Sloane St., SW3, map 15 J7)* and **Joe's Restaurant** *(Harvey Nichols, Knightsbridge, SW1, map 15 I6)*. **Bonne Bouche Coffee Shop** *(2 Thayer St., W1, map 2 E8)* is very French, serves delicious breakfasts and has its own pâtisserie next door.

Pubs

In most countries, it is difficult for even the experienced traveler to visit a strange town and immediately spot a place where it will be possible to relax and, with luck, meet a few friendly natives. English (and Scottish and Welsh) pubs are rooted in their local communities, and each painted sign outside a pub heralds a singularity of identity that is its quintessential charm.

The public house contrives to be unmistakable whatever its origins, and pubs can vary considerably. Being one of England's older cities, London has pubs that grew out of every period of the country's history, and their names reveal their backgrounds. A pub that stands on the site of a colonial Roman taverna may be called The Vines or The Grapes; a hostel for workers on some medieval construction project might be The Builders, The Castle or The Bridge; a monastery hospice for pilgrims, The Angel or The Salutation. Although the term "public house" was not used in official language until the mid-1880s, that's what they all are, whether they were built as coaching inns, Georgian coffeehouses or gin palaces for the new city-dwellers of the Victorian period.

The first purpose of the pub is to provide for conversation in an informal setting, and most London pubs do concentrate on just that, although, as in Shakespeare's time, there are hostelries that present live entertainment. Increasing numbers of pubs serve meals too (indeed some are now better known as restaurants than as pubs), but a good many still employ the impenetrable pork pie as a defense against would-be diners, thus freeing themselves to concentrate on the serving of drink, which is the second purpose of the pub.

WHAT TO DRINK
The fact that England's national liquor is London Dry Gin is easily overlooked, perhaps because the average publican's skills in the matter of mixed drinks don't stretch much further than the addition of tonic.

The true stock-in-trade of the pub is beer. Because London is so close to the hop gardens of Kent, it has long had a tradition of especially "hoppy" beers. Two London breweries, Whitbread and Watneys, are national giants, while the truly local breweries are small firms, Fuller's (London Pride) and Young's. The latter in particular have championed the unique British tradition of having their beer conditioned at the pub, in the cask, whence it is drawn by a hand pump or "beer engine" at a natural cellar temperature. An ale should never be cold, but served like a red wine, which surprises many tourists.

Another puzzler for foreigners is the lack of waiter service, although you may find it in some "lounge" bars. The public bar is where you will find the darts board, and the purist who likes to stand up while he enjoys his pint, and to drink it from a straight, handle-less glass.

DRINKING LAWS
Britain's inconvenient drinking laws, devised during World War I to curb drunkenness, were finally relaxed in 1988. Pubs may now stay open from 11am-11pm Monday to Saturday, and Sunday from noon-3pm and from 7-10.30pm. Within these limits, the exact opening hours are at the discretion of the landlord.

Opening hours tend to be longer in and around obvious tourist attractions. In the financial and commercial heart of the City, pubs may close early and remain shuttered on weekends. Ten minutes before closing, the barman sings out "last orders." Closing time is announced as "time gentlemen please," and customers are given up to 20 minutes to drink up.

CENTRAL LONDON

Anglesea, *Selwood Terrace, SW7 (Kensington). Map* **14***K5.*
On Chelsea borders. Drink outside in summer. Inside, a pewter beer engine dispenses such country specialities as Brakspeare's and Ruddle's. Fairly basic pub snacks. Nearby, the literati and artists favor

the delightfully scruffy **Queen's Elm** *(corner of Old Church St. and Fulham Rd., map 14K5).*

Black Friar, 174 Queen Victoria St., EC4 (Blackfriars). Map 11F14.

The astonishing interior, in marble, alabaster, bronze and copper, with friezes depicting bacchanalia among the friars who gave the neighborhood its name, dates from 1905-24 and is an outstanding manifestation of the later period of the Arts and Crafts Movement. This busy pub, with seats outside, is handy for FLEET STREET and the CITY. Don't miss the tiny nook at the back of the main bar. A good range of real ale is served. Closed Saturday, Sunday.

Bunch of Grapes, 207 Brompton Rd., SW3 (Knightsbridge). Map 15I6.

This pub, w of Harrods, on the way to the VICTORIA AND ALBERT MUSEUM, has a beautiful Victorian interior, with grapes carved in wood, leaded-glass partitions and "snob screens" to prevent bar staff from eavesdropping on your conversation. Pleasantly dark, with an intimate little bar at the back. Country beers from Everard's and Wells. Substantial hot snacks.

Cheshire Cheese, Wine Office Court, EC4 (Fleet St.). Map 10F13.

The pub is on the N side of FLEET STREET, and the few remaining scribes from the street of saints and sinners still favor Dr Johnson's old pub for its low-ceilinged friendliness and Marston's beer, despite its inevitably being a tourist haunt. There are salads and sandwiches in the pub, and the adjoining restaurant offers its famous steak, kidney and mushroom pudding.

French House, 49 Dean St., W1 (Soho). Map 9F10.

The definitively picaresque Soho hangout, in which even the bar staff fits the image. Visitors either adore "The French" or wholly fail to be engaged by its perverse charm, but true Soho-lovers have been loyal for decades. Bare except for fading photographs of French boxers and stage stars, and the pewter water-cooler (for your *pastis*). Indifferent beer and unexciting wine: try the champagne.

"The French," like such neighboring pubs as **The Swiss Tavern** *(Old Compton St., map 9F10),* the **Coach and Horses** *(Romilly St., map 9F10)* and **The Sun and 13 Cantons** *(Gt. Pulteney St., map 9F10),* is a reminder of Soho's ethnic past.

George, 77 Borough High St., SE1 (Lambeth). Map 11H15.

This type of inn, with galleries from which patrons could watch shows presented by strolling players in the courtyard, inspired the layout of the first theaters, including Shakespeare's Globe.

The George is the last galleried inn in London, and only a part of it still stands. It is most attractive and comfortable, with four small bars, one serving bar food, as well as an expensive, oak-beamed restaurant. Wethered's Bitter is dispensed from a recently restored 150-year-old beer engine.

Grenadier, *18 Wilton Row, SW1 (Belgravia). Map 15l7.*
At Hyde Park Corner, down a tiny unpromising mews called Old Barrack Yard. Said to have been the Duke of Wellington's local. You can drink outside this pretty pub, and eat full meals inside at reasonable restaurant prices. Ruddle's County beer.

Guinea, *30 Bruton Place, W1 (Mayfair). Map 8G9.*
In the heart of London, a tiny, basic pub that would pass for a village local if it weren't full of advertising account executives and book editors. Hard to find, down a mews, but worth the effort. The adjoining restaurant serves excellent beef and good Bordeaux, but is very expensive. The Guinea is a Mayfair outpost for Young's brewery in much the way that a nearby mews pub, the **Star Tavern** *(Belgrave Mews West, SW1, map 15I7),* just off Belgrave Sq., is a showpiece in Belgravia for Fuller's brewery.

King's Head and Eight Bells, *50 Cheyne Walk, SW3 (Chelsea). Map 15L6.*
In lovely Cheyne Walk overlooking the river, a pub that is more than 400 years old. 18thC decor, with prints of old Chelsea on the walls. There's a permanent buffet, and Wethered's, Flowers and Marston's Pedigree on tap.

Lamb and Flag, *Rose St., WC2 (Covent Garden). Map 9F11.*
The poet Dryden dubbed this pub "The Bucket of Blood" after being mugged in the adjoining alley. It's as dark and poky as ever, but you will meet none more intimidating than the graphic design crowd, spreading themselves almost into Garrick St.

Red Lion, *2 Duke of York St., SW1 (Piccadilly). Map 9G10.*
Behind Simpson's shop and gentlemanly Jermyn St. Said to be the best example of a small Victorian gin palace. Burton's beer; hot snacks.

Salisbury, *90 St Martin's Lane, WC2 (Trafalgar Sq.). Map 9G11.*
Art Nouveau bronze nymphs and equally decorative predominantly male clientele inhabit this spectacular theaterland pub. Draft Guinness. Cold buffet and hot snacks.

Sun, *63 Lamb's Conduit St., WC1 (Bloomsbury). Map 4D12.*
Speciality beer pub offering never less than a dozen out-of-town brews, usually ranging from Boddington's to Old Peculiar. The manager will proudly show you his cellars *(reserve in advance)* when he is not too busy slaking the thirsts of medics from Great Ormond St. Hospital, or feeding them tasty hot snacks.

Farther along this charming little street is the **Lamb,** said to have been Dickens' local (see DICKENS' HOUSE), which has an attractive Victorian interior. Young's beer is served here.

Windsor Castle, *114 Campden Hill Rd., W8. Map 5H2.*
Popular Notting Hill pub with an open fire in the oak-beamed bar for

winter and a large walled garden for summer. Good British fare, such as roast beef and Yorkshire pudding, fish and chips and the like. Charrington's IPA and Bass are served.

NORTH LONDON

HAMPSTEAD   Bull and Bush, *North End Way, NW3.*
Popularized in song by a star of the 19thC music hall, Florrie Forde. The "Bull" recalls the days when it was the site of a farm, and the "Bush" was a clump of trees planted when it was the home of Hogarth, the cartoonist and moralist. Among the notables who have drunk here, in the intervening years, Dickens perhaps forges the link between the earthiness of the music hall and the artiness of Hampstead. The pub is not far from Hampstead Heath, has its own garden, and serves a range of cask ale, including Tetley Bitter, Burton's and Taylor Walker's. There are two other historically interesting pubs nearby: **Jack Straw's Castle** *(also in North End Way)* and the **Spaniards Inn** *(Spaniards Rd.).*

HAMPSTEAD   Flask, *Flask Walk, NW3.*
Among the well-known Hampstead pubs, this is the best-liked locally. It is a genuine neighborhood pub, with interesting tiling inside and out, a lively regular clientele and Young's beer. It is in a pretty alleyway, near a couple of bookstores, just around the corner from Hampstead tube station.
   Across the Heath there is another **Flask** *(77 Highgate West Hill, N6)*, full of historical interest and serving Tetley Bitter, Burton's and Taylor Walker's. Both take their name from the flasks once used to carry water from wells in Hampstead.

SOUTH LONDON

GREENWICH   Cutty Sark, *Ballast Quay, SE10.*
Named after the famous tea clipper, which is permanently berthed nearby, this pub is Georgian in style and dates from the early 1800s. It serves draft Bass. Another nautical public house located nearby is the **Gipsy Moth** *(60 Greenwich Church St.)*, serving Taylor Walker beer. Greenwich also has a fine Victorian pub in the **Rose and Crown** *(1 Croom's Hill)*, which serves Courage's beer on traditional hand pumps.

SOUTHWARK   Goose and Firkin, *47 Borough Rd., SE1.*
The beer is brewed in the cellar: bitters with names such as Goose, Borough, Dogbolter and Earthstopper bring in an enthusiastic, young clientele. Drinkers can see the brewery through a window at the same proprietor's **Fox and Firkin** *(316 Lewisham High St., SW13)*, farther s. Across town, a third pub in this growing mini-chain is the **Frog and Firkin** *(41 Tavistock Crescent, W11, map 5 E1)*, not far from Portobello Rd. A firkin is a 9-gallon cask.

SOUTHWARK   **Mayflower,** *Rotherhithe St., SE16.*

Close to the jetty whence the *Mayflower* set sail, this well-restored pub, with a veranda over the river and a restaurant, serves Charrington's IPA and Bass. Next door is the Wren church of St Mary's. In the same docklands area is one of Pepys' favorite pubs, the **Angel** *(101 Bermondsey Wall East, SE16),* serving Courage's beer.

WEST LONDON

BARNES   **Sun,** *Church Rd., SW13.*

The village pond lies opposite, alive with ducks and fringed with weeping willows and oak trees. There are seats by the pond, but you could just as well sit outside the pub with a pint of Taylor Walker's beer. Inside, it is low-ceilinged and cozy. Remarkably rural for a place that is a double-decker bus ride *(no.9)* from Piccadilly. Barnes has lots of interesting pubs. Just down the High St. are the **Bull's Head** for jazz and the **White Hart** for its riverside veranda. Both sell Young's beer.

HAMMERSMITH   **Dove,** *19 Upper Mall, W6.*

Riverside pub, with terrace, just upstream from the splendid Hammersmith Bridge. Rich in historical and literary associations: part of the pub was built by George III's son, Prince Augustus Frederick. Fuller's beer. Closer to the bridge is the **Blue Anchor** *(13 Lower Mall, W6),* with a fine pewter bar and enormous beer engine serving Courage's beer.

RICHMOND   **Orange Tree,** *45 Kew Rd., Richmond.*

Theater pub opposite Richmond station *(for details of shows* ☎ *(081) 940-3633).* Victorian, large and rambling, yet somehow intimate. Young's beer and good range of bar meals. Richmond has several good pubs; also especially recommended is the **Old Ship** *(3 King St.),* which faces the main George St., for its Young's beer and its cheering, open fires in winter.

EAST LONDON

EPPING FOREST   **Traveller's Friend,** *496 High Rd., Woodford Green.*

Epping Forest is a rural part of the London area rarely visited by tourists, yet full of interest. This pub, within reach of Woodford Station on the tube *(Central line),* is a good starting point for a visit to the area. It also offers Victorian snob screens and a rare opportunity to sample Ridley's beer.

WAPPING   **Prospect of Whitby,** *57 Wapping Wall, E1.*

Completely refurbished and still desperately touristy pub in old docklands, although the history and location are genuinely interesting. The nearby **Town of Ramsgate** *(62 Wapping High St., E1)* is a more honest-to-badness pub, where hanging once took place.

Nightlife and entertainment

London by night

After dark, the most evident activity in the West End of London (the City dies after the evening rush hour) is theater-going. It is far less formal and self-conscious than in some European cities, but even Broadway can hardly match the elegant bustle of Shaftesbury Avenue as the black cabs deposit and reclaim theater-goers.

Although the best seats for a big show are expensive, the London theater does offer its patrons a wide range of prices, so only the most determinedly philistine visitor fails to catch at least one production. Those with a busy schedule might also note that many theaters present a matinee on Saturday and one midweek day.

THE NOCTURNAL AREAS
For the Londoner, and for the visitor who thinks of it, a drink in a pub or a bar is a likely part of an evening at the theater, either as a rendez-vous beforehand or for a nightcap afterwards; that may depend upon whether you eat before or after the show. Since most of the West End theaters are near either Soho or Covent Garden, these two neighborhoods are the most convenient, and so the most lively, after dark.

Don't be put off by the seediness of Soho; it has lots of reasonably priced Chinese (in Gerrard, Lisle and Wardour Streets) and Italian restaurants, and is a safe place to walk, provided you avoid the darkest alleys. For a simple stroll, Covent Garden might seem more relaxing.

Elegant Mayfair has a villagey enclave called Shepherd Market, with pleasant pubs, restaurants and ladies of the night (or, often, of the broad daylight), whose presence is not excessively assertive. Elsewhere, Mayfair is mostly an area of expensive restaurants, private clubs and casinos.

The young flock around Leicester Square and Piccadilly Circus till the early hours, but the main nocturnal area out of the center of town is outrageous Chelsea; along King's Road and Fulham Road parade the latest trends, strolling in and out of pubs, wine bars and lively restaurants.

PLANNING YOUR EVENING
The closing hours of pubs and restaurants, and the paucity of late-night transport, have won London a reputation that it only partly deserves for being insufficiently nocturnal. Like an aging, dignified actress, London cherishes its beauty sleep, but isn't above the occasional exploit in the small hours.

The essential precaution is to lay plans carefully. Be aware that nightclubs may require membership to be arranged in advance; and after midnight, call for a cab from the restaurant or nightclub, rather than expecting to pick one up on the street.

The performing arts

There is too much choice among London's theatrical riches, even in the recession-hit 1990s. Should you happen to wish to go to a different play, concert, ballet or opera every night for a year without seeing the same show twice or even returning very often to the same venue, then London is the city to pitch your tent in.

More likely, you are looking for a representative cross-section. But where Londoners have a general broad awareness of what's on offer, you probably do not. How to find out?

The best advice is to invest a little time in advance preparation, ideally about two months before you leave from home. Obtain from your local **British Tourist Authority** office in your country the programs for the major theaters (the Royal National Theatre, Royal Shakespeare Company, Royal Opera House, English National Opera, Sadler's Wells Theatre), the main concert halls (the Royal Festival Hall, Barbican Centre, Royal Albert Hall, Wigmore Hall), and any other venues that interest you. Make your choice of performances, and make your reservations through the BTA. Once in London, of course, all these venues can take seat reservations by charge/credit card over the phone.

However, do not worry if your travel plans are too fluid to allow such careful advance planning. There is so much going on that a few inquiries on the day will probably turn up the very show to fit your mood. There are complete listings in the weekly magazines *Time Out, City Limits* and *What's On & Where to Go*. You may find it more convenient to buy tickets through your hall porter or a ticket agency, but be aware that the agent's commission can make quite a difference to the price. Avoid ticket touts at all costs.

THE PRINCIPAL CENTERS

There are three main centers for the performing arts. Most of London's commercial theaters and the two opera houses are in the **West End**. The **South Bank Arts Centre**, across the river near Waterloo Bridge, contains the Royal National Theatre, the Royal Festival Hall and the National Film Theatre. The **Barbican Centre**, home of the Royal Shakespeare Company and the London Symphony Orchestra, is to the N of the City. Other important venues, such as Sadler's Wells, the Royal Court Theatre and the Old Vic, are located away from these areas.

Getting to either the South Bank or the Barbican is less fun than it should be. Consider carrying an umbrella if you intend to approach the South Bank on foot, as there are long, open stretches to walk through from any direction. The best way to get to the Barbican is by taxi; the only serious alternative is to take the tube, which requires some walking once you get there. After late shows, taxis can be scarce at either complex.

BALLET AND OPERA

For true lovers of the opera or ballet, a first visit to the Royal Opera House can resemble a pilgrimage, so dense is the musical history associated with that august establishment. It belongs in the same top league, and its best seats are as costly, as New York's Metropolitan, the Paris Opéra and La Scala in Milan. Sadler's Wells, nowadays a center for visiting opera and ballet companies, is rather more democratic. And the English National Opera at the glorious London Coliseum is refreshingly different: there, opera is sung in English and prices are genuinely affordable (and tickets, as a result, are often scarce).

ROYAL OPERA HOUSE (Royal Opera and Royal Ballet) 𝍐
Bow St., WC2 ☎*(071) 240-1911/1066 (info. and reservations); Curtain Call* ☎*0898-600-001 (24hr info.). Map 9F11. Closed early Aug to mid-Sept.*
Covent Garden was always a nocturnal enclave, and its more recent crop of wine bars and restaurants has helped retain at least a hint of that. "Covent Garden" is Londoners' shorthand for the Royal Opera House, one of the most historically interesting theaters in London, with its Classical facade on Bow St. and its box office in Floral St. It is now one of the world's most important venues for opera and ballet, and the greatest artists appear regularly at the theater.

Originally named the Theatre Royal, its establishment derived from the first permissions granted by King Charles II for the opening of playhouses after the Restoration. The theater of Kean and Kemble was twice burned down before the present building was finally completed in 1858.

The Royal Opera and Royal Ballet both perform at Covent Garden in seasons of alternating productions. Postal reservations open about six weeks before the beginning of a season, and tickets are quickly snapped up, but 65 seats up in "the gods" (very high in this theater) are held until the day of the performance. Each person is permitted only one ticket, and there can be long lines, sometimes overnight.

SADLER'S WELLS THEATRE
Rosebery Ave., EC1 ☎*(071) 278-8916 (info and reservations). Map 4C13.*
It is a strange name for a theater, and Islington is perhaps an unlikely location. The site was originally a garden in which there was a health-giving well, and its owner, whose name was Sadler, opened a "musick house" there in 1683. The theater was the base for the Sadler's Wells Royal Ballet company until its recent move to Birmingham, and now it functions as a venue for international opera, ballet and music companies.

Behind Sadler's Wells is the **Lilian Bayliss Theatre** (☎*(071) 837-4104),* which hosts smaller productions.

LONDON COLISEUM (English National Opera)
St Martin's Lane, WC2 ☎*(071) 240-5258/836-3161 (info and reservations). Map 9G11.*
The theater that houses one of London's largest auditoriums is barely visible from the street, but its illuminated globe stands out in the night skyline. For many years a music hall, it now houses the English National Opera, whose prestigious, reasonably priced, large-scale productions are sung in English. In summer, the company takes a break and international visiting dance companies take over.

OTHER DANCE VENUES
Also important venues for dance are the **Royal Festival Hall** in the **South Bank**

Centre (☎(071) 928-8800), and the **Riverside Studios**, an excellent contemporary arts complex in West London (Crisp Rd., Hammersmith, W6 ☎(081) 741-2251 for information; (081) 748-3354 for reservations).

CINEMA

London has an enormous selection of cinemas, but a lesser choice of movies. Two chains, **MGM** and **Odeon**, dominate, and concentrate on box-office hits. The irritating result, noticeable in Outer London and in other British towns and cities more than in Central and Inner London, is that neighboring cinemas may show near-identical programs.

Art-house films are more likely to be shown by independents, so check the *Evening Standard, Time Out* or *City Limits* for the following:

Camden Plaza   211 Camden High St., NW1 ☎(071) 485-2443, map 2B9
Chelsea Cinema   206 King's Rd., SW3 ☎(071) 351-3742, map **15K6**
Curzon Mayfair   Curzon St., W1 ☎(071) 465-8865, map **8H8**, London's most comfortable cinema
Curzon Phoenix   Phoenix St., off Charing Cross Rd., WC1 ☎(071) 240-9661, map 9F10
Curzon West End   Shaftesbury Ave., W1 ☎(071) 439-4805, map 9F10
Gate   87 Notting Hill Gate, W11 ☎(071) 727-4043, map **5G2**
Minema   45 Knightsbridge, SW1 ☎(071) 235-4225, map **7H7**
Renoir   Brunswick Centre, Brunswick Sq., WC1 ☎(071) 837-8402, map 3D11
Screen on Baker St.   96 Baker St., NW1 ☎(071) 935-2772, map 1E7
Screen on the Green   83 Upper St., N1 ☎(071) 226-3520, map 4B13
Screen on the Hill   203 Haverstock Hill, NW3 ☎(071) 435-3366

Also worth checking out:
- In Brixton, there's the shabby but lovable **Ritzy** (Brixton Oval, Coldharbour Lane, SW2 ☎(071) 737-2121).
- The **Institute of Contemporary Arts** (Nash House, The Mall, SW1 ☎(071) 930-3647, map **9**H10), more commonly known as the ICA, has a cinema. Temporary art exhibitions are also presented at this important avant-garde center.
- The true celluloid freak heads avidly for the **National Film Theatre** (☎(071) 633-0274 for info; (071) 928-3232 for reservations), in the SOUTH BANK ARTS CENTRE. It has two theaters presenting a wide range of films, with retrospectives on the work of individual directors and performers, and the MUSEUM OF THE MOVING IMAGE (MOMI).

CLASSICAL MUSIC

The two most important concert venues are the ROYAL ALBERT HALL and the Festival Hall (in the SOUTH BANK ARTS CENTRE). Each of these belongs to a different era of optimism and grand gestures.

ROYAL FESTIVAL HALL, QUEEN ELIZABETH HALL, PURCELL ROOM ⏛
South Bank, SE1 ☎*(071) 928-3002 (info), (071) 928-8800 (reservations). Map 10G12.*
The Festival Hall, built for the Festival of Britain in 1951, is part of the SOUTH BANK ARTS CENTRE, with the Queen Elizabeth Hall and the Purcell Room. Said by Toscanini to have the finest acoustics in the world, the **Festival Hall** itself, with 3,000 seats, presents concerts by the leading British and international symphony orchestras. The **Queen Elizabeth Hall** has 1,100 seats and stages chamber music, string quartets and other small ensembles. The 372-seat **Purcell Room** presents solo performances and other smaller events.

You can see and hear perfectly from all seats, so the cheaper ones are often a good buy. All three halls offer not only classical music but also jazz and popular concerts. Early-evening conversations with celebrities of the music world are occasionally held in the Chelfield Room of the Queen Elizabeth Hall.

ROYAL ALBERT HALL ⏛
Kensington Gore, SW7 ☎*(071) 589-3203/8212 (info and reservations). Map 14I4.*
The Albert Hall, named after the Prince Consort, is a spectacular manifestation of Victorian architecture, facing Kensington Gardens and the Albert Memorial. It is self-financing, operating independently under Royal Charter.

Its best-known annual event is its "Proms" ("promenade concerts"), founded in 1912 to bring the classics to a wider audience by recapturing the spirit of informal performances in London pleasure gardens. The center of the circular hall is cleared of seats for the Proms season, which runs from mid-July to early September, and a cheap ticket allows you to stand and wander at your leisure while you enjoy the music. Tickets are available at the door on the evening of the performance, except in the case of the Last Night of the Proms, a social event characterized by youthful nostalgia, and booked long in advance.

Although a wide range of classical music is performed at the Albert Hall, its keynote is eclecticism. The Hall also plays host to pop singers, wrestlers, and the annual conference of the Women's Institute, when they all stand up and belt out *Jerusalem.*

OTHER CONCERT HALLS
The **Barbican Centre** *(* ☎*(071) 638-4141 for information; (071) 638-8891 for reservations)* is now the home of the London Symphony Orchestra, which gives concerts regularly throughout the year.

There are several smaller halls. **Wigmore Hall** *(Wigmore St., W1* ☎*(071) 935-2141, map 8F8)* is a famous small concert hall almost within earshot of Oxford St., where international musicians perform chamber music, particularly song and piano recitals and string quartets. Approximately one night a week, debuts are performed. **Kenwood Lakeside** *(* ☎*(071) 973-3427)* is a wonderful venue for large-scale orchestral performances on Hampstead Heath on summer weekends. By the lake near Kenwood House is an orchestra shell that has accommodated the Royal Philharmonic and the London Symphony, among others. It is possible to reserve a deck chair, or to sit on the grass. And performances of chamber music are given in the **Orangery** of **Kenwood House**.

There are also a number of unconventional venues, such as the cushion concerts held at the **Royal Academy** during its Summer Exhibition of paintings: advance tickets are available only to those aged between 14 and 30, but tickets bought on the day are available to everyone *(for times of concerts* ☎*(071) 379-6722).*

There are lunchtime recitals at some of London's most attractive and interesting churches, including **St-Martin-in-the-Fields** *(* ☎*(071) 839-1930 for info; (071) 930-0089 for reservations),* and several of the churches in the City *(* ☎*(071) 260-1456 for info).* Notable among these is **St Anne & St Agnes** *(Gresham St., EC2* ☎*(071) 606-*

4986, map *12*E15), a Wren church (1680) that is the only English-speaking Lutheran church in Central London. The famous boys' choir of **St Paul's** can be heard during Sunday services at the Ca- thedral. Two other lovely venues are **Dulwich Picture Gallery** *(College Rd., SE21* ☎*(071) 693-5254)* and **Leighton House** *(12 Holland Park Rd., W14* ☎*(071) 602-3316).*

FOLK MUSIC

The English Folk Dance and Song Society, at **Cecil Sharp House** *(2 Regent's Park Rd., NW1* ☎ *(071) 485-2206, map *2*A8),* has performances on Saturday at 7.30pm; and there is traditional English Morris Dancing at **Westminster Abbey**, in front of the main gate of Broad Sanctuary, at 8pm on Wednesday in summer.

British, Irish and American folk music is performed in a variety of clubs and pubs, with dates listed in *Time Out* and *City Limits.*

JAZZ

Big-name jazz is always available in London, despite the fact that there are only a few jazz clubs. Almost every well-known name in international jazz has played at **Ronnie Scott's** *(47 Frith St., W1* ☎*(071) 439-0747, map *9*F10).* It looks and feels like a club, and stays open Monday to Saturday until 3am, but anybody can enjoy the jazz; meals and drinks are served during the show. Nearby, jazz and rhythm-and-blues are performed every evening at the **100 Club** *(100 Oxford St., W1* ☎ *(071) 636-0933, map *9*F10).*

Leading British musicians, and occasional guests from other countries, perform every evening at the **Pizza Express** *(10 Dean St., Soho, W1* ☎*(071) 437-9595, map *9*F10)* and at **Pizza on the Park** *(11 Knightsbridge, Hyde Park Corner, SW1* ☎*(071) 235-5550, map *8*H8).*

Jazz cognoscenti have long had an affection for a pub called the **Bull's Head** *(*☎*(081) 876-5241),* despite its unlikely villagey setting on the river at Barnes, SW13. It offers fine jazz nightly, especially Sunday lunchtimes *(noon-3pm),* and serves Young's splendid beer.

Across town is the **Bass Clef** *(35 Coronet St., N1* ☎ *(071) 729-2476),* a packed and steamy basement club.

ROCK   See NIGHTLIFE, page 254.

THEATER

Despite financial pressures, London remains one of the major world centers of theater, and the British still produce many of the greatest actors. The theater scene splits into four broad categories: companies subsidized by the state, in impressive buildings, producing serious drama to the highest standards; commercial theaters, mainly built at the turn of the century in a style of cozy splendor, mounting lighter plays and musicals; Off-West End theaters; and pub/club "fringe" theaters.

Neither of the last two should be ignored by serious theater-goers. The major subsidized theaters usually have several plays in repertory at one time; most others present a single play as long as it is successful.

A booth on the w side of Leicester Sq., WC2, has half-price seats for same-day shows with spare tickets in West End theaters. There is a small service charge, a maximum of four seats per person, and there can be a long line, but it is a good deal. Some shows will have tickets available on the day of performance; otherwise you can try lining up for returns. **First Call** (☎ *(071) 240-7200)*, **Ticketmaster** (☎ *(071) 379 4444)* and **London Theatre Bookings** (☎ *(071) 434-1811)* are efficient charge/credit-card telephone reservations agencies, which can usually provide tickets for the major shows, but will charge a supplement. Avoid touts. Consult the national press and listings magazines such as *Time Out* for what's on where, and watch for reviews in the quality papers.

Many theater bars welcome advance reservations for interval drinks, saving you crush, frustration and thirst. Most theaters close on Sunday. Cheaper seats in some of the older theaters may allow only a partial view.

Subsidized theaters

Denys Lasdun's **National Theatre** (1967-77), though not much loved for its external appearance, has superbly articulated internal space

THE ROYAL NATIONAL THEATRE
Upper Ground, South Bank, SE1 ☎*(071) 633-0880 (info), (071) 928-2252 (reservations). Map 10G13.*
The National Theatre company, originally under the direction of Sir Laurence Olivier, began its life at the Old Vic in the Waterloo Rd. Sir Peter Hall took over in 1973 ready for the opening of the new, custom-built theater, a modern architectural landmark, in the SOUTH BANK ARTS CENTRE. He was succeeded by Richard Eyre in 1988.

"The National" in fact comprises three theaters within one building. The largest auditorium, the **Olivier**, has an amphitheater setting; the **Lyttelton** has a proscenium stage; and the **Cottesloe** is a more spartan studio theater. The three present a wide range of classical and modern British and international works. Before performances there is live music in the foyers, picture galleries are open, there are early-evening lectures, poetry readings and short plays from 6pm, and a good restaurant, **Ovations**, and a ground-floor café. Although many performances are heavily booked, the National always retains some seats for sale on the day, and has reduced-price standby tickets. There are also backstage tours.

BARBICAN THEATRE (Royal Shakespeare Company)
Barbican Centre, EC2. Map 10E15 ☎*(071) 638-4141 (info), (071) 638-8891 (reservations).*
The finest productions of the world's greatest dramatist, many would say. In any case, the RSC enjoys worldwide repute. This is its London base, which complements its Stratford-upon-Avon home (see EXCURSIONS, page 300) where many of the theater's productions originate. Besides Shakespeare, the company also performs a wide variety of standard and new plays. The RSC's stu-

dio theater, **The Pit**, stages a range of smaller-scale productions from Jacobean drama to the present day.

THE ROYAL COURT THEATRE
Sloane Sq., SW1 ☎*(071) 730-1745/2554. Map* **15***J7.*
Despite its name, this theater has a distinguished record of healthily controversial drama and for promoting new

writing. George Bernard Shaw's plays were presented here in the 1920s and 1930s. John Osborne, the original "angry young man," and Arnold Wesker made their names here in the 1950s and 1960s, while John Arden, Edward Bond, David Storey and Caryl Churchill are more recent examples. There is also the **Theatre Upstairs**, a studio space for new writers.

Commercial theaters

The oldest theater in London is the **Theatre Royal, Drury Lane** *(WC2* ☎ *(071) 494-5062, map* **10***F12)*, which specializes in musicals and hit shows. Most elegant is the **Theatre Royal, Haymarket** *(SW1* ☎*(071) 930-8800, map* **9***G10)*, Ed Mirvish's **Old Vic** *(Waterloo Rd., SE1* ☎ *(071) 928-7616, map* **10***H13)* stages quality productions by well-known directors. The 18thC **Richmond Theatre** *(The Green, Richmond* ☎*(081) 940-0088)* stages pre-West End plays.

Other period pieces are the twin **Aldwych** *(WC2* ☎ *(071) 836-6404, map* **10***F12)* and **Strand** *(Aldwych, WC2* ☎ *(071) 240-0300, map* **10***F12)* theaters, designed by W.G.R. Sprague. Most famous is probably the **London Palladium** *(Argyll St., W1* ☎ *(071) 494-5037, map* **8***F9)*, which has a policy of family light entertainment, and plays host to a wealth of national and international stars.

St Martin's *(West St., Cambridge Circus, WC2* ☎ *(071) 836-1443, map* **9** *F11)* stages the world's longest-running play, Agatha Christie's *The Mousetrap.* **Regent's Park Open Air Theatre** *(NW1* ☎ *(071) 486-2431, map* **1** *C7)* presents a diet of Shakespeare throughout the summer.

"Off-West End," fringe and pub theaters

London's Off-West End fringe is alive and kicking, with a number of important theaters doing exciting work. Notable among the first rank are those listed here; *Time Out* has details of many more.

West London has the excellent and well-established **Lyric, Hammersmith** *(King St., W6* ☎*(081) 741-2311)*, a Victorian gem in a modern precinct, and the contemporary arts venue **Riverside Studios** *(Crisp Rd., W6* ☎*(081) 748-3354)*. In North London, there is the **Almeida**, Islington *(Almeida St., N1* ☎*(071) 359-4404)* and the **Hampstead Theatre** *(Avenue Rd., NW3* ☎*(071) 722-9301)* in Swiss Cottage. In East London is the Victorian **Theatre Royal, Stratford East** *(Gerry Raffles Sq., E15* ☎ *(081) 534-0310)*, while in South London is the **Young Vic** in Waterloo *(66 The Cut, SE1* ☎*(071) 620-0411/928-6363, map* **10***H13)* and the **Greenwich Theatre** *(Croom's Hill, SE10* ☎*(081) 858-7755)*.

Pub theater today is more than a small room above a noisy pub. Just for the experience, try the **Gate** at Notting Hill *(above Prince Albert Pub, 11 Pembridge Rd., W11* ☎*(071) 229-0706, map* **5***G2)*, the **King's Head**, in Islington *(115 Upper St., N1* ☎*(071) 226-1916, map* **4***B13)*, **The Bush** *(Shepherd's Bush Green, W12* ☎*(081) 743-3388)* or the **Orange Tree** *(1 Clarence St., Richmond* ☎*(081) 940-0141)*.

Nightlife

While dropping into a pub is kinda going native (see PUBS for an introduction to one of the capital's special pleasures), London has its own distinctive style when it comes to traditional cocktails at one of its luxury hotels. And there are other alternatives to the public house, such as the wine bar, both the traditional and designer variety, and the newer wave of champagne bars.

Not very long ago, the best gaming clubs in town were such courteous, comfortable havens of respectability that it was hard to believe that anything as sinful as gambling went on there. Nowadays, you have to ask your hotel concierge, or, better, know a member. Somewhat more accessible are the nightclubs and discos, many of which have a transient existence, suddenly in the limelight, then equally suddenly gone. Two outstanding exceptions are Annabel's and Tramp, undisputed stars of the nightclub scene for 25 years.

Finally, there is rock. London is one of the world's great rock power-houses — for some, a place of pilgrimage.

BARS

The traditional cocktail bar is most easily found in hotels. The Savoy's **American Bar** inspired the famous *Savoy Cocktail Book* and is believed to have been the first cocktail bar in Europe. Revamped a few years back in Art Deco style, it is sleek, chic and reminiscent of a 1930s Hollywood movie set. Appropriately they mix a mean dry martini. The **Ritz**, **Park Lane Hotel**, **Athenaeum** (for its 54 malt whiskies), **Inn on the Park** and **Hyde Park Hotel**, all in W1, have good cocktail bars, as do many other hotels. **Café Royale** *(68 Regent St., W1, map 9 G10)* has a plush cocktail bar with red velvet seats, glittering chandeliers, and an extensive list of surprisingly reasonably priced cocktails.

Newer cocktail bars, featuring such confections as Sledgehammer, Harvey Wallbanger or Laserbeam, often double as short-order restaurants, and may be obliged by law to ensure that at least a pastrami sandwich is consumed by each drinker. Typical are **Rumours** *(33 Wellington St., WC2, map 10 F12)* and **The Pheasantry** *(152 King's Rd., SW3, map 15 K6)*. The well-known **Groucho Club** *(44 Dean St., W1, map 9 F10)* is a private club, and visitors must be introduced by a member.

A change of mood is offered by the wine bar. The traditional kind, which grew out of wine merchants' shops, is typified by **El Vino's** *(47 Fleet St., EC4, map 10 F13)*, haunt of journalists and lawyers, although much quieter now that the newspaper offices have left The Street. It is a fiercely traditional establishment, where men have to wear jackets and ties, and women are not allowed in wearing trousers.

There was a second growth of wine bars during the 1970s, and these are much more numerous. The most extrovert example, jostling with magazine folk and models, is **Brahms and Liszt** *(19 Russell St., Covent Garden, WC2, map 10 F12)* — Cockney rhyming slang for the risqué "pissed," meaning drunk. For excellent wines and good food, visit the

Cork and Bottle *(44-46 Cranbourn St., WC2, map 9 G11)*. For Knightsbridge or Sloane St. shoppers, the **Ebury Wine Bar** *(139 Ebury St., SW1, map 16 J8)* is pleasant and well run. In Holland Park, **Julie's Bar** *(137 Portland Rd., W11)* is an attractive and sophisticated relic of the 1960s, with ecclesiastical decor. Back in Soho, **Andrew Edmunds** *(46 Lexington St., W1, map 9 F10)*, next to the owner's quaint antiquarian bookstore, is charming in its simplicity, with fresh and excellent food (see also RESTAURANTS A TO Z). It is not necessary to eat in wine bars, but most provide a range of cold and some hot food.

Many of the champagne bars that sprang up all over the West End in the 1980s have since closed. But there are a number of well-established brasseries, excellent for a drink and a bite to eat before the theater. Downstairs at **L'Escargot** *(48 Greek St., W1, map 9 F10)* is comfortable and well placed for the West End theaters, as is the **Soho Brasserie** *(23 Old Compton St., W1, map 9 F10)* and the bar at **Tall Orders** *(2 St Anne's Ct., W1, map 9 F10)*. **Green's** *(36 Duke St., SW1, map 8 G9)* serves some of the best oysters in London in an attractive wood-paneled bar, and **Kettners** *(29 Romilly St., W1, map 9 F10)* also has a pleasant champagne bar. **Café Pelican** *(45 St Martin's Lane, WC2, map 9 G11)* has a friendly ambience and is handy for the Coliseum. **La Brasserie** *(272 Brompton Rd., SW3, map 15 J6)* is very French and perennially stylish.

CASINOS

London does have casinos, but in recent years, faced with the regulatory activity of the Gaming Board, their numbers have declined drastically. Several famous names have vanished, or had their licenses suspended, and the future of others is uncertain.

It is the more urbane type of casino, usually found in the Mayfair or Knightsbridge districts, which has fallen foul of the Board, but one or two brasher places still brightly proclaim their presence in Soho. Those casinos that have remained in business are not permitted to advertise, which includes mentions in guidebooks, but they are usually known well enough to hotel concierges. To visit one, you must either join, which takes 48 hours, or be the guest of a member.

NIGHTCLUBS AND DISCOS

If nightingales still sing in Berkeley Square, their songs are directed at the habitués of **Annabel's** *(no. 44 ☎(071) 629-3558, map 8 G8)*. "The world's best nightclub," says London's most famous gossip columnist, Nigel Dempster. It is hermetically discreet and expensive, and you must be accompanied by a member, or be one yourself. Other smart-set nightspots are:

Raffles   287 King's Rd., SW3 ☎(071) 352-1091, map **14L5**, members only

Roof Gardens   99 Kensington High St., W8 ☎(071) 937-8923, map **13I3**, open Thurs, Sat only, members only

Tokyo Joe's   Clarges St., W1 ☎(071) 409-1832, map **8G8**

Tramp   40 Jermyn St., SW1 ☎(071) 734-0565, map **8G9**, members only

It is the nature of such diversions to be affected by fashion — discos have been known to open and close with alarming swiftness, or to announce a violent shift from one trend to another. Perusal of the gossip columns, in such newspapers as the *Daily Mail* and the *Evening Standard,* the high-class glossies, such as *Harpers and Queen,* and the trendy youth magazines such as *Blitz* should keep you tolerably well informed. Among discos open to anybody are:

Heaven   Under The Arches, Villiers St., WC2 ☎(071) 839-3852, map **9G11**, top gay club

Hippodrome   Charing Cross Rd., WC2 ☎(071) 437-4311, map **9G11**, touristy and a bit tacky

Legends   29 Old Burlington St., W1 ☎(071) 437-9933, map **9G10**, compulsively sleek

Limelight   136 Shaftesbury Ave., W1 ☎(071) 434-1761, map **9F10**, in a converted church

Stringfellows   16 Upper St Martin's Lane, WC2 ☎(071) 240-5534, map **9F11**, pseudo-glamorous

Xenon   196 Piccadilly, W1 ☎(071) 734-9344, map **9G10**, glitzy

Many of the best nightspots for the young or young at heart to meet, to see and to be seen in have live rock bands, as well as disco. They include:

Camden Palace   1a Camden High St., NW1 ☎(071) 387-0428, map **2B9**

Electric Ballroom   184 Camden High St., NW1 ☎(071) 485-9006, map **2A9**

Wag Club   35 Wardour St., W1 ☎(071) 437-5534, map **9G10**

ROCK
London has an ever-lively, ever-changing rock scene. Clubs, concerts and pub dates are listed in *Time Out* and in rock newspapers such as *Melody Maker.* Most of the major rock concert and club venues are 30-45 minutes from the West End. They include the following:

Earls Court Exhibition Centre   Warwick Rd., SW5 ☎(071) 385-1200, map **13K2**

Marquee   105 Charing Cross Rd., WC2 ☎(071) 437-6601, map **9F10**

Mean Fiddler   24-28a Harlesden High St., NW10 ☎(081) 961-5490)

Odeon, Hammersmith   Queen Caroline St., W6 ☎(081) 748-4081

Royal Albert Hall   Kensington Gore, SW7 ☎(071) 589-8212, map **14I4-5**

Town and Country Club   9-17 Highgate Rd., NW5 ☎(071) 284-0303

Wembley Arena   Empire Way, Wembley ☎(081) 900-1234 (tube: Wembley Park)

For further venues, see NIGHTCLUBS, above.

Shopping

Where to go

It is nothing as mundane as shopping that you do in London. It is promenading in the trendy King's Road on a Saturday afternoon after having strolled along the Portobello Road in the morning. It is listening to the spiel in Petticoat Lane's street market on a Sunday morning. It is exploring the world's most famous department store, **Harrods**, in Knightsbridge, and comparing its food with the exotica at **Fortnum & Mason** in Piccadilly. It is window-dreaming of jade and jewels in Bond Street. Depending upon your inclinations, it is the sensation of silk in **Liberty**, or of snuff in Jermyn Street. It is relaxing in Covent Garden and wondering whether you need a French horn from **Paxman** (116 Long Acre, WC2, map 9 F11) or a quill pen from **Philip Poole** (105 Great Russell St., WC1, map 9 E11).

These neighborhoods form a jigsaw stretching five or six miles across the center of London from Chelsea in the west to Petticoat Lane in the east. Each of them is worth half a day of anyone's time, and every one leads to another. None of them is London's principal shopping street, although several of them are linked by it. The main shopping thoroughfare, and the most democratic, is Oxford Street, which runs from west to east (assuming that you see the most traditional end first). It feels like a giant version of the main street of every town in Britain. The stretch from Marble Arch to Oxford Circus is the most interesting, with department stores, including **Selfridges** and the flagship **Marks and Spencer**, and the upmarket enclaves of South Molton Street and St Christopher's Place.

Prices

In London, prices are not generally negotiable, although bargaining is acceptable in some street markets. In most shops, all major charge and credit cards are accepted.

Exemption from Value Added Tax on goods bought for export is sometimes offered. VAT is not negligible: it adds substantially to the price of any item costing a few pounds or more, so do ask. You must show your passport and fill in a form.

Hours

Shops do not stay open as late as in some other countries. Most shops open Monday to Saturday 9am-5.30pm, with "late-night" shopping once a week. The Chelsea and Knightsbridge area stays open until 7pm on Wednesday, and Oxford St. until 8pm on Thursday. Some consolation is that few shops close for lunch. Some shops in Bond St. and a few others in the West End close on Saturday. Central London shops do not as yet open on Sunday, although it is the subject of continuing discussion in Parliament, and many supermarkets and DIY superstores outside the center now open on Sunday.

Although Central London has few "local" or "corner" shops, inner-city neighborhoods have plenty, and they often open until mid-evening, or even midnight, and on Sunday.

Weights and measures

A full set of international clothing sizes appears on page 260. Also useful to know is that some British Imperial measures, such as the gallon, are slightly larger than their American counterparts. For example, one US gallon equals $1\frac{1}{5}$ Imperial gallons.

ANTIQUES

At the top end of the price range, and for the best that money can buy, visit the specialists in **Bond St., W1**, and the adjoining streets and arcades. Examples range from the **Antique Porcelain Company** *(149 New Bond St., map 8 G9)* to **The Leger Galleries** *(13 Old Bond St., map 8 G9)*, for Old Masters, or **Mallet and Son** *(40 New Bond St., map 8 F9)*, for fine English furniture.

The serious buyer will also head out to **Kensington Church St., W8** (map **5** G2-I3), which has several high-quality shops. At the s end of this hilly street, **Simon Castle**, upstairs at no.38b, deals in wooden objects, particularly inlaid boxes and models; **Michael German**, on the ground floor, specializes in walking sticks and firearms; farther up is **The Lacquer Chest**, at no. 75; and at the Notting Hill end, **Philip Dombey** sells antique clocks at no. 174.

Nearby is the **Westbourne Grove, W2** area, for cheaper antiques, and such fascinating shops as **Dodo**, *(nearby at 344a Westbourne Park Rd., W2, map 5 E3)*, which deals in interesting old advertising materials.

The **New King's Rd.** beyond World's End is also peppered with quality antique stores. Farther on, **Wandsworth Bridge Rd.** has shops dealing in pine.

Over the years, several permanent, indoor antique markets have been established. In the **Bond St.** area, at **Gray's Mews Antique Market** *(58 Davies St., and 1-7 Davies Mews, W1, both map 8 F8)*, there are about 300 stalls, in a pleasant, well-appointed former factory building, with a lot of Art Nouveau and Deco, and several excellent stalls for tin toys.

Among the indoor markets, the insiders prefer **Alfies** *(13-25 Church St., NW8)*, rather isolated from shopping areas in Marylebone, selling old lace, antique photographic equipment, genuine antique street signs, etc., with the added interest of the bustle, gossip and dealing.

The other neighborhood for indoor markets is **Chelsea/Kensington**. The **Chelsea Antique Market** *(245-53 King's Rd., SW3, map 14 L5)* is a maze of stalls, run by seasoned dealers in all types of antiques. **Antiquarius** *(135-41 King's Rd., map 15 K6)*, at the corner of Flood St., has always been very conscious of trends, and **Chenil Galleries** *(181-83 King's Rd., map 15 L6)* specialize in fine art and quality antiques. (See also STREET MARKETS, page 264.)

For both antique and modern silver, it's fascinating to explore the **London Silver Vaults** *(53 Chancery Lane, WC2, map 10 E13)*.

AUCTION HOUSES

Auctions are a part of London's metropolitan life. Don't be intimidated by newspaper stories of six-figure bids; most items go for much less, and, if you keep your hand firmly on your lap, you can enjoy the auction without parting with any money. It is not necessary to reserve a seat, and there are always viewing days beforehand. Most renowned are the following:

- **Bonhams** *(Montpelier St., SW7* ☎ *(071) 584-9161, map 15 I6)* is especially good for furniture and paintings. You may pick up a bargain.
- **Christie's** *(8 King St., SW1* ☎ *(071) 839-9060, map 9 H10)* is one of the two great names: fine art, and specialist auctions, including wine sales. Their other salesroom *(85 Old Brompton Rd., South Kensington, SW7, map 14 K4)* has less expensive general items.
- **Phillips** *(101 New Bond St., W1* ☎ *(071) 629-6602, map 8 F9)* has prices usually in the medium range. Objets d'art, and various collectibles.
- **Sotheby's** *(34/5 New Bond St., W1* ☎ *(071) 493-8080, map 8 G9)* is the other great name, and the biggest. Fine art, porcelain, jewelry, clothing, books, Victoriana and decorative arts.

BOOKS

The street for the bibliophile is **Charing Cross Rd., WC2** (map 9F10-G11), with numerous shops, including **Foyle's** (one of the world's biggest) at no. 119, **Waterstone's** next door, and **Books Etc**, with its bargain basement, opposite. In fascinating alleys such as Cecil Court, hours pass quickly in the secondhand bookstores. Regular shops of particular interest are **Zwemmer** at no. 80, for art, architecture and cinema, and **Collet's** at nos. 129-31, for political and philosophical works of the Left.

Away from Charing Cross Rd., the most comprehensive selection is to be found at **Dillon's** *(82 Gower St., WC1, map 3 D10)*. **Hatchards**, in Piccadilly *(map 8 G9)*, is a pleasant, well-stocked general bookstore, and the **Pan Bookshop** *(158 Fulham Rd., SW3, map 14 K5)* is useful for hardbacks as well as paperbacks and stays open until 10pm Monday to Saturday. The excellent and well-laid-out **Economists' Bookshop** *(Clare Market, Portugal St., WC2, map 10 F12)* specializes in economics and other social sciences. The **Children's Book Centre** *(237 Kensington High St., W8, map 13 I2)* has an impressive stock for children up to age 14, and helpful assistants.

Among travel bookstores, **Daunt Books** *(83 Marylebone High St., W1, map 2 E8)* sells literary works alongside guidebooks for each destination; **Stanfords** *(12 Long Acre, WC2, map 9 F11)* is excellent for maps and travel guides; and the **Travel Bookshop** *(13 Blenheim Cres., W11)* also specializes in far-flung places.

For foodies there is the **Cook Book Shop** *(4 Blenheim Cres., W11)*.

The **Countryside Bookshop** *(39 Goodge St., W1, map 9 E10)* is another of many good specialist bookstores in London.

CHEMISTS/DRUGSTORES

Harley Street's supplier, nearby **John Bell and Croyden** *(50 Wigmore St., W1, map 8 F8)*, can meet any pharmaceutical need, and the shop also carries cosmetics. Homeopathic specialist **A. Nelson** *(73 Duke St., W1, map 8 G9)*, by appointment to H.M. the Queen, has wonderful Victorian premises.

For more conventional needs, **Boots**, the major British chain of chemists, has branches all over London. **Bliss Chemist** *(5 Marble Arch, W1, map 7 F7)* stays open daily until midnight.

CHINA

The English invented bone china, and the famous names display themselves proudly in **Regent St., W1**, especially Wedgwood and Spode at **Gered** *(no.158, map 8 G9)*. There is an even more opulent display at **Thomas Goode** *(19 South Audley St., W1, map 8 G8)*, with its Minton elephants within range of the hunting rifles across the road at the gunsmith's **James Purdey & Sons**.

China, glassware, and all sorts of elegant household goods can be found at the **General Trading Company** *(144 Sloane St., SW1, map 15 J7)*, near Sloane Sq., and at department stores such as **Liberty**, **John Lewis**, **Selfridges** and **Harrods** (see page 261). **Chinacraft** *(Regent St., W1, New Bond St., W1, and branches)* has a noteworthy selection.

CLOTHES

That London is one of the world's major contemporary fashion capitals is beyond dispute. But the real lure is the "typically British" accessory, invariably durable and utterly practical, which the English wear with such effortless, casual elegance. Such things as cashmere sweaters, robust raincoats, hand-knitted wool jerseys — outdoor clothes for country pursuits in unpredictable weather — are fashion icons sought after by the world's travelers.

Clothes for women

Young British designers are much in the international limelight these days, and London's role as a fashion center, although not on a par with Paris or Rome, has grown apace of late.

The **Bond St.** area has the premises of international designers such as **Chanel** *(26 Old Bond St., map 8 G9)*, **Karl Lagerfeld** *(173 New Bond St., map 8 G9)*, **Ralph Lauren** *(143 New Bond St., map 8 F9)*, **Saint Laurent** *(113 and 135 New Bond St., both map 8 F9)* and **Valentino** *(160 New Bond St., map 8 G9)*, and of internationally-known British designers such as **Zandra Rhodes** *(14a Grafton St., W1, map 8 G9)*, weaving fantasies from chiffon.

For more accessible creations, nearby **South Molton St., W1** *(map 8 F8)*, is browsily full of interesting clothes and best known for high fashion and sporty items at the several **Browns** shops. Similar lines and accessories abound in shops such as **Nicole Farhi** and **Mulberry** *(St Christophers Pl., W1, map* **8**F8*)*, just across Oxford St. Feminine dresses and separates with a countrified look are still to be found at **Laura Ashley** *(256-58 Regent St., W1, map* **8** *F9, and branches)*, although much more contemporary styles are now in evidence.

Head w via **Knightsbridge, Sloane St.** and **Brompton Rd.**, dropping in at department stores such as **Harvey Nichols** *(Knightsbridge, SW1, map* **15** *I7)*, renowned for high fashion, and **Harrods** (see DEPARTMENT STORES, page 262), en route to Joseph Ettedgui's Sloane St. store **Joseph** (no. 21, also at 77 Fulham Rd.) for trendy stylish clothes. The spacious **Valentino** shop at 174 Sloane St. *(map* **15** *I7)* is exciting if pricey, while **Giorgio Armani** is at no. 178. Top British designer **Katharine Hamnett** sells her designs from no. 20; a shop so striking, with its fish tanks and metal lobster sculptures in the window, wire lights and drapes inside, that it's hard to concentrate on the clothes.

Turn right at Pont St., which leads to **Beauchamp Pl., SW3** *(map* **15** *I6-J6)*. This pretty little street is crammed with fashion, from elegant **Bruce Oldfield** at no. 27, by way of **The Beauchamp Pl. Shop** at nos. 37 (for dressy designer clothes) and 55 (for a more casual look) and ethereal **Monsoon** at no. 53, to smart **Caroline Charles** at nos. 56-7. And go to **Janet Reger** at no. 2 for provocative lingerie.

Head toward **South Kensington**, where the new **Emporio Armani** *(191 Brompton Rd., SW3, map* **15** *I6)* aims to make a designer label more affordable, and British designer **Jasper Conran** has his shop at no. 303. Continue to the **King's Rd., Chelsea, SW3** *(map* **14** *M6-13K7)*, now best known for the bizarre, and often ephemeral, but always offering a wide variety of visual stimuli. Punk was popularized at no. 153, at a shop originally called "Acme Attractions," then renamed **Boy**. Some of the most flamboyant attractions are grouped around a shop named after its location, **World's End** (but remembered by early punks as "Seditionaries"), at no. 430, which now sells Vivienne Westwood's designs; look out for the high-speed clock, which whirls around backward.

(See also DEPARTMENT STORES, page 261. All have women's fashion departments.)

Clothes for men

Savile Row is the place for suits, Jermyn St. for accouterments. These are definitive addresses for the English gentleman.

In **Savile Row, W1** *(map* **8** *F9)*, the appositely named **H. Huntsman and Sons**, at no. 11, is famous for riding clothes and has been a tailor to royalty for more than a hundred years; very expensive, and no charge/credit cards. Other renowned names include **Gieves & Hawkes**, at no. 1, **Anderson & Sheppard** at no. 30, and **Tommy Nutter** at no. 19.

For classic and casual suits, try **Blades of Savile Row** *(8 Burlington Gdns., W1, map* **8** *G9)*. Also nearby is **Austin Reed** *(103 Regent St., map* **8** *G9)*, **Aquascutum** *(100 Regent St., W1, map* **8** *G9)* and **Jaeger** *(200 Regent St., W1, map* **8** *F9)*. **Crolla** *(35 Dover St., map* **8** *G9)* sells wonderfully *outré* clothes for men (and women) in beautiful rococo brocade prints. **Paul Smith** *(41-44 Floral St., map* **9** *F11)*, in Covent Garden, sells

Clothing sizes chart

LADIES
Suits and dresses

Australia	8	10	12	14	16	18	
France	34	36	38	40	42	44	
Germany	32	34	36	38	40	42	
Italy	38	40	42	44	46		
Japan	7	9	11	13			
UK	6	8	10	12	14	16	18
USA	4	6	8	10	12	14	16

Shoes

USA	6	$6\frac{1}{2}$	7	$7\frac{1}{2}$	8	$8\frac{1}{2}$
UK	$4\frac{1}{2}$	5	$5\frac{1}{2}$	6	$6\frac{1}{2}$	7
Europe	38	38	39	39	40	41

MEN
Shirts

USA, UK	14	$14\frac{1}{2}$	15	$15\frac{1}{2}$	16	$16\frac{1}{2}$	17
Europe, Japan							
Australia	36	37	38	39.5	41	42	43

Sweaters/T-shirts

Australia, USA, Germany	S	M	L	XL
UK	34	36-38	40	42-44
Italy	44	46-48	50	52
France	1	2-3	4	5
Japan		S-M	L	XL

Suits/Coats

UK, USA	36	38	40	42	44
Australia, Italy, France, Germany	46	48	50	52	54
Japan	S	M	L	XL	

Shoes

UK	7	$7\frac{1}{2}$	$8\frac{1}{2}$	$9\frac{1}{2}$	$10\frac{1}{2}$	11
USA	8	$8\frac{1}{2}$	$9\frac{1}{2}$	$10\frac{1}{2}$	$11\frac{1}{2}$	12
Europe	41	42	43	44	45	46

CHILDREN
Clothing

UK

Height (ins)	43	48	55	60	62	
Age	4-5	6-7	9-10	11	12	13

USA

Age	4	6	8	10	12	14

Europe

Height (cms)	125	135	150	155	160	165
Age	7	9	12	13	14	15

sought-after menswear, from flamboyant to timeless, often to the stars.

In **Jermyn St., SW1** *(map 8 G9-9G10)*, a man can no longer sweat out a hangover in the Turkish baths, but he can still have a shave and haircut, buy himself a clean shirt and prepare to face the world. It is still a male street, in the debonair sense of the word. Buy moustache wax or even a badger-hair shaving brush at **Trumpers**, no. 20, or an antique meerschaum pipe at **Astleys**, no. 109.

Top-quality shirts are available from **Harvie and Hudson**, at nos. 77 and 97, or the extrovert **Turnbull and Asser**, at nos. 69, 71 and 72. For a bowler hat (a "derby" to Americans) for town wear, where better to go nearby than the originators of the style, **James Lock** *(6 St James's St., SW1, map 8 H9)*? For a tweed cap, visit **Bates** *(21a Jermyn St., map 8 G9)*, where the shop's late cat (it died in 1921) watches you from a glass case. Of the department stores, **Simpson's** *(203 Piccadilly, W1, map 9 G10)* is noted both for menswear and women's clothes.

Out of the way in Fulham, but with the same traditional standards, is **Hackett** *(65a New King's Rd., SW6 , and branches)*, which sells everything the English gentleman needs.

Clothes for children

Britain's maritime tradition is upheld, even for children, by Rowes in the **White House** *(51 New Bond St., W1, map 8 F8)*, which began by making clothes for the children of naval families. This traditional line shares the shop with such children's classics as button-bar shoes and velvet-collared tweed coats.

Visit **Liberty** (see DEPARTMENT STORES, opposite), **Bambino** *(77 New Bond St., W1, map 8 F9)*, **Bananas** *(7 Clarendon Cross, W11)*, **012 Benetton** *(131 Kensington High St., map 13 I2, and branches)*, **Anthea Moore Ede** *(16 Victoria Grove, W8, map 14 I4)* and **Trotters** *(34 Kings Rd., SW3, map 15 K7)*.

Knitwear

The hugely successful Italian chain, **Benetton**, has branches all over London *(including 23 Brompton Rd., SW3, map 15 I6)*. British specialities, such as chunky knits and tweeds, can be bought from the **Irish Shop** *(11 Duke St., W1, map 8 G9)*. **The Scotch House** *(2 Brompton Rd., SW3, map 15 I6, 84 Regent St., W1, map 8 G9, and branches)* is the shop for Fair Isle, Shetland, Pringle, Ballantyne and tartans. More imaginative sweaters are to be found at **Scottish Merchant** *(16 New Row, Covent Garden, map 9 G11)*; it sells handmade designers' sweaters in beautiful patterns and colors.

Visit **Peal & Co.** for cashmere and luxury, in majestic Burlington Arcade, W1 *(map 8 G9)*, one shop for women and men. More economical are **Westaway and Westaway** *(62-5 and 92-3 Great Russell St., WC1, both map 9 E11)*, famous for bargains, and **Marks and Spencer** (see DEPARTMENT STORES, opposite).

Outerwear

For both men and women, tweed jackets, high-quality trench coats and double-breasted raincoats are the specialities at **Aquascutum** *(100 Regent St., W1, map 8 G9)*. Plaid-lined raincoats and fine cashmere coats are the hallmarks of **Burberrys** *(18-22 Haymarket, SW1, map 9 G10)*. For walking stick or umbrella go to **James Smith & Sons** *(53 New Oxford St., WC1, map 3 E11)*.

CRAFTS

Contemporary Applied Arts *(43 Earlham St., Covent Garden, WC2, map 9 F11)* sells original ceramics and jewelry. Also in Covent Garden, on Saturday, is Britain's largest display of crafts, at the **Jubilee Market.** If you feel you need to know a little more before you go shopping for this particular type of merchandise, visit the **Crafts Council** *(44a Pentonville Rd., N1):* not a shop but an exhibition center, but there is a good **Crafts Council Shop** in the V & A.

Other specialist craft stores are the **Craftsmen Potters Shop** *(Marshall St., W1, map 8 F9)*, on the site of William Blake's house in Soho, noteworthy for craftsmen's pots, and the **Contemporary Textile Gallery** *(10 Golden Sq., W1, map 9 G10)*. **The Design Centre** *(28 Haymarket, SW1, map* 9G10) is an essential port of call for those interested in contemporary British products.

DEPARTMENT STORES

Household names abound, especially along **Oxford St.**, where **Selfridges** introduced the American concept of the department store in 1909. Closer to Oxford Circus, a much more British response can be seen in the sober but reliable **John Lewis**. The four shops listed below are tourist attractions in their own right.

- **Fortnum & Mason** *(181 Piccadilly, W1, map 9 G10)* is an aristocratic and exotic grocery store with tail-coated assistants, founded by a footman to Queen Anne, famed for preserves, biscuits, and the like. Have afternoon tea in the Fountain or St James's restaurant. The upstairs floors are devoted to fashion and other items.
- **Harrods** *(Knightsbridge, SW1, map 15 I6: actually in Brompton Rd.)* is the biggest and best-known department store. Imperial flourishes such as the zoo have been trimmed, but the food hall still feels and looks like Britain's greatest provisions merchant. Harrods will get you anything, even if it has to be ordered. In fashion and homemaking, a very wide range of tastes is met.
- **Liberty** *(Regent St., W1, map 8 F9)* gave its name to a design style embracing fabrics, silver, glassware and furniture during the Art Nouveau period. "Liberty prints" and "Liberty silks" are still renowned. This heritage is evident, as are the store's origins as an importer of Oriental goods. But today's range of merchandise is much wider. Worth a visit just for its 1924 mock-Elizabethan building.
- **Marks and Spencer** *(458 and 173 Oxford St., W1, maps 7F7 & 9F10, and branches)* is rapidly becoming better known for food than for knitwear and underwear. Local stores have expanded their food sections (very high-quality convenience food and general groceries)

and contracted their clothing sections. The Marble Arch and Oxford Circus branches, however, concentrate on good-value own-brand clothing, from shoes and suitcases to swimwear. Not a department store in the traditional sense — but what a metamorphosis from the old utilitarian "Marks & Sparks."

FINE ART
The commercial galleries are predominantly in two short and elegant streets in Mayfair, W1, **Cork St.** and **Albemarle St.**, and in nearby parts of **Bond St.** Of special note is **Thomas Agnew & Son** *(43 Old Bond St., map 8 G9)*, selling paintings from all periods.

For contemporary art, go to **Browse and Darby** *(19 Cork St., map 8 G9)*, **Christies** *(8 King St., map 9 H10)* and **Marlborough Fine Art** *(6 Albemarle St., map 8 G9)*, which often deals in the really big names.

A few galleries, such as **Smith's** *(54-6 Earlham St., map 9 F11)* and the **Paton Gallery** *(2 Langley St., map 9 F11)*, exist in Covent Garden, WC2.

FOOD AND DRINK
Don't visit London without "laying down" an English Christmas pudding from one of the great department stores (see above). Their food halls offer an experience that is uniquely metropolitan, even if the biscuits come from Bath or Carlisle, the shortbread and whisky from Scotland, and they all have well-presented gift packs of teas and other specialities. Their hampers, which can be sent abroad, are costly but fabulous.

Gourmet foods also dazzle the eye at **Hobbs** *(29 South Audley St., W1, map 8G8)*. All these shops and food halls incorporate excellent wine merchants. A specialist vintner of note is the long-established **Berry Bros. & Rudd** *(3 St James's St., SW1, map 8 H9)*, whose shop contains a superb pair of antique scales. For the finest selection of Scotch whiskies (single malts, not the commercial blends), go to the **Soho Wine Market** *(3 Greek St., W1, map 9 F10)*.

Other specialist food stores include the following.
- **FOR CHOCOLATES**   **Bendicks** *(55 Wigmore St., W1, map 8 F8, 107 Long Acre, WC2, map 9 F11, and branches)*, which holds the royal warrant; **Charbonnel et Walker** *(28 Old Bond St., W1, map 8 G9)*; and **Prestat**, *(14 Princes Arcade, Piccadilly, SW1, map 8 G9)*.
- **FOR THE BEST ENGLISH CHEESE AND HAM**   **Paxton & Whitfield** *(93 Jermyn St., SW1, map 9 G10)*.
- **FOR HEALTH FOODS, INCLUDING SUPERB BREADS**   **Cranks** *(8 Marshall St., W1, map 8 F9)*, or the extraordinary selection of shops in **Neal's Yard** *(Earlham St., Covent Garden, WC2, map 9 F11)*. The quaintly named **& Clarke's** *(122 Kensington Church St., W8, map 5 H2)* also sells wonderful, unusual breads and fine unpasteurized cheeses, as well as exquisite homemade chocolate truffles.
- **FOR TEAS AND COFFEES**   **R. Twining and Co.** *(216 Strand, WC2, map 10 F13)*; **Drury Tea and Coffee Co.** *(Mepham St., SE1,*

map 10H13); **Algerian Coffee Stores** *(52 Old Compton St., W1, map 9 F10)*.

HOUSEHOLD GOODS

Conran *(81 Fulham Rd., SW3, map 14 K5)* and **Habitat** *(206 King's Rd., SW3, map 15 L6, and branches)* have dominated British household design for two decades. The **Conran Shop**, housed in the stunningly restored Art Nouveau Michelin House *(81 Fulham Rd., SW3, map 14K5)*, is more stylish and impressive than ever. Bauhaus-inspired furniture, Oriental-style flooring, colorful ethnic fabrics and rugs are displayed upstairs, while a vast array of ornaments, accessories, gifts, books and toys are to be found in the basement. There is also an attractive, affordable oyster bar on the ground floor, while Terence Conran's restaurant, BIBENDUM (see RESTAURANTS A TO Z), is upstairs. Habitat is also merged with **Heal's** *(196 Tottenham Court Rd., W1, map , map 3 E10)*.

For more traditional furniture, try **Maples** *(145 Tottenham Court Rd., W1, map 3 E10)*.

JEWELRY

London's diamond center, mainly for the trade, is **Hatton Garden, EC1** *(map 4 E13)*. Some shops, such as **R. Holt**, at no. 98, welcome the public. The royal jewelers are **Garrard** *(112 Regent St., W1, map 8 G9)*.

Anything from a jewel box to a gold-plated toothbrush can be had at **Asprey** *(165 New Bond St., W1, map 8 G9)*; here too is **Cartier** *(175 New Bond St., W1, map 8 G9)*. For fashionable costume jewelry, visit **Butler and Wilson** *(189 Fulham Rd., SW3, map 14 K5, and 20 South Molton St., W1, map 8 F8)*.

The London Diamond Centre *(10 Hanover St., W1, map 8 F9)* has a vast collection of cut and uncut diamonds .

MUSIC

The biggest record stores are **HMV** *(363 & 150 Oxford St., W1, maps 8F8 & 8F9)*, **Virgin Megastore** *(14-30 Oxford St., W1, map 9 F10)*, and **Tower Records** *(1 Piccadilly Circus, W1, map 9 G10)*.

Specialist shops include **Rough Trade** *(130 Talbot Rd., W11)*, some way out of the center, geographically as well as musically; **Collets** *(129-31 Charing Cross Rd., WC2, map 9 F10)*, for Eastern European folk music; **Stern's** *(116 Whitfield St., W1, map 9 E10)*, for African music. Jazz buffs will also want to see the famous **Dobells** *(21 Tower St., off Shaftesbury Ave., W1, map 9 F11)*.

The Gramophone Exchange *(3 Betterton St., WC2, map 9 F11)* specializes in second-hand records.

Classical music is available from **Farringdon Records** *(52 High Holborn, WC1, map 10 E12)*, **Caruso & Co.** *(35 New Oxford St., WC1, map 3 E11)* and **Harold Moore's** *(2 Great Marlborough St., W1, map 8 F9)*.

PERFUMERS

All the international brands are best bought in department stores; **Harrods** boasts one of the largest selections. For English flower perfumes, visit the established **Floris** *(89 Jermyn St., SW1, map 9 G10)* or the fashionably traditional **Penhaligon's** *(41 Wellington St., WC2, map 10 F12)*.

PHOTOGRAPHIC SUPPLIES

For cameras, try **City Camera Exchange***(124 High Holborn, WC1, map 10E12, and branches)* or **Dixons** *(88 Oxford St., W1, map 9 F10, and branches)*. For films, use the **Boots** or **W. H. Smith** chains, which also develop films fast. For emergency repairs: **Advance Technical** *(9 St Anne's Ct., W1, map 9 G10)* and **Sendean** *(105 Oxford St., W1, map 9 F10)*.

SHOES

Fashion shoe stores crowd **Bond St.** and **South Molton St.**, W1. Men who want the best and can wait for it order custom-made boots fit for royalty from **John Lobb** *(9 St James's St., SW1, map 8 H9)*, who keep on the premises a wooden last of every customer. Sturdy, traditional footwear can be bought nearby at **Maxwell's** *(11 Savile Row, W1, map 8 F9)*, and slightly less expensively at **Tricker's** *(67 Jermyn St., SW1, map 9 G10)* and **Church's** *(163 New Bond St., W1, map 8 G9)*.

For women, the most expensive and stylish shoes in London are hand-made and sold by **Manolo Blahnik** *(48-51 Old Church St., SW3, map 14 L5)*. Excellent-quality Italian leather shoes are available from **Ferragamo** *(24 Old Bond St., W1, map 8 G9)*, **Bruno Magli** *(49 New Bond St., map 8 F8, and branches)* and **Rayne** *(15-16 Old Bond St., map 8 G9, and branches)*, where the Queen buys shoes. Well-made shoes at more affordable prices are sold by **Bertie** *(48 South Molton St., W1, map 8 F8)*, **Hobbs** *(47 South Molton St.)* and **Pied à Terre** *(19 South Molton St., map 8 F8)*; all three have other branches in London.

At low price, Marks and Spencer's two Oxford St. stores have a good range of everyday shoes.

SHOPPING CENTERS

Based on the concept of American malls, a number of new centers, which bring together a multiplicity of big name shops, restaurants, cafés, movie theaters and other facilities under one roof, have sprung up over Central London in the last few years. Shopping is made easy, when you can buy everything you need, have a cup of coffee or lunch, and then watch a movie without getting blisters or soaked to the skin.

The most recent and lavish of these is **Whiteleys** *(Queensway, W2, map 5 G3)*, a converted department store, which retains its original sweeping staircase. Other centers in the same mold are **Tobacco Dock** in Docklands and **London Pavilion** in Piccadilly.

STREET MARKETS

The famous ones are still fun, but see some of the others, too. London has 50 or 60 street markets, and it is here that the town best demonstrates its wit, wisdom and elusive code. If you demonstrate your own, you might knock prices down. No charge or credit cards are accepted, only English checks, so take cash.

- **Portobello Road** Saturday antique market is especially well known for its silver. Easy to find — and to explore, since it is basically one street — but it stretches for more than one mile. Start by taking the underground to Notting Hill Gate, and walk via Pembridge Rd., W11, following the crowd. Antiques and junk come first, then freaky shops, and finally food, at the N end.

- **Petticoat Lane** *(Middlesex St., E1)*, a junk market in the East End on Sunday, and only one part of a maze of street trade where the patois embraces Cockney rhyming slang, Yiddish and Bengali. Serious bargain-hunters start at the improbable hour of 4am with the Cheshire St. (E2) and Brick Lane (E1) areas, where the action subsides well before 9am. The more touristic Petticoat Lane itself (real name, Middlesex Street) is in full swing by then, and impossibly crowded by 11am. Take lunch at Bloom's (see RESTAURANTS A TO Z); you'll have to line up, but after that early start, the chicken soup will be manna. The nearest underground stations are Liverpool Street and Aldgate East.

- **Camden Passage** *(Camden Passage, N1, map 4 B14):* Wednesday and Saturday for good-quality antiques; Thursday for books, prints and drawings. Art Deco is something of a theme in the market, especially in the Athenai Arcade. Everyone goes to the Camden Head pub or Natalie's coffee shop for refreshment. Go by tube to Angel and walk up Islington High St.

- **Bermondsey (New Caledonian)** *(Long Lane and Tower Bridge Rd., SE1, maps 12 I16 & 12 I17-H17),* on Friday: the insiders' antique market, where the cognoscenti hunt by flashlight at 5am, grab their purchases by 8.30am at the latest, then retire for breakfast at the Rose Dining Rooms. As if that weren't a sufficiently daunting venture, the market is also hard to find. Thus it is that Bermondsey has remained a market for the seriously interested. Go by underground to London Bridge, and walk down Bermondsey St.

- **Camden Lock** *(Camden High St./Chalk Farm Rd., NW1),* Saturday and Sunday market with an entertaining mix of junk and attractions, including books, musical instruments, crafts, clothing, jewelry and snacks. It stretches for a mile from Chalk Farm underground. The main market is by Regent's Canal.

- **Greenwich Antique Market** *(Greenwich High Rd., SE10),* held on Saturday and Sunday in summer, is devoted to antiques, books and bric-a-brac. **Greenwich Covered Crafts Market** is in nearby College Approach on Saturday and Sunday.

TOYS

The biggest toy store in the world is **Hamleys** *(188 Regent St., W1, map 8 F9)*. Parents who believe play should be educative favor **Galt Toys**, within Liberty (see DEPARTMENT STORES, page 261), and the **Early Learning Centre** *(225 Kensington High St., W8, map 13 I2, and numerous other branches)*. **Frog Hollow** *(15 Victoria Grove, W8, map 14 I4)* has unusual wooden and fabric toys, and **Tiger Tiger** *(219 King's Rd., SW3, map 14 L5)* a good selection of soft animals.

Victorian reproductions are available at **Pollock's Toy Museum** *(21 Scala St., W1, map 9 E10, and Covent Garden Market, WC2, map 9 F11).*

Recreation

London for children

To find out what's on for children, buy the inexpensive *Children's London,* published by the London Tourist Board and Convention Bureau. For specific questions ring **Kidsline** (☎ *(071) 222-8070 Mon-Fri 4-6pm, during school vacations and "half term" 9am-4pm).*

Many museums, such as the BETHNAL GREEN MUSEUM OF CHILDHOOD and the LONDON TOY AND MODEL MUSEUM, have always been directly aimed at a young audience. But by now nearly all of the major museums have discarded their showcase image, recognizing the need to attract children, and consequently many of their exhibits now demand a "hands-on" approach. Some also produce questionnaires to make a child's visit more directly interesting. The SCIENCE MUSEUM, for instance, devotes an entire section to children: in its Launch Pad, children are encouraged to play with the exhibits, which illustrate the basics of science on a simple level that parents too can understand.

In this guide, all museums and places of interest marked with the ♣ symbol are generally suitable for children. Most museums are also reasonably accessible to baby buggies.

WAYS OF SEEING LONDON
An ideal introduction to London, from a child's point of view, is a Round London Sightseeing Tour in a double-decker bus. River trips to HAMPTON COURT and GREENWICH are also popular. (See pages 42 and 47 for departure points of river boats and buses.)

EATING IN LONDON
Most restaurants tolerate children — Italian ones are often the most friendly — and some less expensive restaurants will supply children's portions. Hamburger and other fast-food restaurants are plentiful. The following cater to children:
*   **Wimpy**, **McDonalds**, **Pizza Express**, **Pizza Hut**, **Tootsies** and **Spaghetti House**, all of which have branches all over London
*   **Masseralla's** *(Hamleys, 188 Regent St., W1* ☎ *(071) 734-3161, map 8F9)*
*   **Smollensky's Balloon** *(1 Dover St., W1* ☎ *(071) 491-1199, map 8G9)* and **Smollensky's on the Strand** *(105 Strand, WC2* ☎ *(071) 497-2101, map 10G12),* with children's entertainers at both branches on weekends
*   **TGI Friday's** *(6 Bedford St., WC2* ☎ *(071) 379-0585, map 9G11)*

FARES

On London Transport, children under 5 travel free and children aged 5-16 travel for a reduced fare, although children aged 14 and 15 need a photocard (available from any post office — take a photograph).

CHRISTMAS

Seeing the Christmas lights and decorations in London, particularly in Regent St. and Oxford St., makes a good early evening's entertainment. Children can also see Santa Claus at Hamleys, Harrods and Selfridges and other large department stores during the season. The windows at Selfridges are another special attraction.

PARKS

Hyde Park and **Kensington Gardens** (separated only by a road) are the most central and well-known of London's parks. As well as wide open spaces allowing large-scale games to be played, there are many special attractions. Boats and paddle craft can be rented on the Serpentine, part of which is cordoned off and used as a swimming area in the summer. Kensington Gardens also has unique Sunday entertainments: men sail their model boats on the Round Pond, and there are kites to admire. Nearby is the playground donated by J.M. Barrie with its statue of Peter Pan. Look out too for the beautifully carved *Elfin Oak,* near Bayswater Rd., restored by the fairies (with a little help from Spike Milligan). Puppet shows are staged here on August afternoons.

Regent's Park also has rowboats to rent, but the main attraction is the zoo.

Hampstead Heath, although not particularly central, also offers wide open spaces as well as a deer park, a pond for model boats, an outdoor swimming pool and a playground.

Coram's Fields in Bloomsbury is a park donated to children in London by Sir Thomas Coram — adults are only allowed in if they are accompanied by a child.

Holland Park boasts a wildlife enclosure, with peacocks, Muscovy ducks and Polish bantams, an exciting adventure playground for older children and a toddlers' playground.

Battersea has even more going on: a boating lake, small zoo *(open in summer),* deer park, roller-skating area, and theater events and pony rides in summer.

There are many other supervised adventure playgrounds, which have imaginative materials and equipment created by the children themselves. Information from **Playlink** *(279 Whitechapel Rd., E1 ☎(071) 377-0314).* Younger children can go to the council-run **One O'Clock Clubs** where they can play with the equipment provided. Under-5s must be accompanied by an adult. Information from local borough councils.

THEATERS AND CINEMAS

Some London theaters have special performances for children:
* **The Little Angel Marionette Theatre** in Islington *(14 Dagmar Passage, Cross St., N1 ☎(071) 226-1787)* regularly shows puppet

plays, on weekend afternoons and also on some weekdays during school vacations; performances for small children take place on Saturday and Sunday mornings.

- The **Lyric Theatre, Hammersmith** *(King St., W6 ☎ (081) 741-2311)* shows productions for children every Saturday.
- **Polka Theatre for Children** *(240 The Broadway, SW19 ☎ (081) 543-4888)* stages regular plays for children, and has exhibitions linked to past productions.
- **The Unicorn Theatre** *(6 Great Newport St., WC2 ☎ (071) 836-3334, map 9 F11)* also stages plays suitable for children aged 4-12 on weekend afternoons, and some weekdays during school holidays and "half term," but not in the summer.
- During school vacations in particular, major cinemas show a wide selection of children's movies.
- The **National Film Theatre** cinema (see PERFORMING ARTS, page 247) has children's movie clubs on weekend afternoons.

FAIRGROUNDS AND CIRCUSES
Touring circuses and fairs often come to London for bank holiday weekends (see PUBLIC HOLIDAYS, page 42) and usually set up in the larger parks. Information can be obtained from the **London Tourist Board and Convention Bureau** *(☎ (071) 730-3488)*. Fireworks and other celebrations on November 5 often include fairgrounds.

ATTRACTIONS WITHIN EASY REACH OF LONDON
Bekonscot Model Village *(Warwick Rd., Beaconsfield, Buckinghamshire ☎ (0494) 672919 ▨ open daily late Feb to early Nov 10am-5pm)* is only 40 minutes w of London off the M40 motorway, and is a beautifully landscaped miniature village and model railway. Visitors can wander about in the village and peer into the buildings, which are waist-high to an adult, and see, in fascinating detail, an idealized version of an English village in the 1930s.

   Chessington World of Adventures *(Leatherhead Rd., Chessington, Surrey ☎ (03727) 27227 ▨ open late Mar to late Oct 10am-3.30pm)*, just off the A3, guarantees an entertaining day out, with a host of rides, from *Dragon River* via the *Runaway Mine Train* to Britain's first hanging roller-coaster, *The Vampire*, and its own zoo *(open all year)*.

   Thorpe Park *(Staines Rd., Chertsey, Surrey ☎ (0932) 569393 ▨ open late Mar to late July, mid-Sept to late Oct 10am-3pm, park 10am-5pm; late July to mid-Sept 10am-4pm, park 10am-6pm)* is approximately 40 minutes from London to the w off the M3 motorway, and is a popular family attraction. Rides range from *Thunder River* and *The Flying Fish Rollercoaster* to the *Fantasy Reef*, which incorporates a four-lane waterslide. Less terrifying features include pedalos and canoes, a farm and a traditional fairground carousel.

BRASS-RUBBING
This can be a fascinating way of passing a wet afternoon. In the churches, admission is free but you must pay for your materials.

- The **London Brass Rubbing Centre** *(St Martin-in-the-Fields, Trafalgar Sq., WC2* ☎ *(071) 437-6023, map 9 G11)* has a large collection.
- **Westminster Abbey** *(SW1* ☎ *(071) 222-2085, map 17 I11)* and **All-Hallows-by-the-Tower** *(Byward St., EC3* ☎ *(071) 481-2928, map 12 G17)* also have brass-rubbing facilities.
- There is also brass-rubbing at the TROCADERO.

BABY-SITTERS
- **Babysitters Unlimited** *(* ☎ *(081) 892-8888)*
- **Childminders** *(* ☎ *(071) 935-2049/9763)*
- **Universal Aunts** *(* ☎ *(071) 352-8895).*
- Alternatively you can leave your children at a "children's hotel," **Pippa Pop-pins** *(430 Fulham Rd., SW6* ☎ *(071) 385-2458, map 14 L4)*, where they can stay overnight and/or be well-entertained during the day.

FARMS
There are a surprising number of city farms in the Inner London area. The most interesting (some of which are closed on Monday) are:
- **Freightliners** *(Paradise Park, Sheringham Rd., N7* ☎ *(071) 609-0467)*
- **Kentish Town City Farm** *(1 Cressfield Close, NW5* ☎ *(071) 482-2861)*
- **Mudchute Community Farm** *(Pier St., E14* ☎ *(071) 515-5901)*
- **Spitalfields Farm** *(Weaver St., E1* ☎ *(071) 247-8762)*
- **Stepping Stones Farm** *(Stepney Way, E1* ☎ *(071) 790-8204)*
- **Vauxhall City Farm** *(24 St Oswald's Pl., SE11* ☎ *(071) 582-4204, map 18 K12, entrance in Tyer's St.)*

TOY STORES
See SHOPPING, page 265.

Sports and activities

For information on all sports, contact **Sportsline** (☎*(071) 222-8000 Mon-Fri 10am-6pm*).

ATHLETICS (TRACK AND FIELD)

Major events are held at the **Crystal Palace National Sports Centre** *(Ledrington Rd., SE19* ☎*(081) 778-0131)*. Information from **The British Athletic Federation** *(address: Edgbaston House, 3 Duchess Pl., Hadley Rd., Birmingham B16 8NM* ☎*(021) 456-4050)*.

For keen runners, there is an excellent all-weather-surface 6-lane track at **Battersea Park** *(Albert Bridge Rd., SW11* ☎*(081) 871-7537, map 15M6)* and a synthetic 8-lane track at **West London Stadium** *(Du Cane Rd., W12* ☎*(081) 749-5505)*.

BICYCLING

This can be an effective way of exploring the city and one of the quickest ways of getting around. Cycles can be rented from **On Your Bike** *(52-54 Tooley St., SE1* ☎*(071) 407-1309, map 12H16)*.

For more serious cycling, contact the **British Cycling Federation** *(address: Rockingham Rd., Kettering, Northamptonshire NN16 8HG* ☎*(0536) 412211)* or **London Cycling Campaign** *(address: Tress House, 3 Stamford St., SE1 9NT* ☎*(071) 928-7220, map 10H13)*, which publishes a booklet of routes.

CRICKET

The most baffling of sports to the newcomer, but an integral part of the English summer; from April to September club matches are played all over London, in parks and on greens, mainly on Saturday and Sunday afternoons.

First-class professional matches, also on weekdays, are played at the Middlesex club at **Lord's** *(NW8* ☎*(071) 289-1611)* and the Surrey club at **The Oval** *(SE11* ☎*(071) 735-4911)*. Both stage a yearly test (international) match: Lords in June, The Oval in August or September.

FISHING

Fishing in the Thames is forbidden unless you have a national rod license from the Thames Water Authority, obtainable through the **London Anglers Association** *(Forest Rd. Hall, Hervey Park Rd., E17* ☎*(081) 520-7477)*, which you have to join. It is also possible to fish in Hyde Park: licenses from **The Royal Parks Department** *(The Storeyard, Hyde Park, W2* ☎*(071) 262-5484, map 6H5)*.

FOOTBALL (SOCCER)

Football matches are generally played on Saturday afternoons from August through to April, with some matches on Sunday afternoons and weekday evenings. The FA Cup Final, the most important single match of the football season, is played in April or May at **Wembley Stadium** *(* ☎*(081) 900-1234 ✗ available)*, which is also the scene of England's international matches, usually played on Wednesday evenings. Consult listings magazines such as *Time Out* for details and locations of club matches.

GARDENS

Apart from parks and gardens that are open to the public, the **National Gardens Scheme** *(Hatchlands Park, East Clandon, Guildford, Surrey* ☎ *(0483) 211535)* runs a program that enables private gardens both in London and the country to open to the public for perhaps one day every year.

The **Royal Horticultural Society** holds periodic shows in summer at its home in Vincent Sq., SW1, and stages the massive **Chelsea Flower Show** in May (see CALENDAR OF EVENTS, page 53).

GOLF

Most courses are private and will only allow you to play if you have an introduction from a member or from your own club. Public courses, however, will allow you to play on payment of a green fee, and some will rent out clubs.

One of the nearest professional courses is **Wentworth**, in Surrey. The most central public courses are at:

- **Richmond Park** *(Roehampton Gate, SW15* ☎ *(081) 876-3205, map 19 D3-20 D4.*
- **Wimbledon Common** *(Camp Rd., SW19* ☎ *(081) 946-0294, Mon-Fri),* no clubs for hire, "wear a pillar-box-red top"
- **Royal Mid-Surrey** *(Old Deer Park, Richmond, Surrey* ☎ *(081) 940-1894, map 19 D3, Mon-Fri),* where you must have a handicap or be a member of a recognized club

HEALTH AND FITNESS CLUBS

Gymnasiums, Nautilus machines, aerobics classes, saunas and massages are among the facilities offered by most of the following clubs, where temporary (daily or weekly) membership is available:

- **Earl's Court Gym** *(Upper Floors, 254 Earl's Court Rd., SW5* ☎ *(071) 370-1402, map 13 K3)*
- **Metropolitan Club** *(27-28 Kingly St., W1* ☎ *(071) 734-5002/3, map 8 F9)*
- **The Sanctuary** *(12 Floral St., WC2* ☎ *(071) 240-9635/6, map 9 F11),* women only
- **Westminster Health Club** *(Allington St., SW1* ☎ *(071) 828-3647, map 16 I9)*
- **Westside** *(201-207 Kensington High St., W8* ☎ *(071) 937-5386, map 13 I3)*
- **World Traders Health Club** *(International House, World Trade Centre, St Katharine's Way, E1* ☎ *(071) 488-2400, map 12 G18)*

Perennially popular with office workers in Covent Garden and the West End are the dance/keep-fit sessions at **Pineapple** *(7 Langley St., WC2* ☎ *(071) 836-4004, map 9 F11)* —in conjunction with sister studios **Pineapple Kensington** *(38-42 Harrington Rd., SW7* ☎*(071)* *581-0466, map 14J5)* — and **Danceworks** *(16 Balderton St., W1* ☎*(071) 629-6183, map8F8).*

HORSE-RACING
There are many large racecourses within easy reach of London: to the w, **Ascot** and **Newbury**; to the sw, **Sandown**, **Epsom** and **Kempton Park**. No races on Sunday. There are long overlaps between the summer (flat) and the winter (jumping) seasons.

The best-known annual races, which grip the nation, are the Grand National, held at Aintree near Liverpool in late March, and the Derby at Epsom, Surrey, in early June. All races will be well covered in the daily newspapers, and it is possible to bet from betting shops that are not on the course.

ICE-SKATING
The major public rinks, which will hire out skates, are:
* **Broadgate Ice Rink** *(Eldon St., EC2* ☎*(071) 588-6565, map 12E16),* an outdoor rink open November to March
* **Queens Ice-Skating Club** *(17 Queensway, W2* ☎*(071) 229-0172, map5F3)*
* **Streatham Ice Rink** *(386 Streatham High Rd., SW16* ☎*(081) 769-7861).*

RIDING
Stables are conveniently located near major parks: **Ross Nye's Riding Establishment** *(8 Bathurst Mews, W2* ☎*(071) 262-3791, map6F5),* for Hyde Park; and **Roehampton Gate** *(Priory Lane, SW15* ☎*(081) 876-7089),* for Richmond Park.

Several major show-jumping events are held at **Wembley** *(*☎*(081) 900-1234)* and **Olympia** *(*☎*(071) 603-3344):* for leading examples see CALENDAR OF EVENTS.

ROWING
Rowboats and sailing dinghies may be rented on the Serpentine, in Battersea Park and Regent's Park, as well as on some stretches of the Thames and in Docklands (see WATERSPORTS, overleaf). For rowing events see CALENDAR OF EVENTS. For details contact the **Amateur Rowing Association** *(6 Lower Mall, W6* ☎*(081) 748-3632).*

RUGBY
Rugby Union, a 15-a-side sport with certain affinities to American football, restricts its players to amateur status in the same way that track and field does. Matches are played on Saturday afternoons from September to April.

International and major games take place at the sport's headquarters at **Twickenham** *(Whitton Rd., Twickenham* ☎*(081) 892-8161).* Consult listings magazines such as *Time Out* for details and locations of club matches.

SQUASH
Addresses from **Squash Rackets Association** *(WestPoint, 33-34 Warple Way, W3 ☎ (081) 746-1616).*

SWIMMING
Major indoor pools with all facilities include:
* **Chelsea Sports Centre** *(Chelsea Manor St., SW3 ☎ (071) 352-6985, map 15 L6)*
* **Golden Lane Pool** *(Golden Lane, EC1 ☎ (071) 250-1464)*
* **Fulham Pools** *(Normand Park, Lillie Rd., SW6 ☎ (071) 385-7628, off map 13 L1)*
* **Marshall St. Baths** *(14-15 Marshall St., W1 ☎ (071) 287-1022, map 8 F9)*
* **Oasis Pool** *(32 Endell St., WC2 ☎ (071) 836-9555, map 9 F11),* which also has an outdoor pool

For outdoor swimming during the summer, major pools are:
* **Hampstead Mixed Bathing Pond** *(NW3 ☎ (071) 435-2366)*
* **Parliament Hill Lido** *(NW5 ☎ (071) 485-3873)*
* **The Serpentine** *(Hyde Park, W2 ☎ (071) 262-3751, map 6 H5)*

TENNIS
Information from **The Lawn Tennis Association** *(Queen's Club, Baron's Court, W14 ☎ (071) 385-2366, map 13 K1).* For major annual tennis tournaments see CALENDAR OF EVENTS.

WATERSPORTS
Rowing, canoeing and sailing can be arranged through **Royal Victoria Dock Project** *(Royal Victoria Dock, Gate 5, Dock Rd., E16 ☎ (071) 511-2326, map 20 C5);* windsurfing, through **Peter Chilvers Windsurfing Centre** *(Royal Victoria Dock, Gate 6, Tidal Basin Rd., E16 ☎ (071) 474-2500, map 20 C5);* wet-biking and jet-skiing, through **Docklands Watersports** *(King George V Dock, Woolwich Manor Way, E16 ☎ (071) 511-7000, map 20 C6).*

Excursions

London's hinterland

In Britain, all roads lead to London, and they can also be taken in the opposite direction, as can the commuter railway routes to such historically interesting cities as CANTERBURY, **Salisbury** and **Winchester**. London's hinterland covers the half-dozen "home counties" of the southeast and beyond to cities such as CAMBRIDGE, OXFORD, BRIGHTON and even BATH. These cities, and to an even greater extent STRATFORD-UPON-AVON, repay a weekend visit, with a little exploration on the way. All of them are popular with visitors, and at the height of the summer are over-subscribed to the point of suffocation. This can be even more true of WINDSOR AND ETON, so near to London that it can be difficult to justify missing them.

An interesting alternative or complement to these historical towns and cities is offered by the wealth of **castles and stately homes** that encircle London, and we begin this chapter with a selection of the most interesting and accessible of these.

Stately homes around London

London's own countryside, where the nobility once lived in stately homes, begins in the suburbs, then fans out into Epping Forest, the Thames Valley, the Downs, and the Chilterns. Much of this countryside can be reached by tube, and there are several "country" homes open to the public within the capital, especially in West London (see houses at CHISWICK, HAM, ORLEANS and SYON, and OSTERLEY PARK). Beyond, there are about 50 houses and castles within 100 miles. Most of these close on Monday, but are open on bank holidays, then close the following day.

Audley End House
40 miles (64km) N of London, 15 miles (24km) S of Cambridge ☎ *(0799) 522842. By car, through the pretty Roding Valley on the M11; by train, from Liverpool Street to Audley End, then walk or take a bus. Open Easter-Sept Tues-Sun, bank holiday Mon.*
One of the best examples of a Jacobean mansion, with extensive later work by Vanbrugh and Robert Adam. Much fine 18thC furniture and a collection of stuffed birds. Large grounds, with a miniature railway.

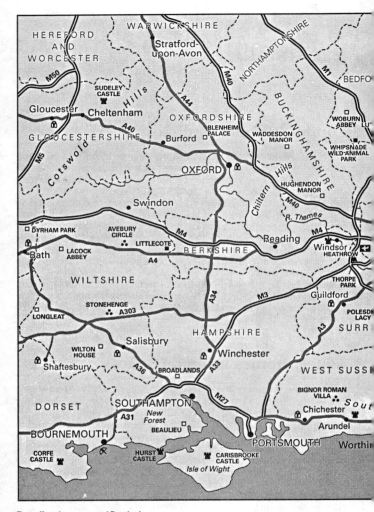

Beaulieu (pronounced Bewlee)
*80 miles (128km) sw of London, 14 miles (22km) s of Southampton ☎(0590)
612345. By car, A3, A31 or M3, A33. By train, from Waterloo to Southampton,
then bus. Open daily.*
World-famous for its **Motor Museum**, with 200 veteran cars, early
Rolls, land-speed record breakers, and a monorail. The house, home of

car enthusiast Lord Montagu, was built as the gatehouse of the 13thC Beaulieu Abbey, the ruins of which visitors can explore. The museum and ruins can be visited all year, as can the stately home. Nearby, just a few miles to the NW, is the **New Forest**, and there is a Maritime Museum at **Buckler's Hard**, a village with shipbuilding associations dating from Nelson's time.

Broadlands

80 miles (128km) sw of London, 6 miles (10km) nw of Southampton ☎(0794) 516878. By car, as BEAULIEU (above). By train, to Southampton, changing for Romsey. Open Easter-Sept Sat-Thurs.

The Prince and Princess of Wales spent part of their honeymoon at Broadlands, the home of the late Lord Mountbatten and, in an earlier time, of Lord Palmerston. Broadlands, a Palladian mansion with landscaping by Capability Brown, is now the home of Lord and Lady Romsey, and there is a **Mountbatten exhibition** in the stable block.

Chartwell

25 miles (40km) s of London, 5 miles (8km) sw of Sevenoaks ☎(0732) 866368. By car, A21, A233, B2026. By bus, from Victoria Coach Station. By train, to Sevenoaks from Charing Cross, then bus to Westerham, then a 25min walk. Open Mar and Nov Wed, Sat, Sun, Apr-Oct Tues-Thurs afternoons, Sat, Sun, bank holiday Mon (closed Tues after bank holiday Mon).

Winston Churchill's country home for 40 years — Victorian, chosen for its tranquility and views. Churchill's study and library can be visited. An unfinished canvas still stands in his studio in the beautiful gardens.

Five miles (8km) away is **Hever Castle**, trysting place of Anne Boleyn and Henry VIII and 20thC home of William Waldorf Astor (with Holbeins and a Titian); **Penshurst Place**, birthplace of Sir Philip Sidney (with a toy museum, costume display, Italian gardens and nature trail), is also nearby.

Hatfield House

21 miles (33km) n of London ☎(07072) 62823. By car, A1000. By train, from King's Cross or Moorgate to Hatfield. House open late Mar to mid-Oct Tues-Sun; grounds open daily.

Royal mementos dating back to Elizabeth I, paintings, tapestries and armor, and special exhibitions on crafts and collectibles. Within the grounds is a part of the palace in which Elizabeth I lived as a girl. Her Secretary of State, Robert Cecil, built Hatfield House, and his descendant, the Marquess of Salisbury, still lives there.

Six miles (10km) n is **Knebworth House**, begun in 1492 and completed in the 1800s, known for its books and manuscripts, paintings and furniture, and narrow-gauge railway.

Leeds Castle

36 miles (57km) se of London, 5 miles (8km) se of Maidstone. By car, A20 and M20. By train and bus, inclusive ticket available from Victoria Station ☎(0622) 765400. Open Apr-Oct daily; Nov-Mar Sat, Sun.

Fairytale medieval castle on two islands in a lake. Built about 1120, restored in the 1800s. Henry VIII converted it into a royal palace; Elizabeth I was a prisoner here. A garden with many species of flowers is named after another resident, Lord Culpeper, who was Governor of Virginia in the 1600s and founder of the herbalist shop.

Luton Hoo

30 miles (48km) n of London, 2 miles (3km) s of Luton ☎(0582) 22955. By car, M1, A1081. By train, from St Pancras Station, then local bus. Open Easter-Oct Tues-Sun, bank holiday Mon.

Fabergé jewels, mementos of Czarist Court, Renaissance jewels, bronzes, porcelain, in a Robert Adam house. Gardens by Capability Brown.

Polesden Lacey
*20 miles (32km) SW of London, 2 miles (3km) NW of Dorking ☎(0372) 452048.
By car, A24. By train, from Waterloo to Box Hill or Bookham, then taxi, or bus
plus walk. Gardens open all year, daily. House open afternoons only, Apr-Oct
Wed-Sun.*

The playwright Sheridan lived, gardened and farmed here, but his
house was demolished in the early 1800s and replaced by a Regency
villa. After having several private owners, the property was bequeathed
to the National Trust. The lovely house, with a much-admired rose
garden, contains a substantial collection of porcelain, and paintings by
Sir Joshua Reynolds and Sir Henry Raeburn.

Waddesdon Manor
*38 miles (60km) NW of London, 5 miles (8km) W of Aylesbury ☎(0296) 651211.
By car, A41. By train, from Marylebone to Aylesbury, then taxi or bus, plus
strenuous walk. House closed for restoration until 1994. Grounds and aviary
open afternoons late Mar to late Dec Wed-Fri, Sat, Sun, Good Fri, bank hol Mon.*
Château-like house built by Baron Ferdinand de Rothschild. Family
mementos, French royal furniture, carpets, paintings. Extensive grounds
in which deer roam.

Wilton House
*80 miles (128km) W of London, 2½ miles (4km) W of Salisbury ☎(072274) 3115.
By car, A30. Train-and-bus excursions by British Rail Awayday from Waterloo
Station. Open Easter-Oct Mon-Sat, Sun afternoons.*
Whimsical Inigo Jones house, with Chippendale and Kent furniture and
Van Dyck paintings. More offbeat attractions include some 7,000 brightly-
painted model soldiers in a diorama setting, exhibition of dollhouses,
reconstructed Tudor kitchens and a lock of Queen Elizabeth I's hair.

City excursions

This section comprises seven excursions, to the following towns and
cities: **Bath**, this page (one-day excursion by train, or weekend by car);
Brighton, page 284 (one-day excursion by train, or weekend by car);
Cambridge, page 287 (one-day excursion by train or car); **Canterbury**, page 291 (one-day excursion by train or car); **Oxford**, page 294
(one-day excursion by train, coach or car); **Stratford-upon-Avon**,
page 298 (one-day excursion or longer, by train or car); and **Windsor
and Eton**, page 301 (one-day excursion by train or car).

BATH
*116 miles (186km) W of London. Population: 85,000. By train, 70mins from
Paddington, trains hourly; by car, 2hrs, M4 to Junction 18, then A46 to Bath
☎code (0225) i Abbey Churchyard ☎462831.*
One-day excursion: an effortless day out by comfortable high-speed
train, with good views of gentle countryside, especially between the
Vale of the White Horse and the Lambourn Downs, and where the

edges of the Cotswolds form a valley with the Marlborough Downs. Fast by car, too, although the temptation is to make it a weekend, with detours into the hills and stops at ancient sites such as **Stonehenge** or **Avebury**, or walks by the Kennet and Avon Canal.

The warm springs that gave Bath its name are said to have been discovered by King Lear's father, but their celebrity can more accurately be dated from the comfort-seeking Romans who developed them in about AD55, calling their settlement Aquae Sulis, after Sul, a local Celtic god.

Aquae Sulis lasted some 400 years, but Bath then had to wait at least another 1,200 years before once again becoming host to a wealthy society set on elegance, ease and pleasure. One woman and three men orchestrated this 18thC Bath: Queen Anne, who simply visited the town and liked it; Richard ('Beau') Nash, a charismatic leader of fashion who became the Master of Ceremonies; and the two architects John Woods, father and son, who, together with others close on their heels, created the honey-colored stone buildings that have since been the glory of Bath.

Bath is easy to explore on foot and, being set amid hills, it best rewards those with willing legs. The center of the city is very crowded in summer, and parking is difficult.

SIGHTS AND PLACES OF INTEREST

A first glimpse of that hillside majesty, embellished with Georgian crescents, is well taken from the train as it slows out of Brunel's tunnel at Box and rumbles toward Bath Spa Station. Out of the station, the immediate impression is uninteresting, but a walk straight ahead down Manvers St. leads to the Georgian Bath in **North** and **South Parades**. A left turn along North Parade leads to **Sally Lunn's Tea House**, after which a traditional English bun is named. It is said to be the oldest house in Bath, and the establishment is reputed to have been a haunt of the dandy and arbiter of social graces Beau Nash himself.

Cut through York St. to the **Abbey Churchyard**, the heart of the city. A Saxon abbey of 791 was followed by a Norman cathedral in 1107, this in turn giving way to today's **abbey**, dating from 1499. On the turrets flanking the w front, carved angels, climbing or descending, are said to represent a dream that inspired the decision to rebuild. Inside, all is height (the nave is nearly three times as high as it is wide), and the superb fan vaulting can be well seen, thanks to the high clerestory windows.

Across the churchyard are the **Roman Baths** and **Pump Room** *(open 9am-5.30pm)*. Public baths, pub, club, health farm, café, temple annex, even tourist lure — all these purposes were served by Aquae Sulis, whose privileged patrons enjoyed not only all the standard facilities of such establishments but also water that was both naturally heated and (although today this is disputed) medicinal. With the departure of the Romans, Aquae Sulis went into decline, finally sinking beneath mud and marsh. In the 18thC, portions reappeared, but it was not until 1878 that the baths were really rediscovered.

A guided tour of the baths affords the opportunity to see the fruits of constant excavations there, ranging from coins to a sacrificial altar. Some years ago it was discovered that Bath's water had been contaminated by

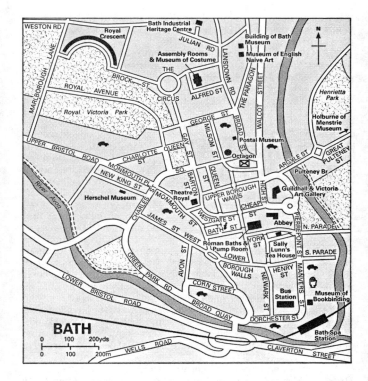

an ameba. Bore holes now reach down below the level of contamination to an uncontaminated source. The water can be sampled from a fountain in the elegant and restful Pump Room, to which came, according to Jane Austen, "every creature in Bath." Since the water tastes, in the words of Dickens' Sam Weller, like a "warm flat iron," it is perhaps as well that the Pump Room serves morning coffee and afternoon tea, sometimes to the accompaniment of string music.

The most spectacular Georgian homes were built on the hillsides to provide their owners with panoramic views. Walk along Bath St. (colonnaded to protect itinerant bathers), turning right at the end, then left into Sawclose, past the lively theater and restaurant area, up Gay St. to The Circus, then along Brock St., to the **Royal Crescent**, Bath's most eye-catching and graceful Georgian feature, begun in 1767. Designed by the younger Wood, it comprises 30 houses and 114 Ionic columns. Cobbles, ironwork and lawns add to the attraction and period atmosphere. The house at **no. 1** opens as a museum in summer *(open Tues-Sat 11am-5pm, Sun 2-5pm)*. Return via The Circus to the **Assembly Rooms** in Alfred St.

The younger John Wood built these elegant rooms in 1771, a German bomb gutted them in 1942, and they were later rebuilt with interior decoration in the original late 18thC style.

The Assembly Rooms also house the **Museum of Costume** *(open Mon-Sat 9.30am-6pm, Sun 10am-6pm)*. Designer and writer Doris Langley Moore started this collection of authentic costumes, which date from 1580 (the oldest complete outfit is a 1660s court dress) to the present day. You may derive light relief if not hilarity from some astonishing underwear.

Royal Crescent

Now return downhill by Lansdown Rd., which in turn becomes Broad St. and then High St., with its Guildhall and covered market, noted for another of the city's culinary delights, the Bath Chap: this turns out to be a pig's jowl!

Such indulgences may subsequently call for a diet of Dr Oliver's remorselessly plain biscuits, for which the city is also known (the more luxurious chocolate-coated version seems at odds with his ascetic intentions), or simply a Bath bun. Determined walkers can shop a little more under cover of Pulteney Bridge, an Italianate delight designed by Robert Adam.

This leads into another fine Georgian street named Argyle St., and thence to nowhere in particular except perhaps, at the end of Forrester Rd., a place where boats can be rented on the River Avon. On weekends, pleasure trips can also be taken on the Kennet and Avon Canal, from Sidney Wharf, near Bathwick Hill, or from the Top Lock, at the far end of North Parade Rd.

Numerous fine museums cater to a wide variery of interests: the **Herschel Museum** *(19 New King St.),* for astronomy and music; the **National Centre of Photography** *(in the Octagon, Milsom St.),* where the building itself merits a visit, in the attractive main shopping street; the **Postal History Museum** *(8 Broad St.);* the **Holburne of Menstrie Museum and Craft Study Centre** *(Great Pulteney St.),* for a fine private collection of silver, decorative art, paintings and miniatures; and the **Building of Bath Museum** and **Museum of English Naive Art** *(both in the Countess of Huntingdon's Chapel, The Vineyard, The Paragon).*

SIGHTS NEARBY

A unique attraction a couple of miles out of the city, at Claverton Down, is the **American Museum in Britain** *(open Tues-Sun 2-5pm).* This has Indian and folk art, interiors of early American homes, including Shaker and Pennsylvania Dutch settings, relics of the West, and gardens that replicate George Washington's at Mount Vernon. Wander through the 18 period-furnished rooms and galleries of textiles, pewter, glass, silver and folk art illustrating American life between the 17th and 19thC. The New Gallery houses a permanent exhibition of the Dallas

Pratt collection of historical maps. The museum bakes its own selection of cakes, cookies and gingerbread, making for a deliciously nostalgic afternoon tea.

Dyrham Park *(8 miles/13km to the N of Bath, open Apr-Nov Sat-Wed noon-5.30pm)* was the site of one of the most decisive battles of early British history, for it was here in 577 that the Saxons defeated the Britons, next advancing to the Severn and finally dividing the Celtic inhabitants of these islands. More than a thousand years later, in the late 17thC, William Blathwayt built his fine home here, a fitting place for a man who was secretary of state to King William III, and one in which he delighted to indulge in the Dutch styles that came over with his new sovereign — leather wall hangings, tapestry, Delftware and some fine pictures by notable Dutch artists.

Lacock Abbey *(12 miles/19km E of Bath, open Apr-Oct 2-6pm, closed Tues)* is well worth the trip. Many a country mansion has its roots in a dissolved religious house, but where Lacock differs is in the way it has preserved the medieval cloisters and much of the conventual buildings of the early 13thC nunnery whose site it usurped. The 18thC brought Neo-Gothic alterations, including a great hall built by the great-grand-father of W.H. Fox Talbot (1800-77), creator of the first photographic negative, commemorated at the abbey entrance by the **Fox Talbot Museum** of early photography. **Lacock Village**, unspoiled and enchanting, is also owned by the National Trust.

Maritime enthusiasts might wish to see Brunel's **SS *Great Britain***, on display in the Great Western Dock in the nearby city and port of **Bristol.** Adjacent is the Maritime Heritage Centre. In the opposite direction, a drive into the spectacular Mendip Hills leads to the small city of **Wells**, with one of Britain's most beautiful Gothic cathedrals and its adjacent Bishop's Palace.

✎   The new **Bath Spa** hotel *(Sydney Rd.* ☎ *444424 ▥▥)* is lavishly appointed in the grand London manner, whereas the **Priory** *(see below ▥▥)* and the **Royal Crescent Hotel** *(▦ ☎ 319090 ▥▥)* are especially comfortable and full of personal touches. The friendly **Pratt's** *(South Parade* ☎ *460441 ▥)* and the more sophisticated **Francis** *(Queen Sq.* ☎ *424257 ▥)* are both centrally placed.

There are many bed-and-breakfast places along **Pulteney Rd.** and **Wells Rd.** A recommended B & B is **Haydon House** *(9 Bloomfield Pk.* ☎ *427351 ▢)*. Also recommended is the delightful **Eagle House** *(Church St., Bathford* ☎ *859946 ▢)*, a Georgian mansion 3 miles (5km) outside Bath, run with care by its friendly owners.

🍴   Rich but subtle sauces feature in the opulent restaurant at the **Priory Hotel** *(Weston Rd.* ☎ *331922 ▥▥)*. The French restaurant **Clos du Roy** run by flamboyant chef Philippe Roy is sited in a small and elegant hotel, **Box House** *(Box* ☎ *744447 ▥▥)*. Its place in Bath has now been taken by **Garlands** *(7 Edgar Buildings, George St.* ☎ *442283 ▥▥)*.

Other highly regarded places are **Beaujolais** *(5a Chapel Row, Queen Sq.* ☎ *423417 ▥)*, which serves good bistro food; **Moon and Sixpence** *(6a Broad St.* ☎ *460962 ▥)*, also relaxed; **Woods** *(9-13 Alfred St.* ☎ *314812 ▥)*; **Circus** *(34 Brock St.* ☎ *330208 ▥)*; and, for a snack or a full meal, **Tarts** *(8 Pierrepont Pl.* ☎ *330280 ▢ to ▥)*. Excellent for breakfast, light lunches or teas is **Canary** *(3 Queen St.* ☎ *424846)*.

BRIGHTON

53 miles (85km) s of London. Population: 145,000. By train, 51mins from Victoria, trains twice hourly: by car, A23, then M23 ☎*code (0273)*
i Marlborough House, 54 Old Steine ☎*23755.*

One-day excursion: the speed and frequency of the trains and the labyrinthine quality of the roads out of South London deter most day-trippers from taking a car, but weekenders might wish to do so to explore the Downs and the Sussex countryside around Brighton.

This seaside resort is beloved by many Londoners for its wry mix of Regency elegance and Graham Greene seediness. A day out in Brighton is a quintessential English experience. The craze for sea-bathing in the late 1700s, and the Prince Regent's subsequent attentions, gave Brighton a social status it never entirely surrendered and to which its residents still cling.

The Regency terraces, squares and crescents provide the elegance, crowned by the extravagant fantasies of the Royal Pavilion. Such an Aladdin's cave of Orientalia is an appropriate centerpiece to a town noted for its antique stores, the most celebrated of which, along with some interesting fish restaurants, are in a neighborhood called The Lanes. Not far away, Volks, an antique electric railway, the first in Britain, runs from one of the town's two Victorian piers along the pebbly beach to the swimming pool and marina. The journey can be continued by open-topped bus, or on foot, to the village of Rottingdean.

SIGHTS AND PLACES OF INTEREST

From the railway station, Queen's Rd. and Trafalgar St. are the boundaries of an antiques-and-boutiques area called **North Laine**, which is less pretty but also less expensive than The Lanes. Within this area, in Upper Gardener St., there is a Saturday-morning flea market.

In the arches below the station at 52-55 Trafalgar St. is the **Sussex Toy and Model Museum** *(open Tues-Sun 10am-1pm, 2-5pm)*. A child's paradise, it boasts perfectly preserved 1930s electric model railways, a miniature *Southern Belle* in chocolate and cream livery (from the legendary Pullman train that ran from London to Brighton until the 1970s), as well as a host of other classic toys, from soldiers and forts to farms, ships, airplanes and buses.

A half-mile walk down Queen's Rd. leads to Church St. on the left and **Brighton Museum and Art Gallery** *(open Mon, Tues, Thurs-Sat 10am-5.45pm, Sun 2-5pm)*, housing major Art Nouveau and Art Deco collections of furniture and decorative art, an award-winning fashion gallery, a fine display of musical instruments, the famous Willett Collection of pottery and porcelain, as well as English watercolors and Old Masters.

Just beyond is the **Royal Pavilion** *(open Jan-May, Oct-Dec 10am-5pm, June-Sept 10am-6pm ✦)*. The royal flourish was bestowed upon Brighton by the Prince Regent, the later George IV, said to have gone there to escape his father. While there in 1785 he secretly, illegally married a Catholic, Mrs Fitzherbert, a twice-widowed commoner. The Pavilion was his summer palace, although he left it soon after its completion.

The bizarre mock-Indian architecture, with its onion-shaped domes and minarets, most of it by Nash, derives from the fashionability of Oriental themes during a period of great trade with the East. There was room for discordance within this preoccupation; the interior was decorated in "the Chinese taste." Although currently undergoing an extensive structural restoration, the Pavilion affords visitors a good hour's browse through eccentric splendor, with huge dragons, exotic birds and chandeliers, in a whole series of room settings.

From the Pavilion one wanders into **The Lanes**, where the fashionable and fascinating shops often close on Sunday, but many stay open late on Thursday. From there it is a few minutes' walk down to the seafront. To the right, about half a mile along the beach, is the **West Pier**, built in 1866, and a century later the memorable setting for the movie *Oh, What a Lovely War*. The pier now stands forlorn, unsafe, closed to visitors, and with an uncertain future. In that direction are some fine Georgian buildings, notably in **Regency Square**, as Brighton blends into its sister town of **Hove**.

In a more central position on the seafront is the **Palace Pier**, built in 1891, a rich symbol of British seaside frolics. Just to the left of the pier is the Aquarium, dating from 1872, but completely refurbished and updated in 1991, and now called the **Sea Life Centre** *(open 10am-6pm, later in summer)*. It incorporates 35 fascinating displays, which include a sandy seabed, alive with skates and stingrays, and an intriguing audiovisual presentation of the world of whales and dolphins.

From here, catch the aforementioned **Volk's Electric Railway** *(open Easter-Oct)*. The railway, named after its founder, was opened in 1883, but at its terminus now is the largest yachting marina in Europe, around which a modern "village" of shops, pubs and restaurants has been built. There are walks along the breakwaters, and pleasure trips and deep-sea angling. Beyond the marina, the resort that once popularized bathing machines now has an area of beach set aside for those who prefer nudity, a bracing facility that's only a whistle away from one of England's most famous girls' schools, **Roedean**, on the way to **Rottingdean**.

SIGHTS NEARBY

Just outside the center of Brighton, to the N of the station, are two sights of interest. At 194 Dyke Rd., the **Booth Museum of Natural History** *(open Mon-Wed, Fri, Sat 10am-5pm, Sun 2-5pm)* contains a marvelous display of British birds in their natural habitats, butterflies, animal skeletons and the bones of a local dinosaur.

Farther N, in Preston Rd., **Preston Manor** *(open Tues-Sat 10am-5pm, Sun 2-5pm)* dates back to 1250, though little of the original house remains. It was substantially rebuilt in the 18thC, extended in 1905, and today its interest lies in its fine collections of furniture, pictures and silver, and the glimpse of "upstairs/downstairs" Edwardian life that it reveals. It has a lovely old-fashioned walled garden and a pets' cemetery.

Walkers enjoy the South Downs, a range of chalk hills that runs just inland from Brighton and stretches N for 80 miles (128km). A bus from the seafront to the crest of **Devil's Dyke** offers superb views and a half-hour walk to the **church at Poynings**.

Another starting point for a number of walks is **Foredown Tower** in Foredown Rd., Portslade *(open Apr-Sept 10.30am-6pm, Oct-Mar Thurs-Sun 10.30am-5pm)*, which was built in 1909 and now acts as a countryside center. At the top, its camera obscura also affords spectacular views of the surrounding country. The Tourist Information Centre has detailed information on walks.

In the Sussex countryside, several towns and villages are worth a visit, including **Lewes**, with a castle, interesting pubs and good walks; **Sheffield Park**, for its Capability Brown gardens and a full-scale steam railway; and another castle, **Arundel**, a sometimes grotesque museum of curiosities, housing an arts festival held in late August.

❧ Brighton has an enormous selection of hotels, and the Tourist Information Centre has a reservations service. Two famous Victorian seafront hotels are the **Metropole** *(☎ 775432 [Fx]207764 ⅢⅢ)* — rather unfairly notorious for furtive weekend couples — and the **Grand** *(☎ 21188 [Fx]202694 ⅢⅢ)*, bombed with tragic consequences by the IRA at the 1984 Conservative Party Conference but since that time renovated and reopened. Both are in King's Rd., as is the **Old Ship Hotel** *(☎ 29001 [Fx]820718 ⅢⅢ)*, which started life as a fishermen's inn, was associated with the escape to France of Charles II, became an important social haunt in Regency times, and has a fine 18thC ballroom.

≡ In The Lanes, **English's Oyster Bar** *(29 East St. ☎ 27980 ⅢⅢ)* is something of an institution. Despite its name, it is a full-scale restaurant, and it is advisable to reserve in advance. A cozy alternative, where the seafood is equally fresh, is **D'Arcys** *(49 Market St. ☎ 25560 ⅢⅢ)*. **Wheeler's** *(17 Market St. ☎ 25135 ⅢⅢ)* is a branch of the famous London chain of fish restaurants, known for its sole. A good vegetarian café is **Food for Friends** *(41 Market St. ☎ 736236 ⅢⅢ)*. At the edge of The Lanes, a tea shop called **The Mock Turtle** *(4 Pool Valley)* sells homemade cakes and lunchtime snacks.

Elsewhere in Brighton, **Langan's** *(1 Paston Pl. ☎ 606933 ⅢⅢ)* and **Le Grand-gousier** *(15 Western St. ☎ 772005 ⅢⅢ)* are good-value bistros.

CAMBRIDGE
54 miles (86km) N London. Population: 105,000. By train, about 75mins from Liverpool Street (direct) or King's Cross (faster route, with a change), 2 or 3 trains hourly; by car, M11, 90mins ☎ code (0223) i Wheeler St. ☎ 322640.
One-day excursion: being linked to London by motorway, Cambridge is easily reached by car. The town is encircled by car parks: cars should not be taken into the center.

The first scholars came from Oxford to Cambridge in 1209, and the first college, Peterhouse, was founded in 1284. Modern times have seen F.R. Leavis, a lion among literary critics, the splitting of the atom by Rutherford, and the work of Crick and Watson in establishing the double helix structure of DNA. For all its architectural similarities to Oxford, this "younger" of Britain's two great university cities is distinguished by the larger scale of its colleges, its lower skyline (it is not, unlike Oxford, an industrial town), its paler stone, and its geographical setting on the edge of flat and water-laced Fen country.

One of the joys of Cambridge is that its plan is so straightforward. For all practical purposes only one street, or sequence of streets, needs to be kept in mind. Starting in the N at the Church of the Holy Sepulchre (a rare medieval round church, but much modernized), the sequence of St John's St. and Trinity St., King's Parade and Trumpington St., splits Cambridge into two. To the w, between this axis and the river, are most of the more interesting colleges, founded between the 13th and 16thC and filling a strip only some 900 yards long. To the E of the road sequence — and hemmed in by an eastern line of 16thC colleges along Bridge St., Sidney St. and St Andrew's St. — crowds inner Cambridge, its market place filled with a colorful collection of stalls.

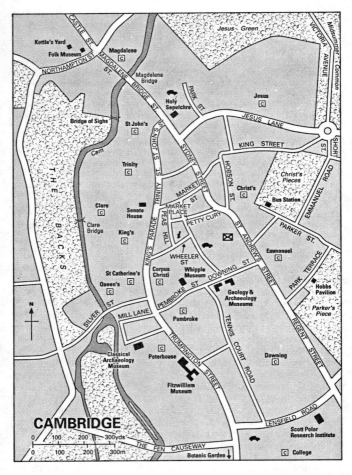

CAMBRIDGE

| 0 | 100 | 200 | 300yds |
| 0 | 100 | 200 | 300m |

C College

If this sightseeing convenience is one advantage that Cambridge enjoys over Oxford, another — and it is a superlative one — is that its small river, the Cam or Granta, flows gently beside some of the most beautiful of the colleges. Landscaped with lawns and trees and offering a dazzling architectural feast, these justly famous Backs are best enjoyed on foot or by boat. In summer the river is crowded with punts, often making their way to **Granchester** village some three miles away, immortalized by the poet Rupert Brooke.

Most of the colleges can be visited except between May and June, and there are daily tours starting from the Tourist Information Centre at 2pm (more frequently in summer). It is advisable to book an hour before the tour starts.

SIGHTS AND PLACES OF INTEREST

Close to the bus station is **Emmanuel College**, where John Harvard was a pupil in the 17thC. Emmanuel's chapel is one of several fine Wren buildings in Cambridge. Across St Andrew's St., in Downing St., are the **Museums of Geology and Archaeology**. Downing St. bends into Pembroke St. and **Pembroke College**, which also has a Wren chapel. Parallel with Pembroke St. is Botolph Lane, beyond which lies **Corpus Christi**, with its fine 14thC collegiate building in Old Court, a place of mellow medieval charm, and the university's best example of a court of this early period.

Turn left from Pembroke St. into Trumpington St. for the **Fitzwilliam Museum** *(open Tues-Sat 10am-5pm, Sun 2.15-5pm)*, which has an outstanding collection, including paintings by Gainsborough, Turner, Rembrandt, Renoir and Degas, drawings by Hogarth, Dürer, Michelangelo and Leonardo, and Blake's illuminated books, as well as Roman, Greek, Egyptian and Eastern antiquities and English pottery and porcelain.

Return along Trumpington St., turning left for the colleges of **St Catherine's** and **Queens'** (1448), the latter with its hall, exuberantly decorated in the 19thC by William Morris, Tudor courtyard, Cloister Court (an intimate 15thC gem in dark red brick), and Mathematical Bridge.

Nearby, at Mill Lane (and farther along, at Magdalene Bridge), rowboats and punts can be rented on the river. Along this stretch of the water are five more colleges, **King's**, **Clare**, **Trinity**, **St John's** and **Magdalene**. The Backs refer to the grassy bank facing the first two of these colleges, a superlative architectural vista.

King's College chapel, unquestioned star of Cambridge, is an outstanding example of Perpendicular architecture, built between 1446-1515, with glass by Flemish craftsmen. Among its treasures is the altarpiece, *The Adoration of the Magi,* by Rubens, given to the chapel in 1961. Satisfying as it is from the outside, it is the chapel's interior that has earned it centuries of acclaim. Perhaps the w end is over-heavy in Tudor decorative motif, but beyond the screen, rows of slim stained-glass windows soar upward to meet a great honeycomb of exquisite fan-vaulting. Nearby, on King's Parade, is the **Senate House**, a Georgian building in which the University's "Parliament" sits.

King's College Chapel vaulting — detail

Clare College was founded in 1326, but the present building, like a perfectly proportioned tiny palace, was built in the 1600s. It has lovely gardens opposite the elegant Clare Bridge. Trinity, with its Great Court, fountain and many-windowed Wren library, is the largest and richest of the colleges. Its alumni have included Bacon, Byron, Macaulay, Tennyson and Thackeray. In the library are manuscripts by Tennyson, Thackeray and Milton. The famous bookstore, **Heffers**, is in Trinity St., as is **Sheratt and Hughes**, which used to be the equally famous Bowes and Bowes, and nearby is **Belinda's**, for excellent teas and cakes.

St John's (1511), with its wedding-cake silhouette and Tudor gateway, is architecturally an acquired taste, but its "Bridge of Sighs" is a splendid gesture. Properly known as New Bridge, it was built in 1831. St John's chapel was also built in the 1800s, by Sir George Gilbert Scott. At the end of this stretch of river, Magdalene College (1524), favored by the aristocracy, has Samuel Pepys' library, in the original bookcases.

Across the road from Magdalene St., in Castle St., the **Folk Museum** *(open Mon-Sat 10.30am-5pm, Sun 2-5pm, closed Mon Oct-Mar)*, in a converted inn, has an engrossing collection of domestic and agricultural objects from Cambridgeshire. In the opposite direction, in Bridge St., is one of only five round churches in England, the **Church of the Holy Sepulchre**, modeled on its namesake in Jerusalem.

From Bridge St., turn left for **Jesus College**, which was once a convent. The windows in the chapel were designed by Burne-Jones and made in the William Morris workshop. Behind the college are Jesus Green and Midsummer Common, separated by Maid's Causeway and Short St. from another stretch of open grass, offhandedly known as Christ's Pieces.

Next to the railway station is another stretch of open grassland called Parker's Piece, with a restaurant called **Hobbs' Pavilion**, popular with students. The restaurant, a converted cricket pavilion, is named after the great batsman Jack Hobbs. Nearby, in Lensfield Rd., is the **Scott Polar Research Institute**, named after the explorer, with relics of expeditions.

Nearby too, off Trumpington Rd., are the University's **Botanic Gardens**. These uncrowded and beautifully scented gardens were laid out in 1846, primarily for the purpose of research. In Northampton St. is **Kettles Yard** *(open Mon-Sat noon-6pm, Sun 2-6pm)*, a museum of 20thC art and sculpture, once a private house and still blessed with a unique atmosphere.

SIGHT NEARBY
The **Imperial War Museum (Air)** *(Duxford Airfield, on A505, 8 miles/13km s of Cambridge; open Mar-Oct 11am-5.30pm.)* This famous Battle of Britain fighter airfield is now the home of historic aircraft, from a Blériot monoplane of 1910 to the Concorde prototype. Several of the aircraft fly, and throughout the season there are special events.

✿ The **Garden House Hotel** *(Mill Lane* ☎ *63421* 🔳*)* is one of the city's best-known hotels, with a better-than-average restaurant, pretty gardens and river views. Also on the river is the smaller, comfortable **Arundel House** *(53 Chesterton Rd.* ☎ *67701* 🔳*)*, in a Victorian terrace.

An excellent guesthouse is **No. 136** *(136 Huntingdon Rd.* ☎ *461142* 🔳*)*. Also recommended is **Gonville Hotel** *(Gonville Pl.* ☎ *66611* 🔳*)*.

▬ There has been a gastronomic renaissance in Cambridge in recent years. Among the newcomers are **Midsummer House** *(Midsummer Common* ☎ *69299* 🔳*)*, which serves imaginative English food in a converted common-keeper's cottage, and **Browns** *(23 Trumpington St.* ☎ *461655* 🔳*)*, an American-style restaurant with polished wood floors, ceiling fans and bentwood chairs, where the fare includes pasta, salads, char-grilled steaks and hamburgers.

In an unremarkable terraced house in Chesterton Rd., **Twenty Two** (☎ *351880* ▥ *)* produces some excellent food, and mouthwatering modern British dishes are served there in an attractive, informal pink dining room. **Hobbs' Pavillion** *(Park Terr.* ☎ *67480* ▢ *)* serves crêpes, salads and its own ice cream; and **Shao Tao** *(72 Regent St.* ☎ *353942* ▥ *)* is one of the city's numerous good Chinese restaurants.

Local pubs serving good food are the **Free Press** *(7 Prospect Row)*, the **Fort St George** on Midsummer Common and the crankily English **Tickell Arms** at Whittlesford, a mere 15 minutes' drive away.

CANTERBURY

61 miles (98km) SE of London. Population: 41,000. By train, about 80mins to Canterbury East from Victoria, trains hourly, about 100mins to Canterbury West from Charing Cross, trains hourly; by car, A2 and M2 ☎ *code (0227)* **i** *34 St Margaret's St.* ☎ *766567.*

One-day excursion: there are good train services to both stations in this famous cathedral city in Kent; and if you come by car, you can park in one of a number of car parks conveniently located in a ring around the city center.

The Romans came to Canterbury first but, not long after their departure, Bertha, Christian queen of Ethelbert of Kent, invited St Augustine to her court in 597. Ethelbert, a remarkably indulgent husband, was soon converted, and a year later Augustine founded his abbey, followed by a church which soon received cathedral status, with Augustine as its first Archbishop.

View of **Canterbury Cathedral** from the southwest.

From this point on the story of Canterbury is essentially that of its cathedral and of the pilgrims (such as those in Chaucer's *Canterbury Tales*) who ceaselessly flocked to it. The cathedral is not all that this ancient city has to offer, however; there are Roman remains, a Norman keep, picturesque medieval houses, the West Gate, and a splendid length of 14th-15thC walls.

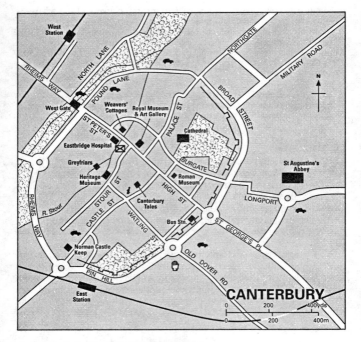

SIGHTS AND PLACES OF INTEREST

A walking tour of Canterbury has to start with the **cathedral** (★), whose great gray towers dominate the city. The mother church of England stands on the site of St Augustine's original church, which was burned down in 1067. Rebuilding began three years later, but the cathedral was not completed until 1503. Historically, Canterbury's most important date is 1170, when the "turbulent priest" Thomas à Becket was murdered in the cathedral, the martyr's shrine in the Trinity Chapel becoming (and remaining until destroyed at the Reformation) one of the most important places of pilgrimage in Britain. The site of the murder, known as the Martyrdom, is in the NW transept.

Among the wealth of detail inside the cathedral are several features which on no account should be missed: the way in which elaborate screens and canopied tombs separate the choir from its aisles; in the Trinity Chapel, the great tombs of Henry IV, the only monarch to rest in Canterbury, and of the Black Prince; the fan vaulting of the Lady Chapel just E of the NW transept; the Great Cloister (c.1400), with its painted bosses; the spacious and lofty Chapter House; the ingenious Norman water tower to the NE of the cloister; the medieval stained glass; and the crypt, where Becket's body was entombed until 1220. Behind the cathedral, within the precincts of King's School, is a **Norman Staircase**, one of the finest pieces of Norman architecture in England.

Almost within the shadow of the cathedral, in Butchery Lane, the **Roman Museum** *(☎ 452747 for opening times)*, a new museum opened in late 1992, is designed around the preserved remains of a Roman mosaic floor, which bears the evidence of under-floor central heating. Cross the pedestrianized High St., turn right and then left into St Margaret's St., where the **Canterbury Tales** *(open Mon-Sat 9am-5.30pm, Sun 9.30am-5.30pm)* brings Chaucer's pilgrims to life through an audiovisual re-creation of the tales.

Retrace your steps back to the High St., and turn left for the **Royal Museum and Art Gallery** *(open Mon-Sat 10am-5pm)*, Canterbury's principal museum, which has both permanent collections and temporary exhibitions, and incorporates the museum of the Royal East Kent Regiment. The archeological material includes Roman and Saxon jewelry and glass. Wander along pretty Palace St. to the N for a worthwhile detour.

Otherwise, turn right out of the museum, up the High St., which soon becomes St Peter's St., and on the right, overhanging the River Stour, are the attractive, well-restored Tudor **Weavers' Cottages**, homes of Flemish and Huguenot refugees, who fled religious persecution and settled here during Elizabeth I's reign to practice weaving and dyeing.

Opposite the cottages is the **Eastbridge Hospital of St Thomas the Martyr** *(open Mon-Sat 10am-5pm, Sun 11am-5pm)*, an ancient hospice for poor pilgrims, founded in 1180, and carefully sited so that the guests could perform their ablutions in the river Stour. Today's visitors see the chapel, Norman crypt, and refectory with an early 13thC mural. Off the High St., Stour St. leads down to **Canterbury Heritage Museum** *(open Mon-Sat 10.30am-4pm, June-Oct Sun 1.30-4pm)*, set in a stunning medieval building on the riverbank, originally an almshouse for elderly priests. The award-winning museum is crammed with treasures covering the city's 2,000-year history. The oldest Franciscan building in Britain, 13thC **Greyfriars House**, the only surviving part of a large Franciscan settlement, spans the river nearby.

At the w end of the city in St Peter's St. is the well-fortified **West Gate**, built in 1380, and the last surviving gate by which travelers used to enter the city, and **West Gate Museum** *(open Mon-Sat 11am-12.30pm, 1.30-3pm)*, featuring arms and armor from the Civil War to World War II. At the E end of the city in Longport, you can see the ruins of the Norman **St Augustine's Abbey** *(open daily 10am-1pm, Easter to Sept 2-6pm, Oct to Easter 2-4pm)*, with a well-preserved crypt.

SIGHT NEARBY

Richborough, 9 miles (14.5km) E of Canterbury, is generally held to be where the Romans landed in AD43, but although there was soon a fort here, the surviving ruins of **Richborough Castle** *(open Easter-Sept daily 10am-1pm, 2-6pm, Oct-Easter Tues-Sun 10am-1pm, 2-4pm)* mainly represent the strengthened defenses put up in the late 3rdC to deter the even bolder Saxons. The site is impressive, a place that even today strikes one as a daunting great square of earthworks and stone.

✍ Beams, antiques, four-poster beds and open fires all combine to continue the welcome that the **County** *(High St.* ☎ *766266* Ⓕⓧ*451512* ▥ *)* has extended to travelers since the 16thC. It is as central and convenient today as its site was nearly 2,000 years ago when the Roman forum stood here. The **Falstaff** *(St Dunstan's St.* ☎ *462138* Ⓕⓧ*463525* ▥ *)* is a former coaching inn dating largely from the early 15thC, and has great character both inside and out, and all mod cons.

From a different era, the **Ebury** *(65-67 New Dover Rd.* ☎ *768433* Ⓕⓧ*459187* ▥ *to* ▥ *)* is a family-run hotel in two Victorian houses, with a big garden, indoor swimming pool and self-catering (efficiency) accommodation available.

☲ In the County Hotel, **Sully's** *(* ☎ *766266* ▥ *)* is a formal restaurant, with attractive decor and a French-influenced menu. **Tuo e Mio** *(16 The Borough* ☎ *761471* ▥ *)* is a smart Italian restaurant, with good fresh food and a convivial atmosphere.

For simpler eating, **Il Vaticano** *(35 St Margaret's St.* ☎ *765333* ▥ *)* and **Pizza Place Ltd** *(87-88 Northgate* ☎ *451556* ▥ *to* ▥ *)* both serve excellent pizzas, and **Caesars** *(46 St Peter's St.* ☎ *456833* ▥ *)* is a popular, lively restaurant serving hamburgers and pasta.

OXFORD

56 miles (90km) NW of London, Population: 109,000. By train, 60mins from Paddington, trains hourly; by car, 90mins, A40, then M40; by coach, Thames Transit Ltd (Horspath Rd., Oxford ☎*(0865) 778849) provides a service between Oxford and London, The Oxford Tube, which operates Mon-Sat throughout the day from Victoria Station, Marble Arch, Notting Hill Gate and Shepherds Bush* ☎*code (0865) i St Aldate's* ☎*726871.*

One-day excursion: a finely-crafted jewel of a city, Oxford has to be protected against invasion by cars. There is a ring of car parks and a "Park and Ride" bus service.

It has been a university town since the 1200s, and has provided Britain with many of its most famous achievers: enough prime ministers to make a cricket team, writers ranging from Wilde to Tolkien, and adventurers from Raleigh to Rhodes. Oxford's colleges and quadrangles dominate the center of the city, rich in their architectural diversity but with a preponderance of Gothic among their turrets, towers and dreaming spires. Some of the colleges are walled, although most of them can be visited in the afternoons (and all day during vacations, usually for a month around Christmas and Easter, and July to September).

As a seat of learning, Oxford also has institutions such as the Bodleian Library and Ashmolean Museum, and famous bookstores. There are the mutual attractions of punting on the river and unstrenuous walks by the waterside. Beyond the city, the countryside reaches out to the Chiltern Hills and Cotswold Hills.

SIGHTS AND PLACES OF INTEREST

An impressive start to a day in Oxford might be at the **Ashmolean Museum** *(open Tues-Sat 10am-4pm, Sun 2-4pm, bank holiday Mon 2-5pm),* one of Britain's finest museums, with riches ranging from Egyptian sculpture to Michelangelo and Raphael drawings, from silverware and musical instruments to John Tradescant's natural-history collection.

Highlights include the 7thC BC Shrine of Taharqa in the Egyptian Sculpture Gallery, the exquisite 9thC Alfred Jewel in the Medieval Room, and the famous Arthur Evans antiquities from Knossos in Crete. Ten galleries are devoted to fine art, displaying works by Tintoretto, Rubens, Van Dyck, Canaletto, Poussin, Hogarth, Reynolds, Burne-Jones, Corot and Daubigny, among others. Look out for Paolo Uccello's fairy-tale *Hunt in the Forest* and Pissarro's *Portrait of Jeanne with a Fan*.

The Victorian Ashmolean building is at the corner of Beaumont St. and St Giles, from which Magdalen St. runs into Broad St., better known as the Broad, the address of the famous **Blackwell's** bookstore (this and Foyle's in London's Charing Cross Rd. are the two most extensive bookstores in Britain), where browsers are welcome. Also housed in this part of Broad St. is an audiovisual display, **The Story of Oxford** *(open daily Apr-June, Sept, Oct 9.30am-5pm, July, Aug 9.30am-7pm, Nov-Mar 10am-4pm),* and a small and friendly pub called the **White Horse**.

On this stretch of walk are the rival colleges of **Trinity**, with charming 17thC buildings and a rose garden, and **Balliol**, founded in the 13thC and especially influential in the development of the university, with a beautiful garden quadrangle. Opposite Balliol on Broad St. is **Exeter College**, the place of conception of the pre-Raphaelite Brotherhood.

To the right off Broad St. is the **Sheldonian Theatre** *(open daily 10am-12.45pm, 2-4.45pm),* the first building designed by Wren, in 1662. The theater, which is modeled on those of ancient Rome, semicircular at one end and with a superb painted ceiling, was named after its benefactor Archbishop Sheldon, and today is used for university functions and concerts.

Nearby in Broad St. is the attractive 17thC building that houses the **Museum of the History of**

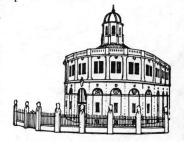

The Sheldonian Theatre, Oxford

Science *(open Mon-Fri 10.30am-1pm, 2.30-4pm)* and its interesting collection of sundials, microscopes, clocks and cameras. Behind the Sheldonian Theatre is the **Bodleian Library** *(open Mon-Fri 9am-10pm, Sat 9am-1pm),* named after Sir Thomas Bodley, who donated his own collection in 1598. Said to be the oldest library in the world, it contains 3 million books. The part known as the Divinity School, with a beautiful late Gothic low-vaulted ceiling, has folios and first editions of works by Shakespeare, Milton, Swift and Pope, among others, and is notorious as the scene of the interrogation in 1555 of Bishops Cranmer, Ridley and Latimer, all burned at the stake opposite nearby Balliol College.

Also within the Bodleian is the **Radcliffe Camera**, a striking domed rotunda designed by James Gibbs in 1739. To the left across Catte St. is **All Souls College**, with its celebrated twin towers by Hawksmoor. Behind All Souls is **New College**, founded in 1379 by William of Wykeham, Bishop of Winchester. Its buildings are fine examples of late 14thC

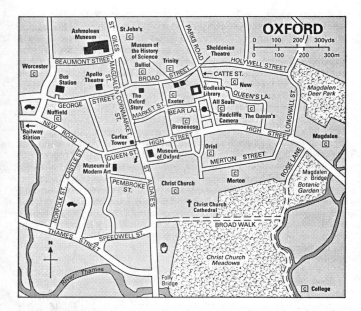

Perpendicular architecture, and it has a magnificent chapel, with a Victorian interior, a painting of *St James* by El Greco and a statue of *Lazarus* by Epstein. Parts of the medieval city wall can be seen in its gardens. Tea shops in nearby Holywell St. serve delicious cream teas.

Holywell St. leads into Longwall, from which the Magdalen deer park can be seen. Where Longwall reaches High St. a turn to the right along Merton St. leads to the mellow and picturesque **Merton College**, with the oldest quadrangle in Oxford, the Mob Quad, dating from the 1300s. The chapel is also the university's oldest, and the library (1378) claims the curious distinction of being the first to store its books on shelves rather than in chests.

A turn to the left, through Christ Church Meadows, leads to **Magdalen College**, the most beautiful of the colleges, with its Perpendicular bell tower from which the choir sings at 6am on May Day morning. Traces of the original Hospital of St John can be found in the Chaplain's Quadrangle and the kitchen, but one of the most attractive and individual parts of the college is the 15th-16thC Cloister Quadrangle, its buttresses decorated with amusing grotesques.

At Magdalen and Folly Bridges punts can be rented. From Rose Lane, a footpath runs around Christ Church Meadow, following the River Thames. Alongside Rose Lane are the **Botanic Gardens**, which date back to 1621, when they were founded as the medical faculty's physick garden. The gateway of 1630 is by Nicholas Stone.

Walk back along High St. and turn left into St Aldate's for the **Museum of Oxford** *(open Tues-Sat 10am-4.40pm)*, where the history of the city is imaginatively told through models, old prints and maps and special exhibitions.

Dodge off to the right down Pembroke St. if you are interested in the **Museum of Modern Art** *(open Tues, Wed, Fri, Sat 10am-6pm, Thurs 10am-9pm, Sun 2-6pm)*, in a converted brewery, and then continue s down St Aldate's to see Oxford's largest college, **Christ Church**, and its **cathedral**. Cardinal Wolsey founded Cardinal College on this site in 1525, razing most of the priory that stood here at that time. Four years later everything stopped when Wolsey fell from power, but in 1532 Henry VIII stepped in to found his own college. Soon, however, this was suppressed to give way in 1545 to the new college of Christ Church.

The 12thC Norman cathedral, the smallest in England, enjoys the curious status of being both the city's cathedral and the college's chapel, and is virtually all that survives of the priory razed by Wolsey. Among a number of points of note are the alternating round and octagonal nave piers, the late 15thC choir ceiling, and the cloister, scene of Cranmer's humiliation when his head was shorn and his vestments were stripped from him. The hall of 1529 is the largest in Oxford and boasts a notable collection of portraits, including those of *King Henry VIII, Queen Elizabeth I* and *Cardinal Thomas Wolsey.*

On the w side of the huge open Great Quadrangle or Tom Quad, much of which dates from Wolsey's time, the college's principal entrance is provided by Wolsey's gateway, topped by Tom Tower, built by Wren in 1681, and famous for its great bell, which tolls 101 times every evening in honor of each member of the original foundation.

Christ Church contains the finest college collection of drawings in its **Picture Gallery** *(open Mon-Sat 10.30am-1pm, Easter-Sept daily 2-5.30pm, Oct-Easter daily 2-4.30pm)*, with an emphasis on 14th-17thC Italian artists, including Leonardo, Michelangelo and Raphael.

SIGHTS NEARBY
Blenheim Palace is 8 miles (13km) N of Oxford. Even without the grand Baroque design of Vanbrugh and the landscaping of Capability Brown, the Churchills' ancestral home and nearby burial place would have a magnetic appeal; but the combination of historic and esthetic interest is irresistible.

The enormous Blenheim Palace and Park *(open mid-Mar to Oct 10.30am-4.45pm)* are at the small town of **Woodstock**, which has resonances quite different from those of its American descendant. There are buses every half-hour from Cornmarket. Apart from its assembly of Churchill artifacts, the palace has a large collection of paintings, tapestries, sculpture and furniture. Perhaps the most magnificent room is the Long Library, which contains more than 10,000 volumes as well as 17thC Oriental porcelain, and has carvings by Grinling Gibbons.

The palace was built by a grateful Queen Anne for John Churchill, First Duke of Marlborough, to mark his victory over the French at the Battle of Blenheim in 1704; groups of trees were planted in the park to form the plan of the battle. Winston Churchill, grandson of the 7th Duke, was born there on November 30, 1874. He is buried in the churchyard at Bladon, on the edge of the park.

✍ For a city that attracts many visitors, Oxford does not flaunt its hotels, but the Tourist Information Centre does have a special telephone accommodation register. Among the city's better-known hotels are the **Randolph** *(Beaumont St.* ☎ *247481* ☒ *791678* ▥*)*, with its Edwardian plush, and **Linton Lodge** *(Linton Rd.* ☎ *53461* ☒ *310365* ▥*)*, which has very pleasant gardens. **Eastgate** *(High St.* ☎ *248244* ☒ *791681* ▥*)* is another delightful hotel, traditional, comfortable, and with an academic ambience.

There are a good number of bed-and-breakfast places around Abingdon Rd., St John's St. and Walton St.

Seven miles (10km) E of Oxford is Raymond Blanc's much-praised and visited hotel and restaurant, **Le Manoir aux Quat' Saisons** *(Great Milton* ☎ *(0844) 278881* ☒ *(0844) 278847* ▥*)*, a 15thC manor house with oak beams, antiques and oil paintings, set in 25 acres of gardens. Beautifully decorated bedrooms enjoy every possible luxury, and Raymond Blanc is still performing culinary miracles in the attractive, airy restaurant.

═ **Gee's** *(61A Banbury Rd.* ☎ *58346* ▥*)* is a Victorian conservatory with a pleasant atmosphere and good Modern British food. The upmarket **Elizabeth** *(84 St Aldate's* ☎ *242230* ▥*)* is an old-established French restaurant, with a superb wine list. **Bath Place** *(4-5 Bath Place, Holywell St.* ☎ *791812* ▥*)* is a family-run restaurant with rooms in a group of converted 17thC cottages; the atmosphere is convivial, the food fresh and imaginatively prepared.

For good-value eating, cold buffet and decent Sunday lunch, **Cherwell Boat-house** *(* ☎ *52746* ▥*)*, on the river off Bardwell Rd., makes for a pleasant experience, as does **Brown's** *(Woodstock Rd.* ☎ *511995* ▥*)*.

STRATFORD-UPON-AVON
96 miles (154km) NW of London. Population: 22,000. By train, about 2hrs 30mins from Paddington, changing at Leamington Spa, 6 trains a day; by train and bus, 2hrs from Euston, changing at Coventry, 7 trains a day; by car, 2hrs 30mins to 3hrs, A40, M40 to Oxford, then A34 ☎ *(0789)* **i** *1 High St.* ☎ *293127, recorded info* ☎ *67522.*

One-day excursion or longer: an awkward journey, but still a seem-ingly inescapable trip for visitors from overseas. Stratford is not really within London's hinterland, belonging less to the South than to the Midlands, and is most comfortably visited as part of a trip taking in **Warwick** or **Kenilworth** castles, **Coventry Cathedral**, or the north-ern part of the **Cotswold Hills**.

In the 16thC, as now, playwrights found their audiences and their milieu in London, and Shakespeare was a metropolitan writer. However, he was born in Stratford, retired and died there, and was buried there. Soon after his death in 1616, people started going to Stratford to see his birthplace, and today they can also watch his plays performed by the Royal Shakespeare Company during its long season.

There is much worth seeing in the town, despite exploitation that would surely draw a satirical sting from the subject of its purported devotions. There is little left of the Forest of Arden, the setting for several of the plays, except for the odd clump, but its trees remain in the timbering of some fine Elizabethan and Tudor buildings.

Essentially what Stratford provides — and provides superbly — is a glimpse (if inevitably only in terms of architecture and period interiors) of the Tudor world of the prosperous provincial market town in which Shakespeare lived and worked. When Stratford's streets are not sighing under the weight of visitors, it is a quiet and peaceful town, especially in the evenings. The sites mentioned in the following description are open throughout the year. For exact opening times consult the Tourist Information Centre.

SIGHTS AND PLACES OF INTEREST

From the railway station, Alcester Rd., Greenhill St. and Windsor St. lead to the half-timbered **Shakespeare's House** in Henley St. where the playwright was born, probably on April 23, 1564. That this occurred in what is unashamedly called the Birthroom is mostly a matter of long-standing tradition. In those days the property was divided into the family home and business wing — a division that generally applies today, with the former furnished in period style while the latter (later used as an inn with the curious name of *Swan and Maiden Head*) houses a **museum** and **visitor center**. The interior of Shakespeare's birthroom has been carefully restored — notice the engraved signatures of such pilgrims as Carlyle, Tennyson and Sir Walter Scott in the alleged room of the birth. In the garden there are trees, plants, herbs and flowers mentioned in Shakespeare's plays.

A short walk along Henley St., High St. (past **Harvard House**, the family home of John Harvard, founder of the university) and Chapel St. is **New Place**, to which Shakespeare retired, and where he died at the age of 52. The house no longer stands, but the garden, laid out in the characteristic Elizabethan "knot" patterns, can still be enjoyed. The foundations of New Place and the gardens are reached by passing through **Nash's House**, once owned by Thomas Nash (who married Shakespeare's granddaughter) and now a museum of local history.

Farther along, when the same thoroughfare has become Church St., is the **Shakespeare Birthplace Trust**, which offers a combined ticket for the several properties that historically are linked to the bard. Another of these properties, just around the corner in Old Town, is **Hall's Croft**. This building is named after John Hall, who married Shakespeare's daughter; however, its principal interest is the fact that Hall was a doctor, and the equipment within provides intriguing insight into the medical techniques of the 17thC.

Old Town meets Trinity St. at the churchyard of **Holy Trinity** where Shakespeare was buried. The gravestone is inscribed with an imprecation, attributed to Shakespeare, to leave him in peace. On the chancel wall is a monument, and at the font is a reproduction of the register recording his baptism and burial. Several of his family lie here too: his wife Anne, his daughter Susanna and her husband John Hall, and Thomas Nash, the first husband of Susanna's daughter.

Back along Southern Lane and Waterside, by the River Avon, is the

Royal Shakespeare Theatre. There were performances in Stratford even in the days of strolling players, but the first serious attempts to honor Shakespeare began in the late 1700s. The original Shakespeare theater was built in 1879, and burned down in 1926. The present red-brick building was opened in 1932, and the Royal Shakespeare Company, one of the world's finest theater companies, presents at least 12 Shakespearean productions in a season stretching from April-January.

The RSC also has a studio theater in the town, known as **The Other Place**, and a new Jacobean-style theater, **The Swan**, which opened in 1986, where lesser-known Shakespearian and contemporary plays are staged. Recorded reservation information for all theaters can be obtained around the clock (☎ *269191; for the box office* ☎ *295623).*

The Royal Shakespeare Theatre has an interestingly informative **picture gallery** of paintings of great actors in Shakespearian costume, in a surviving section of the original building. Tours of the gallery and of the theater backstage take place every afternoon: for details ☎296655. The theater also has extensive gardens; in the part lying near the church are rare trees and a court for Nine Men's Morris, an ancient game mentioned in *A Midsummer Night's Dream;* and the part lying near the Shakespeare monument — **Bancroft Gardens** — makes a nice picnic spot.

Also in Waterside is the **World of Shakespeare**, where, in a darkened auditorium, 25 tableaux supported by dramatic light-and-sound effects illustrate life in the 16thC. Among the subjects are the London plague, Elizabethan sports, Queen Elizabeth I's journey from London to Kenilworth, and bear-baiting.

SIGHTS NEARBY

Two further scenes from the *Seven Ages of Shakespeare* are to be seen just outside the town. **Anne Hathaway's cottage**, her home before her marriage to Shakespeare, is 2 miles (3km) to the w at **Shottery**. The contents include Shakespeare's "second best bed," a four-poster that he willed to his wife. The thatched cottage can be reached by a very pleasant walk along a signposted footpath from Evesham Pl.; there is also a bus service from the bottom of Bridge St.

A longer and sometimes muddy walk along a canal towpath N from Bridgefoot, or a short train journey, leads the 4 miles (6km) to **Wilmcote**, home of Shakespeare's mother, Mary Arden. This typical Warwickshire farmstead, in use in its original capacity until 50 years ago, retains an informality that makes it a revealing museum of English rural life. Visitors can wander around the hall, kitchen, servants' room and massively beamed upper rooms. Outside there are a dovecote, cider mill, pump and, in the outbuildings, a farming museum in which some of the bygones date back to Tudor times.

☞ By custom, the thespian hotel, also enjoyed for its food and drink, is **The Arden** *(at Waterside* ☎*294949* ▯*)*, which has a country-house atmosphere. There are several other hotels in Stratford with this kind of ambience, although the rooms have usually been modernized. In Sheep St. is **Stratford House** (☎*268288* ▯*)*, relaxed and attractively decorated.

For the full modern treatment, try the **Moat House** *(Bridgefoot* ☎*414411* ▯*).*

Payton House *(6 John St.* ☎ *266442* ▢) is a good bed and breakfast; others tend to gather on the roads into Stratford from Oxford, Evesham and Alcester. The Tourist Information Center has an accommodation register.

The **Royal Shakespeare Theatre** *(*♣ ☎ *269191* ▢) has two restaurants and offers a package-deal ticket for a play and dinner. Or reserve in the morning for a pre-theater dinner at **Sir Toby's** *(8 Church St.* ☎ *268822* ▢). After the theater, **Sheep St.** has several late restaurants, Italian and Greek, among which the Greek-biased **Debut** *(*☎ *293546* ▢) is a lively highlight.

In the same street, there are good pub lunches at the **Rose and Crown**, while actors favor the "**Dirty Duck**" (a.k.a. **Black Swan**), at Waterside, near the theater.

WINDSOR AND ETON
21 miles (34km) w of Central London. Population: 30,000. By train, 53mins from Paddington, changing at Slough for Windsor and Eton Central, trains hourly, or 47mins direct from Waterloo to Windsor Riverside, trains twice hourly; by car, 1hr, M4, then A308 ☎ *code (0753) from London* **i** *Central Station* ☎ *852010.*
One-day excursion: Windsor and Eton are compact and busy, and surrounded by walking country. A car is not essential.

With its royal castle and Great Park, on a pretty stretch of the River Thames, and with Eton, famous for its boys' school, just across the footbridge, a visit to Windsor is an almost mandatory day trip for the visitor to London, or worth even a hasty half-day. Hotels are not listed as Windsor is too close to London to warrant an overnight stay.

Opening times for the various sights of interest within Windsor Castle vary slightly from month to month — for exact times consult the Tourist Information Center.

SIGHTS AND PLACES OF INTEREST
Unless you intend to take a long walk in the Great Park or along the river, the places of interest in Windsor and Eton are all within a radius of about a mile. It is possible to take a perhaps brisk look at each in the course of one day, and there are good reasons to plan to see Windsor in the morning and Eton in the afternoon.

From Riverside Station, a walk along Datchet Rd. and Thames St. leads to the castle. Central Station is closer; there is a car park opposite, housed in the ugly King Edward Court shopping center, and a walk up Peascod

St. and Castle Hill leads to the castle. In Central Station you will find **Royalty and Empire** *(open daily 9.30am-5.30pm, 4.30pm in winter)*, a waxwork and audiovisual exhibition on Victorian life taking the occasion of Queen Victoria's Diamond Jubilee in 1897 as its theme, and the Great Western Railway's Royal Station as its setting. Another exhibition marks the 40th anniversary of Queen Elizabeth II's reign.

Close to the castle, the **Toy and Doll Museum** *(15 Church St., open daily 9.30am-5.30pm)* displays old toys manufactured between 1890 and 1969, including a vast collection of Dinky Toys. Farther afield, the **Household Cavalry Museum** *(Combermere Barracks, St Leonards Rd., open Mon-Fri 10am-12.30pm, 2-4.30pm)* tells the story of this colorful and gallant corps.

The **Changing of the Castle Guard** can be seen at 11am Monday to Saturday from mid-March to mid-August and every 48 hours (excluding Sunday) from mid-August to mid-March. The new guard leaves from the Royal Mews at 10.55am and marches to the castle. The old guard returns at 11.30am. On the High St., the **Guildhall**, completed by Wren after the death of the original architect, is open for occasional exhibitions.

Up Church Lane, in Church St., Nell Gwynne's house nowadays is a coffee shop called **The Drury House**. At the top of Church St., King Henry VIII Gate is the main entrance to **Windsor Castle**. Even in William the Conqueror's time Windsor was within a day's march of London, which is why he chose it for the site of one of the nine castles with which he decided to encircle the city. Since the Royal Family still spend time at Windsor Castle, it is both a national monument and a private home, and it is the largest and oldest inhabited castle in the world. The precincts are open to visitors, and there is admission to the State Apartments when the Queen in not in official residence. The best view of the castle is from Long Walk in Windsor Great Park.

Straight ahead within the castle is the finest example of Perpendicular architecture in England, **St George's Chapel**, where several monarchs are buried in the choir. Well-meaning Henry VI (1422-61) heads the list of kings who lie here; his probable murderer Edward IV (1461-83), who started the building of this chapel, lies on the other side of the choir. But if in life Edward was the winner, the role was reversed in death, and it was to the miracle-working tomb of Henry that the pilgrims flocked, placing their gifts in the intricate alms box that still stands here. In one vault the uncouth Henry VIII (1509-47) and the fastidious Charles I (1625-49) make improbable companions, while not far away lie poor mad George III (1760-1820) and his sons George IV (1820-30) and William IV (1830-37). Finally, from the 20thC, there are Edward VII (1901-10), George V (1910-36) and George VI (1936-52). The architectural style of the chapel, with external buttresses providing much of the support, permits a spacious interior, with the light from stained-glass windows filling the magnificent nave. There are elaborate carvings in the nave and stalls.

The chapel's magnificent West Door leads onto Horshoe Cloister, and beyond that is **Curfew Tower**, which remains virtually the same as it was when built (1227-30) by Henry III to defend this NW corner of the castle, although a rather absurd roof was added in the 19thC. It contains eight chapel bells and medieval vaulted dungeons with secret passages through its massive walls.

The **Albert Memorial Chapel** was 13thC in origin. Queen Victoria remodeled it as a memorial to Prince Albert, who died in 1861, but today this eerie place is dominated by the tomb of his grandson, the Duke of Clarence, who died in 1892.

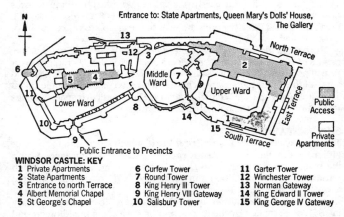

WINDSOR CASTLE: KEY

1 Private Apartments	6 Curfew Tower	11 Garter Tower
2 State Apartments	7 Round Tower	12 Winchester Tower
3 Entrance to north Terrace	8 King Henry III Tower	13 Norman Gateway
4 Albert Memorial Chapel	9 King Henry VIII Gateway	14 King Edward II Tower
5 St George's Chapel	10 Salisbury Tower	15 King George IV Gateway

On the opposite side of the castle precincts are the **State Apartments** which, although dating in part from the 12thC, essentially represent Charles II's palace as remodeled by George IV. A room with nine Van Dycks; another filled with Canalettos; one splendid hall aglow with portraits (mostly by Lawrence) of the high and mighty of Europe who had played a part in the overthrow of Napoleon; another resplendent with Stuart and Hanoverian Sovereigns of the Order of the Garter — this list may indicate the riches awaiting the visitor in this sequence of sumptuous rooms bearing such resounding titles as the Garter Throne Room, St George's Hall, the Queen's Presence Chamber and the King's State Bedchamber. There are also drawings by Leonardo da Vinci and Holbein in the hall near the main entrance to the State Apartments.

Within the same complex is that extraordinary delight, **Queen Mary's Dolls' House**, also near the entrance. This has running water, working elevators and a library with commissioned writings by Kipling and miniature paintings. The house, designed by Sir Edwin Lutyens, is on a scale of 12:1. From the castle, Long Walk runs for 3 miles (5km) through **Home Park** to a statue of George III. Beyond stretches **Windsor Great Park**, with Smith's Lawn, where the Prince of Wales plays polo. Nearby, the **Savill Garden** *(open Mon-Fri 10am-6pm, Sat, Sun 10am-7pm)* has rhododendrons, roses, herbaceous borders and alpine plants, set in 35 wooded acres.

An exploration of the Great Park and Savill Garden may well demand an afternoon, but the alternative is to return to the town, and from Thames

St. cross the footbridge (a pretty Victorian structure in cast iron) to **Eton,** which may prove a less crowded place in which to have lunch. The town of the boating song and playing fields on which Britain's battles were allegedly won instantly proclaims itself; from the bridge, the Eton College boathouses can be seen on the left. In the High St., near a splendid Victorian pillar box, is **The Cockpit,** a timbered building dating from 1420, where cock-fighting used to take place. Note the punishment stocks outside. Among the antique stores in the High St. is **F. Owen,** at no. 113, notable for militaria; covering one wall of the shop are photographs of customers who were Eton boys.

   Eton College *(open Apr-Sept 2-4.30pm, vacations 10.30am-4.30pm; parties of 10 or more must reserve in advance* ☎ *863593),* cradle of great British poets and prime ministers, was founded in 1440 by Henry VI, and some of the oldest parts of the school can be seen in a quadrangle called The Cloisters. The 15thC chapel, built in the Perpendicular style, contains wall paintings from the time of its foundation.

SIGHTS NEARBY
There are walks in **Windsor Great Park**, which stretches s for 6 miles (10km) in the direction of **Ascot racecourse**. A similar distance NW up the willow-fringed river is **Boulter's Lock**, still much as it was when Jerome K. Jerome described it in *Three Men in a Boat* in 1889, and the town of **Maidenhead**.

   A couple of miles farther upriver is **Cliveden House**, built by Barry in 1851, once owned by the Astors, and on occasion a breeding ground for political scandal. The house is now a hotel, but a small section is open to members of the National Trust on Thursday and Sunday afternoons in summer. The magnificent gardens, with beautiful views, can be visited from March to October daily 11am-6pm.

   Cliveden is close to the village of **Cookham**, where the painter Stanley Spencer lived. One of his paintings hangs in the church, and others are in King's Hall.

⇌   Gastronomes will cut short their sightseeing to spend time and money at the **Waterside Inn** *(Bray, near Maidenhead* ☎ *(0628) 20691* ▥ *)*, which is the country establishment of the Roux brothers, owners of Le Gavroche in London (see RESTAURANTS A TO Z). Reserve ahead.

   Windsor itself has plenty of restaurants, though none of particular note, while across the river at Eton you can have a hot pub lunch at **Christopher's**, or a light meal at the **Eton Wine Bar**, both in the High St. For some old-world charm, you may prefer to head out to a pub/restaurant in a pretty Thameside location, such as the **Bel and Dragon** at Cookham, or **Ye Olde Bell Inn** at Hurley.

Index

Bold page numbers indicate main entries. *Italic* page numbers indicate illustrations and maps. See also the LIST OF STREET NAMES on page 321.

List of street names

All streets mentioned in this book that fall within the area covered by our maps are listed below. Map numbers are printed in **bold** type. Some smaller streets are not named on the maps, but the map reference given below will help you locate the correct district.

Abchurch Lane, **12**F16
Abingdon Rd., **13**I2-J2
Abingdon St., **17**I11
Adam's Row, **8**G8
Admiralty Arch, **9**H11
Albany St., **2**B8-D9
Albemarle St., **8**G9
Albert Bridge, **15**L6-M6
Albert Bridge Rd., **15**M6
Aldermanbury, **11**E15
Aldwych, **10**F12
Allington St., **16**I9
Argyll St., **8**F9
Arlington St., **8**G9-H9
Ashley Pl., **16**J9

Baker St., **1**D7-7F7
Balderton St., **8**F8
Ball Court, **12**F16
Bankside, **11**G15
Baron's Court, **13**K1
Basil St., **15**I6-7
Bathurst Mews, **6**F5
Bayswater Rd., **5**G3-7F7
Beak St., **8**G9
Bear Gardens, **11**G15
Beauchamp Pl., **15**I6-J6
Beaufort Gardens, **15**I6
Bedford Pl., **3**E11
Bedford Sq., **3**E10
Bedford St., **9**G11
Beeston Pl., **16**I9
Belgrave Mews West, **15**I7
Belgrave Sq., **15**I7-16I8
Berkeley Sq., **8**G8
Bermondsey St., **12**H16-I17
Berners St., **9**E9-F10
Berwick St., **9**F10
Betterton St., **9**F11
Bevis Marks, **12**F17
Birdcage Walk, **16**I9-17I10
Bishopsgate, **12**E17

Blackfriars Bridge, **11**G14
Blackfriars Lane, **11**F14
Blenheim St., **8**F8
Bloomsbury Sq., **3**E11
Bloomsbury St., **3**E11
Bloomsbury Way, **9**E11
Bond St., **8**F8-G9; see also
    New Bond St. and Old
    Bond St.
Borough High St.,
    11I15-H15
Bow Lane, **11**F15
Bow St., **9**F11
Bread St., **11**F15
Brewer St., **9**G10-F10
Bridge St., **17**I11
Broad Sanctuary, **17**I11
Broad Walk, **2**B8-D8
Broadway, **17**I10
Broken Wharf, **11**G15
Brompton Rd., **14**J6-15I7
Brook St., **8**F8
Brunswick Sq., **3**D11
Bruton Pl., **8**G9
Buckingham Gate, **16**I9
Buckingham Palace Rd.,
    16J8-9
Burlington Arcade, **8**G9
Burlington Gardens., **8**G9
Byward St., **12**G17

Cadogan Gardens, **15**J7
Cadogan Pl., **15**I7-J7
Cadogan Sq., **15**J7
Camden High St., **2**A9-B9
Camden Passage, **4**B14
Camomile St., **12**E17
Campden Hill Rd., **5**H2
Canning Pl., **14**I4
Cannon St., **11**F15
Carey St., **10**F12-13
Carlos Pl., **8**G8

Carlton House Ter., **9**H10
Carnaby St., **8**F9
Cartwright Gardens, **3**C11
Castle Court, **12**F16
Catherine St., **10**F12
Cavendish Sq., **8**F9
Cecil Court, **9**G11
Chancery Lane, **10**E12-F13
Charing Cross, **9**G11
Charing Cross Rd.,
    9F10-G11
Charles St., **8**G8
Charlotte St., **3**E9-10
Charterhouse Mews, **11**E14
Charterhouse Sq., **11**E14
Cheapside, **11**F15
Chelsea Bridge Rd.,
    15K7-16L8
Chelsea Manor St., **15**K6-L6
Chester Sq., **16**J8
Chester Ter., **2**C8
Cheyne Row, **15**L6
Cheyne Walk, **14**M5-15L6
Church St., **6**E5-D5
Clarges St., **8**G8
Cleveland St., **8**D9-E10
Clink St., **11**G15
Conduit St., **8**G9-F9
Cork St., **8**G9
Cornhill, **12**F16
Courtfield Close, **14**J4
Courtfield Rd., **14**J4
Covent Garden, **9**F11
Cowley St., **17**I11
Cranbourn St., **9**G11
Cranley Pl., **14**K5
Craven Hill, **6**F4
Cromwell Rd., **13**J2-14J4
Crutched Friars, **12**F17
Cumberland Ter., **2**B8
Curzon St., **8**H8
Cut, The, **10**H13-14

Davies Mews, 8G8
Davies St., 8F8-G9
Dean St., 9F10
De Vere Gardens, 14I4
Devonshire St., 2E8-D9
Dorset Sq., 7D7
Doughty St., 3D12
Dover St., 8G9
Dowgate Hill, 11G15
Downing St., 9H11
Draycott Ave., 15J6-K6
Draycott Pl., 15K6-J7
Drury Lane, 9F11-10F12
Duke of York St., 9G10
Duke St., 8G9-H10

Earl's Court Rd., 13I2-K3
Earlham St., 9F11
Eastcheap, 12G16
Eaton Sq., 16J8
Ebury St., 16K8-J8
Eccleston Sq., 16J9-K9
Egerton Gardens, 15J6
Eldon St., 12E16
Endell St., 9F11
Euston Rd., 2D9-3C11
Exeter St., 10F12-13
Exhibition Rd., 14I5-J5

Farmer St., 5G2
Farringdon Rd., 4D13-E14
Farringdon St., 11F14
Fenchurch St., 12F16
Field Court, 10E12
Fish St. Hill, 12G16
Fleet St., 10F13-14
Flood St., 15K6-L6
Floral St., 9F11
Folgate St., 12D17
Foster Lane, 11F15
Foubert's Pl., 8F9
Frith St., 9F10
Fulham Rd., 13M3-14J6

Garlick Hill, 11F15
Garrick St., 9F11
George St., 7F6-8E8
Gerrard Pl., 9F10
Gerrard St., 9G10-F10
Gilston Rd., 14L4
Golden Sq., 9G10
Goodge St., 9E10
Gordon Sq., 3D10
Gough Sq., 10F13
Gower St., 3D10-E10
Grafton St., 8G9
Gray's Inn Rd., 4C12-E13
Gray's Inn Sq., 4E13
Great Cumberland Pl., 7F7
Great George St., 17I11
Great Marlborough St., 8F9

Great Newport St., 9F11
Great Portland St., 2D9-8F9
Great Pulteney St., 9F10
Great Russell St., 9E10-11
Great Trinity Lane, 11F15
Great Windmill St., 9G10
Greek St., 9F10-11
Gresham St., 11F15
Grosvenor Gardens, 16I8-J9
Grosvenor Rd.,
  16L9-17K11
Grosvenor Pl., 16I8
Grosvenor Sq., 8G8
Grosvenor St., 8G8-F9
Guildford St., 3D11
Guildhall Yard, 11F15

Halkin St., 17I8
Hallam St., 8D9-E9
Hamilton Pl., 8H8
Hanover Sq., 8F9
Hanover St., 8F9
Harley St., 2D8
Harrington Rd., 14J4-5
Hart St., 12F17
Hatton Garden, 4D13-E13
Haymarket, 9G10
Hays Mews, 8G8
Henrietta St., 9G11
High Holborn, 10E12
Holborn, 10E13
Holborn Viaduct, 10E13
Holland Park, 5H1
Holland St., 5H2-3
Hornton St., 5H2-I2
Horse Guards Parade, 9H11
Horseferry Rd., 17J10-11
Houghton St., 10F12
Hyde Park Corner, 8H8
Hyde Park Gate, 14I4

Inner Circle, 1C7-2C8
Islington High St., 4B13-14

Jermyn St., 8G9-9G10

Kensington Church St.,
  5G2-I3
Kensington Gore, 14I4
Kensington High St., 13I1-3
Kensington Park Rd., 5G1-2
Kensington Sq., 13I3
King St., 9H9-G10
King Charles St., 9H11
King Edward St.,
  11E14-F14
King William St., 12F16
King's Rd., 14M4-15K7
Kingly St., 8F9
Kingsway, 10E12-F12
Kinnerton St., 15I7

Knightsbridge, 7I6-8H8

Lamb's Conduit St.,
  4D12-E12
Lambeth Bridge,
  17J11-18J12
Lambeth Palace Rd.,
  18J12-I12
Lambeth Rd., 18J12-I14
Lancaster Ter., 6G5-F5
Lanesborough Pl., 8H8
Langley St., 9F11
Langton St., 14M4
Launceston Pl., 14I4
Laurence Pountney Hill,
  11G16
Leadenhall St., 11F16
Leicester Sq., 9G11
Leicester St., 9G10
Lexington St., 9F10
Lillie Rd., 13L1-L2
Lime St., 12F16
Lincoln St., 15K7
Lincoln's Inn Fields,
  10E12-F12
Lisle St., 9G10
Lisson Grove, 7E6
Little Britain, 11E14
Liverpool St., 12E16-17
Lombard St., 12F16
London Bridge, 12G16
London Wall, 11E15-12E16
Long Acre, 9F11
Long Lane, 12I16
Lord North St., 17I11-J11
Lothbury, 12F16
Lots Rd., 14M5
Lower Regent St., 9G10
Lower Sloane St., 15K7
Lower Thames St., 11G16
Ludgate Circus, 11F14
Ludgate Hill, 11F14

Maiden Lane, 9G11
Malet St., 3D10
Mall, The, 8H9-9H11
Manchester Sq., 8E8-F8
Marble Arch, 7F7
Marlborough Rd., 9H10
Marshall St., 9F9-10
Marylebone High St.,
  2D8-E8
Marylebone Rd., 1E6-2D9
Meard St., 9F10
Mepham St., 10H13
Middlesex St., 12E17-F17
Milk St., 11F15
Millbank, 17K11-I11
Milner St., 15J6-7
Mincing Lane, 12F17
Monmouth St., 9F11

Montpelier St., 15I6
Monument St., 12G16
Moor St., 9F10
Morgan's Lane, 12H17
Mornington Crescent, 2B9
Mortimer St., 8E9
Moscow Rd., 5G3-F3
Motcomb St., 15I7
Mount St., 8G8
Museum St., 9E11

Neal St., 9F11
Neal's Yd., 9F11
New Oxford St., 3E11
New Bond St., 8F8-G9; *see also Bond St.*
New Row, 9G11
New Sq., 10F12-F13
New Wharf Rd., 4B12
Newgate St., 11E14
North Audley St., 7F7
Northumberland Ave., 9G11
Notting Hill Gate, 5G2

Oakley St., 15L6
Observatory Gardens, 5H2
Old Bailey, 11F14
Old Barrack Yard, 15H7
Old Bond St., 8G9; *see also Bond St.*
Old Broad St., 12E16-F16
Old Brompton Rd., 13L2-14J5
Old Burlington St., 9G10
Old Church St., 14K5-L5
Old Compton St., 9F10-11
Old Park Lane, 8H8
Opera House Arcade, 9G10-H10
Outer Circle, 1 & 8
Oxford Circus, 8F9
Oxford St., 7F7-9F10

Pall Mall, 9H9-G11
Park Crescent, 2D8
Park Lane, 7F7-8H8
Park Rd., 1C6
Park Sq., 2D8
Park St., 7F7-G7
Parliament Sq., 17I11
Parliament St., 9H11-I11
Paternoster Sq., 11F14
Pembridge Gardens, 5G2
Pembridge Rd., 5G2
Penton St., 4B13
Percy St., 9E10
Peter St., 9F10
Petticoat Lane, 12E17
Phoenix St., 9F10
Piccadilly, 8H8-9G10
Piccadilly Arcade, 9G10

Piccadilly Circus, 9G10
Pont St., 15J6-I7
Porchester Rd., 5E3-F3
Portland Pl., 2D8-E9
Portman Sq., 7F7
Portobello Rd., 5G1-2
Portugal St., 10F12
Poultry, 11F15
Praed St., 6F5-E5
Prince Consort Rd., 14I4
Princes Gate, 14I5
Pudding Lane, 12G16
Puddle Dock, 11F14

Queen St., 11F15
Queen Anne's Gate, 17I10
Queen Victoria St., 11F14-15
Queen Victoria Memorial, 8H9
Queen's Gate, 14I4-K4
Queenstown Rd., 16L8-M8
Queensway, 5F3-G3

Regent St., 8E9-9G10
Regent's Park Rd., 2A8
Rochester Row, 17J10
Roland Gardens, 14K4
Romilly St., 9F11
Rose St., 9F11
Rosebery Ave., 4D13-C13
Rotten Row, 6H5-7H7
Royal Hospital Rd., 15L6-K7
Rupert St., 9F10-G10
Russell Sq., 3D11-E11
Russell St., 10F12

St Andrew's Hill, 11F14
St Anne's Court, 9G10
St Christophers Pl., 8F8
St Dunstan's Hill, 12G17
St George's St., 8F9
St James's Pl., 8H9
St James's Sq., 9G10
St James's St., 8G9-H9
St Katharine's Way, 12G18
St Martin's Lane, 9G11
St Martin's Pl., 9G11
St Michael's Alley, 12F16
St Oswald's Pl., 18K12
St Paul's Churchyard, 11F14
St Thomas' St., 12H16-17
Savile Row, 8F9
Scala St., 9E10
Selwood Ter., 14K4-5
Seven Dials, 9F11
Shad Thames, 12H17-18
Shaftesbury Ave., 9G10-F11
Shelton St., 9F11
Shepherd Market, 8H8

Sloane Sq., 15J7
Sloane St., 15I7-J7
Smith Sq., 17J11
Soho Sq., 9F10
South Sq., 10E13
South Audley St., 8G8
South Bank, 10G12
South Molton St., 8F8
Southwark Bridge, 11G15
Stable Yard, 8H9
Stafford Ter., 13I2
Stamford St., 10G13-H14
Stanley Gardens, 5G1
Strand, 9G11-10F13
Stratton St., 8G9
Sumner Pl., 14J5-K5
Sussex Pl., 1D6-7
Swallow St., 9G10
Swan Lane, 12G16
Swan Walk, 15L7

Talbot Yard, 12H16
Tavistock Crescent, 5E1
Tavistock Sq., 3D10-11
Tavistock St., 10F12
Temple Lane, 10F13
Temple Pl., 10F13
Thayer St., 2E8
Threadneedle St., 12F16
Throgmorton St., 12F16
Thurloe St., 14J5-6
Tite St., 15L7
Tooley St., 12G16-I18
Torrington Pl., 3D10-11
Tottenham Court Rd., 3D9-E10
Tower Bridge, 12H17-G17
Tower Bridge Rd., 12I17-H17
Tower Hill, 12G17
Tower St., 9F11
Trafalgar Sq., 9G11
Trinity Sq., 12G17
Tyer's St., 18K12

Udall St., 17J10
Upper Brook St., 7G7
Upper St Martin's Lane, 9F11
Upper St., 4B13
Upper Thames St., 11F14-12G16
Upper Woburn Pl., 3C10-D11
Uxbridge St., 5G2

Vere St., 8F8
Victoria Embankment, 10G12-13
Victoria Grove, 14I4
Victoria St., 16J9-17I10

KEY TO MAP PAGES

1-18 CENTRAL LONDON
19-20 LONDON ENVIRONS

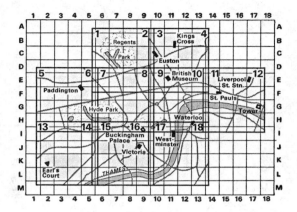

KEY TO MAP SYMBOLS

City Maps

▨	Place of Interest or Important Building
▦	Built-up Area
░	Park
⊞	Cemetery
✝	Church
☾	Mosque
✡	Synagogue
⊞	Hospital
ⅰ	Tourist Information
⊠	Post Office
☝	Police Station
🚗	Car Park
⊖	Underground Station
→	One-way Street
▭	Footpath / Arcade
3	Adjoining Page No.

Area Maps

▪	Place of Interest
▨	Built-up Area
░	Wood or Park
=○=	Motorway (with access point)
= =	Motorway under construction
——	Dual Carriageway / Four-lane Highway
——	Other Main Road
—	Secondary Road
⇌	Railway
✈	Airport
✦	Airfield

```
0    100   200   300   400   500yds
0    100   200   300   400   500m
```

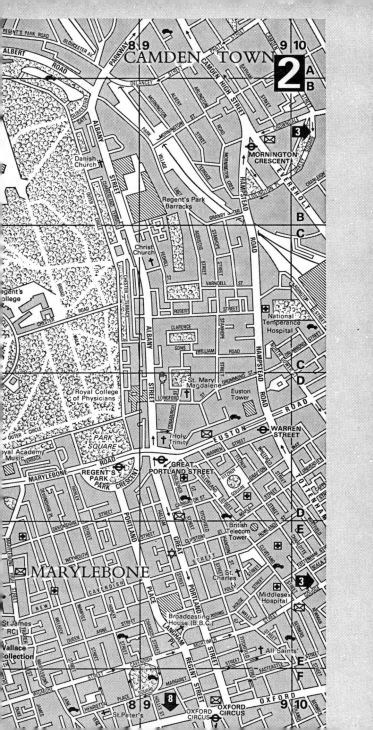

RAILWAY YARDS

St. Pancras Hospital

ST. PANCRAS GARDENS

Grand Union Canal

GOODS WAY

King's Cross Station

EVERSHOLT

2
B

C

St. Mary's

St. Aloysius

New British Library

Shaw Theatre

St Pancras Station

EUSTON ROAD

National Temperance Hospital

E. Garrett Anderson Hospital

German Lutheran Church

Holy Cross

Presbytery

Euston Station

St Pancras

C

HAMPSTEAD ROAD

D
Friends House

British Medical Association

Sch. of Pharma

EUSTON SQUARE

University College London

Jewish Museum

Institute of Archaeology

Brunswick Centre

WARREN STREET

Christ the King

Percival David Foundation

WOBURN PLACE

Coram Foundatio

UCL Hospital

RUSSELL SQUARE

Royal Academy of Dramatic Art

BLOOMSBURY

St George the Martyr

D
E

GOODGE STREET

University of London

British Museum

TOTTENHAM COURT ROAD

Middlesex Hospital

St George's

8

BLOOMSBURY

All Saints'

CENTRE POINT

NEW OXFORD STREET

HOLBORN

TOTTENHAM COURT ROAD

SOHO

French Protestant

ST GILES HIGH ST.

St Giles

9

F

OXFORD STREET

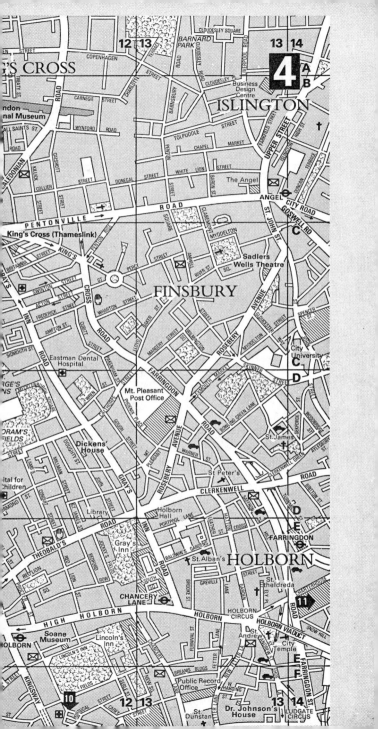

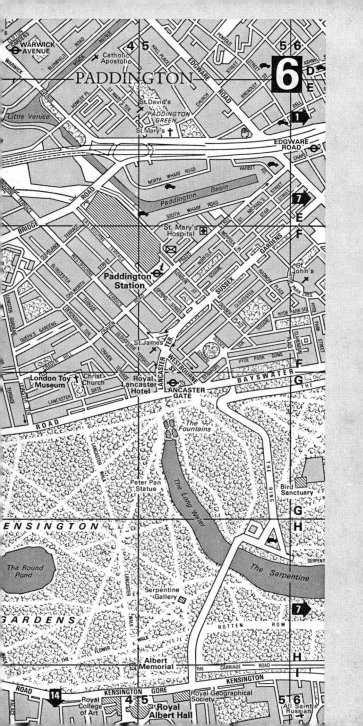

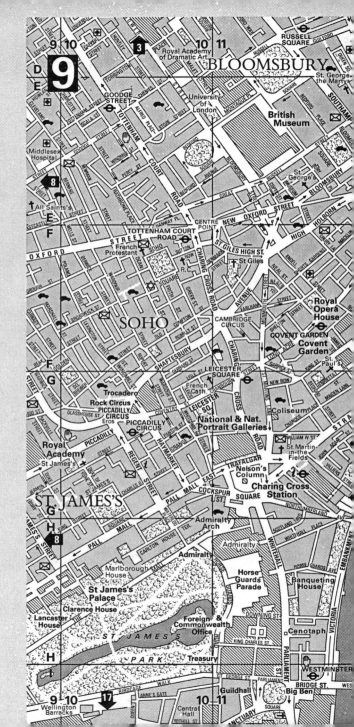

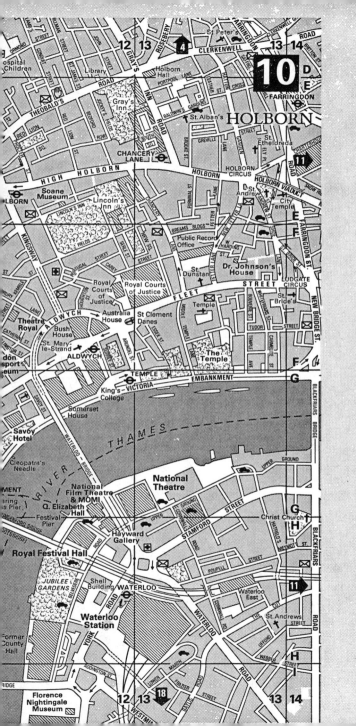

CLERKENWELL ROAD
St. Peter's

FARRINGDON

HOLBORN

Library
Holborn Hall
PORTPOOL LANE

THEOBALD'S ROAD

Gray's Inn

BALDWIN'S GARDENS

St. Alban's

St. Etheldreda

CHANCERY LANE

HIGH HOLBORN

HOLBORN

HOLBORN CIRCUS

HOLBORN VIADUCT

SNOW HILL

11

Soane Museum

Lincoln's Inn

St. Andrew

City Temple

E

LINCOLN'S INN FIELDS

BREAMS BLDGS

FARRINGDON ST.

Public Record Office

W. HARDING

NEW SQ.

KINGSWAY

St. Dunstan

Dr. Johnson's House

LUDGATE CIRCUS

Royal Courts of Justice

FLEET STREET

St. Bride's

NEW BRIDGE ST.

Theatre Royal

Bush House

Australia House

St Clement Danes

Temple

ALDWYCH

St. Mary-le-Strand

TUDOR STREET

F

London Transport Museum

The Temple

TEMPLE

VICTORIA EMBANKMENT

G

King's College

Somerset House

Savoy Hotel

THAMES

BLACKFRIARS BRIDGE

Cleopatra's Needle

RIVER

UPPER GROUND

National Film Theatre & MOMI

National Theatre

Q. Elizabeth Hall

Festival Pier

Christ Church

G
H

Hayward Gallery

UPPER GROUND

STAMFORD STREET

Royal Festival Hall

JUBILEE GARDENS

Shell Building

WATERLOO

WATERLOO ROAD

Waterloo East

11

Former County Hall

Waterloo Station

YORK ROAD

St. Andrews STREET

WEBBER

H

Florence Nightingale Museum

D

E

HOLBORN

St. John's

St. Bartholomew's
Medical School

GOSNELL

Charterhouse

FARRINGDON
COWCROSS ST.

BARBICAN

Beech Street

Barbican
Centre

SILK ST.

CHISW

St.
Etheldreda

Smithfield
Market

St. Bartholomew
the Great

BARBICAN

St Giles

FORE

HOLBORN
CIRCUS

HOLBORN
VIADUCT

LONG LANE

West
Smithfield

Little Britain

**Museum of
London**

LONDON — WALL

City
St.
Temple

St.
Andrew

E

SNOW HILL

St. Bartholomew's
Hospital

National
Postal
Museum

St.
Botolph's

KING EDWARD ST.

St. Anne &
St. Agnes

ALDERMANBURY

FARRINGDON STREET

F

10

OLD BAILEY

NEWGATE ST.

Holy
Sepulchre

NEWGATE

ST. MARTIN'S

LE GRAND

GRESHAM

Goldsmith's
Hall

Guildhall

Central
Criminal Court

ST.
PAUL'S

PATERNOSTER
SQUARE

St Vedast

St. Martin's

**St. Paul's
Cathedral**

CHEAPSIDE

CITY

POULT

LUDGATE
CIRCUS

LUDGATE HILL

ST. PAUL'S CHURCHYARD

NEW CHANGE

WATLING

St. Mary
le Bow

St Ste

TREET

St
Bride's

WHITEFRIARS

NEW BRIDGE ST.

CARTER LANE

St Andrew

St Paul's
Thameslink
Stn.

College
of Arms

BREAD ST.

BOW LANE

St Walbr

CANNON STREET

St. Mary
Aldermary

TUDOR

STREET

CARMELITE ST.

St Paul's
Thameslink
Stn.

Mermaid
Theatre

QUEEN

St Nicholas
Cole
Abbey

St Benet

VICTORIA

MANSION
HOUSE

St. James
Garlickhythe

QUEEN

**Cannon
St.
Station**

CANNON

F

G

BLACKFRIARS

Blackfriars
Station

UPPER

THAMES

St Michael

P. Royal

River Bus

UPPER GROUND

BLACKFRIARS — BRIDGE

BANKSIDE

**Shakespeare Globe
Museum**

SOUTHWARK BRIDGE

St
Over
CLIN

G

H

Christ
Church

BLACKFRIARS ROAD

HOPTON ST.

SUMNER

Bear Lane

STREET

GREAT GUILDFORD

PARK

PARK

ST.

SOUTHWARK

HATFIELDS

MEYMOTT

STREET

SOUTHWARK

GRAVEL

STREET

SOUTHWARK BRIDGE ROAD

STREET

10

UNION

NELSON

COPPERFIELD STREET

SUFFOLK ST.

ST HAWKS

All
Hallows

UNION

STREET

St. Andrews
STREET

SQUARE

POCOCK STREET

GT. SUFFOLK STREET

BOROUGH

BOROUGH

H

I

WEBBER

STREET

WEBBER

STREET

BOROUGH

GT. SUFFOLK STREET

SNOW STREET

LANCASTER

St.
Alphage's

QUAKER ST

WORSHIP STREET

FOLGATE ST

SPITAL SQUARE

CITY ROAD

FINSBURY

EARL ST

CLIFTON ST

WILSON ST

SUN ST

APPOLD ST

APPOLD ST

NORTON FOLGATE

STEWARD ST

Old Spitalfields Market

COMMERCIAL

Christ Church

BROADGATE
Liverpool Street Station

BRUSHFIELD STREET

WHITE'S ROW

ORGATE

St. Mary Moorfields

ELDON ST

FINSBURY
CIRCUS

LIVERPOOL ST

All Hallows

St. Botolph

NEW ST

WORMWOOD ST

TURNER ST

WENTWORTH

BELL LANE

MOORGATE

FINSBURY

THROGMORTON AV.

LONDON WALL

BLOMFIELD ST

OLD BROAD ST

E F

Nat. West Tower

St. Ethelburga's

BEVIS MARKS

HOUNDSDITCH

Margaret's

THROGMORTON ST

Bank of England

Stock Exchange

BISHOPSGATE

CAMOMILE ST

St.Helen

ALDGATE
St. Botolph

CUTLER ST

DUKE'S PLACE

MIDDLESEX ST

HIGH ST

WHITECHAPEL

THREADNEEDLE

Royal Exchange

STREET

St Katharine Cree

Baltic Exchange

ALDGATE HIGH STREET

ALDGATE

MANSELL STREET

CORNHILL

St Michael's

St Peter's

Lloyds

LEADENHALL

STREET

VINE ST

BANK

Mansion House

LOMBARD

St Edmund's

Leadenhall Market

FENCHURCH AVE

MINORIES

KING WILLIAM

St. Clement's

FENCHURCH

Fenchurch St. Stn.

CRUTCHED

CROSSWALL

St Mary Abchurch ST

MINCING LANE

ROOD LANE

All Hallows Staining

St.Olave's

Tower Gateway

F G

MONUMENT

EASTCHEAP

St. Margaret Pattens

ST. MARY AT HILL

Corn Exchange

MARK LANE

SEETHING LANE

Trinity House

SEETHING LANE

TOWER HILL

TOWER HILL

The Monument

St. Mary at Hill

St. Dunstan-in-the-East

BYWARD

STREET

EET

mongers Hall

LOWER THAMES STREET

St.Magnus Martyr

All Hallows by the Tower

an l. ar

Custom House

LR. THAMES ST

Tower of London

TOWER BRIDGE APPR.

RIVER

Tower Pier

Traitor's Gate

THAMES

St Katharine's Dock

G H

London Bridge City Pier

Hay's Galleria

H.M.S. Belfast

TOWER BRIDGE

Greenwich

Butlers Wharf

nwark edral

London Dungeon

SHAD THAMES

London Bridge Station

TOOLEY

STREET

VINE LANE

Tower Bridge Museum

ROAD

H I

Guy's Hospital

THOMAS STREET

SNOWS FIELDS

KIPLING ST

CRUCIFIX LANE

St.Olave's

TOOLEY

STREET

ELIZABETH

BRIDGE

LONG

LEATHERMARKET ST

WESTON ST

BERMONDSEY

TANNER STREET

TOWER BRIDGE ROAD

KENSINGTON GARDENS

ROTTEN ROW

THE FLOWER WALK

Albert Memorial

THE CARRIAGE ROAD

KENSINGTON

KENSINGTON GORE

Royal Geographical Society

All Saints Russian

PALACE GATE

ROAD

Royal College of Art

Royal Albert Hall

PRINCE'S

CONSORT ROAD

KENSINGTON

EXHIBITION ROAD

ENNISMORE GARDENS

15

NG

HYDE PARK GATE

Holy Trinity

PRINCE

KNIGHTSBRIDGE

QUEEN'S GATE TER.

QUEEN'S

Imperial College

GARDENS

Victoria & Albert Museum

GLOUCESTER

ELVASTON PLACE

IMPERIAL INSTITUTE ROAD

Science Museum

BROMPTON

GARDENS

ROAD

QUEEN'S GATE

Natural History Museum

Earth Galleries

THURLOE PLACE

THURLOE SQ.

St.Stephen's

CROMWELL ROAD

CROMWELL ROAD

Ecole Française

THURLOE STREET

SOUTH TERRACE

GLOUCESTER ROAD

GARDENS

STANHOPE

GARDENS

HARRINGTON

ROAD

SOUTH KENSINGTON

PELHAM STREET

FELHAM CRES.

J K

GARDENS

GDNS

ROAD

ONSLOW

PELHAM PLACE

POND PLACE

ELYSTAN

ROAD

ROSARY GDNS

OLD

CRANLEY

GARDENS

ONSLOW SQUARE

St. Paul's

FOULIS TER.

CALE

ROAD

BROMPTON

DRAYTON

ROLAND GARDENS

SELWOOD TER.

CRESS ST.

Brompton Hospital

St. Luke's

THE BOLTONS

GARDENS

SOUTH TERRACE

TREGUNTER

CHELSEA

SYDNEY STREET

Mary's

EVELYN GARDENS

ELM PARK GARDENS

CHURCH STREET

CARLYLE SQ.

K L

GILSTON ROAD

CAMERA

ROAD

MANRESA ROAD

GORE

REDCLIFFE ROAD

BEAUFORT

ELM PARK

THE VALE

KING'S ROAD

OLD CHURCH STREET

PLACE

HOLLYWOOD ROAD

LIMERSTON

CHELSEA PARK GDNS

WALK

PAULTON'S SQUARE

15

St. phen's

ROAD

STREET

BEAUFORT STREET

UPPER CHEYNE ROW

R.C.

GERTRUDE STREET

LAWRENCE ST.

MALLORD ST.

Carlyle's House

Chelsea Old Church

L M

KING'S

Crosby Hall

CHEYNE

WALK

Roper's Garden

BATTERSEA BRIDGE

River

Bus

4 5 6

14 H I

15

J

J K

K

K L

L

L M

M

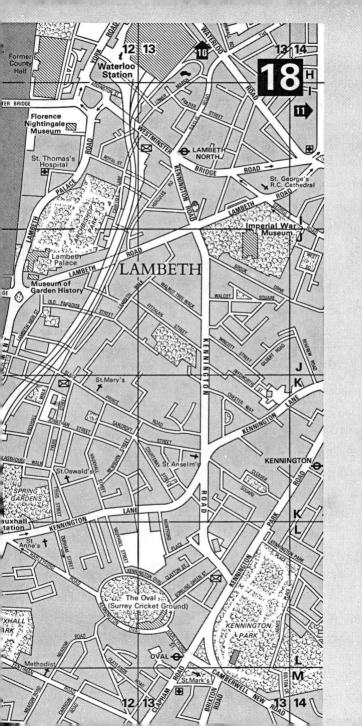

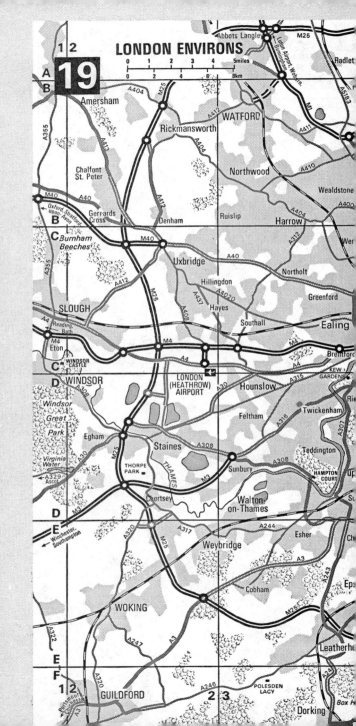

Abbots Langley
M25
Radlet

Luton Airport, Welwyn, Birmingham

A5183

A404
M25

Amersham

A404

Rickmansworth

WATFORD

A412

A411

A355

A413

A404

Chalfont
St. Peter

A410

Northwood

Wealdstone

A404

A400

M40

A40

Oxford, Stratford
upon-Avon

A412

B

Gerrards
Cross

Denham

Ruislip

Harrow

A312

C
Burnham
Beeches

M40

A355

A412

Uxbridge

A40

Northolt

Wer

M25

Hillingdon

A4020

Greenford

SLOUGH

A437

A408

Hayes

Southall

Ealing

A4

Reading,
Bath

M4
Eton

M4

A4

Northolt

WINDSOR
CASTLE

C*

A4

M4

A4

Brentfor

KEW
GARDENS

D
WINDSOR

A308

LONDON
(HEATHROW)
AIRPORT

A30

Hounslow

A315

Windsor
Great
Park

Egham

A308

Feltham

A316

Twickenham

Ri

A30

A307

Teddington

Virginia
Water

A329
Ascot

M25

THORPE
PARK

Staines

THAMES

A308

HAMPTON
COURT

Up

M3

Sunbury

Su

Chertsey

Walton-
on-Thames

D

E

Winchester,
Southampton

A320

A317

M25

A244

Esher

Ch

Weybridge

A3

A307

A243

Eps

Cobham

M25

A329

WOKING

A322

A247

A3

Leatherhe

A24

E

F

A320

POLESDEN
LACY

Box H

1 2

GUILDFORD

A246

2 3

Dorking

A3

Portsmouth,
Chichester

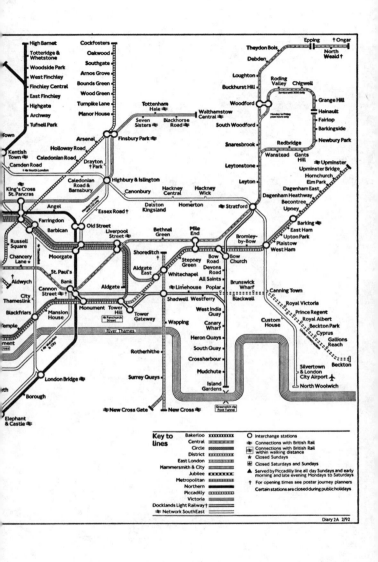

What the papers said:

• "The expertly edited American Express series has the knack of pinpointing precisely the details you need to know, and doing it concisely and intelligently." (*The Washington Post*)

• "*(Venice)* ... the best guide book I have ever used." (*The Standard* — London)

• "Amid the welter of guides to individual countries, American Express stands out...." (*Time*)

• "Possibly the best ... guides on the market, they come close to the oft-claimed 'all you need to know' comprehensiveness, with much original experience, research and opinions." (*Sunday Telegraph* — London)

• "The most useful general guide was *American Express New York* by Herbert Bailey Livesey. It also has the best street and subway maps." (*Daily Telegraph* — London)

• "...in the flood of travel guides, the *American Express* guides come closest to the needs of traveling managers with little time." (*Die Zeit* — Germany)

What the experts said:

• "We only used one guide book, Sheila Hale's *Amex Venice*, for which she and the editors deserve a Nobel Prize." (Eric Newby, London)

• "Congratulations to you and your staff for putting out the best guide book of *any* size *(Barcelona & Madrid)*. I'm recommending it to everyone." (Barnaby Conrad, Santa Barbara, California)

• "If you're only buying one guide book, we recommend American Express...." (*Which?* — Britain's leading consumer magazine)

What readers from all over the world have said:

• "The book *(Hong Kong, Singapore & Bangkok)* was written in such a personal way that I feel as if you were actually writing this book for me." (L.Z., Orange, Conn., USA)

• "Your book *(Florence and Tuscany)* proved a wonderful companion for us in the past fortnight. It went with us everywhere...." (E.H., Kingston-on-Thames, Surrey, England)

• "I feel as if you have been a silent friend shadowing my time in Tuscany." (T.G., Washington, DC, USA)

• "We followed your book *(Los Angeles & San Francisco)* to the letter. It proved to be wonderful, indispensable, a joy...." (C.C., London, England)

• "We could never have had the wonderful time that we did without your guide to *Paris*. The compactness was very convenient, your maps were all we needed, but it was your restaurant guide that truly made our stay special.... We have learned first-hand: *American Express — don't leave home without it.*" (A. R., Virginia Beach, Va., USA)

• "Much of our enjoyment came from the way your book *(Venice)* sent us off scurrying around the interesting streets and off to the right places at the right times". (Lord H., London, England)

• "It *(Paris)* was my constant companion and totally dependable...." (V. N., Johannesburg, South Africa)

• "I could go on and on about how useful the book *(Amsterdam)* was — the trouble was that it was almost getting to be a case of not venturing out without it...." (J.C.W., Manchester, England)

• "We have heartily recommended these books to all our friends who have plans to travel abroad." (A.S. and J.C., New York, USA)

• "Despite many previous visits to Italy, I wish I had had your guide *(Florence and Tuscany)* ages ago. I love the author's crisp, literate writing and her devotion to her subject." (M. B-K., Denver, Colorado, USA)

• "We never made a restaurant reservation without checking your book *(Venice)*. The recommendations were excellent, and the historical and artistic text got us through the sights beautifully." (L.S., Boston, Ma., USA)

• "We became almost a club as we found people sitting at tables all around, consulting their little blue books!" (F.C., Glasgow, Scotland)

• "This guide *(Paris)* we warmly recommend to all the many international visitors we work with." (M.L., Paris, France)

• "It's not often I would write such a letter, but it's one of the best guide books we have ever used *(Rome)* — we can't fault it!" (S.H., Berkhamsted, Herts, England)

American Express Travel Guides

spanning the globe....

EUROPE
Amsterdam, Rotterdam
  & The Hague
Athens and the
  Classical Sites · ‡
Barcelona, Madrid &
  Seville #
Berlin, Potsdam &
  Dresden * (‡ as Berlin)
Brussels
Dublin
Florence and Tuscany
London
Moscow & St Petersburg *
Paris
Prague #
Provence and the
  Côte d'Azur *
Rome
Venice #
Vienna & Budapest

NORTH AMERICA
Boston and New
  England *
Los Angeles & San
  Diego
Mexico #
New York
San Francisco and
  the Wine Regions
Toronto, Montréal and
  Québec City #
Washington, DC

THE PACIFIC
Cities of
  Australia
Hong Kong
  & Taiwan
Singapore &
  Bangkok * ‡
Tokyo

* Paperbacks in preparation # Paperbacks appearing August 1993
‡ Currently available as hardback pocket guides

*Clarity and quality of information, combined
with outstanding maps — the ultimate in
travelers' guides*